The
Commodity
Futures
Game

The Commodity Futures Game

WHO WINS?   WHO LOSES?   WHY?

Abridged Edition

Richard J. Teweles
Charles V. Harlow
Herbert L. Stone

McGRAW-HILL BOOK COMPANY

New York   St. Louis   San Francisco   Auckland   Bogotá
Düsseldorf   Johannesburg   London   Mexico   Montreal
New Delhi   Panama   Paris   São Paulo   Singapore
Sydney   Tokyo   Toronto

First McGraw-Hill Paperback edition, 1977
    45678910   MUMU   89876543210

Library of Congress Cataloging in Publication Data

Teweles, Richard Jack, date.
    The commodity futures game.

    Edition for 1969 published under title: The
commodity futures trading guide.
    Bibliography: p.
    Includes index.
    1. Commodity exchanges. 2. Speculation.
I. Harlow, Charles Vendale, joint author. II. Stone,
Herbert L., date, joint author. III. Title.
[HG6046.T452]   332.6′44   77-1853
ISBN 0-07-063727-X

Dedicated to

Bill	*Jeff*	*Leslie*
Ted	*Pam*	*Brian*
	John	

Contents

Preface

To prophesy is extremely difficult,
especially with respect to the future.
CHINESE PROVERB

As the quote above notes with delectable irony, the commodity futures game, like the stock-trading game, is not easy to play well. Consistent, profitable trading is a demanding exercise that requires superior knowledge, intelligently and consistently applied. Perhaps it is because we are old (over 30) and irascible, but it seems that the sun never sets on a day when there has not been an appalling volume of utter nonsense on the subject of trading stocks and commodities. The torrent of misinformation seems to be quite durable, despite occasional perceptive attacks on its flanks. Indeed, the sheer weight of ignorance reminds us of the truth of James Bryant Conant's remarks that bad theory is never overthrown merely by uncovering facts to the contrary, no matter how impressive their number; rather, bad theory is purged only by better theory.

The Commodity Futures Game: Who Wins? Who Loses? Why? attempts to organize much of what is known about commodity futures and allied disciplines mixed liberally with a total of more than forty years of trading experience, and to transmit a package in readable form to people who are, have been, or will be trading commodity futures. The idea is simply to provide the intelligent layman with a level of understanding that might take many years to acquire by his own experience.

To accomplish this, the book is divided into four sections and a bibliography. Section 1 introduces the basics of the game to the reader. The experienced trader is urged not to skip these early chapters. Chapter 4, for example, will arouse a special interest in the professional who may have explored some of its contents subjectively. The neophyte may find the concepts discussed here somewhat difficult on the first reading, but he may be assured that additional time spent in acquainting himself with the essential behavior of prices and the nature of the markets is far from wasted. Section 2 presents the most definitive treatment of actually playing the commodity futures game that has appeared to date. The trader is taken through the decision-making process in a thorough, decisive manner. He constructs his own trading curve, explores the fundamental and technical approach (including spreads and options), and is presented with a detailed discussion of the game plan, including an in-depth treatment of money management.

Section 3 details the state-of-the-art in understanding why losers lose and why winners win. Satire and serious research are combined to analyze the results of the players, including the behavioral aspects of the game. Section 4 can well serve as a blueprint for broker and client awareness of a relationship that should entail more than a modicum of mutual trust. The bibliography is the most complete to be found in any work to date. References have been organized so that virtually all relevant material on commodity futures and related fields may be consulted. The hard cover predecessor of this edition of *The Commodity Futures Game* contains a fifth section which may be of interest to some readers. It consists of detailed discussions of over 25 specific commodities and may prove valuable as a continuing reference for both brokers and clients.

Indebtedness for a book like this must run wide and deep, and therefore no attempt has been made to enumerate individually all those to whom we owe our thanks. However, in addition to those mentioned in *The Commodity Futures Trading Guide*, the successful sire to this work, some special notes of appreciation are in order.

The Food Research Institute of Stanford University has long been a source of consistently excellent work in the commodity futures field. Special thanks are due Holbrook Working and Roger Gray for their considerable contribution to the level of understanding of the futures markets.

The excellence of the chapter "The Technical Approach" is owed to James Aliphier, whose tireless efforts culminated in what we consider the definitive survey of technical analysis extant. In addition, his extensive comments and criticisms on other portions of the book were of continuing help.

Stephen Greenberg's decision to take time out from a busy schedule to review the entire manuscript resulted in several helpful suggestions and was a labor of love much appreciated. Helmut Weymar, President of Commodities Corporation, kindly supplied updated figures for the cocoa analysis in Chapter 6, and Walter Emery of the Commodity Research Bureau graciously provided us with considerable tabular material and chart data. John Howe kindly lent assistance in the early development of the Trading Profile Interview. Jack Salmon, Keith Morgan, Warren Nelson, Lester Abbott, and Bill Bowen of the Clayton Brokerage Company, St. Louis, assisted in many continuing ways. Ted Teweles, Neal Oberg, Al Hammond, and Tom Garland spent hours gathering data for tables and figures. Special thanks go to Donna Doughty, who bravely served as translator for rough manuscript drafts, and to Margaret Buck, who helped in the final preparation. A note of thanks must go to all those who have taken Finance 488 at CSULB, where a blend of enthusiasm and intellectual curiosity has made the commodity markets exciting subjects for serious inquiry.

Finally, each of us would be remiss if we failed to express our enduring gratitude to our wives and children, who gave cheerfully of portions of the time to which they were most clearly entitled.

In spite of all the help received, implicity and explicity, errors of omission and commission inevitably will remain. These are the sole province of the undersigned, who promise to give cheerful consideration to their remedy at some time in the future.

Richard J. Teweles
Charles V. Harlow
Herbert L. Stone

**The
Commodity
Futures
Game**

Basics of the Game

A stock and a commodity trader were good friends and compared notes often on trading philosophies. When the stock trader fell on bad times with a series of losses, he was forced to sell his membership. Before leaving for another line of work, he reflected with his commodity trader friend. "Your trouble is that you weren't over here with me trading commodities," confided the friend. "But I don't know anything about commodities," the crestfallen stock trader replied.

In one way or another the advice, "You've got to know the territory," has been proffered for centuries. The four chapters in this section are an effort to introduce the reader to "the territory" of commodity futures.

In Chapter 1, "Why Trade Commodity Futures?," the idea of speculation, as well as the specific evolution of trading in commodities, is discussed. Because many potential commodity traders have had experience in securities, specific similarities and differences in the two areas are noted.

Chapter 2, "The Nature of the Commodity Futures Markets," places the trader in the environment in which he is to operate. The nature of contracts, the markets for those contracts, who plays the game, and the nature of cash and futures prices are discussed in order that the trader may appreciate the relationships involved in market and trader performance.

Chapter 3, "The Mechanics of Commodity Trading," helps the trader to choose a broker and to understand clearly the procedures of opening and maintaining a commodity trading account. Contract information, types of order, regulatory requirements, and tax considerations are not heady stuff, but avoiding problems in these areas is imperative.

Chapter 4, "The Behavior of Commodity Futures Prices," lays the vital groundwork for a clear understanding of the behavior of prices, the relation between past and future price changes, and the question of trends.

CHAPTER ONE

Why Trade Commodity Futures?

> When asked why he continued speculating, James R. Keene, a famous speculator, replied, "Why does a dog chase his thousandth rabbit? All life is a speculation. The spirit of speculation is born with men."
> BERNARD BARUCH, *Baruch: My Own Story*

INTRODUCTION

This is a book about trading commodity futures. Trading is an activity that cuts across many disciplines — economics, sociology, and psychology are three of the most obvious. Futures trading is carried on by individuals involved with the cash commodity and by floor traders and speculators as well. Speculators account for more than half the dollar value of the open interest in commodity futures, yet perhaps there is no other field in which there is more interest and less knowledge among the participants.

In this first chapter the economic role of the speculator and the history of trading from Phoenician beginnings are presented. Attacks on trading as an institution are included and speculation as an activity is analyzed, as are the specific differences between commodities and securities. A final section, "Should you speculate?", leads the trader to considerations that, although personal, must include general criteria.

ECONOMIC FUNCTION OF THE SPECULATOR

The usual justification made for speculation in commodities is simple. Futures trading is beneficial to the public which ultimately consumes the goods traded in the futures markets. The benefit most often considered primary is the probability that the hedging of commodities allows the risk of price changes to be shifted; hence the cost of production, marketing, or processing is reduced. If this is true, and if the cost savings achieved are passed on to consumers, futures trading will benefit the consumers on whose behalf the economy is supposed to function. Futures markets provide other important benefits, such as continuous, accurate, well-publicized price information and continuous liquid markets. Without the speculator futures markets could not function; therefore, if the futures markets operate for the social good, the speculator who makes the operation possible must also contribute to the social good. Speculators attempt to anticipate what prices are going to do and, by taking appropriate positions in the futures markets, make a profit if their judgment proves correct. They may or may not be correct and therefore may or may not make a profit, but in their very effort to do so they do enough trading to provide the necessary base for liquid futures markets and thereby raise the efficiency of commodity marketing. Sometimes speculators are accused of making markets unstable by virtue of their speculation, but it is not necessary for them to prove that they earn their profits, if they do earn any, by stabilizing or destabilizing prices; they earn the opportunity to profit merely by being in the market, hence making the market possible. Furthermore, there is no proof that speculators destabilize prices, and at least one study has demonstrated that the speculator probably moderates rather than accentuates price volatility.[1]

Not only is the volume of business done by trade hedgers at any given time frequently too small to provide the liquidity necessary for an efficient market, but a preponderance of hedgers frequently tends to want to buy at the same time or sell at the same time, and the speculator is needed to take the other side of some of these trades.

SPECULATING OR GAMBLING?

There are many who regard "speculation" and "gambling" as synonymous terms. One hears of "investing in securities" and "gambling in commodities." Even some relatively sophisticated investors consider commodity trading to be one step removed from a Nevada casino. Others regard speculation and gambling as distinctly different activities. The usual differentiation is based on the nature of risk and the social good. Gambling involves the creation of a risk for the sole purpose of someone taking it. The horse race, poker game, and roulette wheel themselves create risks that would not be present without them. Gamblers are willing to accept these risks in return for the opportunity to win some money. No particular social good is accomplished unless one believes that gambling provides a needed outlet for the gamblers whose needs might be satisfied by something worse if they could not gamble.

---

[1] *Margins, Speculation, and Prices in Grains Futures Markets,* Economic Research Service, U.S. Department of Agriculture, 1967.

Speculation, on the contrary, deals in risks that are necessarily present in the process of marketing goods in a free capitalistic system. As a soybean crop grows and is harvested, concentrated, and dispersed, the obvious risks of price changes must be taken by those who own the soybeans or have commitments to buy them, either in their original form or as oil or meal. These risks would be present whether futures markets existed or not. If the speculator were unwilling to take them, someone else would have to do so. Unlike the gambler who causes a game to be created merely to satisfy his desire to gamble, the speculator does not inject risk into the economy merely because he is willing to speculate.

The truth of the matter seems to lie somewhere between these two points of view. If hedgers operated in the futures markets solely to reduce their risks, passed their savings on to consumers, and the speculator made this all possible, there could be little quarrel with the argument that his services had social value. Actually, hedgers operate in the futures markets primarily to increase their profits and not just to reduce their risks. If they believe that to hedge against their inventories or to make forward sale commitments is the best course of action, they will do so. If they believe that a partial hedge is adequate, they might well hedge only part of their risk. In some cases, if they are quite certain that their judgment of the future course of prices is correct, they might carry their entire risk unhedged. Such selective hedging is far more common than is implied in many standard texts, which indicate that all risks are hedged and that most hedges work perfectly or nearly so.

Furthermore, many firms are not above attempting to take advantage of apparent opportunities in the futures markets by taking positions parallel with their cash positions—which, of course, amounts to speculations that increase risk rather than hedges that reduce it. If such speculation is successful, it works for the good of the company and its owners, and insofar as the economy is benefited by the health of companies and their owners it is also benefited by the speculation. If speculation of this kind proves unsuccessful, however, and the company, its owners, and its customers are damaged, it is difficult to argue that the speculators who took the other side of the trade and made it possible benefited anybody.

The motivation of many individual speculators could well be identical with that of gamblers; that is, they are willing to take relatively large risks in return for the chance to gain large profits. In addition, they may derive some pleasure from the activity of trading, just as the gambler derives excitement from his game and not just from the monetary result of his gambling. The major difference is that the activities of commodity speculators are essential to hedging, which, on balance, is apparently beneficial to the social good.

THE EVOLUTION OF FUTURES TRADING

Trade carried on over great distances is an ancient activity of mankind. The great trade networks of the Phoenician, Greek, Roman, and Byzantine empires were primary sources of economic power for these old civilizations. Because of the great distances and the hazards of travel, trading was done only on barter and cash-and-carry bases.

The decline of the Roman Empire in Europe resulted in the rise of disorganized and hostile European feudal states. This system of self-sufficient feudal manors undermined the basic exchange of goods among peoples of widely separated lands. When the urban tradition of Rome disappeared in early medieval Europe, only a few cities in the south of France and in Italy retained their ties with distant Eastern trade depots. During the Middle Ages economic and political stability slowly returned. In the eleventh and twelfth centuries several feudal monarchs succeeded in expanding their land holdings and their authority and thereby sowed the seeds of the modern European state system.

By the twelfth century two great trading centers had begun to flourish on the European continent as a result of a general revival in trade. In northern Italy the cities of Venice, Florence, Genoa, Pisa, and Milan competed for trading rights with the Orient and also sought to expand their trade throughout Europe. At the same time northern European trade centered about the region of Flanders (now Holland and Belgium). This area, known since Roman times for its fine cloth, developed strong economic ties with England, which was then the most important wool-producing area in Europe. The Italian traders, specializing in such luxuries as fine silk, spices, rare metals, and exotic perfumes, crossed the paths of the Flemish traders of cloth, wine, salt fish, lumber, and metalware on land held by the Counts of Champagne. Evidence shows that as early as 1114 the Counts of Champagne had established trade fairs to encourage mercantile activity from which they extracted fees. It was at these markets in Champagne during the twelfth century that the first use of forward contracts in Europe probably occurred.[2]

Once established, the market fairs became the chief centers of international exchange in Europe. Traders came not only from Flanders and Italy but from Scandinavia, England, and even Russia. The Counts of Champagne provided the traders with protection, money changers, and even storage facilities. Trade fairs were eventually held on a year-round basis, rotating initially among several raw materials and manufactured goods but eventually specializing in only one or a few related commodities; for example, linen and wool at Troyes and leather and skins at Reims.[3]

Generally, the last few days of each fair were reserved for paying bills and settling the bargains struck during the fair. Because traders at the fairs often came from widely dissimilar geographical and ethnic back-

---

[2] J. K. Sowards, *Western Civilization to 1660*, St. Martin's Press, New York, 1965, pp. 10, 384, and 391; Lee Dee Belveal, *Commodity Trading Manual*, Chicago Board of Trade, 1966, p. 3-a.

[3] Henry H. Bakken, *Theory of Markets and Marketing*, Mimir Publishers, Madison, Wis., 1952, p. 317.

grounds, disputes often arose over the settling of accounts, and because of these disputes a code of commercial law, called the "law merchant," was slowly developed. Violators of the code were taken before "courts of the fair" which were manned by the merchants themselves.

This emerging medieval code of mercantile law performed much the same function as the regulations established by today's commodity exchanges. It defined contract terms, determined methods of sampling, inspecting, and grading the commodity in question, and set down the location and date for delivery of the goods. Although most transactions were of a spot nature, an innovation of the medieval fairs was the use of a document called a *lettre de faire* as a forward contract which specified the delivery of goods at a later date.[4] Although these *lettres de faire* were first issued only in the sale of cash commodities between a single buyer and seller, they later evolved into negotiable documents which might be transferred to several parties before arriving at the warehouse where the specified goods were stored. Because of the difficulties of travel, many merchants preferred to bring only samples of their merchandise to the fairs, and the *lettre de faire* helped to make trade by sample satisfactory to both buyer and seller. Its functions became similar to the bill of exchange widely used today.[5] In addition, it had some characteristics of the modern warehouse receipt. Signed by a reputable merchant in a distant city to indicate that a specified commodity was being held in his warehouse, the receipt *(lettre de faire)* could be sold to a third party who would, in turn, either sell or take possession of the purchased goods. The forward contract trading by merchants in the late Middle Ages was in many respects like the modern commodity futures contract but differed in that the forward trades were not standardized and were consummated on a more personal basis.

Following the establishment of the Champagne market fairs, and later others like them at Bruges, Antwerp, and Amsterdam, and the proved viability of the representative sample as the basis for a commodity transaction, England created year-round meeting places at which traders could buy and sell commodities and manufactured goods. These meeting places were known as exchanges, an early example being the Royal Exchange opened in London in 1570. The Royal Exchange was later divided into specialized exchanges known as a group as the London Commodity Exchange.

Dealers soon began acting in the London commodity exchanges as middlemen willing to absorb price risks that the merchants wished to avoid in return for the opportunity to profit in forward transactions. Although spot, or cash, trades remained the essential part of the market, increasingly large numbers of traders took advantage of the forward contracts.

---

[4] W. C. Labys and C. W. J. Granger, *Speculation, Hedging, and Commodity Price Forecasts,* D. C. Heath and Co., Lexington, Mass., 1970, p. 3.

[5] Belveal, *loc. cit.*

As the system evolved, sellers sold their goods to middlemen who would, in turn, seek out a prospective buyer. In this way sellers were almost certain to dispose of their goods at reasonable prices and buyers could expect standardized levels of quality from dealers who offered goods for resale. At this point in the development of the marketing process grading systems and true futures contracts had not yet been devised, but they were on the horizon.

DEVELOPMENT OF THE FUTURES CONTRACT

The first recorded case of organized futures trading occurred in Japan during the 1600s.[6] Wealthy landowners and feudal lords of Imperial Japan found themselves squeezed between an expanding money economy in the cities and their primarily agrarian-based resources. The rents that they collected from their feudal tenants were paid in the form of a share of each year's rice harvest. This income was irregular and subject to uncontrollable factors such as weather and other seasonal characteristics. Because the money economy required that the nobility have ready cash on hand at all times, income instability stimulated the practice of shipping surplus rice to the principal cities of Osaka and Edo, where it could be stored and sold as needed. In an effort to raise cash quickly, landlords soon began selling tickets (warehouse receipts) against goods stored in rural or urban warehouses. Merchants generally bought these tickets in anticipation of their projected needs (they also suffered at times from the fluctuations of uncertain harvests).[7]

Eventually "rice tickets" became generally acceptable as a form of currency to facilitate the transaction of business. At times, however, stored rice reserves were inadequate to meet the needs of the nobility, and when this happened many merchants extended credit at interest to the landlord before the actual sale of the rice tickets.

During the late seventeenth century the Japanese Dojima rice market was characterized by the fact that only trading in futures contracts was permitted. By 1730 the Tokugawa Shogunate, or Imperial government, designated and officially recognized the market as *cho-ai-mai*, or, literally, "rice trade on book." A number of rules of the *cho-ai-mai-kaisho* (the market place) were strikingly similar to the rules of modern American futures trading[8]:

1. Contract term duration was limited.
2. All contracts within any term were standardized.
3. A basic grade for any contract period was agreed on beforehand.
4. No contract could be carried over into a new contract period.

[6] Henry H. Bakken, "Futures Trading–Origin, Development and Present Economic Status," *Futures Trading Seminar,* Vol. II, Mimir Publishers, Madison, Wis., 1953, p. 9.

[7] *Ibid.,* p. 10.

[8] *Ibid.,* p.11.

5. All trades had to be cleared through a clearinghouse.

6. Every trader had to establish a line of credit with the clearinghouse of his choice.

The major difference between the *cho-ai-mai* market and today's futures market was that delivery of cash commodites was never actually permitted. This "futures trading only" concept caused the futures cash-price relationship to function improperly and resulted in erratic price fluctuations. In 1869 this discrepancy between prices in the spot (cash) market and those of the futures market prompted the Imperial government to order trading stopped. Testifying to the essential futures trading function of maintaining an orderly market, fluctuations in the cash price of rice reached chaotic proportions less than two years after the discontinuance of the *cho-ai-mai* futures market, and a disgruntled Imperial regime was forced to reopen it.[9] Significantly, physical delivery of goods was then allowed, and as a result the Japanese futures market was effectively wedded to the cash market, thus eliminating its initial instability.

It appears that the practice of tying the cash market to the futures market in Japan may have been influenced by Western trading practices on the Oriental rice-ticket market. As the economy in the United States expanded during the early part of the nineteenth century, commodity exchanges evolved from unorganized club-type associations into formalized exchanges, the first of which was the Chicago Board of Trade, established in 1848 with 82 members. Trading in Chicago was encouraged considerably by the trading standards, inspection system, and weighing system prescribed by the board.

It was on the Chicago Board of Trade on March 13, 1851, that the first time contract was recorded. This contract authorized the delivery of 3,000 bushels of corn to be made in June at a price one cent per bushel below the March 13 price.[10]

The major commodity exchanges in the United States were established and are still situated in Chicago and New York. These sites were logically chosen because of their proximity to the major transport routes. New York, with its port located on the major ocean shipping routes, was ideally suited for international trade. Chicago, situated at the hub of rail and canal routes extending into the agricultural heartlands of the United States, inherited the bulk of internal trade.

Around the mid-nineteenth century forward contracts known as "to arrive" contracts, similar in nature to the medieval *lettre de faire,* gradually made their appearance. It was the accumulation of excess supplies at some times and their shortage at others in the expanding American money economy that caused the modification of the traditional cash-and-carry

[9] Labys and Granger, *op. cit.,* p. 6.

[10] H. S. Irwin, *Evolution of Futures Trading,* Mimir Publishers, Madison, Wis., 1954.

transaction. The first of these time contracts was not much more than a verbal agreement or a simple memorandum exchanged by both parties.

Because of the increase in the volume of trading at Chicago, the risk in forward contracts became too great to be transferred to middlemen or specialized dealers, which was the common practice in the London markets at the time, but if another kind of middleman—a third party—could be induced to assume the risk the effect would be the same, namely the assurance of a fair price for the seller and a reasonably uniform quality of product.

Although the first "to arrive" contracts were not transferable, the printed documents that were developed to specify the grade, quantity, and time of delivery of the goods soon were.[11] These alterations to the "to-arrive" contracts resulted in the creation of a futures market in this country in which a contract was readily tradeable before delivery. The middleman drawn into the newly evolved marketing structure in the United States was the speculator on whom the risk was placed.

Because of the volume of the futures contracts traded at Chicago and the replacement of the London-type dealer by the speculator, additional rules for orderly and fair futures trading had to be drawn[12]:

1. The commodity selected for trading had to be easily graded.

2. The grading of commodities had to be maintained by regular governmental inspection.

3. Payment had to be set at the time of delivery.

4. Prices had to be reported openly and be equally accessible to all traders.

5. Buyers and sellers were required to establish financial responsibility.

6. The number of buyers and sellers had to remain large enough to provide continuous opportunities for trade.

As already noted, the rules established in Chicago were much like those of the Japanese rice futures market of earlier date.

Futures trading on the Chicago Board of Trade quickly reached sizeable proportions and was rapidly adopted by other exchanges. In New York futures trading had begun on the New York Produce Exchange and on the New York Cotton Exchange by 1870. That same year futures trading was initiated on the New Orleans Cotton Exchange, and by 1885 the New York Coffee Exchange was actively trading in futures. Since the second half of the nineteenth century a number of other commodity exchanges have been founded.

During America's history of futures trading some commodities, such as wheat, have retained their popularity with the trading public. Others, such as silk, butter, and pepper, have lost favor because of insufficient trading volume for a variety of reasons. Some, such as cotton and coffee,

---

[11] Bakken, *op. cit.*, p. 104.
[12] Labys and Granger, *op. cit.*, p. 6.

failed in interest for a number of years but regained popularity later. The American commodity futures market has now developed into a vast and complex institution consisting of 10 major and about a dozen minor exchanges on which approximately 40 commodities are traded and a large clearing-house system. It is based on widely acceptable standardized futures contracts. With the exception of a short period during World War II, when the markets were closed, the growth of this institution has been continuous since about 1865 and in recent years has accelerated enormously. The history of the commodity futures trading in the United States, however, has not been problem free.

ATTACKS AGAINST FUTURES TRADING

Futures trading has been subject to varying degrees of criticism as long as it has been in existence. Opposition grew particularly severe during the 1890s, when considerable legislation was proposed to restrict loose business practices of many kinds. In Germany all futures trading in grains was actually forbidden by a law passed in 1896, although the law was repealed four years later.

In the United States commodity exchanges were widely considered to be gambling dens full of parasitic speculators who drained off money that should have gone instead to producers or consumers of products. There were, and sometimes still are, attempts by the federal and certain state governments to abolish futures trading in whole or in part. In 1867 the Illinois Legislature passed an act that provided that the parties to futures contracts, referred to in the act as gambling contracts, should be fined $1,000 and imprisoned up to one year in the Cook County Jail. Seven members of the Board of Trade in Chicago were actually arrested under this act. Although it was repealed the following year, many more than 100 other bills to abolish futures trading have been introduced in the United States Congress alone.

In 1890 one Congressman Butterworth of Ohio introduced a bill to place a prohibitive tax on dealers in futures, and, during the ensuing debate, Representative Funston of Kansas described the futures market as follows:

> Those who deal in "options" and "futures" contracts, which is mere gambling, no matter by what less offensive name such transactions be designated, neither add to the supply nor increase the demand for consumption, nor do they accomplish any useful purpose by their calling; but on the contrary, they speculate in fictitious products. The wheat they buy and sell is known as "wind wheat" and doubtless for the reason that it is invisible, intangible, and felt or realized only in the terrible force it exerts in destroying the farming industry of the country.

Although Congressman Butterworth's bill failed to pass, agitation continued, and in 1892 Senator Washburn, speaking in the United States Senate, asserted:

As near as I can learn, and from the best information I have been able to obtain on the Chicago Board of Trade, at least 95% of the sales of that Board are of this fictitious character, where no property is actually owned, no property sold or delivered, or expected to be delivered but simply wagers or bets as to what that property may be worth at a designated time in the future. . . . Wheat and cotton have become as much gambling tools as chips on the faro-bank table. The property of the wheat grower and the cotton grower is treated as though it were a "stake" put on the gambling table at Monte Carlo. The producer of wheat is compelled to see the stocks in his barn dealt with like the peas of a thimblerigger, or the cards of a three-card-monte man. Between the grain-producer and loaf eater, there has stepped in a "parasite" between them robbing them both.[13]

Another bill that would have imposed a prohibitive tax on all futures trading in farm products failed to pass Congress in 1893 only because final action before Congress adjourned required a suspension of the rules of the House of Representatives and the necessary two-thirds majority vote failed by the narrow margin of 172 to 124. A similar bill considered by the next Congress actually passed the House but this time failed to gain approval of the Senate.[14]

Almost all the bills designed to abolish or restrict futures trading died before reaching a vote or were defeated. After World War II, however, the continuing demands for restrictive legislation were largely concentrated on two unrelated markets: onions and potatoes. In both cases the futures markets were blamed for causing wide fluctuations in prices that inflicted severe losses on the producers, processors, and marketers of these products. In previous attacks on futures trading those engaged in the production and marketing of the products traded were among the most vocal defenders of the futures markets. This time they were among the attackers. In particular, trading in onions was attacked by those who were supposed to benefit from the existence of the market as well as by the usual unsuccessful speculators. The market had few defenders other than the Chicago Mercantile Exchange, whose members did not relish losing the futures market in one of the products traded exclusively on that exchange.

After several years of argument Congress passed a bill in 1958 to prohibit futures trading in onions. The onion crop is a minor one, grown only in limited areas, but those engaged in the business of trading futures did not take the prohibition lightly. The Chicago Mercantile Exchange appealed to a United States District Court to get the prohibition set aside as unconstitutional, but the attempt failed. Some believe that those engaged in the onion trade who attacked futures trading were really concerned, as they

[13] From a speech entitled "Regulation and Supervision of Futures Trading," by Bernard P. Carey, Chairman, Chicago Board of Trade, delivered at a futures trading seminar April 28–30, 1965, at the Chicago Board of Trade.
[14] Holbrook Working, *"Futures Markets Under Renewed Attack."* Reprinted from *Food Research Institute Studies,* 4, No. 1 (1963).

maintained, about the wide fluctuations in price. Others believe that they were actually more interested in having accurate price information somewhat less publicized in order to capitalize on the ignorance of the farmers and consumers. The truth will probably never really be known, but there is some suspicion that the latter provided at least some basis for the trade's lack of enthusiasm for the futures market.

A similar law to prohibit trading in potatoes was considered several times during the years that followed. Although it was given serious consideration, it was not passed.

Although the equating of speculation in the futures markets with gambling is somewhat illogical, there were other reasons for the hue and cry. There has always been a widespread feeling that profits from speculation are somehow immoral, compared with profits from other seemingly more productive activities, although the concept of compensation received by other risk bearers, such as insurance companies, does not seem to cause similar resentment. This is the same sort of vague opposition that many people feel toward selling a commodity or security short. Somehow they believe that a price going up is good and a price going down is bad, and, furthermore, that the short seller not only thinks that it will go down but makes it do so by selling short.

There are consistent and loud complaints by those who have lost money in commodities and who are reluctant to believe that their losses are caused by their own failings. They prefer to blame factors beyond their control, which helps to restore their faith in themselves, if not their money.

For long periods of time the United States witnessed falling commodity prices even as the prices of finished goods rose. This divergence was caused by a number of factors which were difficult to understand by many and proved even more difficult to correct by those who did understand. It was easy for the farmer, who believed that he was paying too much for his food and clothing, to blame the speculator, who appeared to be making considerable money without growing or producing anything tangible.

A common criticism of commodity speculation is that it causes violent price moves, which work considerable hardship on those engaged in more productive pursuits. Wide publicity is given to the relatively rare but highly dramatic manipulations that cause many to conclude that speculation is not only gambling but that the game is dishonest besides. Almost any public speaker talking about commodity trading can be sure that someone in the audience will ask about "that big soybean oil scandal of a few years ago" or some similar incident.[15]

Speculators can point to equally scandalous events in all types of busi-

[15] The Allied Crude Vegetable Oil Refining Corp., under the leadership of its president, Anthony De Angelis, went bankrupt in 1963 and caused substantial losses to a large number of prominent banks, brokers, and commodity dealers and is considered to be one of the largest business frauds in recent history. The scandal was, however, based primarily on the issuance of fraudulent warehouse receipts rather than on any failure of the commodity futures markets.

ness at all times and in all countries, but no responsible person wants to declare all types of business activity illegal. Manipulative devices, such as artificial corners, wash sales, spreading of false rumors, and the "bucketing" of orders are illegal. All such activities are an abuse of speculative practice and certainly not an integral part of it. Nor does the fact that speculators are essential to the operation of commodity futures markets mean that they dominate these markets. Major price movements are usually caused by basic changes in the supply or demand, or both, for a given product and only rarely by a group of speculators successfully creating self-fulfilling prophecies.

Considerable research has been done in an attempt to prove that speculation does or does not cause excessive price movement. No final conclusions can yet be drawn on this subject, but the weight of evidence indicates that speculation probably does more to smooth price fluctuation than to increase it. Even the demise of the much maligned onion market did something to prove this point. The fluctuations in the price of cash onions apparently were greater both before there was a futures market and after it was prohibited than while the market was functioning. There is no doubt that the presence of speculative traders results in more transactions than would take place without their activities, but to conclude that more transactions in themselves cause more price variation than there would otherwise be is unwarranted by the facts.

WHY DO SPECULATORS SPECULATE?

The specific motivation or combination of motivations of all the millions of speculators could not be discussed here in any detail even if reliable data were available. The broad incentives that attract most speculators are quite clear, however, and can be summarized briefly.

Certainly the greatest is the opportunity to make an important amount of money in relation to the capital base used. Not many speculators are naïve enough to compare their activities with those of investors. Most of them are well aware of the risks that they take in return for the large and quick profits possible, although there are some who, like gamblers, are so convinced that they will win that they are unable to admit even to themselves that they might lose. Most of them learn all too quickly that it is a rare opportunity indeed that provides an important potential profit without an attendant large risk.

Other speculators are attracted almost as much by the stimulation of the speculation itself as they are by the opportunity for profit. For some it is the sheer excitement of the game; for others, it is the dynamics of the involvement with world politics, trade, currency fluctuation, wars, and other events that come to affect their own positions rather than just provide newspaper headlines. Aside from those who receive some masochistic pleasure from losing, it seems likely that even those motivated in large part by the desire to have something to get up for in the morning find the pleasure of speculating more satisfying when they win than when they lose.

SPECULATE IN WHAT?

The desire of man to speculate has always been so strong and widespread that hundreds of examples could be mentioned. Historically, there are some that are difficult even to comprehend today. One of the more fantastic is the trading that took place in tulip bulbs in Holland in 1634 to 1637. The high regard for the tulip held by society leaders spread throughout the country and reached the point at which everybody seemed willing to part with almost anything for rare tulip bulbs. Trading became frantic, and prices rose until entire fortunes were paid for bulbs. When the mania had run its course, the economy of Holland was shattered and it was years before it recovered.

Similar effects were felt in the eighteenth century from the Mississippi land schemes of John Law in France and the South Sea Bubble that was perpetrated on the English public. The latter created a mood that fostered a rash of some of the most fantastic schemes in the history of finance and caused the ruin of thousands of people. There was the huge subscription for a company that was to manufacture a perpetual-motion wheel. A company was formed to repair and rebuild parsonage and vicarage houses, and among others were companies to supply London with sea coal, rebuild every house in England, settle the island of Blanco and Sal Tarthgus, repave the streets of London, insure horses, and transmute quicksilver into a malleable fine metal. The most preposterous of all was "A company for carrying on an undertaking of great advantage, but nobody to know what it is." Subscribers were to buy 5,000 shares at 100 pounds each, with a 2-pound deposit. An annual return of 100 pounds for each share was promised, details to be announced in a month. The issue was oversubscribed in five hours, and the promoter left for the Continent that same night and was never heard from again.[16]

In the United States the Florida land boom of the 1920s was comparable to its predecessor bubbles. The results of the worldwide 1929 stock break are well known.

Some areas of speculation have been popular for many years. These include land, precious stones and metals, natural resources such as oil, rare items such as stamps, coins, and paintings, and securities, such as stocks, bonds, warrants, and options to buy or sell stocks.

The types and degree of skill needed for success may vary among these areas, as will the amount of capital required and the mechanics of buying and selling the items. In each case, however, the attraction is the profit possible, the stimulation received from the activity, or their combination. Certain of these items have characteristics that attract some speculators and repel others. The general characteristics of the commodity futures markets are, in some respects, unique.

---

[16] Charles Mackay, *Extraordinary Popular Delusions and the Madness of Crowds,* London, 1841. Reprinted in 1932 by L. C. Page & Co., Boston, p. 55.

COMMODITY FUTURES VERSUS SECURITIES AND OTHER SPECULATIONS

One reason for the popularity of commodity trading is undoubtedly the ease with which it may be done. Most brokerage houses deal in commodity futures as well as in securities. Some have research departments of their own and others subscribe to various services, but in either case the speculator looking for a suggested commodity position will have little difficulty in finding one. Some individual registered representatives choose not to handle commodity trades, preferring to specialize in securities or mutual funds, but in such cases other registered representatives in the same office are likely to be available. Few are really expert in commodity trading nor do they claim to be, but most are at least able to enter or close out positions efficiently and to pass pertinent information on to the trader if he wants it. In addition to full-line wire houses, there are firms that specialize in the handling of commodity business. They usually have a considerable amount of factual information available and are especially adept at the order and clerical end of the business, but there is no reason to believe that their market opinions are any better or worse than anyone else's.

Commodity speculators who prefer to make their own decisions may be attracted by the relative ease of securing information. Important political and economic information is readily available in general and trade newspapers. Vital supply and demand information concerning specific commodities is published in large quantities by various government departments and bureaus (particularly the Department of Agriculture) and is made available at frequent intervals. In addition to being mailed at low or no cost to anybody who requests it, such information is widely publicized in financial journals and on news wires. An adequate amount of accurate information about the handful of commodities that trade actively is considerably easier to obtain than about the tens of thousands of stocks, bonds, and mutual funds that are available. The problem faced by those who gather basic information about stocks or commodities is quite similar. To date no model clearly superior to a random walk has been published to describe the behavior of stock and commodity futures prices. Stock traders, however, may be able to take advantage of some slight trend tendencies and long-run cycles and commodity traders may be able to isolate some conditioned seasonals. Traders in stocks and commodities are both faced with the results of information that becomes available while markets are closed, which means that markets are as "active" then as they are when they are open. In both securities and commodities there are significant covariances among the prices of stocks representing related industries and among interrelated commodities such as feeds or edible oils.[17]

A basic difference between commodity and stock markets is that commodity markets are primary and stock markets are secondary. The com-

[17] Labys and Granger, *op. cit.*, pp. 268–270.

modity speculator in the long run must be concerned primarily with the real forces of supply and demand. The speculator in stocks must know the markets of the company in whose stock he is speculating and the market for the stock itself, in which case he must be concerned with the influence of floor specialists whose influence on price is somewhat controversial but exists to some significant degree with little doubt.

Like the stock trader, the commodity trader has an advantage in his liquidity over speculators in most other areas. There is seldom any difficulty in finding a buyer or seller at any time for even large positions, although, of course, the price may not be so favorable as desired. Positions can normally be acquired or disposed of within a minute or two when the exchanges are open, but if markets are active an actual report of the transaction might not be received that promptly. There is no need to search out a buyer or seller or wait for an auction, as there would be in trading in paintings, and no loans to arrange or escrows to close, as in trading property.

The commodity trader, unlike the stock trader, must consider the limits that restrict the amount a commodity price can rise or fall in one day and the range over which it may trade. These "limit moves" probably concern the unsophisticated trader far more than they should. For one thing the typical trader will seldom encounter them in a commodity in which he actually has a position. In addition, of course, he is hardly anxious about limit moves in a direction favorable to him. His freedom of action is also not restricted by an adverse limit move that does not carry beyond the level of risk he was prepared to assume.

What does worry him is the possibility of an adverse limit move that will prevent him from liquidating his position with a reasonable loss. It should be made clear that a limit move does not cause a market to close; it merely prohibits trades at prices beyond the limit. On reaching the maximum possible advance or decline a market may trade any number of times at that level or trade in away from the limit. The purpose of limiting a move is to prevent unreasonable price moves based on undue reaction to news. Securities markets deal with similar situations either by suspending trading until a fair and orderly market is again possible or by allowing prices to move over a large and (it may be noted) unlimited range. For a trader liquidity under the first condition is no better than in the commodity markets when a market has advanced its permissible limit.[18]

Commodity margins differ from stock margins both in concept and method of computation. Stock margins constitute a partial payment to the broker. The remainder, or debit balance, in a margin account is a debt owed to the broker on which interest is charged. The amount of the debt is limited by the Federal Reserve, the stock exchange, or the broker himself. Commodity margins are actually good-faith deposits to protect a broker

---

[18] C. V. Harlow and R. J. Teweles, "Commodities and Securities Compared," *Financial Analysts Journal* (September–October 1972), 65–66.

against risk in the event of adverse price moves in the interim between the establishment of a position and its limitation either by delivery or offset. Payment for the cash commodity need be made only in the highly unlikely event that delivery is actually made or taken.

Stock margins required typically fluctuate in a range of 50 to 90 percent, although both limits of this range have been exceeded for brief periods. Commodity margins are based on fixed minimums per bushel or per contract established by the commodity exchanges, but individual brokers may require larger amounts if they believe the minimum involves undue risk for themselves or their clients. Requirements amounting to 5 to 10 percent of contract value are common, although the amount may be even less than 5 percent in low-risk spread positions. The margin on 5,000 bushels of corn, for example, might typically be about 6 to 8 cents a bushel, with corn selling at $1.25 to $1.50. On a contract value of as much as $7,500 the deposit required would be only $300 to $400. If 5,000 bushels of May corn were bought against the sale of 5,000 bushels of July corn, the total margin required might be as low as $100 for the entire position. When markets become unusually volatile, margins may be raised to protect the broker from his client and, perhaps, the client from himself. Even at such times margins of as much as 20 percent of the contract value are unusual.

The low margins not only provide the opportunity to establish large positions on a small capital base but also give the commodity markets their somewhat undeserved reputation for extreme price volatility. Commodity prices frequently remain in quite narrow ranges for long periods of time and are not more volatile than typical security prices in similar price ranges. The price movements of commodities, however, relative to margin required, can create large profits or losses relative to the available trading capital. If a trader finds the moves too great for his capital or nerve, all he need do is utilize more margin than is required and trade on a more conservative basis. Too many traders take advantage of the possible potentials without accepting or recognizing the accompanying risks by fully utilizing the available leverage. This is why it is often maintained that bulls or bears can trade profitably, but not hogs.

The cost of trading commodities is low in relation to trading in other areas. Commissions paid are usually less, considering the value of the merchandise traded, than those in land, precious goods, paintings, prints, or securities. Computation is simpler because commissions are based on the number of contracts bought or sold and are unrelated to the amount of money involved in a transaction, as they are in the security markets; for example, regardless of its price, the commission on 5,000 bushels of wheat, which is equivalent to a security round lot, is a total of $30 which covers both the purchase and sale. The entire $30 is charged against the customer's account when he liquidates his position rather than $15 at the time of entry and $15 on liquidation.

The amount of record keeping required by a commodity trader is minimal unless he holds a position so large that it must be reported to the Commodity Exchange Authority. Reportable and maximum limits are so great that they are only of academic interest to most traders.

Tax rules covering profits and losses on commodity positions are quite similar to those covering securities in that both are capital items. There are fewer long-term gains in commodities because so many traders take their profits or losses more quickly than stock traders, but nothing precludes their waiting for long-term capital gains if conditions permit. In contrast to the case for securities, there are no state or federal taxes on the purchase or sale of commodity positions.

The commodity markets operate under regulations of the exchanges and the Commodity Futures Trading Commission (CFTC). In 1975 the CFTC superseded the Commodity Exchange Authority (CEA), an arm of the Department of Agriculture. There is no trade association operating in a manner comparable to the NASD.

There are those who are fond of pointing out that the commodity trader who is long in a contract of a commodity in the spot month risks getting delivery of a commodity that he really does not want. They usually refer to a person, whom they invariably do not know personally, who forgot that he owned wheat and came home to find it piled on his front lawn. In reality, the commodity trader has less to worry about concerning deliveries than the security trader. If he is short, he cannot get delivery at all. If he is long, he can avoid delivery merely by selling his position before the contract month arrives. If he carries his position into the contract month, there is still no certainty that he will get delivery; but if he does he most often has the remainder of the trading session during which he will get delivery to dispose of his position. Even if he fails to do so, the cost of carrying the delivered position for short periods is small and it can usually be sold when desired. The security trader might well have far greater delivery problems if he misplaces his securities. There is considerable time and trouble involved in disposing of securities if they are misplaced, as well as the expense of paying for a bond to protect the broker if they are found and sold by somebody else. This cost may be particularly high in the case of bearer bonds.

Trading in commodities is more like trading in securities than other types of speculation, but it should be noted that although there are differences among all these fields commodity trading is almost always the simplest. This, of course, does not imply that successful results in commodity trading are more certain. The fact remains, however, that the commodity trader is not concerned with dividends, interest, rents, royalties, stock dividends, rights offerings, handling certificates, proxies, ex-dividend dates, voting, call dates, conversions, or any other of the host of factors that might burden a security trader. The commodity trader incurs lower costs of trading relative to the amount of money that he is trading because there are no direct taxes or fees on transactions. Because the money he deposits as margin is a good-faith deposit and not a down payment, he owes his broker no money, hence pays no interest. His cost of trading, of course, could become high if he trades relatively often.

SHOULD YOU SPECULATE?

It is hardly proper for the authors of a book, brokers, or financial advisers to advise individuals to speculate or not to speculate. Some speculators make important amounts of money by speculating. They would not have been served well by someone who persuaded them not to risk losing any money and thus prevented their success. Similarly, it seems improper to suggest that everybody should speculate when it is known that most speculators are unsuccessful and therefore that the odds favor any particular new speculator losing. The decision to be conservative or aggressive with his funds is best made by the person who is going to try to acquire more at the risk of losing part of what he has. The logical basis for making the decision can be discussed productively, however.

The most common advice to a would-be speculator by many advisers is that he should speculate only when all of his financial responsibilities have been met, that is, when his insurance program is adequate, when there is an adequate equity in his home, when his children's education is complete or provided for, and when some money is available for emergencies. This approach is certainly cautious enough, but it might make some wonder what the purpose of speculating would be. The reason for increasing an individual's net worth is primarily to raise his standard of living. If he has funds available to accomplish everything that is important to him, successful speculation can do little to improve his situation significantly, whereas unsuccessful speculation could leave him in a far worse condition than that from which he began. In short, he has much to lose and little to gain.

In contrast, one with relatively little capital might appear to be irresponsible if he entered a speculative venture with the little that he has; but if a loss would not leave him despondent an aggressive program might not be altogether out of the question for him. If he succeeded, he might improve his financial condition impressively, whereas if he lost, he would be little worse off than he was before.

Regardless of the amount of capital available to a trader for speculative purposes, his own nature is probably even more important than his capital. There are those who are simply unable to take a loss or allow enough time for a profitable position to grow to its full potential. Some people are able to make a logical plan and follow it with a high degree of discipline. Others prefer to take things as they come rather than follow a rigid program. There are certainly activities to which the latter are well adapted, but speculation is not one of them.

There are those who find that the tension of carrying a position is so great that it interferes with their work or other activities to a degree that any profit they might gain is not worth the anguish of realizing it. It is well and good to suggest "selling down to a sleeping point," but there are those who are so emotional that they cannot sleep if they have any position at all because they are so concerned about where the market will open in the morning. If it is necessary to trade on such a small scale that the chance for important gains is lost, it hardly seems reasonable to expend the energy needed to trade at all.

Each person must consider his own capital position along with the responsibilities he must meet and must decide whether he wishes to risk part of what he has to try to gain more. He must also take adequate stock of himself to determine whether the cost in time and energy involved in trading is worth expending for any profits that might be achieved. Speculating in commodites might prove to be an expensive mistake for some, but not speculating might prove equally or even more expensive for others in terms of opportunity lost. It is not the function of this book to convince the reader that he should or should not speculate in commodities. The purpose is rather to provide information about the nature and behavior of commodity markets, the procedures used by successful traders and the pitfalls they face, fundamental and technical considerations, and information about specific markets to help the reader make an intelligent decision for himself.

CHAPTER TWO

The Nature of the Commodity Futures Markets

> Futures markets are an anomaly to those economists who study them least, an anachronism to those who study them a little more, and an annoyance to those who study them most. . . .
>
> ROGER GRAY, "Fundamental Price Behavior Characteristics in Commodity Futures," *Futures Trading Seminar*

INTRODUCTION

Trading commodity futures is a skill, and no skill develops powerfully when one is wearing blinders. For that reason the prospective trader must understand, insofar as it is possible, the nature of the environment in which he is to pit his skill against those of others who play the same game.

This chapter, then, discusses the nature of the contract the participants hold while playing the game, the nature of the organized markets for those contracts, the nature of the open interest (i.e., the kinds of participant in the game), and the nature of cash and futures price relationships. The last includes a detailed analysis of the structure of the hedging process. Finally, a discussion of market performance contains an analysis of the many connections between futures markets and price variability.

NATURE OF THE CONTRACT [1]

Regardless of whether the user of the futures contract is a hedger or speculator, the common bond is the nature of the contract itself. That contract is a firm legal agreement between a buyer (or seller) and an established com-

---

[1] The following discussion draws on Henry B. Arthur, "The Nature of Commodity Futures as an Economic and Business Instrument," *Food Research Institute Studies in Agricultural Economics, Trade, and Development,* 11, No. 3, 257–260.

modity exchange or its clearing house in which the trader agrees to deliver or accept during a designated period a specified amount of a certain commodity that adheres to the particular quality and delivery conditions prescribed by the commodity exchange on which that commodity is traded. The contract, if allowed to run to its termination, is fulfilled by a cash payment on the delivery date based on the settlement price for that day in return for delivery of the commodity.

During the time that the contract is open the trader must agree to a series of conditions with a qualified broker (or the clearing house if he is a member) which calls for an initial margin deposit, a prescribed margin level that protects the broker from possible losses resulting from adverse price movements, and the right to close out (offset) his contract at any time simply by properly instructing his broker to do so. The last condition is a bilateral one that permits the broker to close out the trader's position if margin is seriously impaired.

This basic commitment has several ramifications. Although the contract defines the quantity, quality, and location at which the commodity will be delivered, there are, as a rule, alternatives available to the seller that will allow him to make delivery of a commodity with substantial deviations from the par specifications. The seller faces a scale of premiums or discounts in price because of such deviations, which might include different locations of delivery or variations in the unit weight of delivery or the deliverable grade. Deliveries must be made during the delivery month traded, but the actual day of the month is selected by the seller who issues a notice of his intention in the form of a warehouse receipt, shipping certificate, or a bill of lading.

The trader holding a contract will be dealing most often through a futures commission merchant (broker) who is a member of an exchange and who will charge for his services a minimum commission set by the exchange. It is the member broker who is responsible for the fulfillment of the contract if he is a clearing member of the exchange. If he is not a clearing member, he in turn must have his trades cleared by a clearing member.

The contracts themselves are subject to legal provisions and the rules of the various exchanges such as the setting of hours and trading regulations and the daily trading limits beyond which a particular commodity cannot move. These and other attributes of each commodity contract traded on all major exchanges are reviewed fully in Chapter 3.

There are, then, two major elements of the commitment assumed when a trader enters into a commodity futures contract. The first is a promise of actual delivery of the commodity at a designated date in a way that meets exchange specifications. The second is a promise to respond financially to daily price changes by payment, if necessary, of cash to a member broker who must in turn respond to a call for cash from the clearing house, the operation of which is discussed in the following section. This daily settlement process maintains the viability of the first promise of delivery, for if any trader wishes to cancel his commitment to accept or effect delivery of the actual commodity he may merely enter the market and offset his present position. More than 98 percent of all futures contracts are settled by offset rather than by deliveries.

Until actual delivery a transaction in a commodity futures contract does not involve anything beyond the daily process of generating profits or losses against a good-faith margin deposit with a broker. No purchase or sale is required, and there is no debit balance; hence no interest is charged. All net balances are on the credit side and are marked to the market after each day's trading. The act of buying or selling occurs only after an intent to deliver occurs, when a specific buyer and seller are paired at the current settlement price.

NATURE OF EXCHANGE OPERATIONS

The need for holding commodity futures contracts has grown at a rapid pace in recent years. To facilitate this growth about 40 commodities are presently trading actively on about 15 exchanges in the United States and a much larger number in the rest of the world. Table 2-1 and Figure 2-1 illustrate the growth cycle of futures contracts trading on American exchanges, in both regulated and nonregulated commodities, since 1954.

TABLE 2-1 ANNUAL VOLUME OF
CONTRACTS TRADED ON U.S.
COMMODITY EXCHANGES,
1954–1972* (MILLION CONTRACTS)

Year	CEA regulated	Nonregulated	Total
1954	4.00	0.26	4.26
1955	3.86	0.25	4.11
1956	4.27	0.26	4.53
1957	3.73	0.38	4.11
1958	3.52	0.35	3.87
1959	3.40	0.41	3.81
1960	3.52	0.36	3.88
1961	5.79	0.27	6.06
1962	4.90	0.28	5.18
1963	6.38	0.76	7.14
1964	5.63	0.80	6.43
1965	6.99	1.43	8.42
1966	8.67	1.79	10.46
1967	6.76	2.69	9.45
1968	7.72	1.61	9.33
1969	9.35	1.86	11.21
1970	11.54	2.08	13.62
1971	11.81	2.75	14.56
1972	14.34	3.99	18.33

* Contracts are counted once, not twice, for each transaction.

SOURCE: Association of Commodity Exchange Firms, New York.

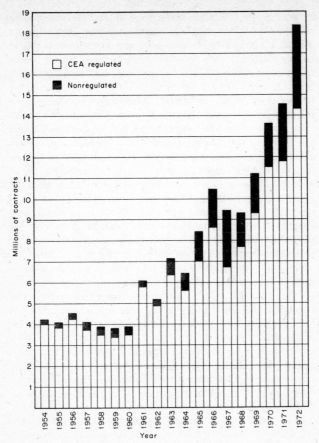

FIG. 2-1   Annual volume of trading on U.S. commodity exchanges, 1954–1972 (million contracts).

More than 18 million futures contracts at an estimated dollar value of approximately $200 billion were traded in 1972. That the volume of futures trading dominates that of physical cash trading in commodities may be seen by the fact that usually fewer than 2 percent of all those holding futures contracts take delivery and by production statistics that indicate that more than 20 times the actual crop may be traded before the expiration of the crop year. The size and value of each contract varies widely according to each commodity, as summarized in the contract facts discussion in Chapter 3.

Commodity exchanges may perform many functions, such as supplying accommodations for trading, handling, and grading cash commodities, but basically they exist to provide their members with facilities for trading commodities for future delivery. It is important to note that the exchanges themselves do not trade commodity contracts, nor do they set prices at which contracts are traded. They merely furnish a place where people in the commodity business, speculators, or their representatives can meet to buy and sell commodity futures contracts.

Most exchanges are voluntary associations of members whose primary business is the production or marketing of the commodities traded on the exchanges. The number of memberships ranges from a few dozen to the approximately 1,400 on the Chicago Board of Trade. Memberships are usually acquired from other members, subject to the approval of the exchange. In some cases an exchange may wish to expand membership and so sells memberships itself. In other cases an exchange may wish to reduce the membership and thus retires them as they become available.

Trading generally takes place in a pit or around the outside of a ring. Each exchange differs in some respects from the others, but the similarities are many. All futures orders received by member firms are transmitted to the exchange floor for execution and are filled according to bids and offers in the respective pits by open outcry to all members present at the time. Only one commodity is traded in a pit or around a ring unless the volume is too small to justify so much space. Customarily, those trading the same delivery contract of a commodity gather in the same area of the ring or on the same step of the pit so that a broker with an order can find his market as quickly as possible.

Whenever volume is high and price changes of a commodity are rapid, it is not uncommon for different prices to be bid and offered for the same delivery in different parts of the trading area at the same time. The trader must remember that these conditions might result in executions at prices that are never officially quoted or, even more difficult to understand, might cause return of an order marked "unable," even though the price on the order was well within the range of trading in that commodity. Conversely, to avoid forcing brokers to stand around the pit or ring with little to do when markets are inactive, some exchanges post orders on a blackboard. When a broker gets an order, he can find the highest bid or lowest offer on the blackboard and make his transaction against it.

Immediately after each transaction on the exchange the pit recorder, who is an employee of the exchange, writes out a record of the transaction and time-stamps it for possible future reference. The report includes the commodity traded, the month, the price, and the time of sale. The volume of each sale is not recorded as it is on stock exchanges, because it has been observed that the execution of orders in active markets would be delayed. The information from the pit recorder is transmitted to a quotations room, from which it is sent out on ticker systems for the information of those off the exchange.

Some markets start each day's trading with an open auction and continue to trade in that manner all day. Under this system all months in a particular commodity begin trading at the opening bell. Others open and close on a call basis, which means that each contract is called in turn until all orders currently on hand for that contract, except limit and stop orders away from the market, are filled.[2] After all contracts are opened, the market continues on an open auction or on the blackboard until halted by the closing call. All this makes little difference to the individual trader, except that he must remember that spread orders in call markets (e.g., silver) cannot be filled on the opening or close because only one contract at a time is being traded. The client may have a spread order limited to a given difference in price, which he has noted on the tape or a broker's board early or late in the day. When his broker tells him that he was unable to fill the order, the customer sometimes blames him unfairly for missing the market, not realizing that the order could not possibly have been filled.

At the end of each day the clearing house, which is a subsidiary of the exchange, assumes one side of all open contracts: if a broker is long, the clearing house has the other, or short, position; if a broker is short, the clearing house assumes the other, or long, side. The clearing house guarantees its members the performance of both sides of all open contracts. Each broker, therefore, who is long or short a futures contract deals only with the clearing house after initiating his position and not with the broker who actually took the other side of the trade. In effect, all obligations to receive or deliver commodities are with the clearing house and not with other brokers or individuals.

The clearing house does not care about the prices at which each trade was entered, because, as already mentioned, all profits and losses are settled daily in cash according to the latest settlement price. Because the clearing house always has a zero net position, it can operate easily without any reference to entry or exit prices for the individual trades on its books. Only the customer and his broker are interested in these matters.

The total long or short positions (which are always equal) outstanding at a given moment is called the "open interest." A broker who is long a futures contract can meet his obligation either by accepting delivery of the commodity during the delivery month or by selling his position to someone else who chooses to be long. If he sells his position to someone who replaces him, the open interest is unchanged. If he sells his position to a short who is buying in his position, the open interest is accordingly reduced. A broker who is short a futures contract can meet his obligation by making delivery of the commodity or by buying in his position either from someone else who wishes to be short or from a broker on the long side who is selling out his position. The total size of the open interest and volume indicates the degree of current liquidity in a given market and is tabulated daily by the exchanges and by the Commodity Futures Trading Commission (CFTC). The

---

[2] These and other orders are discussed in detail in Chapter 3.

CFTC also publishes monthly and annual figures. The attempt by technicians to relate changes in open interest to simultaneous, preceding, or lagging changes in volume and price is discussed in Chapter 7.

Commodities may be traded for delivery during any future month, but a few months of the year ordinarily become active, usually in accordance with trade needs or customs, such as the normal harvest time of a crop. All months in which each commodity is traded are listed with other pertinent contract facts in Chapter 3.

Some commodity exchanges, such as the Chicago Board of Trade and The Chicago Mercantile Exchange, handle long lists of commodities, whereas others, for example, the New York Cocoa Exchange, handle only one. Sometimes the same commodity is traded on more than one exchange. This is usually a matter of regional requirements, as in the case of wheat, in response to which Soft Red is traded in Chicago, Hard Red in Kansas City, and spring wheat in Minneapolis. Sometimes more than one type of a commodity can be delivered against an exchange contract; for example, Hard Red wheat is deliverable against the Soft Red contract in Chicago.

NATURE OF THE OPEN INTEREST

Although commodity exchanges differ in commodities traded, location, size, and details of their operations, the people who trade on them are all similarly motivated. Basically, there are floor traders of various types, outside speculators, and hedgers. Speculators and hedgers, unlike floor traders, may or may not be members of the exchanges on which they trade, but whether they are or not primarily affects their commission and margin requirements and not the manner in which they trade or their reasons for trading. Because the remainder of the book centers on the activities and techniques of the market participants, they can be introduced briefly at this point.

Speculators. A commodity speculator is interested in profiting from a price change in a commodity futures contract. He is not interested in taking delivery or making delivery of the commodity in which he trades, although he may do so sometimes in connection with his speculating. Speculators may trade from the floor of an exchange if they are members or through a broker if they are not. They differ from one another in several ways. Some trade small positions and some quite large positions, even up to the limits imposed on speculative positions by the CFTC or by the exchanges, as illustrated in Chapter 3. Some prefer to trade from the long side, some from the short side, and some prefer to trade spreads rather than net positions. Spreading, like security arbitrage, is usually done by the more sophisticated traders.

One of the great differences among speculators is the length of time during which they are prepared to hold a position. A small number prefer to wait for a full move, which could take months, a year, or even more to develop, and will hold a position for as long as necessary. Position traders of this kind generally trade from the long side of the market, in order, when their trades are successful, to take advantage of the favorable long-term gain provisions of the Internal Revenue Code. Most traders hold their positions for much shorter periods, and there are some who, whenever possible, get out the day they get in. These day traders are sometimes called "scalpers." Although they are seldom able to realize large gains in so short a time, neither do they often sustain large losses. In addition, day traders receive more favorable margin requirements and, on many exchanges, benefit from a materially reduced commission rate. Unfortunately many unsophisticated day traders develop a practice of liquidating only their day trades that go in the right direction and maintaining positions that go wrong, with the inevitable eventual record of an accumulation of many small profits which are more than countered by some large losses. The number of successful day traders in relation to the number who try day trading is probably quite small.

Floor traders. Floor traders are members of the exchange who make their transactions in the pit or around the ring on the exchange floor itself, as contrasted with other members who choose to trade off the floor through member brokerage houses. A floor trader, like a nonmember speculator, can trade for his own account. He can take long-term positions, "scalp" over short periods for day trades, or even trade several times a day. He may work in one commodity or several. His advantage is the speed with which he can take positions or liquidate them, but this is in itself no assurance of a profit. A bad position quickly taken is bad nonetheless. There are some floor traders who specialize in spreads by taking opposite positions between options when the price difference appears abnormal. Floor traders have the advantage of the lower commissions available to all members of exchanges. Floor traders trading for their own accounts are sometimes referred to as "locals." Some become quite prosperous; many others do not, despite the market letters of some brokers, which leave the impression that locals almost never lose.

Some members on the floor handle orders for others but seldom or never trade for themselves. These brokers specialize in orders emanating from futures commission merchants or from customers in the trade, such as processors, exporters, and warehousers. They receive only a small part of the commissions paid by the customer to his commission house, but a broker who handles the orders for a large commission house may be involved in a substantial volume of business and his total income can be quite impressive. The orders held by this broker at any given time are referred to as his "deck." He is allowed to trade for his own account if he chooses, but must not trade in such a way that anything he does could be in conflict with his deck. As in any fiduciary business, the customers' interests are to be placed first.

Hedgers. Futures trading grew out of the needs of the manufacturers, merchants, and dealers engaged in the business of producing, merchandising, and processing commodities. Some of the earliest markets featured the grains, and most of them are important today. Their salient point was that they existed primarily for delivery and therefore were characterized by rules governing merchandising transactions, standards ensuring grade and delivery terms, and clearing arrangements. Futures contracts soon came to be viewed as temporary substitutes for cash contracts, and traders found it rewarding to be able to establish prices for a future date.

The most important role played by early futures markets was in the hedging of inventories. During the peak marketing season tradesmen often bought more than enough to fill their current orders to be sure of being able to meet the demands of their customers until new supplies became available. The merchant and dealer of those grains incurred the risk of unfavorable price changes that could easily outweigh the other risks, such as fire, theft, or windstorm, he faced as a matter of course. Grain prices, then as now, were notoriously volatile because they were subject not only to the vagaries of supply and demand but were also affected to an unusual degree by weather, unexpected political developments, and sometime illogical changes in public psychology. Merchants and dealers with heavy inventories of an unsold crop could face disastrous losses in the event of a material drop in prices. Those same participants who made forward sales based on current cash prices and who relied on purchasing inventories later to meet their commitments rather than pay storage charges for the cash grain would have a similar problem if prices rose sharply.

The hedging function, then, naturally focused on the role of transferring the risk of drastic inventory price changes to other holders in the futures markets. The other side of the transaction necessary to accomplish this might well have been taken by another hedger who was offsetting an opposite risk or was liquidating another hedge as a result of a change in his position in the cash market. More often than not it was taken by a speculator attempting to make a profit. It would appear, on the surface, as if this risk of price change would not be important in the long run because of the windfall profits that would compensate for disastrous losses. Most businessmen learned in those early years, however, that they would gladly forego large profits to avoid large losses because of the danger that they might not survive the large loss to enjoy the large profit if the loss should come first. There was also the danger that a number of losses might precede a number of profits.

The traditional risk transferral concept of hedging has evolved into a dynamic concept of risk management which accents the maximization of expected return as well as the position of merely minimizing risk. In this regard hedging is now viewed by many sophisticated users as an important management tool which can facilitate buying and selling decisions and give greater freedom for business action in markets not only dominated by the necessity of carrying inventories from one period of time to another but also in nonstorage markets. The evolution of the hedging process and an analysis of the motivation and mechanics of hedging are covered in a subsequent section.

Distribution of the open interest. It is of considerable use to the trader to examine the distribution of the value of the total open interest among the participants over a wide range of markets for a significant period of time. Table 2-2 provides such data reported semimonthly for CEA-regulated commodities over an 18-year period.[3] The analysis does not include the unregulated markets at the time of the study, such as pork bellies, sugar or cocoa, or markets that have since come into being and reflect important volume, such as cattle, plywood, lumber, orange juice, or silver. Even

---

[3] Charles Rockwell, "Normal Backwardation, Forecasting, and the Returns to Commodity Futures Traders," *Proceedings of a Symposium on Price Effects of Speculation in Organized Commodity Markets, Food Research Institute Studies,* Supplement, 7 (1967), 107–130. Rockwell's approach is the only published study that utilizes the commitments of reporting speculators, hedgers, spreaders, and nonreporting traders prepared by the CEA in a broad coverage of both markets and time. An earlier study by Hendrik Houthakker, "Can Speculators Forecast Prices?" *The Review of Economics and Statistics* (May 1957), reported evidence based on three markets over a shorter time period.

TABLE 2-2   VALUE OF GROUP COMMITMENTS AS A PERCENTAGE OF THE VALUE OF THE TOTAL OPEN INTEREST

Trading groups*	Percentage of the value of total open interest for 25 CEA-regulated markets, 1947–1965
Nonreporting (small) traders	
Small traders, long	53
Small traders, short	39
Reporting (large) traders	
Large speculators, long	11
Large speculators, short	5
Spreaders, long	18
Spreaders, short	18
Hedgers, long	18
Hedgers, short	38

* The CEA requires that reports be filed for each day on which a trade is made, for the day before, during, and one day after a certain level of positions are held. These reportable positions, by commodity, are listed in Chapter 3.

SOURCE: Charles Rockwell, "Normal Backwardation, Forecasting, and the Returns to Commodity Futures Traders," *Proceedings of a Symposium on Price Effects of Speculation in Organized Commodity Markets, Food Research Institute Studies,* Supplement, 7 (1967), 117.

though many markets no longer viable, such as bran, middlings, shorts, onions, and butter, are included in the study, it is reasonable to assume that the three broad conclusions[4] that follow continue to be applicable.

The first conclusion is that on the average both small (nonreporting) and large (reporting) speculators are net long and that reporting hedgers are net short. Large speculators, then, tend to be on the same side of the market as the small traders and opposite that of the hedger. The implications of this distribution in regard to the effectiveness of the futures market for hedging and to the rates of return to the participants are discussed later.

Second, the data indicate the degree of balance between the long and short positions of each group. The short-to-long position ratio is 74 percent for small traders, 45 percent for large speculators, and 47 percent for hedgers. As a group, then, it would seem that large speculators and hedgers have expectations that are more unbalanced than those of small traders. Whether the greater homogeneity in large trader expectations accompanies generally superior or inferior trading results is discussed in Chapter 12.

Third, the data in Table 2-2 confirm the long-suspected notion that large speculators form an elite population. Although the percentage of the total open interest attributed to the large speculator may vary considerably from market to market, the fact is that for all markets the holdings of the large speculator's total long and short positions are less than 20 percent of the total holdings of the small traders. If it can be conservatively assumed that the average large speculator holds a position at least 10 times as large as the average small trader, then large speculators probably constitute less than 2 percent of the total futures trading population.

NATURE OF CASH AND FUTURES PRICE RELATIONS

Introduction. There is a basic truth about commodity futures contracts. They are temporary substitutes for cash commodities. The realization that, if held to maturity, delivery of the real goods is guaranteed impresses upon the speculator, both small and large, that speculation in commodity futures is not just a numbers game which is conducted in Wonderland. Because of this, the trader should understand the relation between cash and futures prices. Perhaps this clarification can be made by indicating the complexities of the role of hedging in the futures markets.

There can be no serious exceptions to the statement that futures trading depends on hedging. Markets simply do not come into existence solely to furnish a speculative arena, nor do they persist if hedgers, the inhabitants of the land, do not find it rewarding to continue to use those markets. The

[4] *Ibid.,* 117, 118.

higher the level of hedging, the higher the level of futures business. The relation between hedging and speculation is discussed in the final section of this chapter.

The trader should be apprised that the literature on hedging in commodity futures markets is not the essence of clarity. It is often disjointed and the thoughful work is not generally available to the casual trader. In an attempt to define and develop the controversies as they have appeared, four classes of hedging theory are discussed,[5] each of which differs in the assumptions made about the attitudes of hedgers toward risk and motivation for using the futures markets.

Hedging carried out to eliminate the risks associated with price fluctuations. The risk-elimination view of hedging usually begins with a naïve illustration of the two kinds of hedge. A processor holds 100,000 bushels of cash wheat at $2.00 a bushel and is fearful of a decline in price. He immediately sells 100,000 bushels of futures contracts at $2.00 and is thereby short hedged. If the feared decline materializes and wheat drops to $1.85 a bushel, the profit on the short sale of futures exactly offsets the loss on the inventory. A long hedge is illustrated in much the same manner. A commercial business with a commitment to sell 100,000 bushels of wheat at a specific price and time in the future, which it has neither bought nor contracted to buy, can protect itself by buying a futures position equal in amount to its forward sale and thereby fix its forward costs. Thus the hedging process is said to eliminate the risk of price fluctuation.

In real life hedging decisions are neither really so simple nor mechanical. The grade of the commodity owned or sold forward by the prospective hedger may not be the same as that of the contract grade traded on the futures exchange. There might also be variations in the discounts or premiums of "off" and "on" grades which have been hedged in relation to the basic contract grade. Trade houses serving or buying from local areas might be confronted with conditions somewhat different from those affecting markets elsewhere. Sales and purchases of the cash commodities do not always correspond exactly with futures market contract units. Merchants and dealers might prefer to sell in amounts geared to contract units, but there is inevitably some variation. If elimination of risk is to be a reality, buyers in the field must report their purchases to be hedged before the market closes. Cash business can still be conducted after the futures close or before they open, which means that either some hedging must be delayed until the following day or, as noted later, some must be done in *anticipation* of further cash business.

Because of the "equal but opposite" connotation implied in the naive

---

[5] This approach was employed by Roger W. Gray and David J. S. Rutledge, "The Economics of Commodity Futures Markets: A Survey," *Review of Marketing and Agricultural Economics*, 39, No. 4, reported by the Food Research Institute, Stanford University, Stanford, Calif. 1972.

view of hedging, the concepts of hedging and insurance seem to be analogous. In fact, apart from the problems just discussed, the hedger is insured against price risk only if cash and futures prices move in parallel. The literature is replete with examples that indicate that cash and futures prices do *not* move in parallel.[6] The naïve view of risk elimination must, then, give way to a risk-reduction concept.

Hedging carried out to reduce the risks associated with price fluctuations. Even though it has often been found that cash and futures prices do not parallel one another, researchers have been able to muster considerable support for the proposition that a change in cash prices frequently results in a *similar* change in futures prices, particularly if some unexpected event causes a violent price change. Cash and futures prices, it has been ascertained, will not always move exactly together, but a material movement by them in opposite directions is quite unusual.

BASIS. The arithmetical difference between the cash and futures prices at any time is known as "*the* basis." The usual difference reflects a premium or discount of the cash price versus the nearby future; for example, No. 1 Soybeans in June might be quoted at 5 cents over the August future, in which case the basis would be expressed as "5 over." On the other hand, the individual hedger, concerned primarily with his own position, would be inclined to speak of "my basis." "*My* basis," refers to the difference between the price of "my" commitment in the actual product expressed as a premium or discount from the specific future contract in which the individual hedger has effected a short hedge. "My basis" remains unchanged as long as the established price relationships remain in effect. The size of the premium or discount provides a benchmark against which the closeout prices of both positions may be measured. If the spread between "my" cash commitment and the nearby future contract remains unchanged or moves to a more favorable close-out basis, "my" transactions will have been successful.[7]

Nothing, of course, precludes the basis from being quoted in distant options. Besides the current cash price being above or below that of futures options, nearby futures market prices may be above or below those more distant prices that reflect the same crop. In seasons in which supplies are normal or large the later contracts generally show a premium. Such a market is referred to as a "carrying-charge market." When supplies are tight, nearby contracts may reflect the scarcity of the cash market by selling at premiums over more distant contracts, in which case the market is said to

[6] A readily available source for the trader is *The Hedger's Handbook,* published by Merrill Lynch, Pierce, Fenner & Smith, Inc., 165 Broadway, New York, N.Y., 10006, pp. 21, 33, 37, 49.

[7] A complete discussion of "basis" is given by Henry B. Arthur, *Commodity Futures As a Business Management Tool,* Division of Research, Graduate School of Business Administration, Harvard University, Cambridge Mass., 1971, pp. 64–69.

be "inverted." Whether the current cash market is above or below prices in the futures market and whether the futures market is at carrying charges or inverted, and by how much, is vital to hedgers making price decisions. The same conditions can also influence speculators, who might attempt to make their decisions partly by considering what hedgers are likely to do.

If the risk reduction premise is accepted as the major reason for indulging in the hedging process, the usefulness of any market must depend on how closely cash and futures prices move together. The methodology employed in such a search is predictable. First changes in cash prices and then changes in the basis must be measured. If the variation in cash prices is larger than the variation in the basis, the futures market can be considered an effective tool for reducing the risks associated with price fluctuations. Studies employing this kind of analysis have confirmed that there is considerably less variation in the difference between cash and futures prices than there is in cash or futures prices alone.[8] That there is a significant positive correlation between cash and futures prices is now regarded as the first axiom of the hedging process.

At this point the usual definition of the hedger as an aloof onlooker rather than a participant in the speculative market pricing process begins to blur. Indeed, the trader begins to understand that in most circumstances hedging is merely a form of speculation—speculation on the basis. The hedger differs from the speculator only because the variation in his outcome is generally less. What the hedger accomplishes is the specialization of risk, not the elimination of it. The short hedger, for example, passes to the speculator the risks of anticipating changes in absolute prices and retains the "basis risk," that is, predicting the demand for stocks. If he can forecast the volume and timing of demand for his product for a given level of risk, a short hedger might well be able to hold a much larger volume of hedged inventory than he could hold unhedged. Such a thought raises the possibility of hedging for profit as well as reduced risk.

Hedging carried out to profit from movements in the basis. If a merchant or processor feels that he has a comparative advantage in anticipating the yield on his inventory, the important question is no longer how *closely* cash and futures prices move together (the stability of the basis) but rather whether such movement is *predictable*. Working[9] produced

[8] L. D. Howell authored two such studies for the USDA, *Analysis of Hedging and Other Operations in Grain Futures,* Technical Bulletin No. 971, August 1948, and *Analysis of Hedging and Other Operations in Wool and Wool Top Futures,* Technical Bulletin No. 1260, January 1962. He also coauthored, with L. J. Watson, *Relation of Spot Cotton Prices to Futures Contracts and Protection Afforded by Trading in Futures,* USDA Technical Bulletin No. 602, January 1938.

[9] Holbrook Working, "Hedging Reconsidered," *Journal of Farm Economics,* 35, No. 4 (November 1953), 544–561.

data on wheat prices that indicate that basis fluctuations are predictable. A recent study has provided supporting evidence for corn and soybeans.[10] Working's conclusions invited a significant expansion in the possible motivations of hedging:

1. It facilitates buying and selling decisions. When hedging is practiced systematically, there is need only to consider whether the price at which a particular purchase or sale can be made is favorable in relation to other current prices; there is no need to consider also whether the absolute level of the price is favorable.

2. It gives *greater freedom for business action.* The freedom most commonly gained is that of buying; for example, when a particular lot of the commodity is available at a relatively low price, regardless of its absolute level (this freedom is related to but distinct from the facilitation of decision mentioned above): often, moreover, the freedom gained is to make a sale or purchase that would not otherwise be possible at what is judged a favorable price level, as when a cotton grower sells futures in advance of harvest, or a textile mill buys futures because cotton prices are judged to be favorable, but the desired qualities of cotton cannot be bought immediately in the spot market.

3. It gives a *reliable basis for conducting storage of commodity surpluses.* The warehousing of surplus commodity stocks is a very uncertain and hazardous business when based on trying to judge when the price is favorable for storage; hedging allows operation on the basis simply of judgment that the spot price is low in relation to a futures price.

4. Hedging *reduces business risks.* There is usually reduction of risk when hedging is done for any of the previous three reasons (though often not under the second reason), but any curtailment of risk may be only an incidental advantage gained, not a primary or even a very important incentive to hedging.[11]

The enlarged concept of hedging, which emphasizes the expected returns rather than simply reducing risk, came to be called "arbitrage hedging" and stemmed from the belief that hedgers develop a sophisticated understanding of factors that determine prices in the commodities in which they deal.

Working developed the concepts of "selective" and "anticipatory" hedging to deal with actions based on expectations. Selective hedging is partial hedging which occurs when the hedger has made a subjective determination on a price rise or fall in a coming period. Because of this determination, the hedger may leave some or all of his inventory unhedged. Thus a firm would employ short hedging only when a price decline is expected and would not carry short hedges at all when a price increase is expected. Anticipatory hedging would involve the purchase or sale of futures in antici-

---

[10] R. G. Heifner, "The Gains from Basing Grain Storage Decisions on Cash-Future Spreads," *Journal of Farm Economics,* 48, No. 5 (December 1966), 1490–1495.

[11] Holbrook Working, *op. cit.,* 560–561.

pation of a formal merchandising commitment to be made later, and the operator would carry an open position in the futures market for a time without an offsetting cash commitment.

An excellent example of arbitrage hedging is reflected by soybean processors' use of the markets for soybeans, soybean meal, and soybean oil. The relation between the soybeans and their products enables processors to set hedging policies, for example, according to expectations of a large crop, short crop, processing margins, and the relative demand for meal or oil.

The major considerations of a hedger in making his decisions revolve around his particular basis and the premiums or discounts among forward future contracts. The literature developing these relationships has come to be known as the "supply of storage" theory.[12] The objective of the theory is to explain intertemporal (over time) price differences between cash and forward prices or between cash and expected future cash prices in commodities with continuous inventories. Until recently futures trading was limited to commodities that could be stored for relatively long periods; hence a significant body of knowledge was built up. Price relationships for seasonally produced commodities with discontinuous inventories, such as Maine potatoes, or for continuously produced commodities in which no inventories are held at all, such as fresh eggs or live cattle, must emphasize the forward pricing function.

The costs of holding inventory include carrying charges, such as interest and insurance, and the risk of price fluctuation. The benefits of holding inventory have been referred to broadly as the convenience yield, which arises from holding, per se, a certain level of inventory. If a processor, for example, inadvertently runs out of inventory, his sales may drop precipitously and he may not cover his overhead expenses. Insuring that inventory does not drop below a given level reduces the chance of incurring such out-of-stock costs. A processor may wish, too, to maintain a relatively stable re-

[12] M. J. Brennan, "The Supply of Storage," *American Economic Review*, 47 (March 1958), 50–72; Paul H. Cootner, "Speculation and Hedging," *Proceedings of a Symposium on Price Effects of Speculation in Organized Commodity Markets, Food Research Institute Studies*, Supplement, 7 (1967), 65–105; Nicholas Kaldor, "A Note on the Theory of the Forward Market," *Review of Economic Studies*, 7 (June 1940), 196–201; John Maynard Keynes, *The General Theory of Employment, Interest and Money*, New York, Harcourt, Brace, 1936; Lester G. Telser, "Futures Trading and the Storage of Cotton and Wheat," *Journal of Political Economy*, 66 (June 1958), 233–55; Holbrook Working, "Price Relations Between July and September Wheat Futures at Chicago Since 1885," *Wheat Studies*, 9 (March 1933), 187–238; Holbrook Working, "Price Relations Between May and New Crop Wheat Futures at Chicago Since 1885," *Wheat Studies*, 10 (February 1934), 183–228; Holbrook Working, "Theory of the Inverse Carrying Charge in Futures Markets," *Journal of Farm Economics*, 30 (February 1948), 1–28; Holbrook Working, "The Theory of the Price of Storage," *American Economic Review*, 31 (December 1949), 1254–1262.

tail price level for a product, even though raw material prices fluctuate considerably. He can accomplish this more efficiently if he has a sizable inventory base that will allow a more stable average price. The convenience yield can offset some or all of the carrying costs associated with stocks. As soon as a short hedge, for example, is placed, the processor has fixed the rate of return he will earn if he holds both the cash and the futures contract to maturity. For this reason the relation between the futures price and the cash price must be sufficient for the processor to recoup the net costs of storage from one time period to another.

If the first axiom of hedging is that cash and future prices tend to move in the same direction, the second general principle is that the price of the cash commodity and its futures price must become equal in the delivery month. If the futures price were higher than the cash price, the cash commodity would be bought, the futures sold, and delivery made. If the cash price were higher than the futures price, the processor would buy the futures and take delivery as the most desirable source of supply. Many traders notice, however, that cash prices are usually higher than the futures during the delivery month, and they wonder why they cannot buy the futures, take delivery, sell the commodity in the cash market, and pocket the difference. There are several reasons for the cash premium.[13] One is that cash and futures are not perfect substitutes until the last day of the month, which occurs after futures trading in that particular contract has ceased. Until that point, because delivery is made at the seller's option, the precise time of delivery is not known. This uncertainty can inject a premium into the cash commodity, which tends to decrease as the delivery month progresses. Factors among others that may be included are not knowing the precise quality of commodity that will be delivered and the possible inclusion of load-out or switching charges.

The trader should remember that there need be no particular incentive to deliver just because there is a gap between cash and expiring future prices. If he anticipates lower demand, the early month deliverer may reason that the recipient (most likely a speculator) will have no use for the actual commodity and will have to redeliver (perhaps many times), while relieving the deliverer of storage charges. The merchant can deliver early in the month, fully expecting to stand for delivery again later in the month.

Tactics formulated by hedgers attempting to profit from movements in the basis revolve about four basic possibilities which may accompany either the short or long hedge. A selling hedge or a buying hedge can be placed in a carrying charge market or an inverted market, and price levels may increase or decrease after the placement of the hedge. Table 2-3 summa-

---

[13] As discussed by Thomas A. Hieronymus, *Economics of Futures Trading*, Commodity Research Bureau, New York, pp. 152–53.

rizes the possible outcomes from differences in cash and futures price movements. Generally, in a carrying charge market, which is most common,
merchants and dealers will buy the cash product freely because they are
able to sell futures contracts favorably against their cash position, knowing
that the premiums on the forward futures contracts will pay part or all of
their carrying charges. The futures contract chosen will depend on the
length of time that the merchant expects to hold his cash position and on
which of the futures months traded is most favorably priced in relation to
the others at the time the hedge is placed. A dealer or merchant who is long
in the cash market and short hedged is, in effect, "long the basis"; that is,
if the basis increases because the cash price gains on the futures month in
which the hedge is placed, the hedger will make a profit by the amount of
the improvement. Similarly, a merchant who has made a forward commit-

TABLE 2-3   VARIATIONS IN GAINS OR LOSSES RESULTING
FROM DIFFERENCES IN CASH AND FUTURE PRICE
MOVEMENTS

Price Movements		Results			
		to one who is "long" in the cash market		to one who is "short" in the cash market	
Cash price	Future price	Unhedged	Hedged	Unhedged	Hedged
Falls	Falls by same amounts as cash	Loss	Neither profit nor loss	Profit	Neither profit nor loss
Falls	Falls by greater amount than cash	Loss	Profit	Profit	Loss
Falls	Falls by smaller amount than cash	Loss	Loss, but smaller than unhedged loss	Profit	Profit, but smaller than unhedged profit
Falls	Rises	Loss	Loss but greater than unhedged loss	Profit	Profit, but greater than unhedged profit
Rises	Rises by same amount as cash	Profit	Neither profit nor loss	Loss	Neither profit nor loss
Rises	Rises by greater amount than cash	Profit	Loss	Loss	Profit
Rises	Rises by smaller amount than cash	Profit	Profit, but smaller than unhedged profit	Loss	Loss, but smaller than unhedged loss
Rises	Falls	Profit	Profit, but greater than unhedged profit	Loss	Loss, but greater than unhedged loss

SOURCE: B. S. Yamey, "An Investigation of Hedging on an Organized Produce Exchange,"
Manchester School 19 (1951), 308.

ment to sell a cash commodity and places a long hedge by buying a futures position against his commitment is "short the basis." If cash prices drop in relation to the futures month in which the hedge is placed, he would profit; if they gained, he would lose.

When forward months are selling at discounts to nearby months, a buyer of the cash commodity has an especially difficult problem. If he places his short hedges in months selling at a discount, he does so knowing that cash and futures prices will tend to draw together as time passes and that there will not be a significant difference when the forward month becomes the cash month. This means that the basis will almost certainly become smaller, and because he is long the basis he will lose accordingly. The difficulty of hedging in such markets is even more apparent when it is noted that the degree of inversion is virtually unlimited, whereas in a carrying charge market, as already discussed, the degree of the carrying charge is limited by the possibilities of arbitrage.

Even under such conditions hedging may take place. Many hedges are placed for short periods, during which the unfavorable basis may not change or may become even more unfavorable, in which case a basis profit may even be realized. Alternatively, a cash dealer could buy "hand-to-mouth," perhaps buying only to fill orders in hand, or, if he has orders for future delivery, he can cover his commitment by buying the relatively cheap forward futures contracts rather than the presently high-priced cash commodity. This places him in the position of having a long hedge, which makes him short the basis. Later he can meet his commitment by buying in the cash market and selling his futures contract or taking delivery against his long futures position if the time, grade, and location of delivery all meet his requirements satisfactorily.

An oversimplified example illustrates the possible actions of a dealer in cash corn. Assume that in November he has bought some cash corn from the country at $1.15 a bushel. Pending its sale to a processor or exporter, the dealer decides for any of myriad reasons, to place a short hedge, assuming that he has no commitment for the sale of the corn. Perhaps corn for March delivery is then selling for $1.21 on the Chicago Board of Trade and he regards the March contract as most satisfactory for hedging purposes. The dealer therefore may decide to sell an amount of March corn approximately equal to his cash position. Having placed a short hedge, he is now long the basis. When he sells his corn, the hedge will be removed, or lifted. If the price of corn in the futures market has moved up or down by the same amount as that of cash corn, the cost of hedging to the dealer is his commissions. In practice, of course, the dealer must consider related costs, such as moving the corn into storage, holding it, and moving it out again, all of which could have been avoided by selling the corn immediately after buying it. Typically, the cash and futures prices will move in the same general direction but not in exactly the same degree. If the cash price gains on the future, the basis will have widened and there will be a basis profit on the hedge itself. If the basis narrows, there will be a basis loss by the amount that it narrowed. With so little time between November and March, a material loss resulting from the cash price losing in relation to the futures is unlikely because in March they should differ by little or nothing. A large basis loss is therefore not a great risk.

The sale of the March futures contract could be made to another hedger who is short the cash market, to a hedger long the cash market who has sold his cash position and is now lifting, or buying in, his hedge, or to a speculator who is going long or covering a short position. The short position in the March contract can ultimately be eliminated in one of two ways. The dealer can wait until March and deliver his corn against the contract, or he can sell his cash corn on the cash market and lift his hedge either by offsetting it by purchase or by transferring the position to the new holder of the cash corn, who might also choose to be hedged in the March futures month. The latter procedure is so common that the transfer of the futures position itself frequently forms the basis for determining the selling price of the cash position: for example, a sale may be made at "3 cents under March," but exactly what is March? The price of March corn might vary several cents during the course of one trading day. A determination can be made simply by the dealer buying in his own March position for the purchaser of his cash corn and setting the price from that transaction. Such deals are given different names on different exchanges, such as "ex-pit transactions" or "sales against actuals." In these transactions the brokers agree to report identical prices to the clearing house without actually executing the trades.

If, in the example, March arrived and the cash corn which had been hedged was not yet sold, the hedger still might not deliver against his futures contract. He might conclude that the cash market was too low and, noting that the premium of the May futures contract over the March was favorable, might choose to buy in his March contract (offset) and remain hedged by selling May. This is called "rolling forward." If the dealer had known in November what he came to know in March, he could, of course, have saved a commission by selling the May corn as a hedge in the first place. It is obvious that if the basis narrowed while the dealer was in a hedged position—that is, cash lost on the future—a loss on the basis would have been suffered.

Like speculators, hedgers must deposit margin against their positions, although normally their margin requirements are considerably less than those required for speculators. Sometimes margin may be handled by the hedger's bank. In such cases confirmations or statements involved in transactions will be provided to the bank as well as the hedger. Hedging involves certain costs, such as commissions and interest on margin requirements, but these may be regarded as costs of doing business. Most banks are willing lenders for hedging purposes and may be cautious about making loans to firms carrying large unhedged positions in the commodity markets. To some hedgers the ease of procuring cash loans may be the most important advantage of using the futures markets.

Because price relations are complex and the users of futures markets include producers, warehousemen, merchants, and processors, hedging carried out to profit from movements in the basis requires detailed knowledge and skill in interpretation to be successful. An excellent summary of the specific needs, practices, and behavior of the individual trade user is offered by Hieronymus[14] and Arthur.[15]

Hedging carried out to maximize expected returns for a given risk (variability of return) or minimize risk for a given expected return. Recent studies have applied portfolio theory to hedging behavior.[16] The hedger is viewed as being able to hold several assets: for example, unhedged inventory, inventory hedged by a sale of futures, or inventory hedged by a forward cash sale are all possible decisions by the hedger, depending on the probability of the rate of return on each asset. The hedger himself is considered as acting in concert with his own utility for risk and reward and the inevitable playoff between the two at any given time in much the same way as the individual trader responded, as described in Chapter 5.

The theoretical studies are an attempt to formalize a discussion of hedging behavior and are based on the Markowitz theory of portfolio selection.[17] Further discussions of the models suggested in the literature are technical and are beyond the scope of this book. The implication of portfolio theory for understanding the nature of the futures markets are clear, however. The theory emphasizes that "risk is inherent in all marketing and processing strategies, not only those in which hedging does not take place, i.e., that futures markets facilitate 'risk management' rather than 'risk transferral.'"[18]

Any business contemplating the use of the commodity futures markets as a management tool for choosing between various sets of marketing and processing strategies should answer initially several questions simply as a test of relevance.[19] These questions should include, What business are we in? What are the critical profit factors? How do price changes affect the critical factors? How do price change impacts compare with changes in the

[14] *Ibid.,* 171–240.

[15] Arthur, *op cit.,* pp. 137–314.

[16] David J. S. Rutledge, "Hedgers' Demand for Futures Contract: A Theoretical Framework with Applications to the United States Soybean Complex," *Food Research Institute Studies,* 11 (1973), 237–256.

[17] H. Markowitz, *Portfolio Selection—Efficent Diversification of Investments,* Yale University Press, New Haven, 1959.

[18] Rutledge, *op. cit.,* p. 254.

[19] Henry B. Arthur, "The Many Facets of Commodity Futures as a Tool of Management," *Workshop/72,* Coffee and Sugar Exchange, 1972, p. 36.

futures markets? Assuming that the answers to these questions indicate that risk management incorporating commodity futures can contribute to the overall business objectives, varying points of view in developing hedging policies may be considered. Exhibit 2-1 attempts to structure these views.[20] Each of the column headings relates to a business management function or interest; for example, the first column assumes total independence of cash and hedging considerations. Hedging is employed merely to offset all or some of the net inventory price risks as they occur. The second column begins building the futures contract into the business operation, columns 3 and 4 include specific procurement and marketing functions which accent decision making by those responsible for the operations, and column 5 reflects the most sophisticated use of hedging. The vertical shading of the first panel is suggestive of the degree of risk incurred which increases as the listings progress from top to bottom. The range includes an attempt at risk avoidance on the one hand to brash opportunism on the other. Real-world practices lie somewhere in between.

Critical comment. The main purpose of including a discussion of the theory and practice of hedging is to educate the trader in the singular truth that futures trading depends on hedging. Two additional purposes must share top priority, however. The first is that the treatment of the vast majority of literature with which the trader is most likely to come in contact is naïve, if not outright incorrect. The most charitable judgment one can make of these approaches is that they are exactly what they claim to be— oversimplified examples. Many commission house offerings, as well as much of the early literature, tend to perpetuate pleasant myths in the interest of obviating the need for their own understanding and that of their readership.

The second purpose of a discussion of hedging is to impress on the average trader the probable futility of attempting to relate a significant amount of this knowledge to the improvement of his own record. The differences of opinion and practices as well as the intricacies of the variables involved make it all but impossible to reduce the outcomes to general rules for the improvement of trading effectiveness. Better by far that the trader applaud the consistent use of well-traveled markets by the trade, the expansion of those markets that may have fallen into comparative disuse, and the emergence of new markets, for example, for live hogs, orange juice, and cattle, which consolidate, renew, and expand opportunities for rewarding speculation.

NATURE OF MARKET PERFORMANCE

The trader has been introduced to the nature of the futures contract and the considerable recent growth in its use. The nature of the exchanges that

---

[20] *Ibid.*, p. 42, *op. cit.*, pp. 336–337.

EXHIBIT 2-1   Points of View in Developing Hedging Policies

Primary guide or → purpose / Shading from protection to exposed position	Net position control (inventory risk)[1]	Gross position[2] (total commitment factors—"a larger market")	Procurement tool (time and cost)	Marketing tool (time and price)	Profit margins and incentives[3]
	1. Fully hedged (zero net position) Large volume "basis" operators	1. Maximize turnover without net exposure	1. Take delivery on futures markets to get needed goods	1. Deliver actuals on futures market	1. Lock in margin where actuals are bought or sold on formula price to be based on later futures quotations
	2. Partial hedge (constant, not zero, net position) Examples: Exclude Lifo base; hedge only seasonal accumulation	2. Spreading and arbitrage[4]	2. Lock in margin through low-costing raw material (to cover a sale commitment)	2. Sell futures to lock in realization on goods in inventory	2. Deal in basis this covers a wide assortment of specialized applications
	3. Variable hedge (planned or budgeted net position) Examples: Headquarters managed hedge; discretionary position within limits	3. Hedge excess over Lifo base	3. Assure repurchase of temporarily liquidated Lifo base stocks	3. Sell futures to assure price for anticipated production	3. Use price or margin targets to determine how much business will be done, as in deciding how much to store or process
	4. Variable hedge (deliberate variances to profit from price swings) Examples: Cyclical position taking; leaning into the wind; special position taking situation	4. Hedge seasonal storage	4. Anticipate storage accumulation by purchase of new crop futures	4. Cover risks on unpriced sales, requirements contracts, or "price date of delivery"	4. Pin down other half of a cash commodity trade in futures, awaiting opportunity to fulfill with actuals
		5. Use of futures to economize cash tied up in inventories, or to shorten exposure without sacrificing current throughout	5. Use futures to attain a target exposure when actuals not available	5. Liquidate unwanted risk by selling futures when cash won't move	5. Buy low, sell high, wherever the opportunity presents itself – all cash, all futures, or a mix including discretionary position taking
		6. Disregard business needs; straight speculation	6. Pin down attractive cost for anticipated needs	6. Sell futures farther ahead than actuals can be booked in the market	
			7. Reach out, speculate regardless of commercial needs		

[1] This column assumes a commercial operation in which all decisions are based on cash market considerations. The net cash positions (or portions of them) are then hedged in futures.

[2] This column assumes that added cash positions will be undertaken simply because they can be hedged.

[3] The column for profit margins and incentives relates to operations in which the primary focus is not on protection from general price swings, but on earnings from residuals and differentials (basis), or even from deliberate position taking.

[4] Includes earning of storage by holding deliverable cash product against short futures. This is sometimes referred to as "cash and carry."

SOURCE: Henry B. Arthur, Commodity Futures as a Business Management Tool, Division of Research, Graduate School of Business Administration, Harvard University, Cambridge, Mass., 1971, pp. 336–337.

trade these contracts have been discussed and a portrait of the speculator and hedger which included the impact of each on the open interest have been drawn. Cash and futures price relationships were analyzed to give the trader an appreciation of the complexities of the hedging process.

At this point it might help to ask, "How well do the markets function?" The experienced trader may retort wryly, "Too well. They're *so* tough to beat." He, of course, is referring to the behavior of futures prices which is of such importance that Chapter 4 is devoted entirely to a discussion of the characteristics of price changes. In a general sense, however, there has always been an implicit benchmark for judging whether futures markets should receive high or low performance marks. Because agricultural and raw materials commodities, which are featured in most futures markets, are subject to considerable price fluctuations (many are beyond the control of the producer or processor), markets that receive high performance marks are those in which there has been a noticeable reduction in price variability.

The question of price variability may be viewed generally from two positions — either that futures trading, in an institutional sense, tends to dampen or increase price fluctuations or that speculation itself significantly influences the variability of price changes. The various attacks on potato and onion futures trading as an institution [21] seemed to make more headway when price levels were depressed, just as similar investigations of the coffee, copper, and sugar markets were launched when prices were high. Some scholars have wondered about the pattern that exhibits concern for the *producer* of domestic commodities and the *consumer* of imported commodities. [22] Apart from such obvious bias, there is a continuing question whether the institution itself is worthy of the increasing trust that has been shown in its regard. A discussion of speculation and price variability follows later in the section.

One of the early dissatisfactions with market performance centered around the question of manipulation, which featured corners and bear raids in the finest robber baron tradition. [23] Activity by such men as Hutchinson, Leiter, and Patten in the years just before the turn of the century resulted in short-term price distortions, frequently because of inadequate supplies of a grain in the delivery position. The effectiveness of such corners gradually diminished as competitive balance appeared in the market, aided by legislation that now rewards the manipulator with five years imprisonment, a $10,000 fine, or both.

Historical evidence of the effects of futures trading on price fluctuations is not conclusive. Perhaps the most voluminous example of the divergent

---

[21] See Chapter 1.
[22] Gray and Rutledge, *op. cit.*, p. 32.
[23] C. H. Taylor, *History of the Board of Trade of the City of Chicago,* Robert O. Law Co., Chicago, 1917.

findings were those of the United States Federal Trade Commission,[24] which in part concluded:

> Frequently attempts have been made to deal with the question of the stabilizing effect of future trading by comparing periods prior to the practice of trading in futures with periods since there has been such trading. Such a comparison, in order to prove anything, must first prove that the other things are equal — either that there have been no other changes between the two periods or that any other changes that may have occurred had no effect on the fluctuation of grain prices. Obviously, no such proof can be offered in the case under consideration . . . (Vol. VI, p. 261).
>
> It seems to be conclusively proved by this bit of analysis that futures trading under existing conditions itself generates certain elements of risk and uncertainty. In other words, it causes some fluctuations. Its stabilizing influence must, therefore, depend upon its stilling or checking other causes of fluctuation that are more important than those it creates (Vol. VI, p. 264).

More recent studies of onions tend to support the contention that a futures market diminishes the variation in cash prices[25] as well as the seasonal range in prices.[26] In the latter study an index of seasonal price variations was computed for a period before the advent of futures trading, during the actual trading period, and for a four-year period following the ban on futures trading. The periods before and after futures trading registered similar harvest lows of about 75 and a subsequent spring high reading of about 145. During futures trading those figures were 87 and 118, respectively.

As the trader may surmise by now, there can be no single meaning in the term "price variability." A look at continuous and discontinuous inventory futures markets will illustrate the variations.[27] In continuous inventory markets the price of storage theory ensures that the level of prices for *all* months responds to change in information as it develops. Of course, the interrelations between cash prices and futures prices (the basis) change, but these changes are generally much smaller than absolute price changes, as discussed earlier. When no inventories are carried, the function of a futures market is to conduct "forward pricing" (forecasting), and the relations among prices differ from the first case. Figures 2-2, 2-3, and 2-4 present price behavior in three crops in which production decisions take place in the spring before a fall harvest—corn, soybeans, and potatoes.

[24] U.S. 56th Congress, 2nd Session, House, *U.S. Industrial Commission Report* (1900–1901), House Doc. 94.

[25] H. Working, "Price Effects of Futures Trading," *Food Research Institute Studies,* 1, No. 1 (1960), 3–31.

[26] Roger W. Gray, "Onions Revisited," *Journal of Farm Economics,* 45, No. 2 (May 1963), 273–276.

[27] As developed by William G. Tomek and Roger W. Gray, "Temporal Relationships Among Prices on Commodity Futures Markets: Their Allocative and Stabilizing Roles," *American Journal of Agricultural Economics,* 52, No. 3 (August 1970).

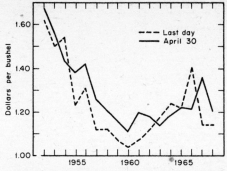

FIG. 2-2   Closing prices of December corn contract on April 30 and expiration date, 1952–1968. (W. G. Tomek and R. W. Gray, "Temporal Relationships Among Prices on Commodity Futures Markets: Their Allocative and Stabilizing Roles," *American Journal of Agricultural Economics*, vol. 52, no. 3, August 1970, pp. 374–375.)

In each case the closing prices for December corn, November soybeans, and November potatoes on April 30 are compared with expiration prices for a number of years. Corn and soybeans prices depict a tendency to move together (low variability), whereas the last day (cash) price of potatoes is clearly much more variable than the futures price throughout the years analyzed. The implications from the standpoint of the *growers'* ability through hedging to reduce price variability from year to year are interesting. Because no potato stocks are carried from May to November, the market in the spring cannot forecast any price other than the mean November

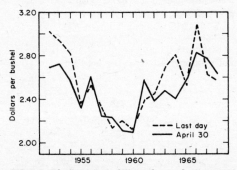

FIG. 2-3   Closing prices of November soybean contract on April 30 and expiration date, 1952–1968. (W. G. Tomek and R. W. Gray, "Temporal Relationships Among Prices on Commodity Futures Markets: Their Allocative and Stabilizing Roles," *American Journal of Agricultural Economics*, vol. 52, no. 3, August 1970, pp. 374–375.)

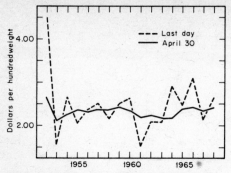

FIG. 2-4   Closing prices of November Maine potato contract on April 30 and expiration date, 1952–1968. (W. G. Tomek and R. W. Gray, "Temporal Relationships Among Prices on Commodity Futures Markets: Their Allocative and Stabilizing Roles," *American Journal of Agricultural Economics*, vol. 52, no. 3, August 1970, pp. 374–375.)

price until new crop information emerges. A forecast at the mean value of past observations, when coupled with a near zero variance in springtime prices, provides an excellent basis for hedging. On the other hand, as in the corn and soybean markets, routine hedging may not be helpful in reducing annual price variability because the variance in the springtime prices is about equal to the variance in the cash prices at maturity. In summation, then, as Gray and Rutledge note in their survey,

> . . . the potato grower can greatly reduce *his* price variability through hedging, as the corn and soybean grower cannot. But it is implied on the *other* sides of these coins that corn and soybean price variabilities have been reduced (through generalized production and inventory response) as potato price variability has not.[28]

The question whether speculation itself significantly influences the variability of prices is one of long standing. Many unresolved questions owe their longevity primarily to problems of measurement, and the role of speculation is no exception. An example of the data on open interest, available monthly from the CEA, is presented in Table 2-4; the reported commitments are divided into large (reporting) traders and small (nonreporting) traders. Hedgers are assumed to be numerous enough to be included in the reporting category, and small traders are considered residual, which is equal to the difference between the total open interest and that reflected by large speculators plus hedgers. All categories include the holdings of both the long and short positions. The monthly data also include the net change in the long and short positions for each group to reflect changes in the rela-

[28] Gray and Rutledge, *op. cit.*, 35.

TABLE 2-4   EXAMPLE OF MONTHLY REPORTED FUTURES
COMMITMENTS

*Soybeans**

Classification	July 31, 1971		Net change from June 30, 1971	
	Long	Short	Long	Short
		(in thousand bushels)		
Large traders				
Speculative				
Long *or* short only	17,390	7,240	− 510	− 3,035
Long *and* short (spreading)	97,415	97,600	+16,625	+16,810
Total	114,805	104,840	+16,115	+13,775
Hedging	107,815	96,595	− 1,395	− 5,890
Total reported by large traders	222,620	201,435	+14,720	+ 7,885
Small traders				
Speculative and hedging	73,365	94,550	− 5,165	+ 1,670
Total open contracts	295,985	295,985	+ 9,555	+ 9,555
Percent held by large traders	75.2	68.1	+ 2.6	+ 0.5
small traders	24.8	31.9	− 2.6	− 0.5

Frozen Pork Bellies†

Classification	July 31, 1971		Net change from June 30, 1971	
	Long	Short	Long	Short
		(in contract units of 36,000 pounds)		
Large traders				
Speculative				
Long *or* short only	1,416	2,276	− 329	− 1,398
Long *and* short (spreading)	3,124	3,124	+ 230	+ 230
Total	4,540	5,400	− 99	− 1,168
Hedging	476	787	− 1,278	− 1,218
Total reported by large traders	5,016	6,187	− 1,377	− 2,386
Small traders				
Speculative and hedging	9,891	8,720	− 5,518	−4,509
Total open contracts	14,907	14,907	− 6,895	−6,895
Percent held by large traders	33.6	41.5	+ 4.3	+ 2.2
small traders	66.4	58.5	− 4.3	− 2.2

* Commitments of traders, Chicago Board of Trade, July 31, 1971.
† Commitments of traders, Chicago Mercantile Exchange, July 31, 1971.
SOURCE: Commodity Exchange Authority.

tive levels of hedging and speculative activity for the preceding period. The CFTC publishes a yearly summary, *Commodity Futures Statistics,* which includes a bimonthly (1st and 15th) report of futures commitments and other useful statistical information.

Because the terms "excessive" speculation and "undue" price fluctuations are subjective and the CFTC figures are the sole source of reference, the trader can appreciate the problem of assessing the impact of the speculator. Because the positions of the nonreporting traders are *not* available, the total amounts of hedging and speculating in the market cannot be accurately known. The simplest solution is to assume that all nonreporting traders are speculators. Working, however, attempted to reclassify these nonreporting traders as hedgers or speculators and preceeded to construct a "Speculative Index."[29]

The Speculative Index may be understood more easily by first referring to Table 2-2. On the average, long hedging does not equal short hedging; therefore for market balance long speculation is required to offset net short hedging. If H_L = long hedging commitments, H_S = short hedging commitments, and S_L = long speculating commitments, the degree to which short hedging is balanced by long hedging = H_L/H_S and the degree to which short hedging is balanced by long speculation = S_L/H_S. Together these ratios measure the hedging and speculative responses to short hedging.

The Speculative Index (T) isolates the amount of *net* short hedging (H_s^μ), which must be carried by long speculation (S_L),

$$T = \frac{S_L}{H_s^\mu},$$

where S_L = long speculating commitments,
$\quad H_s^\mu$ = unbalanced short hedging commitments.

In other words, long hedging (H_L) is subtracted from short hedging (H_S) to give the unbalanced short hedging commitment (H_s^μ). If a commodity has more long speculation (S_L) than needed to carry net short hedging (H_s^μ) requirements, the Speculative Index will exceed 1.

The trader must bear in mind that the Speculative Index does not distinguish between markets in which long speculating commitments are greater than short speculating commitments or vice-versa. The ratio indicates only that unneeded speculation is becoming more or less important when compared with unbalanced hedging. A more serious limitation of the Speculative Index is that it ignores spread or matching positions, which can be a significant percentage of the total open interest shown in Table 2-4 for soybeans and pork bellies. Working simply defined the problem away when

[29] Holbrook Working, "Speculation on Hedging Markets," *Food Research Institute Studies,* 1, No. 2 (May 1960), 199 ff.

he limited speculation to the holding of a net long or net short position for gains,[30] and Larson developed a technique for estimating the classification of the total open interest.[31] However, precise measurement of the speculative commitment and its subsequent effects on price variability will have to wait for a more detailed publishing classification of open interest.

Because of these problems in measurement, the trader would expect difficulty in reaching a consensus regarding the impact of speculation on price behavior. In one study of the grains the following was concluded for soybeans:

> Clearly, this evidence does not support the hypothesis that "excessive speculation" causes or is even associated with market periods containing "unwarranted or undesirable price fluctuation." Of the 52 separate, semi-monthly dates on which classification of total open interest indicated that the unneeded speculative fraction was high relative to hedging requirements, 39 cases were identified as markets in which prices showed little movement. However, in 36 out of the 40 cases for which the calculated Speculative Index was low, price behavior was entirely different. Prices in these particular markets moved over wide ranges, sometimes rising and falling rapidly during a relatively short period of time, and often showing wide daily price ranges over an extended period of time.[32]

A recent study of 186 monthly observations from 1950 to 1965 computed the hedging ratios and the Speculative Indexes for potatoes, cottonseed oil, soybean meal, corn, soybean oil, soybeans, rye, wheat, and oats.[33] Most of the hedging ratios (H_L/H_S) were near 0.5, which reflects a situation in which long hedging is not sufficient to cover short hedging requirements. All Speculative Indexes were greater than 1, ranging from 1.12 for oats to 1.31 for soybeans, leading to the conclusion that the market had a tendency toward imbalance, with speculation as the dominant force.

Because the futures markets are growing at such a pace, it seems reasonable to conclude that the markets of the future will require greater, not lesser, levels of speculation in order not only to survive but to thrive. The failure of some futures contracts can be traced directly to the failure of sufficient speculative activity which in turn led to the unbalanced or lopsided markets discussed in Chapter 4. The behavior of commodity futures prices is significantly affected by the levels of hedging and speculation in the markets, and it is safe to say that if no speculation marked the trading landscape the hedging interests would have to create a statistical equivalent to the speculator at great cost.

[30] *Ibid.*, p. 187.

[31] Arnold Larson, "Estimation of Hedging and Speculative Positions in Futures Markets, *Food Research Institute Studies*, 2, No. 3 (November 1961).

[32] *Margins, Speculation, and Price in Grain Futures Markets*, Economic Research Service, U.S.D.A., Washington, D.C., 1967, p. 35.

[33] Labys and Granger, *op. cit.*, 127.

CHAPTER THREE

The Mechanics of
Commodity Futures Trading

> The man who says he knows all the answers does not
> know all the questions.

INTRODUCTION

Many people are reluctant to trade commodities because they believe that
the mechanics of trading are much more complicated than they really are.
There are good reasons why some people should not trade commodities,
but the complexities of taking positions or understanding the bookkeeping
are not among them. Some of the mystery is probably created by individual
registered representatives of brokerage firms who are loath to spend the
time necessary to understand the technology themselves because of their
more immediate interest in securities and mutual funds.

Perhaps if a new commodity trader making his first trade is followed,
some confusion can be cleared away.

THE BROKER

Unless the trader is actually a member of the commodity exchanges himself, it will be necessary for him to deal through a member brokerage firm.
Normally firms that handle public business are futures commission merchants registered as such with the Commodity Exchange Authority. Such
firms are usually called brokers, commission houses, or wire houses. Brokers are of two general types, but their methods of operation are similar.

52

One type of broker is the mixed wire or commission house, which normally emphasizes listed securities but has other departments dealing with over-the-counter securities, bonds, puts and calls, mutual funds, and, in addition to commodities, a variety of other financial merchandise. The other is the specialized broker who deals exclusively in one, several, or all commodities. Some of these houses were originally cash commodity firms that went into the futures business to add to their incomes. Many already had sufficient investment in memberships and wire facilities to make the addition of customer brokerage relatively inexpensive. Most clients who have traded in securities and have become interested in commodities find it convenient to begin trading through the same broker through whom they trade securities if the broker is an integrated house. Others select specialty firms because they believe that they are given more varied and current information and better guidance by them.

After the firm has been chosen, the trader must select the salesman with whom he chooses to do business. This person may be a partner or stockholder of the firm or an employee variously referred to as a "solicitor," "registered representative," "customer's man," "account executive," "investment executive," or some other euphemism for "salesman." The salesmen frequently refer to themselves as "brokers" although this term technically describes their employers. Most customers spend little time or effort in their selection of this man or woman, which is probably an error. Trading may involve a significant portion of one's net worth, and the salesman is almost certain to have some effect on the results of trading in any account he handles.

In order to make his selection intelligently, the customer should give a little thought to what he wants the registered representative to do for him. If he wishes to make his own decisions and does not want to be solicited to make trades, he is primarily concerned with the service he is going to get. In this case, the customer may be satisfied with a relatively young but well-trained registered representative. Although such a man has little experience, he does have considerable time and is grateful to have his few clients. Therefore his services can be relatively good. A little time should be spent with this representative before beginning to trade to determine whether a good personal relationship will develop. There is no need to trade with a man simply because it happens to be his "floor day" in the office or because he is next in line to open a new account when the customer happens in.

If the client is going to rely on his registered representative to guide his trading, the care given to his selection is even more important. In addition to his ability to render good service, the broker will need good judgment and some personal knowledge about commodity trading. This is not easy to evaluate, but neither is it impossible. One can choose one's broker as one would choose a lawyer or physician; that is, by referral from people who have been satisfied with his performance. Another criterion is the broker's success with his own trading. If he has had good results, he may not necessarily continue to have them, but this is better than having to account for continuously poor performance over a significant period of time. If the broker does not trade his own account, one might wonder why. Presumably he is economically motivated or he would not be in the brokerage business. If he is not allowed to trade because of the rules of his firm or because of his own conservative financial objectives, of course, these are mitigating circumstances.

If a customer decides to deal with a firm with which he has had no experience, he might also ask some questions about its research department. It is not enough to know that there are some people in New York or Chicago who send out wires or prepare attractive-looking market letters and special reports. It is also important to learn that they know what they are talking about, as indicated by their results.

OPENING THE ACCOUNT

Once the brokerage house and registered representative have been selected, the opening of the individual brokerage account is a simple procedure. Various papers need to be signed, which will vary somewhat from broker to broker, but the following are typical.

The basic form is the customer's margin agreement, in which the client agrees to be responsible for any losses in his trading, just as he is in a securities account. The form may be signed by an individual client or by more than one, in which case the clients must specify whether they wish to be joint tenants or tenants-in-common. If they choose to act as joint tenants with right of survivorship, the broker will accept instructions from all joint tenants. In the event of the death of any of them, the equity in the account belongs to the survivors. If the customers act as tenants-in-common, they own the account in specified shares. Typically, a husband and wife will be joint tenants, whereas unrelated customers, such as business partners, will open their accounts as tenants-in-common.

The other form usually required is the authority to transfer funds. When the broker opens an account for a commodity client, he is in reality opening two accounts. One is for trading in commodities regulated by the Commodity Futures Trading Commission (CFTC) and the other for trading in unregulated commodities. Both accounts will have the same basic account number but will be differentiated in some minor way, such as "Type 1" and "Type 2" or "Type A" and "Type B." As trading takes place in various commodities, the broker will transfer the necessary funds from one account to the other as needed. It is these transfers that necessitate the authority to transfer funds.

Commodities may also be traded by partnerships and corporations. In a partnership all partners must agree to allow the account to be opened and must designate which partners can act for all. Corporate charters must allow commodity trading, and the broker must be told which officers of the corporation are to be allowed to trade the account. Minors may be prohibited from trading by some brokers, but others permit accounts in the name of a minor if guaranteed by an adult.

Some brokers require that a minimum deposit of funds which ranges between $1,000 and about $2,500 be made available for margin. Other brokers require only the margin specified by the commodity exchanges for a particular position, which can be as low as $100. Customers who deposit bare minimums to cover only the required initial margin would have to be concerned with the regulations covering the required deposit of additional funds in case of adversity. Some brokerage firms allow somewhat more impairment than others and some are inclined to press for additional deposits more aggressively than others. Exchanges specify the maximum impairment possible and the maximum time allowed to collect additional funds, but some brokers have house rules more stringent than those of the various exchanges. A small number of wire houses require a statement of net worth and/or much higher than the usual initial minimum margins from commodity clients to make certain that they can afford to take the necessary risks inherent in commodity trading.

If an account is to be managed by someone other than the client investing the capital, the broker will require a limited power of attorney, or trading authority, which allows him to take orders from that other person. A general power of attorney permits the account manager to withdraw money as well as to trade the account. There is seldom any reason to use this kind of document for trading purposes. Managed accounts are subject by some exchanges to minimum capital requirements somewhat in excess of those required of accounts not so managed. The client is responsible for all losses in his account, even though in a managed account the positions are taken by someone else, and he should be cautious before he signs a trading authority, particularly if his account manager has any conflict of interest in the trading, such as an interest in the commissions generated. Those who wish to have their accounts managed or who wish to manage the accounts of others should take the time to note the latest exchange, state, and Commodity Exchange Authority rules applicable to such accounts.

CONTRACT INFORMATION

The decision-making processes by which a trader chooses the commodity in which to trade and how he selects the particular contract month best for his purposes are discussed at length in subsequent chapters of this book, but a summary of basic information can be indicated profitably at this point. The list in Table 3-1 is not complete, but it does indicate the major commodity exchanges in the United States, typical commodities most actively traded on them, and pertinent contract and commission data concerning these commodities. From time to time changes occur in commissions, delivery months, opening times, closing times, and, of course, the list of commodities popularly traded. Most brokers will have updated information available which is designated as "Contract Facts" or "Contract Informa-

TABLE 3-1 CONTRACT INFORMATION

Commodity	Name of exchange	Exchange hours CST	Usual par contract grade(s)	Delivery months*	Contract size	Prices quoted in	Minimum fluctuation	Dollar value of one tick	Dollar value of one 1¢ move	Maximum daily limits above or below previous day's close		Round turn commissions		
										Cents	$	Regular	Day trade	Spread
Wheat	Chicago Board of Trade	9:30 1:15	#2 Soft Red winter #2 Hard Red winter #1, 2 north spring	NUZHK	5,000 bu	¢/bu	⅜¢/bu	$12.50	$50	20¢/bu	1,000	$30.00	$20.00	$36.00
Corn	Chicago Board of Trade	9:30 1:15	#2 yellow	ZHKNU	5,000 bu	¢/bu	¼¢/bu	12.50	50	10¢/bu	500	30.00	20.00	36.00
Oats	Chicago Board of Trade	9:30 1:15	#1 white #1, 2 heavy white #3 extra heavy white	ZHKNU	5,000 bu	¢/bu	¼¢/bu	12.50	50	6¢/bu	300	25.00	17.00	36.00
Soybeans	Chicago Board of Trade	9:30 1:15	#2 yellow	XFHKNQU	5,000 bu	¢/bu	¼¢/bu	12.50	50	20¢/bu	1,000	30.00	20.00	36.00
Soybean meal	Chicago Board of Trade	9:30 1:15	44% protein	VZFHKNQU	100 tons (2,000 lb/ton)	$/ton	10¢/ton	10.00	1	1,000¢/ton	1,000	33.00	22.00	44.00
Soybean oil	Chicago Board of Trade	9:30 1:15	Regular—one grade	VZFHKNQU	60,000 lb (one tank car)	¢/lb	$\frac{1}{100}$ ¢/lb	6.00	600	1¢/lb	600	33.00	22.00	44.00
Broilers, iced	Chicago Board of Trade	9:15 1:05	USDA Grade A 2½ to 3½ lb whole eviscerated	FHKMNQUX	28,000 lb (60- to 65-lb boxes)	¢/lb	$\frac{2.5}{100}$ ¢/lb	7.00	280	2¢/lb	560	30.00	20.00	36.00
Silver	Chicago Board of Trade	9:00 1:25	0.999 fine	CJMQVZ	5,000 troy oz (5 bars)	¢/oz	$\frac{1}{10}$ ¢/oz	5.00	50	20¢/oz	1,000	30.00	15.00	32.00
Plywood	Chicago Board of Trade	10:00 1:00	½" CDX—standard exterior 4-5 ply 48% group 1	FHKNUX	69,120 sq ft 36(60-piece units) (one boxcar load)	$/M sq ft	10¢/M sq ft	6.91	0.691	700¢/M sq ft	484	30.00	20.00	40.00
Stud lumber	Chicago Board of Trade	10:00 1:00	8' 2x4s 10/15% utility	FHKNUX	100,000 bd ft (two boxcar loads)	$/M bd ft	10¢/M bd ft	10.00	1	500¢/M bd ft	500	33.00	22.00	44.00
Pork bellies	Chicago Mercantile Exchange	9:30 1:00	USDA seedless Green—square Cut.—standard	CHKNQ	36,000 lb (12- to 14-lb bellies)	¢/lb	$\frac{2.5}{100}$ ¢/lb	9.00	360	1.5¢/lb	540	45.00	27.00	48.00
Feeder cattle	Chicago Mercantile Exchange	9:05 12:40	USDA—minimum 80% choice and maximum 20% good	HJKOUVZ	42,000 lb (650-lb average)	¢/lb	$\frac{2.5}{100}$ ¢/lb	10.50	420	1¢/lb	420	40.00	25.00	43.00
Cattle, live	Chicago Mercantile Exchange	9:05 12:40	USDA choice "Live steers	GJMQVZ	40,000 lb (1050-lb average)	¢/lb	$\frac{2.5}{100}$ ¢/lb	10.00	400	1¢/lb	400	40.00	25.00	43.00
Hogs, live	Chicago Mercantile Exchange	9:20 12:50	USDA 1, 2, 3, 4 Barrows and gilts	GJMNOVZ	30,000 lb (220-lb average)	¢/lb	$\frac{2.5}{100}$ ¢/lb	7.50	300	1.5¢/lb	450	35.00	22.00	38.00
Eggs, shell (fresh)	Chicago Mercantile Exchange	9:15 12:45	USDA extras 90% Grade A Large white	All	22,500 doz (750 cases; one carload)	¢/doz	$\frac{5}{100}$ ¢/doz	11.25	225	2¢/doz	450	40.00	25.00	43.00
Milo	Chicago Mercantile Exchange	9:30 1:15	#2 yellow	NUZHK	400,000 lb (7142.8 bu)	¢/cwt	$\frac{1}{4}$ ¢/cwt	10.00	40	15¢/cwt	600	30.00	20.00	33.00
Potatoes (Idaho Russett)	Chicago Mercantile Exchange	9:00 12:50	USDA No. 1 Size A 2" diameter	FHJKX	50,000 lb (500 sacks)	¢/cwt	1¢/cwt	5.00	5	35¢/cwt	175	30.00	20.00	33.00
Lumber	Chicago Mercantile Exchange	9:00 1:05	Kiln or air dried Random 2x4s Hem—fir construction	FGHKRNUX	100,000 bd ft (two boxcar loads)	$/M bd ft	10¢/M bd ft	10.00	1	500¢/M bd ft	500	40.00	25.00	43.00
Copper	New York Commodity Exchange (Comex)	8:45 1:10	Electrolytic ASTM standards	FHKNUVZ	25,000 lb	¢/lb	$\frac{5}{100}$ ¢/lb	12.50	250	5¢/lb	1,250	36.00	18.00	50.40
Mercury	Comex	8:50 1:30	99.9% pure	HKNUZ	10 flasks (76 lb each)	$/flask	$1/flask	10.00	0.10	500¢/flask	50	40.50	20.00	56.00
Silver	Comex	9:00 1:15	0.999 fine	FFHKNUZ	10,000 troy oz (10 bars)	¢/oz	$\frac{1}{10}$ ¢/oz	10.00	100	20¢/oz	2,000	45.50	23.00	64.00

Commodity	Exchange	Hours	Grade	Months	Contract Size									
Potatoes (Maine or Idaho)	New York Mercantile Exchange	9:00 12:30	USDA No. 1 Size A 2" diameter	FHJKX	50,000 lb (1000–50-lb sacks)	$/cwt	1¢/cwt	5.00	5	50¢/cwt	250	30.00	15.00	32.00
Platinum	New York Mercantile Exchange	8:45 12:30	99.8% pure sheet or bar	FJNV	50 troy oz (1 sheet or bar)	$/oz	10¢/oz	5.00	0.50	1.000¢/oz	500	45.00	22.50	45.00
Silver coins	New York Mercantile Exchange	8:50 1:20	Dimes, halves, quarters pre-1965 United States	FJNV	$10,000 (10 bags)	$/bag	$1/bag	10.00	0.10	15,000¢/bag	1,500	35.00	17.50	35.00
Palladium	New York Mercantile Exchange	9:20 11:55	99.8% pure	HKMQUXZ	100 troy oz (4 sheets or ingots)	$/oz	5¢/oz	5.00	1	400¢/oz	400	{40.00 / 52.00}	{20.00 / 26.00}	{40.00 / 54.00}†
Cotton #2	New York Cotton Exchange	9:30 2:00	U.S. Middling 1-1/16" white	FHKNVZ	50,000 lb (100 bales)	¢/lb	$\frac{1}{100}$ ¢/lb	5.00	500	2¢/lb	1,000	{45.00 / 55.00}	{22.50 / 27.50}	{54.00 / 66.00}†
Frozen Concentrated orange juice	New York Cotton Exchange	9:15 1:45	USDA Grade A Brix—51° 3% solids	FHKNUX	15,000 lb (44/55 gallon drums)	¢/lb	$\frac{5}{100}$ ¢/lb	7.50	150	3¢/lb	450	45.00	25.00	54.00
Wool	New York Cotton Exchange	9:00 1:30	64's 2¾"	HKNVZ	6,000 lb (clean weight)	¢/lb	$\frac{1}{10}$ ¢/lb	6.00	60	10¢/lb	600	50.00	27.00	60.00
Liquified propane gas	New York Cotton Exchange	9:05 2:10	NGPA-HD-5	FKNUZ	100,000 gal (pipe line bulk)	¢/gal	$\frac{1}{100}$ ¢/gal	10.00	1,000	1¢/gal	1,000	40.50	20.00	45.00
Cocoa	New York Cocoa Exchange	9:00 2:00	Standard (beans)	HKNUZ	30,000 lb (200 bags)	¢/lb	$\frac{1}{100}$ ¢/lb	3.00	300	4¢/lb	1,200	60.00	30.00	70.00
Coffee (C)	New York Coffee and Sugar Exchange	9:30 1:45	Columbian (beans)	HKNUXZ	37,500 lb (250 bags)	¢/lb	$\frac{1}{100}$ ¢/lb	3.75	375	2¢/lb	750	{25.00 / 80.00}	{15.00 / 42.75}	{30.00 / 96.00}†
World sugar #11	New York Coffee and Sugar Exchange	9:00 2:00	Raw Bulk 96% average polarization	FHKNUV	50 long tons (112,000 lb)	¢/lb	$\frac{1}{100}$ ¢/lb	11.20	1,120	1¢/lb	1,120	{42.00 / 62.00}	{21.00 / 31.00}	{42.00 / 62.00}†
Wheat	Kansas City Board of Trade	9:30 1:15	#2 Hard Red or Hard Yellow winter	NUZHK	5,000 bu	¢/bu	$\frac{1}{8}$ ¢/bu	6.25	50	25¢/bu	1,250	22.00	22.00	30.00
Rye	Winnipeg Commodity Exchange	9:30 1:15	#1, 2 Western Canadian	VZKN	1,000 bu 5,000 bu	¢/bu	$1\frac{1}{8}$ ¢/bu	1.25 6.25	10 50	10¢/bu	100 500	4.50 22.50	4.50 22.50	9.00 45.00
Flaxseed	Winnipeg Commodity Exchange	9:30 1:15	#1, Western Canadian	VZKN	1,000 bu 5,000 bu	¢/bu	1 ¢/bu	1.25 6.25	10 50	30¢/bu	300 1,500	5.50 25.00	5.50 25.00	11.00 50.00
Rapeseed	Winnipeg Commodity Exchange	9:30 1:15	#1 Canadian	UXFHM Vancouver VXZKN Thunder Bay	1,000 bu 5,000 bu	¢/bu	$1\frac{1}{8}$ ¢/bu	1.25 6.25	10 50	20¢/bu	200 1,000	5.50 25.00	5.50 25.00	11.00 50.00
Wheat	Minneapolis Grain Exchange	9:30 1:15	#2 Northern Spring U.S. 13.5% protein	NUZHK	5,000 bu	¢/bu	$\frac{1}{8}$ ¢/bu	6.25	50	20¢/bu	1,000	30.00	15.00	36.00

*Chicago Board of Trade commodity month symbols for the current year listed in crop-year order when applicable:

January F	March H	May K	July N	September U	November X
February G	April J	June M	August Q	October V	December Z

Chicago Board of Trade commodity months symbols for subsequent years when needed:

January A	March C	May E	July L	September P	November S
February B	April D	June I	August O	October R	December T

†There are different commissions for different price levels.

SOURCE: Clayton Brokerage Company.

NOTE: Similar information is available for all other futures not shown here, such as those traded on the International Money Market (IMM) and the London and other foreign exchanges.

tion." There is no need for a customer to memorize the exact contract size of all commodities traded or the times at which the various exchanges open and close. He can refer to his copy of "Contract Information" and keep pertinent information in mind only for the positions in which he is currently interested.

Commodity prices appear on broker's quote equipment and on the financial pages of newspapers much as common stock prices appear in the same places. In stock trading the unit of trading is usually 100 shares; and in bond trading it is five bonds. Commodities, however, trade in terms of contract units specified by the exchanges. For most grains and soybeans the unit of trading is 5,000 bushels. Traditionally, traders do not speak in terms of being long two contracts of corn, but rather 10,000 bushels. The broker's board, quote machines, and newspapers indicate the value of grains and soybeans in terms of dollars, cents, and eights. Corn at $1.12½, for example, merely means that corn is valued at that price per bushel. It can be ascertained from "Contract Information" that a change of 1 cent per bushel on the standard contract of 5,000 bushels would represent a profit or loss to a corn trader of $50 on each contract. A change of ¼ cent is $12.50 on a 5,000-bushel contract.

DAILY TRADING LIMITS

To prevent extreme price changes in one day all exchanges limit the amount that prices are allowed to move daily. Basically there are two limitations. One restricts the amount that a price may move above or below the settlement price of the preceding day. This is usually called the "daily limit." The other is a restriction on the maximum range over which the price may move during one day. This is sometimes called the maximum permissible "daily range." Sometimes the daily limit and daily range are the same and sometimes the daily range is twice the limit; for example, in cattle the daily limit is 1 cent per pound and the daily range is 2 cents. If cattle closed at 33.55 cents on one day, then 34.55 cents would be "limit up" and 32.55 cents "limit down." However, if the price moved up to 34.55 cents, it could trade all the way down to 32.55 cents because its permissible range is twice its limit. For orange juice, however, the daily limit and range are both 3 cents per pound; therefore, if May orange juice closed at 44.70 cents and then traded up to 46.20 cents the next day it could not then trade below 43.20 cents. Any amount of trading can take place at the limit or the market can move down from limit up or up from limit down. Despite widespread misconception on this point, a market does not close because a daily price limit is reached; it merely cannot trade past that point. In the current month restrictions on limits may be modified to allow more flexibility, and directors of an exchange can change limits under conditions deemed to be an emergency. Daily trading limits and ranges are indicated in Table 3-2. As in "Contract Information," there may be changes from time to time and the trader is well advised to maintain current data which are available from his broker.

Many traders who began by trading stocks are quite concerned about the possibility of being "frozen in" by an adverse limit move. It should be noted, however, that the alternative is an *unlimited* adverse move which may provide far less comfort.

TABLE 3-2 DAILY TRADING LIMITS

Price limitations are imposed by the various exchanges to prevent extreme price changes in any one day. When prices reach the trading limit, trading beyond that limit is stopped for that day. In nearly all markets the Board of Directors or Governors has the power to change the limits in emergencies.

In the current month the limitations are broadened in certain future contracts by permitting wider price changes and in others, by removing limitations entirely.

	Usual range above or below previous close	Usual range between high and low
Grains		
Oats (CBT)	6¢ per bu.	12¢ per bu.
Corn	10¢ per bu.	20¢ per bu.
Rye, Winnipeg	10¢ per bu.	20¢ per bu.
Grain sorghum, Milo	15¢ per bu.	30¢ per bu.
Rapeseed, Winnipeg	20¢ per bu.	40¢ per bu.
Soybeans	20¢ per bu.	40¢ per bu.
Wheat (CBT, MGE)	20¢ per bu.	40¢ per bu.
Wheat (KC)	25¢ per bu.	50¢ per bu.
Flaxseed, Winnipeg	30¢ per bu.	60¢ per bu.
Metals		
Copper (NY)	5¢ per lb.[a]	10¢ per lb.[a]
Mercury	$5 per flask[b]	$10 per flask[b]
Palladium	$4 per oz.[c,d]	$8 per oz.[c,d]
Platinum (NY)	$10 per oz.[d]	$20 per oz.[d]
Silver (CBT)	20¢ per oz.[a]	40¢ per oz.[a]
Silver (NY)	20¢ per oz.[a]	40¢ per oz.[a]
Silver Coins (CME)	$120 per bag[d]	$240 per bag[d]
Silver Coins (NY)	$150 per bag[d]	$300 per bag[d]
Others		
Propane	1¢ per gal.[d]	2¢ per gal.[d]
Cattle	1¢ per lb	2¢ per lb
Soybean oil	1¢ per lb[a]	2¢ per lb.[a]
Sugar #11	1¢ per lb.[e]	2¢ per lb.[e]
Sugar (London)	10 £ per long ton[a]	20 £ per long ton[a]
Hogs	1.5¢ per lb.	3¢ per lb.
Pork bellies	1.5¢ per lb.	3¢ per lb.

TABLE 3-2   (Continued)

	Usual range above or below previous close	Usual range between high and low
Broilers	2¢ per lb.*a*	4¢ per lb.*a*
Cocoa (NY)	2¢ per lb.*a*	4¢ per lb.*a*
Coffee (C)	2¢ per lb.*a*	4¢ per lb.*a*
Cotton #2	2¢ per lb.*a*	4¢ per lb.*a*
Eggs (shell)	2¢ per dz.	4¢ per dz.
Orange juice	3¢ per lb.*f*	3¢ per lb.*f*
Lumber	$5 per M bd. ft.*a*	$10 per M bd. ft.*a*
Wool	10¢ per lb.*f*	20¢ per lb.*f*
Potatoes (Maine)	50¢ per cwt.*d*	$1.00 per cwt.*d*
Soybean meal	$10 per ton*a*	$20 per ton*a*
Plywood (CBT)	$7 per M sq. ft.*a*	$14 per M sq. ft.*a*

*a*Limit is removed from spot month on first notice day.

*b*Limit is removed from spot month on first day of delivery month.

c$5.00 and $10.00 per ounce above or below preceding close during spot month.

*d*Limit is removed from spot month on last trading day.

*e*Limit is removed from calendar month prior to delivery month.

*f*Limit is removed from spot month on eighth day of delivery month.

TAKING A POSITION

When the account has been opened, the customer can take a position in one of the approximately 40 commodities traded in futures markets.

The procedure, as far as he is concerned, is almost exactly like trading a security. He gives his order to his registered representative, who transmits it to his firm's wire room, from which it is sent to the exchange on which the selected commodity is traded. The report of the trade is then sent back to the office from which it originated and given to the customer. Orders may be placed by customers personally or by telephone, letter, or wire. Most of them are placed by telephone.

The broker is required to mail the customer a confirmation of the trade as promptly as possible. This is usually done on the same day the trade is made. A confirmation of a new position indicates the exchange on which it was made, the date, the price, and the size of the position. The confirmation of a position being liquidated contains the same information but in addition indicates the amount of profit or loss on the transaction and the total commission charged for entering and liquidating the position. This differs somewhat from a security confirmation of a closing transaction. Such confirmations do not indicate the profit or loss because the broker may not have access to this information. A stock can be bought at one brokerage house, held for years, and then sold at another. Commodity positions are held for relatively brief periods and may not be readily transferred from one brokerage house to another. Commodity transactions indicate the entire round-turn commissions on the liquidating side, whereas security confirmations indicate one commission on the entry and another on the liquidation.

LIQUIDATING A POSITION

A speculator who has established a long position may liquidate it in one of two ways; he may offset it with a sale or he may accept delivery of the commodity. One who has established a short position also has two possible routes to follow; he may cover his short position by buying or make delivery of the cash commodity if he has it in deliverable form and location or can acquire it. For virtually all speculators offset is the liquidation route chosen. Most do not want the cash commodity nor have it available for delivery. Their purpose in being in the markets is rather an attempt to take advantage of price change, not to deal in cash products.

If delivery is to become a factor, it is usually of more concern to the speculator with a long position than for one with a short position because it is the latter who has the choice of whether to make delivery and when. Sometimes the holder of a long position holds his position into the delivery month, hoping that the amount of deliverable cash product is too small or too tightly held to make his risk of receipt of any great concern. In such a case he should familiarize himself with the rules of the exchange on which he is trading to appraise his odds of receiving early deliveries if any are made. Notices of delivery are posted on dates and at times specified by exchange rules. These notices are sometimes given to the long with the oldest position in terms of the date on which it was established and sometimes to the brokerage house with the oldest net long position. The latter might well mean that a trader with a long position held with a brokerage house which itself was net short could not get delivery at all. Considering the cost and trouble that an unwanted delivery can cause, a trader who is not highly sophisticated in commodity market operations might do well to liquidate his long positions routinely before the first date that notice of delivery is possible. These dates are available from any well-informed brokerage firm.

The trader who does choose to hold his position into a delivery month must also be aware of the last day of futures trading after which offset is impossible and delivery is the only route open. Some typical rules covering notice days and the last day of trading are indicated in Tables 3-3 and 3-4, respectively.

TYPES OF ORDERS

A commodity may be bought or sold at the market, which means that the floor broker on the exchange must execute the order promptly at the most favorable price possible.

A limit may be imposed by the customer, which precludes the floor broker

TABLE 3-3 NOTICE DAYS

Commodity	Notice or first notice day
Sugar #11 (NY)	14th calendar day of month preceding the delivery month[1]
Sugar (London)	15th calendar day before 1st day of the delivery month[1]
Cocoa (NY)	7 business days before 1st day of the delivery month
Cotton #2 Propane Wool	5 business days before 1st day of the delivery month[2]
Coffee (C)(NY)	3 business days before 1st day of the delivery month
Copper Mercury (Comex) Silver	2 business days before 1st day of the delivery month
Broilers Corn Oats (CBT) Plywood (CBT) Silver (CBT) Soybeans Soybean meal Soybean oil Stud lumber (CBT) Wheat (CBT, KC, MGE)	Last business day before 1st business day of the delivery month
Cocoa (London) Coffee (London) Eggs (shell) Grain sorghum, Milo Pork bellies Silver coins (CME) Winnipeg grains	1st business day of the delivery month
Cattle Hogs	M, Tu, W, Th, business day on or after the 6th calendar day of the delivery month[3]
Lumber (CME) Orange juice[2] Palladium Platinum Potatoes (Maine) Silver coins (NY)	1st business day after the last trading day of the delivery month

[1-4] See footnotes of Table 3-4.
SOURCE: Clayton Brokerage Company.

from paying more on a buy order or selling for less on a sell order. This limit assures the trader that he will get at least the price he wants if the order is executed but means that he will run the risk of not getting the order executed at all if the floor broker finds it impossible to fill it at the specified limit. Unlike the trader of listed security round lots, the commodity trader who sees the correct price of a commodity "sell through his limit" on the tape, board, or quote machine cannot assume that his order has been filled.

TABLE 3-4 LAST DAY OF TRADING

Commodity	Last day of trading
Coffee (C)	5th calendar day before 1st day of the delivery month[1]
Sugar #11 (NY) Sugar (London)	Last business day before 1st day of the delivery month
Potatoes (Maine) Wool Cotton #2	5th business day of the delivery month 11th last business day of the delivery month 17th last business day of the delivery month
Palladium Platinum Silver coins (NY)	14th calendar day of the delivery month[1]
Lumber (CME) Propane	15th calendar day of the delivery month[1]
Orange juice	10th last business day of the delivery month
Cattle[1.] Copper (NY)[4] Hogs[1] Mercury[4]	20th calendar day of the delivery month
Cocoa (NY) Corn Eggs (shell) Grain sorghum, Milo Oats (CBT) Plywood (CBT) Soybeans Soybean meal Soybean oil Stud lumber (CBT) Wheat (KC, CBT, MGE)	8th last business day of the delivery month
Pork bellies Silver coins (CME)	6th last business day of the delivery month
Broilers Silver (CBT) (NY)	4th last business day of the delivery month
Cocoa (London) Coffee (London) Winnipeg grains	Last business day of the delivery month
London metals	Last business day prior to prompt date for delivery

[1] Or business day immediately preceding.
[2] At least 5 business days prior to day of delivery.
[3] No holiday or business day prior thereto.
[4] Or the full business day immediately thereafter.
SOURCE: Clayton Brokerage Company.

Because there are no floor specialists on the commodity exchanges, it is possible and often reasonable for a transaction to take place too far away from a floor broker to allow him to complete it. This is not considered "missing the market" unless there is some evidence of carelessness.

Stop orders are often confused with limit orders but are actually quite different. A "buy stop" instructs a broker to execute an order when the price of a commodity rises to a specified level above the current market. The difference between a buy limit order and a buy stop order is exemplified as follows. A customer is inclined to buy December sugar, which is then selling at a price of 5.43 cents per pound. He tells his broker to buy him a contract at a price not to exceed 5.35 cents. This is a "buy limit." Another customer under the same circumstances tells his broker to buy a contract of December sugar but not until the price rises to at least 5.55 cents, at which point the order will be executed at the market. The buy limit order is usually placed below the current market and must be executed at the limit or better. The buy stop order is placed above the current market and may be executed at the price specified on the stop, above it, or below it, because it is executed at the market after the stop price is touched, at which point the stop is said to be "elected."

A "sell stop" instructs a broker to execute an order when the price falls to a given level, at which point it is to be executed at the market. Unlike a typical sell limit order, it is below the current market level and may be executed at a price at, above, or below the specified stop when it is elected.[1]

A sell limit order may be used to establish a new position or to liquidate an old one. A buy limit may be used to establish a new long position or to liquidate an old short.

A stop order may be used to limit a loss, protect a profit, or establish a new position. In the first case a client may have bought his sugar at 5.45 cents per pound and has instructed his broker to sell it if it falls to 5.37 cents in order to limit his loss to eight points. In the second case the sugar may already have risen from 5.45 to 5.65 cents and the customer places his sell stop at 5.53 cents because he wants to keep his position if the price continues to rise but does not want to lose back all his paper profit if the price declines. Some clients will raise their stops as the price advances in an effort to gain as much as possible from a major move, while making certain that they can probably lose back only a little of the gain. This device, frequently called a "trailing stop," has great appeal to new traders but works considerably better in theory than in practice for reasons discussed in Chapter 4. Many major price moves seem to have an uncanny tendency to elect all the trailing stops just before going into their accelerating phase. In the third case a client with no position believes that if the current price declines from 5.45 to 5.36 cents it will continue to decline

---

[1] Some exchanges prohibit stop orders from time to time or allow only stop limit orders when they fear stops might aggravate unusually volatile markets.

substantially and he would like to take a short position, although not until it declines to that point. He thereupon tells his broker to sell his contract of sugar at 5.36 cents stop. Buy stops are used for similar reasons; that is, to limit a loss, protect a profit on a short position, or establish a new long position but only after the price begins to rise.

A somewhat more complex order is the stop limit. The client might instruct his broker not to buy sugar until it rises to 5.53 cents per pound and not to pay more than 5.55 cents. This is unlike the unlimited stop, which becomes a market order when the stop price has been touched. The limit price may be the same or different from the specified stop.

A "market-if-touched (M.I.T.) order" is used somewhat like a limit order but with a minor difference. The limit order must be executed at the limit price or one more favorable to the client. The M.I.T. order is executed at the market when the market has traded at the price specified on the order, and so it may be filled either at that price, above it, or below it. This order is often used by chartists who believe that a particular price is at the extreme of a trading range and who want to take a position immediately if that price level is reached with no risk of missing the market. M.I.T. orders are sometimes called "board orders"; for example, a client long pork bellies at 45.60 cents per pound who preferred to take his profit on a limit order might say, "Sell my July pork bellies at 48.50 cents." This instructs the brokerage firm to sell the contract at 48.50 cents or more. The order may be entered for one day, a specified period, or open (good until canceled). Another client with a similar position who preferred M.I.T. orders would instruct his broker to sell his position at the market whenever a transaction took place at 48.50 cents or higher.

Sometimes a customer may wish to take a position within a short time but would like the broker on the floor of the exchange to use some of his personal judgment in the timing of the fill. The broker will do this if the order indicates that he is to fill it at the market but is to take his time and will not be responsible if by waiting too long or not waiting long enough the price is unsatisfactory to the customer. Such orders are marked "Take your time" (T.Y.T.), "Not held" or both. Customers may also specify the time at which they wish their orders filled; that is, "on opening," "on close," or at a particular specified time.

"Alternative orders" provide for one of two possible executions: a customer may order 5,000 bushels of corn at $1.45 a bushel and 5,000 bushels of wheat at $2.56 a bushel, but not want both. A far more common example of the alternative order is the placing of an objective and a stop, with instructions to cancel one if the other is filled; for example, having bought one contract of soybean oil at 14.50 cents a pound, a customer may order his broker to sell the oil either at 14.95 or 14.25 cents stop, whichever occurs first, and then immediately cancel the remainder of the order to avoid inadvertently reversing his position. This second kind of alternative order is popular with the trader who has carefully determined his objective and maximum loss point for a position and prefers to enter the order rather than watch the market and have to hurry to place one order or another as the market approaches one of the two points. Such an order also helps overcome the temptation to overstay positions.

"Scale orders" are used to establish or liquidate positions as the market moves up or down. The sugar trader may instruct his broker to buy a contract of sugar at 5.45 cents and another contract each time the price drops five points from that level until he has accumulated six contracts. When he sells out his position, he may order the broker to sell one contract at 5.70 cents and another contract each time the price rises five points until his six contracts have been sold.

"Contingent orders" are filled by the broker after the price of another contract or even another commodity reaches a specified level; for example, "Sell one July pork bellies at the market when August bellies have sold at 32.60." This order is used when the customer believes that August bellies will set the tone of the market but that profits will be maximized in the July contract.

"Spreads" may be established at a fixed difference rather than at specified prices because the spreader is concerned only with the difference rather than the level. He may therefore order his broker to "buy one July pork bellies and sell one February bellies at 80 points difference or more, premium February." Such an order could be used to establish a new spread position, which the trader believes will narrow, or to take the profit in a position at a narrower difference and be satisfied with the profit at 80 points difference.

DAILY OPERATING STATEMENT

It is essential that a trader be completely aware at all times of the status of his account. He must realize that it is the equity that is most important, not the closed profits and losses to date. Failure to accept this allows the trader to convince himself that he is ahead when he has taken some small profits but is keeping positions with large open losses in the hope that the markets will reverse and his losses will be recovered.

To avoid overextending an account the trader should distinguish his gross power from his net power. "Gross power" is the capital (credit balance or ledger credit) in a commodity account increased or decreased by adjustments from all trades open at a particular time. The adjustments consist of margin requirements, commissions, and open profits or losses. Gross power can be used to margin new positions or can be withdrawn from the account. It is sometimes called "buying power" or "free credit."

"Net power" is gross power adjusted by the risk in open trades. This risk may be measured by the loss that would be suffered if all trades open were stopped out.

A trader, for example, has an account with $5,000 and no open positions. For the moment, $5,000 is his gross power. Let us assume that he has bought two contracts of cotton at 31.25 cents a pound, which require a margin of $900 per contract or $1,800 for the entire position. The commission expense for the transaction is $90. His gross power is therefore reduced to $3,110. If cotton moves up 20 points a contract to 31.45 cents, the open profit of $200 can be added to gross power, which would then be $3,310. As far as the broker is concerned, this amount can be used for new positions or withdrawn from the account. It a stop loss order has been entered at 30.80 cents, it would be possible for each cotton contract to drop at least 65 points before it is sold. If the drop occurs, the value of the account would decline by $650. A cautious trader, therefore, would regard only $2,660 as really available for use. This is his net power.

Traders use different devices to make certain that they are always aware of their equity. Some go to the length each day of withdrawing any excess

EXHIBIT 3-1   Daily Operating Statement
(Five weeks from _____ to _____)

	M	Tu	W	Th	F
Capital (includes unrealized gains and losses)					
Margin on open trades					
Gross power					
Risk on open trades					
Net power					
Additions and withdrawals					

	M	Tu	W	Th	F
Capital (includes unrealized gains and losses)					
Margin on open trades					
Gross power					
Risk on open trades					
Net power					
Additions and withdrawals					

	M	Tu	W	Th	F
Capital (includes unrealized gains and losses)					
Margin on open trades					
Gross power					
Risk on open trades					
Net power					
Additions and withdrawals					

	M	Tu	W	Th	F
Capital (includes unrealized gains and losses)					
Margin on open trades					
Gross power					
Risk on open trades					
Net power					
Additions and withdrawals					

created by improvement in their equity and depositing a check for the amount of the equity loss at the end of any day during which they suffer adversity. This makes them constantly aware that they are dealing in real money and not merely debits and credits.

A somewhat simpler method, and one calculated to make the trader more popular with his broker, is to maintain a simple ledger sheet (see Exhibit 3-1). If the fluctuations in an account are alarmingly large, or if the trader is overextended, this statement will make the danger clear before, rather than after, a margin call or sell-out notice is received.

BUYING POWER

Sometimes a client may wish to know how much is available for new trades or how much cash can be withdrawn from his account. This amount is called "buying power," "excess," "excess margin," or "gross power," and in either case would be the same at any given moment. To arrive at the figure it is necessary to subtract margin requirements on open positions from the equity in the account. This is just a way of saying that what is not being used is free to be utilized or withdrawn. The figure is computed by taking the credit balance, adjusting it by the open profit or loss, including commissions, on open positions to arrive at equity and then subtracting margin requirements to arrive at the buying power or free balance. A well-run brokerage firm should be able to provide its clients with his buying power, equity, and open profit or loss almost immediately on request.

THE MONTHLY STATEMENT

The monthly statement sent by the broker to his customer lists the changes that took place in the account during the month. Such changes may result from the deposit or withdrawal of funds, the establishment or liquidation of positions, or the changes in the prices of commodity positions held during the month and still held when the statement is mailed. The client must be familiar with the following terms to have a reasonably good understanding of his statement.

Credit or cash balance represents the funds deposited into the account, modified by the realized profits or losses from positions that have been closed out. The credit balance is not affected by open positions even though they may represent paper profits or losses. The only way the original credit balance represented by the customer's deposit of margin may be affected is by an additional deposit, a withdrawal, or closing out a position at a profit or loss. The margin requirements established by the broker to support open positions do not appear on the statement but merely reduce the amount of the credit balance left free to take other positions.

Equity is the amount of money the account would be worth if all open positions were liquidated. If there were no open positions in an account, credit balance and equity would be identical. If there were positions, equity would be determined by adding open profits less commissions to the credit balance and subtracting open losses plus commissions. A few firms indicate the net open profit or loss on statements to show their clients exactly where they stand. This plays havoc with the common practice of ignoring open losses in the hope that they will go away but is a desirable way to make certain that the client knows what he has. A statement that indicates the net open profit or loss is frequently called an "equity statement."

Transfers of funds made between the customer's regulated and unregulated commodity accounts are also shown on the monthly statement. Most brokers keep funds in the regulated account until the customer trades in a commodity not regulated by the CFTC. A transfer will be indicated by a debit to the regulated account balanced by a credit in the unregulated account. The statement will show credit and open positions separately in the two types of account. Most firms give both on different parts of the same statement form. A few use separate statements. Transfers of funds within the accounts do not change the overall credit balance or equity but are just routine accounting entries to comply with federal regulations.

REGULATORY REQUIREMENTS

In addition to the rules of the various exchanges, a trader may be concerned with some of the regulations imposed by the CFTC, which has many of the same functions relating to commodity exchanges and trading as the SEC has to security exchanges and trading. Most of these regulations, some of which require certain capital and bookkeeping procedures, apply to brokerage houses, but sometimes an individual trader may be directly concerned. One of the most common is that transactions in commodities regulated by the CFTC, as opposed to the unregulated, be accounted for separately. This is the reason why two monthly statements may be necessary and why most brokers encourage their clients to sign the "Authority to Transfer Funds." Unregulated commodities include those that trade on foreign exchanges not regulated by the CFTC, such as Winnipeg.

To provide accurate information on the activities of large and small traders, the CFTC requires large traders to file reports that can be compared with the number of open positions available from clearing houses to arrive at a total of small positions. These reports are easily prepared and need be of no concern to the trader who chooses to comply. Some brokerage houses will help to prepare the forms or even perform the entire task if assured that a client is not trading elsewhere, which could lead to an inaccurate report. Current CFTC reportable positions are listed in Table 3-5. These reports are made on forms supplied by the CFTC's regional offices. The CFTC has also set maximum limits, well above the specified reportable positions, that may be held by one person directly or indirectly through his control of other accounts. These limits are indicated in Table 3-6.

TABLE 3-5   CFTC REPORTABLE PORTIONS

The Commodity Futures Trading Commission requires that reports be filed for each day on which a trade is made, for the day before, during and one day after the following positions are reached by a person in the aggregate of all accounts which that person owns or controls:

Regulated commodities	Reportable position
Eggs (shell or frozen)	
Pork bellies	
Cattle	
Hogs	
Lumber	25 contracts
Orange juice	
Potatoes	
Soybean meal	
Soybean oil	
Wool	
Corn	
Grain sorghum, Milo	
Oats	40 contracts
Soybeans	
Wheat	
Cotton	50 contracts

SOURCE: Clayton Brokerage Company.

TAX CONSIDERATIONS

A commodity position in the futures market represents a contract to buy or sell and does not represent ownership of a commodity, as discussed in Chapter 2. The margin required by a broker may be viewed as a performance deposit and not as a payment in the usual sense of the word. When the contract is liquidated, the profit or loss merely represents the price difference from the level at which the contract was made, less the commission. There are those who quarrel with designations of commodity positions as "property," but they have been generally accepted as such and are considered to be capital assets. Although they are not regarded as securities (chiefly because they are seen as primary rather than secondary investments, hence do not depend on the performance of others), commodity contracts are subject in general to the same tax treatment as other capital assets, including securities.

Commodity trading does not create the deductible interest expense that stock trading on margin does because no interest is charged on commodity accounts unless they are in deficit or undermargined to the degree that the broker must deposit his own funds with the clearinghouse, pending receiving adequate funds from the client, in which case he may charge interest.

No state or federal taxes are charged directly on transactions. The cost of a trade for tax purposes includes the commissions charged.

TABLE 3-6   CFTC POSITION LIMITS

The Commodity Futures Trading Commission has established the following limits on the positions that may be held or the daily trades made by a person in the aggregate of all accounts he owns or controls in any one contract month or in all contracts combined.

Commodity	Position limit	Daily position limit if different
Eggs (shell)	150 contracts[a]	
Pork bellies	250 contracts[b]	375 contracts[c]
Broilers		450 contracts
Cattle		
Cotton	300 contracts	
Plywood		
Stud lumber (BOT)		
Potatoes	350 contracts[d]	
Oats	400 contracts[e]	
Wheat	400 contracts[e]	
Soybean oil	540 contracts	
Grain sorghum	550 contracts[f]	
Corn	600 contracts	
Soybeans		
Soybean meal	720 contracts	
Hogs	750 contracts[g]	1,125 contracts[h]
Lumber (CME)	1,000 contracts[g]	2,000 contracts[i]
Silver		
Copper (Comex)	2,000 contracts[j]	
Mercury		

[a] In addition to the limitations of 150 carlots on total net long or short position, no person shall hold a net long or short position in excess of 100 carlots in the October egg future, 75 carlots in the November egg future, 50 carlots in the December egg future, or 50 carlots in the January egg future.

[b] 150 contracts in February, March, July, August, 200 contracts in May.

[c] 225 contracts in February, March, July, August, 300 contracts in May.

[d] 150 carlots in March, April, May—300 carlots in others.

[e] To the extent that the net position held or controlled by any one person in all futures in any one grain on any one market is shown to represent spreading in the same grain between markets, the limit on net position in all futures may be exceeded on such contract market, but in no case shall the excess result in a net position of more than 3,000,000 bushels in all futures combined nor more than 2,000,000 bushels in any one future.

[f] 825 net contracts in all months combined.

[g] 300 contracts in any one contract month.

[h] 450 contracts in any one contract month.

[i] 600 contracts in any one contract month.

[j] 4000 net contracts in all months combined.

In addition to the above CFTC limits, certain limits are imposed by some of the commodity exchanges.

SOURCE: Clayton Brokerage Company.

Holding period rules are similar to those for securities; that is, transactions are considered to be first-in, first-out, unless a different choice is specified on the orders given to the broker: for example, if a trader buys one contract of May potatoes at 4.52 cents a pound in January, a second contract at 5.53 cents in March, and then instructs his broker to sell one contract in April when the price is 5.80 cents, the transaction will be closed on the earlier purchase at 4.52 cents. If the client prefers to close the transaction against his later purchase at 5.53 cents, he may do so, but he must ask the broker specifically to use the later purchase before the sale is made. Reasons for such requests usually involve tax or morale motives. There is no problem with physical delivery of certificates because there are none. There is no provision in the commodity markets for short sales against the box.

Capital gains treatment. The tax treatment of a commodity position depends on whether it was speculative or a hedge. Hedging carried on in day-to-day dealings of a business results in current operating expenses or credits and therefore in fully taxable operating profits and losses rather than capital gains or losses.[2]

Just where hedging ends and speculation begins is most difficult to determine. There appears to be little question that bona fide hedges are benefited by lower margin requirements and that losses resulting from them are fully deductible and gains fully taxable as ordinary income. It is less clear, however, just what is "bona fide" and even what is a "hedge." The definitions used by the CEA and IRS differ materially.[3]

Speculative profits and losses have consistently been held to be long-term or short-term capital gains, depending on whether the positions were held for more or less than six months and whether they were long or short positions. The holding period of a commodity futures position begins on the day after acquisition and ends on the day it is liquidated. There is no settlement period of several days, as there is in securities, which may be important to the trader who liquidates his position during the last few trading days of the calendar year. If delivery of a cash commodity is taken, the holding period consists of the time that the futures contract was held added to the time that the cash commodity is held, because a commodity futures contract and the commodity delivered against it are usually considered to be substantially identical.

As in securities, all profits on speculative short positions are regarded, with only rare exceptions, as short-term gains, regardless of how long the positions are held, in that short positions can hardly be considered to be

[2] Henry B. Arthur, *Commodity Futures as a Business Management Tool,* Division of Research; Graduate School of Business Administration, Harvard University, Boston, 1971, p. 41.

[3] Thorough discussions can be found in the Commodity Exchange Act As Amended, Section 4a, and in the Internal Revenue Code of 1954. The latter is summarized in *Standard Federal Tax Reporter,* Code Volume, Commerce Clearing House, New York, Chicago, and Washington, D.C., 1969. See especially Code sections 1221 and 1233.

capital assets. Of course, a long position is usually taken to liquidate the short position, but it is considered to be instantaneously liquidated.

In a closed-out loss reinstated by a similar position within 30 days of the date on which the loss was realized the law is not so obvious as it is in securities, where such a loss is clearly not deductible. One Circuit Court of Appeals has ruled that wash-sale rules apply and another has ruled that they do not. The decisions have not been clearly reconciled. In practice, many commodity traders apparently assume that the rule does not apply because most commodity trades are quite short-term and the government's revenue is unlikely to be materially affected in the long run.

Substantially identical nature of different commodity contract months. Although a commodity futures contract and the commodity it represents are substantially identical, with little doubt, it should be noted that there is some difference in court decisions concerning whether different contract months of the same commodity are substantially identical. This has important implications for those who trade spreads, whether motivated by speculation or tax considerations. Ultimate settlement of this point, along with others, such as whether commodity futures and options (puts and calls) are securities, could have a drastic effect on the conduct of the commodity business. These questions are difficult to resolve but will undoubtedly be settled by the courts sooner or later.[4]

If different delivery months of the same commodity are not considered to be substantially identical, as is usually presumed by most traders and their tax consultants, then a trader who is long March cotton and short May cotton is able at the same time to realize a long-term gain on the March cotton if he holds the position more than six months. If a trader is long with a substantial profit, which he is inclined to take, but needs only a short time more to be eligible for long-term capital gain treatment, he can sell another futures contract against his position without jeopardizing his holding period. There is no certainty, of course, that this procedure will ensure complete success. If the market should decline drastically, the profit on the long position would be replaced by a profit on the short side. Furthermore, the spread position itself involves the possibility of a loss on the difference and the certainty of greater commission expense. A spread of exactly the same commodity in the same delivery month on two different exchanges would certainly be considered substantially identical and therefore obviously offers no tax advantage.

Tax spreads. Much has been written about the possibility of using commodity spreads to convert short-term gains from any source into long-term gains, postponing one year's short-term gains to the next year, either in whole or in part, converting one year's short-term gain into a long-term gain the following year, or, possibly, transferring a gain from one entity to

[4] Laurence Goldfein and Lester Hochberg, "Use of Commodity Straddles Can Effect Impressive Tax Savings," *The Journal of Taxation* (December 1968), 342.

another. Such spreads are not easy to manage, and the United States Internal Revenue Service has a long, often successful, record of attacking transactions whose obvious purpose is to secure a tax advantage rather than a profit. A trade may yield a tax advantage and no profit, but at least a profit should have been a reasonable possibility. Spread trading for tax purposes is no area for the amateur. A poor choice of spread positions or mismanagement of the positions chosen can result in losses to a client well beyond any possible tax savings. Many clients in this position may be considered unsophisticated in the commodity area and the brokerage employee may be inexpert in taxes (and perhaps in commodities), with distinct adverse legal implications to the broker. A particular problem is caused when a short position is placed in the early month of a spread and a long position in the later month. This may result in a severe loss if a strong market in the nearby month gained substantially on the distant month. It is unlikely that an unusually strong market will cause a distant month to rise materially on the nearby.

Aside from the difficulty of selecting and timing the trades, the trader and his adviser should make certain of a high degree of probability that the commissions, interest loss on margin, and risk of loss on the trade itself are overcome by enough potential saving to justify the economic risk inherent in every trade, no matter how carefully conceived and executed.

Tax rules vary among individual speculators, among businesses that deal primarily or partly in commodities, and among dealers in commodities. Important changes are made in the rules as new court decisions are handed down. The investor or trader would do well to consult his tax adviser before making any important assumptions about his tax exposure.

CHAPTER FOUR

The Behavior
of Commodity Futures Prices

Truth is allowed only a brief interval of victory
between the two long periods when it is condemned
as paradox or belittled as trivial.
ARTHUR SCHOPENHAUER,
From Copernicus to Einstein

INTRODUCTION

An important step toward successful commodity trading is an understanding of the behavior of commodity futures prices. This chapter promotes
such an understanding by describing and analyzing some of the important
facts that are known about short- and long-run characteristics of futures
prices.

Initially a review will be presented of the statistical evidence that supports or denies the random walk theory, which suggests that short-run price
changes in speculative markets like commodity futures are difficult to forecast with only past prices as a guide.

Even if the random walk model approximates reality in the short run,
speculators can still profit from long-run changes in prices if, for example,
the average upward price change is greater than the average downward
price change. If such trends are present, do speculators profit solely and
simply for bearing the risks that hedgers transfer to them or do they profit
because they can forecast prices successfully? The "risk premium" concept
is a common point of departure in the literature of futures price behavior,
and the case for and against the existence of such a premium is analyzed.

Whether a risk premium, as such, exists, there are observable biases in
commodity futures that can lead to speculator profits, and some of these,
as well as evidence that some speculators can forecast prices, are discussed.
The process of decision making which precedes these forecasts is the subject of Chapters 6 and 7.

THE THEORY OF THE RANDOM WALK

Although the fundamental laws of supply and demand have been generally
accepted as determining the long-run price behavior of commodity futures
prices, they have certainly failed in the short run to provide a similar in-

sight. Most traders will agree that in the short run there is simply no significant correlation between "fundamentals" and prices, yet it is precisely in the short run that traders establish open profits and receive open losses.

Premises. Most discussions of short-run speculative price behavior take the "random walk hypothesis" as their point of departure. This theory suggests that successive price *changes* in commodity markets are independent and that past prices are not a reliable indicator of future prices. One of the major premises of the random walk theory is based on the concept of an "efficient" market. An efficient market is defined as one in which there are large numbers of equally informed, actively competing people attempting to maximize profits. In such a market, at any moment in time, price reflects all available information, as well as those events *expected* to transpire in the foreseeable future. Holbrook Working was the first in the commodity futures field to offer a theory of expectations that rests on the premise that futures reflect *anticipated* changes in supply and demand rather than on their immediate values.[1]

In an efficient market actual prices approximate anticipated or intrinsic value. In a world of uncertainty intrinsic value is elusive. Disagreements will cause random discrepancies between intrinsic value and actual prices. If the market is highly efficient, actual prices will move randomly about the intrinsic value.

Of course, intrinsic values change. Soybeans *do* move from $2.85 to $3.50 a bushel, and there is nothing in the random walk theory to suggest that superior intrinsic value analysis is useless in an efficient market. The trader will always do well if he can identify long-run supply-demand changes before such expectations are reflected in actual price changes. On the average, however, competition will cause most of the effects of new information regarding intrinsic values to be reflected quickly in commodity prices. It is the random quality of new information and not changes in supply or demand that is responsible for the irregular behavior of futures prices. The duration and extent of such price adjustments will be random variables that will cause prices to overadjust, underadjust, sometimes precede the information, and sometimes follow it in a manner that successive price changes are independent. Such a market has come to be known as a "random walk" market.

Behavior of traders. If price changes are formed according to anticipations of supply and demand, it is important to analyze in more depth the behavior of traders in response to news. In a *totally* efficient (hypothetical) market, when no new information is available, no new market position would be taken and there would be no price changes. A general price equilibrium would be established in which no trader who had the will to buy or sell had the power and no trader who had the power (one who held

---

[1] Holbrook Working, "A Theory of Anticipatory Prices," *American Economic Review Proceedings,* 48 (May 1958), 191.

an open position or the funds to establish one) had the will. As new information emerged, all traders would analyze it. If a change in positions were
dictated, those changes would be effected rapidly and a new level of equilibrium would be established. In such a market a trader would be successful only if he were better at analyzing and interpreting the information
currently available to all traders because the history of equilibrium levels
would tell him nothing about tomorrow's new input of information.

Moving from such an ideal market, an analysis can be made of the after
math of the input of new information on a more realistic market consisting
of "insiders" and "outsiders." The first group is made up of traders who
by training or position learn about new developments quickly. The second
group obtains new information only after the insiders have heard about it.
Such a market would be less than strongly efficient.

As new information becomes available, a double response occurs: Insiders react first and outsiders' reactions follow. The first response is clear.
If the new information is bullish, insider response would push prices higher.
Conversely, if the new input is bearish, prices would fall. The later outsider
response cannot be disposed of so simply. If the new information is bullish,
prices could rise again, remain unchanged, or drop. The first possibility
could occur if the demand by the outsiders exceeded the supply offered by
the insiders at the higher price established by the insiders. The second
possibility could occur if outsider demand were exactly offset by insider
desire to sell at the higher price. The third possibility is that outsider demand could not offset some increased insider selling at a higher price. The
second case reflects the most efficient market, that is, when insiders correctly predict subsequent outsider behavior. Even if this response is not
always forthcoming and the insiders do not perfectly anticipate the outsiders, the insiders are as likely to overestimate as to underestimate the
outsiders' response to market news. Thus on each input of bullish news a
trader could not establish a long position and expect prices to work higher,
nor could he take a short position directly after the issuance of bearish
news and have a high probability of profit.

The random walk theorists agree that it is unlikely that their model describes the behavior of commodity price changes exactly. Yet they assert
that although successive price changes may not be strictly independent
the amount of dependence is unimportant. If there is no such strategy,
then a simple policy of buy and hold will equal the results from any sophisticated procedure for timing. Therefore, unless a trader can improve on the
buy-and-hold policy, the independence assumption of the random walk
model is an adequate description of reality.

All this does *not* mean that short-term traders will not or cannot make
money trading commodity futures; it *does* mean that, on the average, those
traders will not beat a buy-and-hold strategy with information they obtain
from historical data.

Perhaps the clearest method of testing the random walk theory is to assume for the moment that it is *true* and that it does present an excellent "jumping off point" for the analysis of the behavior of commodity futures prices. To many traders this assertion may be heresy, yet if the theory is not backed by significant statistical evidence it can be withdrawn as a serious candidate.

EMPIRICAL STUDIES

Introduction. Those who have argued that commodity price changes are random in nature have based their assertion on the following principles: (1) price changes are such that they could have been generated by independent trials from a simple chance model such as a roulette wheel; (2) no one has been able to show that price changes exhibit a systematic pattern, even though present statistical techniques are capable of detecting data that have come from a significantly nonrandom process.

The first point is merely suggestive because it is impossible to prove the existence of randomness. Holbrook Working, writing as early as 1934 observed:

> It has several times been noted that time series commonly possess in many respects the characteristics of cumulated random numbers. The separate items in such time series are by no means random in character, but the *changes* between successive items tend to be largely random. This characteristic has been noted conspicuously in sensitive commodity prices. . . .[2]

In support of this position it has been suggested that the output of a simple roulette wheel could duplicate many of the characteristic features of commodity futures price movements. Results of this approach are illustrated in Figures 4-1 and 4-2. Although the illustration is based on price changes of a securities index, the principle is clear. Figure 4-1 represents the daily changes in closing prices of the Dow-Jones Industrial Average for the year 1956. Figure 4-2 represents changes generated by the output of a random number table. Even though the chance model demonstrated in Figure 4-2 cannot duplicate history in any sense other than one evening at a gambling casino duplicates another, the similarity of both series is striking enough to startle the would-be trader. Certainly the plotting of a series of price changes that could be generated from a random number table is not calculated to inspire confidence in the recurring "patterns" supposedly imbedded in price history.

In testing the random walk assertion, statisticians have brought to bear several kinds of tests. In the pages that follow results of runs analysis, serial correlation, filter rules and spectral analysis are presented as evidence in the controversy.

Analysis of runs. If a change in price (daily, weekly, monthly) is positive,

[2] Holbrook Working, "A Random-Difference Series for Use in the Analysis of Time Series," *Journal of the American Statistical Association,* 29 (1934), 11.

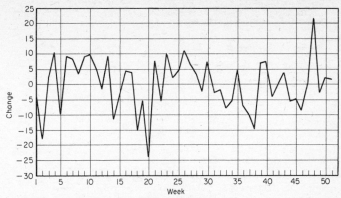

FIG. 4-1 Changes from Friday to Friday (closing), January 6, 1956, to December 28, 1956, Dow-Jones Industrial Index. (Harry Roberts, "Stock Market 'Patterns' and Financial Analysis: Methodological Suggestions," *Journal of Finance*, March 1959, p. 4.)

it can be denoted by "$+$." A negative change can be labeled "$-$." A "run" is a consecutive sequence of the same symbol. Assume the following sequence of $+$'s and $-$'s on a close-to-close basis:

$$- - + + - + + + + - + - - - + + - - + - + -.$$

The first four runs of this sequence are $- -, + +, -, + + + +.$ There are 13 runs in the entire sequence.

The purpose of a runs test is to determine whether the number of consecutive days of price movement in one direction is close to that expected by pure chance. Table 4-1 summarizes the observed versus the expected runs

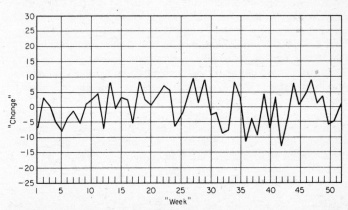

FIG. 4-2 Simulated market changes for 52 weeks. (Harry Roberts, "Stock Market 'Patterns' and Financial Analysis: Methodological Suggestions," *Journal of Finance*, March 1959, p. 5.)

TABLE 4-1   DISTRIBUTION OF LENGTHS OF RUN OF
DAILY JULY CORN AND SOYBEAN FUTURE PRICES,
SUMMARY, 1957–1968

Length of run (days)	July soybeans			July corn		
	Observed run		Expected run	Observed run		Expected run
	Up	Down	Up or down*	Up	Down	Up or down*
1	359	364	345	359	365	361
2	202	169	172	201	185	180
3	82	88	86	78	75	90
4	26	48	43	40	40	45
5	8	12	22	12	12	23
6+	10	15	22	13	7	23
Total	687	696	690	703	684	722

* Expected on the assumption of 0.5 probability of rise or fall and 2,755 close-to-close observations for July corn and 2,888 observations for July soybeans.
SOURCE: Richard Stevenson and Robert Bear, "Commodity Futures: Trends or Random Walks?" *Journal of Finance*, No. 1 (March 1970), 74.

in a recent study of daily futures prices of July soybeans and July corn over an 11-year period. Examination of these actual price changes shows that in this sample there were slightly more short (one- and two-day) runs than expected and slightly fewer long runs (five and six or more days) than would have occurred, on the average, by pure chance. The difference, however, is not significant and *could* have occurred by chance. The trader will note that these results, although slightly favoring a tendency toward reversals, in the main confirm the absence of identifiable nonrandomness in the length of runs through the 12 years observed. Also, as expected, the number of "up" runs of any given duration was about equal to the number of "down" runs of the same duration. Results of other statistical tests using runs have also been generally consistent with the hypothesis of independent price changes.[3]

Serial correlation. Serial correlation measures the correlation between a series of numbers like commodity futures prices with lagging numbers in the same series. Many different lags and many different time periods can be used to draw data for serial correlation tests. The presence of trends or reversal tendencies in commodity futures prices can be detected with this approach. The object is to find patterns in short-term price changes that can be used to trade more profitably than a naïve buy-and-hold strategy. If an up-move in price is followed more often than not by another up-move, positive serial correlation is present. If the converse is true, the trader has isolated a tendency for negative serial correlation or a reversal characteristic.

[3] See Holbrook Working, "Prices of Cash Wheat and Futures at Chicago Since 1883," *Wheat Studies*, 2, No. 3 (November 1934), 75–124, and Sidney Alexander, "Price Movements in Speculative Markets: Trends or Random Walks," reprinted in Paul Cootner, Ed., *The Random Character of Stock Market Prices*, The M.I.T. Press, Cambridge, Mass., 1964, pp. 199–218.

Following Working's discovery that fluctuations of futures prices are economically warranted responses to new information, itself unpredictable, came a study that showed a slight nonrandom characteristic in price movements. Brinegar,[4] using a new statistic, found a weak but statistically significant tendency toward "continuity" of a trend (positive serial correlation) in the prices of wheat, corn, and rye, ranging from 4 to 16 weeks. The amount of continuity varied from commodity to commodity and from time period to time period and was especially associated with periods of large price movements. A second important conclusion from Brinegar's study is the evidence of a slight "reaction tendency" (negative serial correlation) for short intervals of apparently one to two weeks.

Larson[5] expanded these findings by studying the day-to-day changes in corn prices for two 10-year periods, 1922–1931 and 1949–1958. His contribution was to measure the pattern followed by prices after inputs of new information. Larson found that on the average about 81 percent of the price effect of new demand and supply information occurs on a single day, presumably the day of changes in news. There is then a reaction, averaging about 8 percent dispersed over four days, away from the initial price movement, even though the first movement is not sufficient to discount all the news. Finally, an additional 27 percent dispersed over 45 days results in a total price movement that is just appropriate. Many markets may operate as Larson's study suggests, differing from an ideal random walk market principally in that traders react with varying skills to varying sources of information. For that reason some of the response to price making may be delayed, even though the delay is a small fraction of the total response and is dispersed over a considerable number of days in an unpredictable pattern.

Larson's evidence was important because, as Working later indicated,

> Economic reasoning suggests that the larger hedging orders should be expected to produce fairly large dips and bulges, of considerable duration. Experience of hedgers seems to bear out that reasoning. But Larson's evidence was the first to indicate clearly, from the behavior of prices, that these larger dips and bulges occurred frequently, in a large range of sizes and durations, their durations extending often to three or four days.[6]

Houthakker[7] has made a study that deals with the relative profitability of varying stop-loss order percentages as an indicator of serial correlation. Theoretically, if price changes were random, a trader who tried to limit

---

[4] Claude Brinegar, "A Statistical Analysis of Speculative Price Behavior," *Food Research Institute Studies*, Supplement, 9 (1970).

[5] Arnold Larson, "Measurement of a Random Process in Futures Prices," *Food Research Institute Studies*, 1, No. 3 (November 1960).

[6] Holbrook Working, "Tests of a Theory Concerning Floor Trading on Commodity Exchanges," *Food Research Institute Studies*, Supplement, 7 (1967), 16.

[7] Hendrik Houthakker, "Systematic and Random Elements in Short-Term Price Movements," *American Economic Review*, 51 (1961), 164–172.

his losses by selling (buying) whenever the price of a commodity falls (rises) by a fixed percentage below (above) his initial price would not find his average results better over a number of years than if he used no stops at all. If successive price changes were independent, a price decline (rise) of, say, 5 percent, which might be necessary to trigger a stop-loss, would not affect subsequent price changes. On the other hand, if a particular stop-loss percentage can be discovered, the use of which increases average net profit, then an instance of persistence in price trends will have been indicated. If the use of stop orders can lead to nonrandom outcomes for the trader, the problem becomes one of discovering what stop percentage is relevant. Stops placed too close to the entry price are activated by "noise," whereas if stops are placed too far away from the market losses may be too great to be adequately offset by profits.

For his analysis Houthakker chose wheat and corn futures during the periods October 1, 1921, to October 1, 1939, and February 1, 1947, to October 1, 1956. It was assumed that a trader bought or sold May wheat or corn on October 1, the September contract on February 1, and the December futures on June 1, liquidating each trade after four months unless stopped out beforehand. Commissions were not calculated.

Tables 4-2 and 4-3 summarize trading results for varying stop-loss percentages. A stop percentage of 5 means that the trader sells out at 95 percent of his purchase price, and a stop percentage of 0 means that any adversity below (above) a given entry point resulted in liquidation. A consistent long position in all three contracts of both wheat and corn was profitable, which implies a possible positive expected value over the periods covered.

In analyzing the stop percentages between 0 and 100, Houthakker cites

TABLE 4-2   TRADING RESULTS IN WHEAT FUTURES (1921–1939, 1947-1956) FOR VARIOUS STOP PERCENTAGES, IN CENTS PER BUSHEL

Stop percentage	Long positions				Short positions			
	May	Sept.	Dec.	Combined	May	Sept.	Dec.	Combined
100	+127	− 99	+ 59	+ 87	−127	+ 99	−59	− 87
20	+104	−126	+ 55	+ 33	−100	+112	−16	− 4
15	+ 96	−130	+ 69	+ 35	− 83	+ 73	−24	− 34
10	+132	−123	+ 90	+ 99	− 68	+ 90	+10	+ 32
7½	+135	− 74	+126	+187	− 55	+ 57	+27	+ 29
5	+122	− 47	+140	+215	− 34	+ 83	+79	+128
4	+133	− 15	+ 65	+183	− 19	+ 94	+53	+128
3	+116	− 5	+ 78	+189	− 19	+ 94	+70	+146
2	+ 42	− 4	+ 84	+122	− 24	+ 71	+30	+ 77
1	− 2	− 27	+ 73	+ 44	− 27	+ 60	−11	+ 22
0	+ 18	0	+ 27	+ 45	0	0	0	0

SOURCE: Hendrik Houthakker, "Systematic and Random Elements in Short Term Price Movements," *American Economic Review*, 51 (1961), 166.

TABLE 4-3   TRADING RESULTS IN CORN FUTURES (1922–1939,
1947–56) FOR VARIOUS STOP PERCENTAGES IN CENTS PER
BUSHEL

Stop percentage	Long positions				Short positions			
	May	Sept.	Dec.	Combined	May	Sept.	Dec.	Combined
100	+79	− 83	+112	+108	− 79	+ 83	−112	−108
20	+75	−114	+108	+ 69	−111	+ 94	− 36	− 64
15	+95	− 94	+119	+120	− 80	+ 91	− 48	− 37
10	+83	− 73	+141	+151	− 37	+107	− 47	+ 23
7½	+57	− 97	+151	+111	− 45	+103	− 27	+ 31
5	+21	− 47	+127	+101	− 23	+104	− 19	+ 62
4	+35	− 34	+125	+126	− 28	+117	− 56	+ 33
3	+36	− 11	+139	+164	− 12	+115	− 68	+ 35
2	+ 9	− 17	+156	+148	− 10	+105	− 53	+ 42
1	+29	− 24	+170	+175	− 9	+ 66	− 27	+ 32
0	+29	+ 2	+ 70	+100	0	0	0	0

SOURCE: Hendrik Houthakker, "Systematic and Random Elements in Short Term Price
Movements," *American Economic Review*, 51 (1961), 166.

some evidence of nonrandomness, even though the improvement is not
always large.[8] The study notes that long positions in May corn give better
results when stop percentages are relatively large but that the opposite is
true for December corn. Results for being long May and December wheat
and short September corn also favor a moderate stop percentage. Stop-
losses, of course, tend to reduce losses rather than increase profits. The
trader could not expect a stop-loss policy, no matter how efficiently formulated, to furnish him with a profitable trading record.

The best published evidence to date of attempting to scalp at least the
larger dips and bulges of prices is presented in a study by Smidt, whose
analysis of daily soybean prices produces interesting evidence of the presence of positive or negative serial correlation over a 10-year period.[9] The
data used were the daily high, low, and closing prices for May soybeans
for the 10 consecutive contracts expiring May 1952 through May 1961.
Each trading period was terminated 10 days before the contract expired,
and the length of the period available for trading varied from 137 to 188
days a year.

Table 4-4 represents some characteristics of the data and indicates that
prices at the beginning of the first trading period at 289.500 were only
21.5 cents a bushel less than the 311.000 price in May 1961. The portion

[8] Roger Gray and S. T. Nielsen, "Rediscovery of Some Fundamental Price Behavior Characteristics" (paper presented at a meeting of the Econometric Society, Cleveland, Ohio, September 7, 1963). The authors supplied additional data, using the same "stop-loss" technique,
which indicated that Houthakker's results were not necessarily typical of the markets analyzed. The tendency for trends was attributed by Gray and Nielsen to the influence of the
government price support program and Houthakker's use of distant contracts.

[9] Seymour Smidt, "A Test of the Serial Independence of Price Changes in Soybean Futures,"
Food Research Institute Studies, 5, No. 2 (1965).

TABLE 4-4 SOME CHARACTERISTICS OF THE MAY SOYBEANS
FUTURES CONTRACT PRICE SERIES USED TO TEST TRADING
RULES (CENTS PER BUSHEL, EXCEPT AS OTHERWISE
INDICATED)

Year ending	Length of time series,* trading days	Closing prices			Within trading period			
		10 days from			Maximum		Minimum	
		beginning	end	Change	Price	Day	Price	Day
1952	192	289.500	296.500	+ 7.000	309.750	50	281.500	166
1953	157	299.500	301.000	+ 1.500	311.000	41	280.000	91
1954	157	270.250	393.500	+123.250	422.000	141	268.750	11
1955	161	282.250	252.250	− 30.000	299.000	24	247.250	134
1956	161	236.750	321.500	+ 84.750	340.000	148	234.000	40
1957	161	248.250	240.375	− 7.875	269.500	43	238.000	142
1958	204	250.500	226.625	− 23.875	251.750	13	222.625	148
1959	208	233.250	229.625	− 3.625	233.500	28	217.375	110
1960	203	222.000	213.875	− 8.125	233.500	70	211.000	185
1961	201	225.750	311.000	+ 85.250	334.500	174	220.500	76
Total	...	......	......	+228.250				

* Exceeds "trading period" by 10 days at the beginning and 10 days at the end.

of the year that was arbitrarily chosen exhibits a strong trend upward. Indeed, without regard for the capital necessary to carry intrayear adverse price movement, a trader could have earned $2 a bushel if he had instituted the simple strategy of buying May soybeans at the beginning of each year's trading period and selling them 10 days before the contract expired in May of each year.

POSITIVE SERIAL CORRELATION. Traders often remark that they want to buy strength and sell weakness on the theory that strength or weakness in a given price structure tends to perpetuate itself. To check this viewpoint Smidt formulated and tested two rules, using May soybeans data from 1952 to 1961. Twenty examples of each of these tests are summarized in Tables 4-5 and 4-6. The study is designed so that the trader can utilize only two market positions, long one contract or short one contract. The only time a cash position is allowed is before the initial commitment. For both rules a moving average of N daily closing prices is computed in which N takes on values $1, 2, 3, 5, 10$; that is, the rules are tried by using moving averages of $1, 2, 3, 5,$ and 10 days, respectively.

The first rule of action specifies that the trader buy (sell) soybeans if the N-day moving average should move up (down) by K cents or more in any given day; for example, if the trader selected an $N = 3$-day moving average and a $K = 2$ cents required price change before taking a position, he would follow the decision rule, "Buy (sell) one contract of May soybeans whenever the 3-day moving average advances (declines) by 2 cents or more on any day." In the study described the required change K was given the values shown in Section A of Table 4-5. The prices at which the buys (sells) were executed were statistically determined by defining a random price variable

TABLE 4-5 RESULTS OF SOYBEAN RULES TESTING POSITIVE CORRELATION, WITH ACTION SIGNALS BASED ON ABSOLUTE SIZE OF CHANGE IN THE MOVING AVERAGE

A. Summary
Total profits or losses° (cents per bushel)

Action signals		1952–1961		After commission, in year with		After commission, number of years†		Commission, cents per bushel	Total number of moves
Length of moving average N, days	Change required, K, cents per bushel	After commission	Before commission	best profits	worst losses	with profits	with losses		
1	1.0	−476	−338	1	−112	1	9	138	384
1	2.0	−176	−112	18	−108	3	7	64	117
1	3.0	− 59	− 29	100	− 66	4	5	30	83
1	4.0	146	163	91	− 19	7	2	17	46
2	1.0	− 12	52	104	− 40	4	6	64	178
2	2.0	3	28	83	− 46	4	5	25	69
2	3.0	71	84	93	− 44	5	3	13	37
2	4.0	36	44	51	− 19	3	4	8	21
3	1.0	112	154	142	− 27	4	5	42	116
3	2.0	75	89	108	− 50	7	3	14	40
3	3.0	67	73	61	− 42	4	3	6	18
3	4.0	20	23	41	− 16	1	2	3	9
5	0.5	9	57	52	− 53	3	7	48	133
5	1.0	110	131	72	− 54	7	2	21	57
5	1.5	102	112	43	− 20	6	2	10	28
5	2.0	149	155	77	− 22	6	1	6	18
10	0.5	25	47	65	− 50	5	5	22	61
10	1.0	197	203	100	− 14	7	1	6	17
10	1.5	124	127	113	− 45	3	2	3	7
10	2.0	58	60	54	− 29	2	1	2	5

° Profits and losses rounded to the nearest cent.

† Total does not always equal 10 because of years in which profits or losses were less than half a cent per bushel, or in which no trading occurred.

such that any value between the high and low price on the day following the signal was equally likely. For illustrative purposes the midrange price, or the price midway between the daily high and low, will suffice. Results using the described decision rule for $N = 1, 2, 3, 5, 10$ and for K as shown are summarized in sections A and B of Table 4-5.

Reading from section A of Table 4-5 and continuing the preceding example with $N = 3$ and $K = 2$, it can be seen that during the entire period from 1952 to 1961 the trader made 75 cents a bushel profit after commissions, the highest profit being $1.08 a bushel and the largest loss being 50 cents a bushel. The decision rule was profitable in 7 of the 10 years, commission costs were 14 cents a bushel, and 40 positions were taken by the trader. A breakdown by years is listed in section B of Table 4-5.

TABLE 4-5   *(Continued)*

B. Annual profits and losses‡ after commissions, cents per bushel

N	K	1951–1952	1952–1953	1953–1954	1954–1955	1955–1956	1956–1957	1957–1958	1958–1959	1959–1960	1960–1961	Total
1	1.0	−86	−60	− 42	−110	− 1	−29	−16	1	−21	−112	−476
1	2.0	−41	−15	18	− 48	− 1	11	− 5	− 4	17	−108	−176
1	3.0	−35	−24	100	8	−39	3	−14	0	8	− 66	− 59
1	4.0	4	−19	91	− 17	25	12	20	0	1	29	146
2	1.0	−17	−37	104	2	46	−26	−25	−21	2	− 40	− 12
2	2.0	−46	−31	83	7	−10	12	18	0	− 2	− 28	3
2	3.0	−20	−44	93	− 3	19	6	18	0	2	0	71
2	4.0	− 9	−19	28	− 16	51	13	0	0	0	− 12	36
3	1.0	−22	5	142	0	53	−27	5	− 6	−21	− 17	112
3	2.0	−11	4	108	14	− 4	1	11	0	2	− 50	75
3	3.0	−19	19	45	− 42	61	13	0	0	0	28	67
3	4.0	0	0	−16	0	− 5	0	0	0	0	41	20
5	0.5	−18	−11	46	− 53	52	−14	−13	− 4	− 3	27	9
5	1.0	−26	−54	61	5	15	12	17	0	8	72	110
5	1.5	−20	12	43	− 15	35	9	0	0	3	35	102
5	2.0	−22	2	77	16	35	14	0	0	0	27	149
10	0.5	−50	10	55	− 37	65	−31	−10	− 4	7	20	25
10	1.0	−14	1	100	34	35	16	0	0	1	24	197
10	1.5	−10	0	113	− 45	37	0	0	0	0	29	124
10	2.0	0	0	54	0	33	0	0	0	0	− 29	59
Average per year		−23	−15	65	− 15	25	0	0	− 2	0	− 6	29

‡ Profits and losses rounded to the nearest cent.

The second rule of action is the same as the first, except that the required change is now a proportion P of the largest of the 10 past daily price ranges. This innovation is based on the hypothesis that the price volatility, as measured by the daily price range, might be an indication of the variability of future price changes. For the study P took on the values indicated in section A of Table 4-6, in which the results of trading by this rule are shown. Section B of Table 4-6, the counterpart of section B of Table 4-5, lists results year by year.

The data summarized in Tables 4-5 and 4-6 show that for the period and commodity tested a large number of the trading-decision rules (i.e., for various values of N and K or of N and P) lead to significant returns after commissions. For any given length N of moving average, gain (or loss) is a function of K (or P). The trader can immediately see that this is so; for example, a small value for K will generate more trades and therefore more commissions.

If the microscope rather than the telescope is applied to the results of soybean trading rules, interesting insights develop. Even for the most profit-

TABLE 4-6 RESULTS OF SOYBEAN RULES TESTING POSITIVE CORRELATION, WITH ACTION SIGNALS BASED ON RELATION OF CHANGE IN MOVING AVERAGE TO LARGEST PAST 10 DAILY PRICE RANGES

A. Summary
Total profits or losses* (cents per bushel)

Action signals		1952–1961		After commission, in year with		After commission, number of years†		Commission, cents	Total number
Length of moving average N, days	Change required, P (fraction of maximum range)	After commission	Before commission	best profits	worst profits	with profits	with losses	per bushel	of moves
1	0.2	−460	−264	26	−105	1	9	196	544
1	0.5	−114	− 41	15	− 58	4	5	73	204
1	0.7	128	161	90	− 32	6	4	33	93
1	1.0	153	161	114	− 22	4	5	8	23
2	0.2	− 7	88	129	− 44	4	6	95	265
2	0.5	162	184	110	− 27	5	5	22	62
2	0.7	93	101	110	− 44	5	4	8	23
2	1.0	− 14	− 13	12	− 26	1	1	1	2
3	0.2	110	172	104	− 27	3	6	62	173
3	0.5	173	183	119	− 30	5	5	10	27
3	0.7	107	110	81	− 11	5	3	3	9
3	1.0	0	0	0	0	0	0	0	0
5	0.2	134	167	101	− 28	5	5	33	92
5	0.5	57	60	80	− 28	4	4	3	8
5	0.7	0	0	0	0	0	0	0	0
5	1.0	0	0	0	0	0	0	0	0
10	0.05	125	161	58	− 32	7	3	36	99
10	0.10	108	136	84	− 43	5	5	28	77
10	0.15	181	199	122	− 26	7	3	18	50
10	0.20	227	237	122	− 33	7	3	10	29

*Profits and losses rounded to the nearest cent.

†Total does not always equal 10 because of years in which profits or losses were less than half a cent per bushel, or in which no trading occurred.

able decision rules most of the individual years generate losses or small profits, and it is left to a few years to produce extraordinary profits. In fact, even the highly profitable rules would not attract a trader if the one most profitable year were deleted. Large profits are concentrated in the major bull market years of 1954, 1956, and 1961.

From Table 4-4 it can be seen that only in 1953–1954, 1955–1956, and 1960–1961 was the intracontract range in May soybeans $1 a bushel or more. Each of these years produced unique supply and demand factors. In 1953 insufficient rains severely damaged the soybean crop and prices leaped up in response to an acute shortage. The 1955–1956 soybean price move did not originate from drought or reduced production but rather

TABLE 4-6 *(Continued)*

B. Annual profits and losses‡ after commissions, cents per bushel

N	P	1951–1952	1952–1953	1953–1954	1954–1955	1955–1956	1956–1957	1957–1958	1958–1959	1959–1960	1960–1961	Total
1	0.2	−73	−70	26	−105	−2	−50	−19	−21	−69	−77	−460
1	0.5	−36	1	15	−36	21	0	4	−5	−20	−58	−114
1	0.7	−32	−18	90	−10	53	23	−26	4	5	39	128
1	1.0	0	−8	114	−26	48	12	−22	−17	−11	63	153
2	0.2	−34	−43	129	−14	30	−38	17	0	−10	−44	−7
2	0.5	−27	−8	110	−16	56	−2	−8	4	5	48	162
2	0.7	−19	−44	110	0	61	13	−6	−11	−22	11	93
2	1.0	0	0	12	−26	0	0	0	0	0	0	−14
3	0.2	−28	−25	104	−21	62	−27	−3	0	−12	60	110
3	0.5	−17	−24	119	15	61	−30	−3	2	−26	76	173
3	0.7	−2	0	12	17	−8	0	11	−11	7	81	107
3	1.0	0	0	0	0	0	0	0	0	0	0	0
5	0.2	−14	−8	101	−21	52	3	−28	4	−3	48	134
5	0.5	−5	−2	12	−28	−8	2	0	0	6	80	57
5	0.7	0	0	0	0	0	0	0	0	0	0	0
5	1.0	0	0	0	0	0	0	0	0	0	0	0
10	0.05	−32	2	54	3	58	−10	−10	4	0	56	125
10	0.10	−44	3	84	−13	65	−13	−21	3	−1	45	108
10	0.15	−15	4	122	−22	78	−26	4	8	3	25	181
10	0.20	−7	11	122	−33	68	−32	6	14	5	73	227
Average per year		−19	−11	67	−17	35	−9	−5	−1	−7	26	58

‡Profits and losses rounded to the nearest cent.

from a heavy foreign demand for edible oil that almost completely absorbed a tremendous crop. A major bull move also occurred in soybeans during the 1960–1961 season because it was the year of a second consecutive short crop. Beginning stocks were much smaller in 1960–1961 than they were in 1959–1960, and so a limited crop had a significantly bullish effect on prices.

The supply and demand factors peculiar to these years are mentioned to underline the possibility that the distribution of price changes for those three bull-market years had a positive expected value, and therefore the gains shown for those years do not necessarily support a hypothesis of positive serial correlation. One might argue that a fundamentalist, in erecting a supply-demand model, might have good reason to project higher soybean prices in each of these three years and that he might have predicted the positive expected value.

On the other hand, nothing is quite so certain as hindsight, and the assumption could be advanced that fundamental factors are known with varying degrees of uncertainty before the fact. Could a trader take a responsible position based on a certain demand situation that he hopes will materialize or could he depend on crop damage to provide the impetus for a major bull move? Building a reliable model of expected future value is extremely difficult at best. If one rejects the assumption that it is possible to identify in advance those years in which there will be a positive expected value in soybean prices, one might argue that the profits that resulted from the application of the described rules are bona fide evidence in support of the existence of positive serial correlation in soybean prices over the period covered by the data.

NEGATIVE SERIAL CORRELATION. It remains to examine the possibility that a rewarding futures price strategy might be to sell rallies and buy declines rather than to bank on the continuation of price strength or weakness. Smidt reversed the previously described trading rules so that the trader was to buy on price dips and sell on price rises.

Table 4-7 summarizes the results of countertrend trading by using the two most profitable countertrend rules. Interestingly enough, both rules are characterized by the fact that small price changes are required to switch the trader from long to short. Profits before commissions are higher than those generated following any rule considered earlier, and profits are distributed much more evenly over time than they were following their counterparts. Results would not be altered significantly, even if the most profitable year were eliminated. After showing that the observed profits would have been statistically unlikely if the price changes were not nega-

TABLE 4-7 ANNUAL PROFITS OR LOSSES, BEFORE AND AFTER
COMMISSIONS OF TWO MODIFIED TRADING RULES TESTING
NEGATIVE CORRELATION (CENTS PER BUSHEL, EXCEPT AS
OTHERWISE INDICATED)

	$N = 1, P = 0.2$			$N = 1, K = 1$		
		Profits or losses[*]			Profits or losses[*]	
Year	Number of moves	before commission	after commission	Number of moves	before commission	after commission
1951–52	64	50	27	59	64	43
1952–53	49	52	34	39	46	32
1953–54	44	−42	−58	52	23	4
1954–55	54	86	66	54	91	71
1955–56	38	−11	−25	28	−10	−20
1956–57	53	31	12	35	16	4
1957–58	62	− 3	−25	32	4	− 7
1958–59	62	− 1	−23	13	− 5	−10
1959–60	65	46	22	23	13	5
1960–61	53	58	39	49	94	76
Total	544	266	69	384	336	198

[*] Profits and losses rounded to the nearest cent.

tively correlated, Smidt concludes that the evidence supports the hypothesis that May soybean futures can profitably be traded on the basis of selling strength and buying weakness under selected conditions.

The most successful strategy summarized in Table 4-7 which produced 336 cents a bushel gross return was simple: sell following any price advance, close-to-close, of more than 1 cent a bushel; buy following any close-to-close price decline of more than 1 cent a bushel. If the initial purchase or sale was to be x bushels, each purchase or sale following the initial one would have been $2x$ bushels, thus keeping the trader continuously long or short x bushels. This rule would have resulted in gains of nearly $\frac{9}{10}$ cent a bushel before commissions for the 10-year period.

Characteristic	Five effective years*	Five ineffective years
Number of transactions	253	131
Aggregate net gain in cents per bushel of continuous holding (alternately long and short)	318	18
Gain per bushel, cents	1.26	0.014

* Classed by the criterion that the trading rule produced an average holding interval of less than four days. The years were 1952 to 1955, inclusive, and 1961.

SOURCE: Holbrook Working, "Tests of a Theory Concerning Floor Trading on Commodity Exchanges," *Food Research Institute Studies*, Supplement, 7 (1967), 16.

Working selected Smidt's results showing negative serial correlation for a pertinent comment.[10] He tabulated them according to the average length of each trade rather than by financial return and found that Smidt's rule worked well in 5 of the 10 years with the result that the average gain for those years was 1.26 cents a bushel. In the other five years, as noted later, gains and losses were almost equal. Those years in which the rule worked well and which led to an average trading period of less than four days reflected generally higher prices and wilder fluctuations than usual.

Because very short-run rules similar to those tested by Smidt become popular from time to time, the trader is cautioned that consistent profits utilizing such negative serial correlation are not easy to amass for the following reasons. First, few traders execute trades physically on the floors of the exchanges. Orders must be written to buy or sell on a market-on-close basis, leading to significant execution costs for local traders willing to execute them. These costs are generally seriously underestimated (see Chapter 10). Working alludes to the problem by indicating that the profes-

[10] Holbrook Working, "Tests of a Theory Concerning Floor Trading on Commodity Exchanges," *Food Research Institute Studies*, Supplement, 7 (1967), 16, 17.

sional scalper must buy or sell when a "dip" or "bulge" is *actually* forming, for it is only at that time that favorable prices can be obtained.[11] Such a consideration is paramount when it is realized that Smidt's best rule, after commissions, results in approximately ½ cent a bushel average profit per trade. Any effort to buy *after* a dip or bulge has formed could seriously impair the already minuscule profit margin.

Second, because of the small margin of profit expected on the average, a trader may be tempted to increase the number of bushels he trades, thereby substantially increasing his risks on any one trade. Unless the trader has considerable financial means, several losses on balance could do irreparable harm, both financially and psychologically. The question, then, not only of average profits but of average losses to be sustained deserves serious consideration in the setting of stop-losses.

Filter rules. It remains to inquire into the possibility of applying filter techniques to commodity futures prices. A major reason for examining filters develops from the concern that any dependence in the form of recognizable and usable price patterns will be so complicated that standard statistical analyses such as runs tests or short-run serial correlation tests will fail to uncover them. If prices exhibit patterns that persist over long periods of time, it can be concluded that the markets *have* a memory, that past price movements can help to forecast future price changes, and therefore that price changes are not independent. Such trend-following strategies, if successful, may eliminate or reduce the problems of commission costs, execution costs, and small average profits that have plagued the trader in results examined to date.

Most of the early work in trying to simulate technical trading rules centered on security prices. Alexander[12] developed a filter technique in order to apply a criterion similar to that used by some traders. The filter was defined as follows: as soon as the closing price moves up x percent from some initial point, the security is bought and held until its price moves down x percent from a high subsequent to the first purchase, at which time the long position is abandoned and a short position instituted; the short position is maintained until the closing price again rises x percent above a low subsequent to the previous sell, at which time the short position is covered and a long position is entered. Alexander used filters with varying values of x between one and 50 percent and applied the technique to American industrial stock price averages from 1897 to 1959. He concluded that his filter rule yields positive results for filters ranging from $x = 5$ to $x = 30$ percent. In other words, he finds a tendency for a price change in a stock price average to be followed by a subsequent price change in the same direction. The

[11] *Ibid.*

[12] Sidney Alexander, "Price Movements in Speculative Markets: Trends or Random Walks," No. 2, reprinted in Paul Cootner, Ed., *The Random Character of Stock Market Prices*, The M.I.T. Press, Cambridge, Mass., 1964, pp. 338–372.

profitability of this filter technique may imply similar results for other trend-following techniques, but, because the data consisted of changes in stock price *averages* and because changes in price *averages* have behavioral characteristics that differ from those of changes in the price of an individual stock, Alexander's results would not necessarily be meaningful in a pragmatic trading situation.

Cootner[13] examined the results of a rule that permitted much more rapid response to changes of direction than Alexander's strategy. The decision rule was stated as follows: buy the stock when the price exceeds a 40-week moving average by more than a given percentage (threshold amount) and sell the stock whenever the price dips below the moving average by *any* amount; sell the stock short whenever it falls below the moving average by more than the threshold amount and cover the short sale whenever the price rises above the moving average by *any* amount. This rule was applied to the weekly closing prices of a sample of 45 stocks listed on the New York Stock Exchange over a period that generally included the years 1956 to 1960.

Rates of return using a zero and 5 percent threshold rate were provided, the latter rate lowering the excessive transactions that tend to occur when the stock price remains in a narrow range. Both strategies were superior to buy-and-hold *only* if gross profits were considered. After commissions neither strategy outperformed the simple investment rule.

In a careful analysis covering all the individual stocks of the Dow-Jones Industrial Average Fama and Blume[14] tested 24 filters ranging from ½ to 50 percent over daily data for approximately five years ending in 1962. When commissions are included, the largest profits under the filter technique are those of the broker. When commissions are omitted, the returns from the filter technique are improved but are *still* inferior to buy-and-hold for all except two securities of the 30 — Alcoa and Union Carbide. In addition, empirical evidence is presented which indicates Alexander's results tended to overstate the actual profitability of the filter technique versus buy-and-hold. Such bias, it is believed, appears because the use of indices overstates the profitability of short sales. Because short sellers must incur the cost of paying all dividends, the index is reduced by dividend payments, and therefore the time spent in being short will introduce a bias estimated at about 2 percentage points in favor of the filter technique.

A recent study by Stevenson and Bear[15] reveals some success in applying

[13] Paul Cootner, "Stock Prices: Random vs. Systematic Changes," reprinted in Paul Cootner, Ed., *The Random Character of Stock Market Prices,* The M.I.T. Press, Cambridge, Mass., 1964, pp. 231–252.

[14] Eugene Fama and Marshall Blume, "Filter Rules and Stock-Market Trading," *Journal of Business,* 39 (Supplement 1966), 226–241.

[15] Richard Stevenson and Robert Bear, "Commodity Futures: Trends or Random Walks?", *Journal of Finance,* 21, No. 1 (March 1970), 65–81.

varying filters in July corn and July soybeans over the 12-year period, 1957–1968. Three trading techniques are simulated. Trading technique 1 assumes that the trader buys the future at the opening on the first day of trading and enters a stop-loss order x percent below the purchase price. If the stop-loss is not executed, the future is sold on the last day of the contract. If the stop-loss is executed, no further position is taken until the following July contract begins trading. The reader will recognize this rule as similar to the one tested earlier by Houthakker.

Trading technique 2 is divided into Plan A and Plan B. Plan A waits for the closing price to move up or down x percent and then establishes a position in the *direction of the market move*. A stop-loss order is placed x percent below (above) the established position. If price moves in favor of the trader, the stop is moved each day so that the trader never risks more than x percent from the high closing price. If prices move against the trader, the stop-loss order is not moved. When a trade is closed out, the trader repeats the process. Plan A, then, to be successful requires a tendency toward a move of x percent to be followed more often than not by another move of *more* than x percent. Plan B uses the same procedure, except that it establishes a position *against* the market rather than *with* the market. This rule should help indicate whether the tendency in the markets tested is toward price reversals.

Trading technique 3 establishes a position *with* the market when price moves up (down) x percent and holds the position until a move occurs, either up or down, of x percent. Profits are not allowed to run.

For each of the trading techniques 1½, 3, and 5 percent filters were tested. Commissions were charged on all transactions, and the dollar returns in Tables 4-8 and 4-9 reflect a commitment of 10,000 bushels or two contracts. A buy-and-hold policy over the 12-year period resulted in a profit in soybeans of $8,545 or about an average of 3.5 cents annually. However, if it were not for the large profit of $10,654 realized in 1966 (about 53 cents a bushel), there would have been a sizable loss. Buy-and-hold results for corn over the same period produced a $5,328 loss.

Trading technique 1 with a 5 percent filter worked well in soybeans but did not result in a profitable corn trading rule, even though all filters reduced the loss accruing to the buy-and-hold strategy.

Trading technique 2 (Plan A) provided the best results for both corn and soybeans. As the size of the filter increased, profitability increased when positions were established *with* the market, until results were optimized with a 5 percent filter. Eight of 12 years were profitable with the largest filter in soybeans, and 7 of 12 years yielded profits in corn. Plan B produced nearly inverse results when compared with Plan A, yet confirmed some tendency toward reversals in the shorter run price movements.

Trading technique 3 did not perform so well as the other strategies. After commissions, only a 5 percent filter in soybeans did well.

TABLE 4-8 RETURNS FROM TRADING TECHNIQUES USING VARIOUS SIZED FILTERS, JULY CORN FUTURES, SUMMARY TABLE FOR 1957–1968

	1½% Filter				3% Filter				5% Filter			
	Profit	Loss	Net	Years profit	Profit	Loss	Net	Years profit	Profit	Loss	Net	Years profit
Buy and hold	$2,955	$8,283	$(5,328)	5	$2,955	$8,283	$(5,328)	5	$2,955	$8,283	$(5,328)	5
Trading technique 1	1,187	1,940	(753)	2	1,187	3,440	(2,253)	2	2,849	4,277	(1,428)	4
Trading technique 2 (Plan A)	460	9,397	(8,937)	1	2,915	2,381	584	7	3,990	1,577	2,413	7
Trading technique 2 (Plan B)	2,978	5,358	(2,380)	5	5,259	4,332	927	6	2,422	3,241	(819)	4
Trading technique 3	203	8,833	(8,630)	1	2,728	4,235	(1,507)	6	2,527	3,178	(651)	6

SOURCE: Richard Stevenson and Robert Bear, "Commodity Futures: Trends or Random Walks?", *Journal of Finance*, **21**, No. 1 (March 1970), 77.

TABLE 4-9 RETURNS FROM TRADING TECHNIQUES USING VARIOUS SIZED FILTERS, JULY SOYBEAN FUTURES, SUMMARY TABLE FOR 1957–1968

	1½% Filter				3% Filter				5% Filter			
	Profit	Loss	Net	Years profit	Profit	Loss	Net	Years profit	Profit	Loss	Net	Years profit
Buy and hold	$21,210	$12,663	$ 8,547	4	$21,210	$12,663	$ 8,547	4	$21,210	$12,663	$ 8,547	4
Trading technique 1	10,556	3,132	7,424	3	10,556	5,832	4,724	3	21,210	6,784	14,426	4
Trading technique 2 (Plan A)	4,502	11,159	(6,657)	3	15,744	3,428	12,316	7	19,241	2,140	17,101	8
Trading technique 2 (Plan B)	9,098	8,942	156	5	4,676	13,550	(8,874)	3	5,635	16,107	(10,472)	2
Trading technique 3	3,589	15,858	(12,269)	3	2,380	11,518	(9,188)	3	16,462	4,130	12,332	8

SOURCE: Richard Stevenson and Robert Bear, "Commodity Futures: Trends or Random Walks?", *Journal of Finance*, **21**, No. 1 (March 1970), 78.

Spectral analysis. Spectral analysis is a modern statistical technique for decomposing a time series like commodity futures prices.[16] This idea itself is not a new one because breaking down a time-series into a "trend," plus a "cycle," plus a "seasonal" component, plus the unexplained remainder has been studied by standard economic procedures for many years. The trend is a very smooth, slow-moving component, corresponding to a very low frequency, and therefore seldom occurs. The cyclical component, which corresponds to the next lowest frequency, is followed by the seasonal (12-month) component and finally by all other shorter term frequencies.

Spectral analysis can be compared with the swinging of the dial of a radio across a waveband. The signals received, however, are not words or music. At any particular frequency only the total *power* of the signal is measured. The static between "stations" would correspond to a purely random signal and would register as a small, constant amount. The "stations" themselves correspond to the frequencies of the transmission as well as the *strength* of each signal. Spectral analysis shows the size of the amplitude of each frequency found in a time series.

Monthly futures prices for a number of commodities for January 1950 through July 1965 were examined by Labys and Granger by spectral analysis.[17] In general, the series was flat and exhibited the behavior expected from a random walk market. The only commodity that showed a slightly significant seasonal tendency which the authors would confirm was wheat. Cotton oil, potatoes, eggs, cocoa, corn, flax, lard, soybeans, soybean meal, soybean oil, cotton, rye, and oats generated the type of spectra that would generally confirm the random walk model. Similar analysis was applied to weekly and daily futures prices. Fifteen years of weekly prices for corn, oats, rye, wheat, and soybeans were examined and the shape of the spectra of these futures also confirmed the random walk model. One year of daily prices for coffee, corn, oats, rye, rubber, soybeans, sugar, wheat, cocoa, and cotton was tested and all but the last two indicated that the random walk model provides a good explanation of price behavior. A small amount of negative serial correlation existed for cocoa and cotton.

THE QUESTION OF TREND

Even if the random walk model results in a crude approximation of the truth when it comes to explaining price changes in commodity futures, a trader can still profit. He can isolate, quantify, and trade those short-run, nonrandom changes that he can validate as offering, after commissions, a profit. This approach is discussed in detail in Chapter 7. A trader can still profit even if successive price changes are independent if their expected

[16] An excellent summary of spectral analysis is given in Walter C. Labys and C. W. J. Granger, *Speculation, Hedging and Commodity Price Forecasts,* D. C. Heath and Co., Lexington, Mass., 1970, Chapter 2.

[17] *Ibid.,* p. 66–70.

value is not zero. In other words, traders can make money in commodity futures even if they cannot predict short-term price changes consistently. A trader can simply follow a trend.

Risk premium concept. The first explanation advanced to indicate how the idea of an efficient market and a trend might coexist centered around a risk premium concept. Keynes first advanced the hypothesis in an essay in the Manchester Guardian Commercial in 1923 in which he suggested that anyone could reap handsome profits by simply holding long positions in cotton futures throughout the crop year, year in and year out.[18] This affirmation came to be regarded as the "Keynesian theory of normal backwardation."[19]

Though for years severe problems in semantics were to persist in the literature, the theory in essence stated that, although markets sometimes reflect carrying charges and sometimes are inverted, in either case a risk premium is a normal and continuing part of the difference between cash prices and futures prices. In other words, the theory required that the futures price be lower (biased downward) than the price expected to prevail at the later delivery period by an amount representing the speculators reward for bearing the risk of price change in the interim. The implication here is that short hedging will predominate, thereby leaving the speculator net long.

In its simplest form the theory predicted that under certain conditions it was necessary, *on the average,* for the price of futures contracts to rise. Early in the development of the theory there were three necessary conditions:

1. Speculators are net long.
2. Speculators are risk avoiders; that is, they require a history of profits if they are to continue to trade.
3. Speculators are unable to forecast prices.

It is clear that all these assumptions can be met if there is a rise, on the average, in futures prices during the life of each contract. It is equally clear that if speculators are net long, require a history of profits to continue the game, and have no ability to forecast the direction or extent of future price changes then obviously all profits that accrue to them must unambiguously be considered as a reward for the bearing of risk, not unlike the flow of insurance premiums between an insurance company and the insured. The speculator is guaranteed an expectation of gain, on the average, by making it possible for the hedger to hedge. The size of his speculative gain, under

---

[18] Quoted in Roger W. Gray and David J. S. Rutledge, "The Economics of Commodity Futures Markets: A Survey," *Review of Marketing and Agricultural Economics,* 39, No. 4, 9.

[19] "Backwardation" is a British trade term which in American usage refers to the premium present in an inverted market or a situation in which cash prices exceed futures prices. "Contango," the opposite word, refers to a carrying charge market in which futures prices exceed cash prices. Thus Keynes considered that risk cost (backwardation) was to be considered "normal" in both kinds of markets, inverse or carry.

these assumptions, hinges *only* on the size of his position and not on his competence.

STATISTICAL EVIDENCE. Stone stated as early as 1901[20] in a report for the U.S. Congress that, among several commodities, an analysis of the cotton markets did not sustain the contention that the futures price is always less than the spot price:

> . . . if, for example, we compare October futures in July with the spot price realized in October. Out of fifty-seven different futures . . . compared with spot prices realized . . . in the N.Y. cotton market from 1881–82 to 1899, in twenty-nine cases the futures proved to be higher than the spots realized 3 months hence, and in twenty-eight cases the futures prices were lower than the spots at maturity—that is, the speculative judgment anticipated the realized value of cotton a little too favorably in half of the cases and not quite favorably enough in the other half . . . in the long run the speculative quotations for future delivery are neither uniformly above nor below the level of the proper cash value of cotton as determined at the future date, but . . . they are tentative anticipations of such realizable value as the conditions of the supply and demand are most likely to determine at the time when the future contract matures.

In the same report results for 15 years (1883–1898) of Chicago wheat prices confirmed that if the speculator were to rely on the Keynesian postulate of earning substantial profits by merely running risk and allowing one season's results to be averaged against the others he would not have fared well.[21]

A later report by the Federal Trade Commission[22] introduced evidence on which Working was later to comment:[23]

> One of the most critical and painstaking inquiries into the subject was that made by the Federal Trade Commission. It attacked the problem in several different ways. All the methods produced evidence, in price data subsequent to 1896, of some 'downward bias' in futures prices of wheat and corn but not of oats; but for the 10-year period prior to 1896, the indicated bias was in the opposite direction for all grains. The method which the Federal Trade Commission appeared to regard as quantitatively most trustworthy . . . yielded for wheat, 1906–16, the estimate that it amounted to −2.39 cents (about 2.4 percent) for a twelve-month interval.

Early in the controversy considerable doubt was raised that a speculator could amass consistent and substantial profits by merely being net long. In spite of the evidence, it does not seem that the theoretical discussion ever turned to the statistics of the organized markets for confirmation. When

---

[20] U.S. 56th Congress, 2nd Session, House, *U.S. Industrial Commission Report* (1900–1901), House Doc. 94, reviewed in Gray and Rutledge, *op. cit.*, 14–15.

[21] *Ibid.*

[22] U.S. Federal Trade Commission, *Report on the Grain Trade,* 7 volumes, Washington, D.C., 1920–1926.

[23] Holbrook Working, "Theory of the Inverse Carrying Charge in Futures Markets," *Journal of Future Economics,* 30, No. 1 (February 1948), 9.

other commodities were examined in due course, it became evident that hedgers could be net long for considerable periods of time. The implication that net short hedging would predominate was not always realized. Because the level of the net short positions of hedgers may vary considerably, so will the size of offsetting speculative long positions. Therefore speculators may possibly have a history of profits *without* prices rising on the average: for example, prices rise 5 cents in the first period and fall 5 cents in the second period; speculators are long 20 contracts in the first period and only 10 contracts in the second period. Such action is still consistent with the assumed inability of speculators to forecast price changes. The opposite situation may be true also; that is, a rise in prices may not result in profits for traders who are long. Speculators may be long 10 contracts during a price rise of 5 cents and long 30 contracts during a decline of 3 cents.

The arena became packed with clamoring voices, and the ensuing controversy was instructive because it led the academic community to test what traders commonly refer to today as "seasonals." Indeed, if the presence of a trend in a commodity is to be related to the risks of carrying an inventory in that commodity, then any such trend *must* be related to the pattern of hedging.

Cootner has presented several examples[24] in support of the contention

---

[24] Paul Cootner, "Speculation and Hedging," *Food Research Institute Studies,* Supplement, 7 (1967), 84–103.

TABLE 4-10   WHEAT AVERAGE GAIN PER YEAR
1947–1965 UNDER INDICATED STRATEGIES

Specifications	Strategy I	Strategy II	Strategy III
Cents per bushel			
Short only	7.8°	8.5°	6.2
Long only	8.6°	9.4°	8.6
Long and short	15.9°	17.9†	14.8
Per cent of price			
Long and short	7.7	8.7	7.3

Strategy I. Go short at bimonthly point when reported short hedging first drops below 3,000 contracts. Cover short sales and go long at bimonthly point when reported short hedging first rises above 3,000 contracts. Sell long positions when you go short. All positions are taken in the nearest future in which the position can be held for the entire period.
Strategy II. Same as Strategy I except that all positions are liquidated at the point prior to the change in the balance of hedging.
Strategy III. Same as Strategy I except that all short positions are initially taken in May and are switched to the July future (if necessary) on April 30. Long positions are initially taken in March and switched to May if necessary. Not tested for significance.
    ° Significant at the 5 per cent level.
    † Significant at the 1 per cent level.
    SOURCE: Paul Cootner, "Speculation and Hedging," *Proceedings of a Symposium on Price Effects of Speculation in Organized Commodity Markets, Food Research Institute Studies,* Supplement, 7 (1967), 89.

that risk premiums can exist in commodity futures. From 1946 to the present, bimonthly hedging and speculative positions are available for "large traders" as defined by the CEA. Table 4-10 provides the results of three strategies of initiating long and short positions in wheat futures based on short hedging levels. All strategies are profitable for both long and short positions for the 19-year period. These results indicate that it was possible for speculators to profit merely by being long after the peak of net short hedging and short after the peak of net long hedging.

Table 4-11 presents some evidence for a seasonal in soybeans. The period covered is from the autumn of 1949 to the autumn of 1960. Details of the strategies are given in the notes to Table 4-11. The long and short strategy keeps the trader long for six months and short for almost the same period of time. This strategy offsets what otherwise might be considered an inflationary bias. The average gains for the years 1949 to 1960 are impres-

TABLE 4-11   SOYBEANS: AVERAGE GAINS PER YEAR, 1949–1960*

Positions	(cents per bushel) Autumn 1949 to autumn 1960†
Long positions	
From peak in visible supply to April 30	18.2
From peak in hedging to April 30	21.3
Short positions	
From April 30 to September 20	14.7
Long and short positions	
Long from October 20 to April 30 and short from April 30 to September 20	38.7

* Since soybeans have been in shorter supply than wheat during this period, long hedging has tended to predominate earlier in the crop year than was the case for wheat even though it is earlier in the soybean crop than in the wheat crop year.

Long positions were always taken in the May future.

Short positions were taken in the September future except in 1949–1950 and 1950–1951, when the September future was not used. In those years the position was taken in the November future.

The September 20 terminal date was near the last day of trading in the September future. The last day was chosen because the long hedging positions in that month are usually taken to protect against late or poor harvests. The harvest usually begins late in September and the hedging position is generally liquidated very late. It is the late September results which truly indicate the outcome. A smaller but still significant profit is obtained by terminating the short position on August 30.

† All results are significant at the 0.1 per cent level.

SOURCE: Paul Cootner, "Speculation and Hedging," *Proceedings of a Symposium on Price Effects of Speculation in Organized Commodity Markets, Food Research Institute Studies,* Supplement, 7 (1967), 97.

sive, even though they *omit* the 1960–1961 crop year which provided about 100 cents profit on the long side and 80 cents profit on the short. It is interesting to note that the peak in visible supplies is a good proxy for the peak in hedging.

Traders have long considered the possibilities of trading "intermarket" spreads, that is, being simultaneously long and short in different markets in which the impact of hedging comes at different periods of time. One spread is the relation between oats and corn reflected in Table 4-12. The domestic oats crop harvest is started in the spring and frequently lasts through the summer. The corn harvest, on the other hand, begins in September and is usually completed by the onset of winter. For corn, then, short hedging generally increases in the period just before the December contract goes off the board. Oats, during the same period, is a market in which the customary activity is one of hedge lifting. Again, details of the strategies are indicated in the notes to Table 4-12.

TABLE 4-12 OATS—CORN: CHANGE
IN PRICE DIFFERENTIALS OF
DECEMBER CONTRACTS, 1947–1964

| | Mean annual change (cents per bushel) | |
Strategy°	To December 15	To November 30
1	4.79†	2.67
2	5.62†	3.45‡
3	3.84†	1.67
4§	2.37	−1.20
5§	− .54	−1.72

° Hedging-oriented strategies: buy two bushels of December oats and sell one bushel of December corn on bimonthly date when

(1) reported oats net short hedging first exceeds reported corn net short hedging.

(2) reported oats net short hedging exceeds 2,000 contracts,

(3) reported oats net short hedging minus reported corn net short hedging reaches peak. When oats short hedging always meets the conditions, trades are initiated on April 15.

Calendar strategies: buy two bushels December oats and sell one bushel December corn on

(4) July 30,

(5) April 15.

† Significant at the 5 percent level.

‡ Significant at the 10 percent level. All other numbers are not statistically different from zero.

§ The figures are not significant at the 10 percent level.

SOURCE: Paul Cootner, "Speculation and Hedging," *Proceedings of a Symposium on Price Effects of Speculation in Organized Commodity Markets, Food Research Institute Studies,* Supplement, 7 (1967), 100.

The trader should note that strategies 4 and 5 show a much smaller tendency for the price differential to rise because they are computed on a calendar rather than a hedging basis. Thus, although buying two contracts of December oats and selling one contract of December corn on a hedging pattern resulted in an average rise of about 5 cents a bushel from 1947–1964, a similar strategy on a calendar basis yielded only about 2 cents a bushel. These results tend to support the existence of a risk premium.

Houthakker found, based on monthly price observations, that his sample of speculators actually made money trading commodity futures.[25] These findings required additional changes in the risk premium theory. The trader will remember that the original risk premium concept required that speculators

(a) be net long,
(b) refuse to trade if they lost money in the long run,
(c) be unable to forecast price changes.

The only price behavior that apparently would tolerate all three conditions was one of rising prices on the average. The first breach in this concept occurred when it was discovered that short hedging did *not* predominate at all times for all commodities and that speculators *could still* obtain a risk premium even if prices did not rise on the average. A speculator could simply be net long when hedgers were net short and net short when the hedgers were net long. Houthakker not only indicated that speculators earned profits but he devised a method of estimating the share of profits that should be attributed to actual forecasting skill versus the premium that would be received for merely bearing risk. The insurance premium analogy was no longer adequate in itself to explain speculators' profits. Of course, not everyone accepted these findings. Telser,[26] for one, rejected Houthakker's evidence of the ability to forecast on the basis that commissions were not charged against speculator income, the study was limited to only nine years (1937–1939 and 1946–1952), and the method of estimating profits and losses was hampered by not including the changes in prices that were available to speculators in each month.

Rockwell recently enlarged on Houthakker's study in an important analysis covering 7,900 semimonthly observations over 25 markets for the 18-year period, 1947 to 1965.[27] Among other pertinent inquiries, Rockwell attempted to define the proportion of dollars flowing to speculators that could be attributed to the presence of a risk premium. In other words, how much money would accrue to a naïve trader who is long when hedgers are net short and short when hedgers are net long? Two important conclusions emerged. First, prices rose consistently when speculators were net short,

[25] H. S. Houthakker, "Can Speculators Forecast Prices?", *Review of Economics and Statistics*, 39, No. 2 (May 1959), 143–151.

[26] L. G. Telser, "Futures Trading and the Storage of Cotton and Wheat," *Journal of Political Economy*, 66, No. 3 (June 1958), 233–255.

[27] Charles Rockwell, "Normal Backwardation, Forecasting and the Returns to Commodity Futures Traders," *Food Research Institute Studies*, Supplement, 7 (1967), 107–130.

causing them considerable losses. Second, the profits that accrue to the naive speculator when he is net long are so small that no significant tendency toward normal backwardation is observed. Rockwell pointed out, however, that these conclusions do not imply that there can never be strong upward or downward price tendencies in different markets or in different periods within a market. In other words, even though the overall generalization might be that the futures price is an unbiased estimate of the ultimate spot price, such a statement is critically dependent on the markets which are selected.

Rockwell's study is critically important for another reason, however. If his study indicated rather conclusively that the risk premium theory is not viable for traders in a general way, his findings clearly promise a flow of profits to some traders solely on the basis of their forecasting skill. It is possible to define two levels of forecasting skill. First, a basic skill can measure the ability to be long in markets in which prices generally rise over the period examined and short when prices fall. Second, a special forecasting skill measures a trader's ability to forecast price movements that are shorter than the total period observed. The trader can see that these two definitions loosely parallel what might be called the fundamental and technical approaches to market forecasting. After developing these two approaches to decision making in greater detail in Chapters 6 and 7, the trading results of the players in the game—hedgers, large speculators, and small speculators—are fully analyzed to answer to the all important question of who wins, who loses, and why? It is of interest to note at this point that traders might participate, without the prerequisite of any basic or forecasting skill, in biases that may be present without heavy reliance on whether or not there is a risk premium.

Other causes of bias. That there might be fruitful excursions into the question whether price action could be lopsided for reasons other than the existence of a risk premium being paid to speculators has been stressed by such scholars as Gray. Gray has measured statistically the general tendency for futures prices to rise over extended periods of time for which the beginning and ending cash prices are generally unchanged.[28] If a trader holds a long position in a future, routinely rolls his position forward on maturity, and is able to generate consistent profits or losses when the cash price stays virtually unchanged, then that market may be said to be unbalanced, lopsided, or biased. Gray finds that corn, wheat, oats, beans (post-1955), and cocoa (post-1955) are examples of markets that do *not* offer the speculator a profitable bias. Soybeans (pre-1955), cocoa (pre-1955), wheat (Minneapolis), and coffee are examples of markets that *do* offer a significant bias over a considerable period of time. Markets that offer these biases are referred to as "thin" markets or markets in which the amount of speculation

[28] Roger Gray, "The Characteristic Bias in Some Thin Future Markets," *Food Research Institute Studies,* 1, No. 3 (November 1960).

does not keep pace with hedging requirements. Some markets outgrow their biases, such as soybeans and cocoa, and others do not. The latter, such as the markets for bran and shorts, fall into disuse and die. The futures market in coffee underlines the kind of pattern that characterizes a thin market. For many years after World War II coffee prices were high by historical standards, and prices for the near future were highest, followed by lower quotations for deferred contracts. This kind of pattern produces rather routine profits for the longs and losses for the shorts. It is interesting to note that in Rockwell's work, cited earlier, the markets with the smallest open interest displayed the largest bias, thus reinforcing Gray's analysis.

Another predictable bias can enter into the futures markets under the influence of a government loan program. Futures prices in wheat, for example, have regularly risen toward the guaranteed loan price, and even though that movement is predictable it cannot take place until the movement into government hands has occurred. As Gray and Rutledge observe: "So long as the movement into loan is *anticipated*, it would be an irrational price which reflected it, for such a price, incorporating the anticipation, would prevent the event."[29] It is perhaps fitting that the chapter should close as it began, with a description by Working which illustrates the underlying premise of a futures market:

> The idea that a futures market *should* quote different prices for different future dates in accordance with developments anticipated between them cannot be valid when stocks must be carried from one date to another. It involves supposing that the market should act as a *forecasting* agency rather than as a *medium* for rational price formation when it cannot do both. The business of a futures market, so far as it may differ from that of any other, is to anticipate future developments as best it may and to give them due expression in present prices, spot and near futures as well as distant futures.[30]

NOTES FROM A TRADER

The random walk hypothesis is really a simple theory. It merely says price changes are unpredictable when only previous price changes, not *all* available information, are used. Those holding that the random walk model describes reality better than any other model do *not* say that the trader cannot make money—they merely promise him the fight of his life to beat the naive strategy of buy-and-hold after paying for the privilege of trying.

The tests that have been published so far lend a great deal of credence to the theory as an excellent "jumping off point" to explain the short-run behavior of commodity futures prices. This is not to say that all possible strategies have been tested and have failed to provide consistent profits.

[29] Gray and Rutledge, *op. cit.,* 22.
[30] Holbrook Working, "Theory of the Inverse Carrying Charge in Futures Markets," *Journal of Farm Economics,* 30, No. 1 (February 1948), 14.

The ingenuity of traders in this regard has barely been scratched. Most of them feel they have 25 trading rules that will bring them riches beyond the dreams of avarice. But the present state of the statistical art warns — "Don't look around. Something's gaining on you. It's the random-walk theory, the new 'King of the Hill.'"

A stand such as this at the *beginning* of a section devoted to *successful* trading may be considered by many as unadulterated heresy. Men make markets, and men do not release cherished falsehoods any more easily in the area of markets than they do in the area of science or philosophy. The fact that "patterns," usually described in an invincibly vague fashion, lead to profits about one-half the time they are traded does not dissuade the user. Instead, the capacity for definition is affirmed, and a new term "false breakout" is coined. Indeed, the collection of empirical contradictions to any theory, albeit impressive, never succeed solely by their presence in overturning the theory they contradict. Rather, it is a better theory that must be advanced, or error simply becomes institutionalized by the collection of reams of "exceptions to the rule."

If short-run price behavior is described crudely by the random walk hypothesis, then the theory itself becomes fair game. That it sets the tone for the game makes beating it a delicacy, never expected with certainty, yet always savored. The assumption of its tenets sharpens the trader for the battle. He *can* win, but only if he discovers the truth of the biblical injunction, "Broad is the path that leadeth to destruction." Financial salvation is a narrow gate through which pass only those traders who believe very little in luck as the cornerstone of their success. Sooner or later each trader affirms with Damon Runyon that "the race doesn't always go to the swift or the battle to the strong, but that's the way to bet." Indeed, one of the greatest contributions to traders' welfare made by advocates of the random walk hypothesis is the presentation of objective evidence that shows how difficult it is to make money consistently in the markets.

In moving from trading the markets in the short-run to taking positions to profit from expected trends, the trader should realize that the work in this area affirms that, generally speaking, the market does not habitually shower loose dollars on the casual trader who plays the game. As someone remarked, a trader will have to leave his mouth open a long time before a roast pigeon falls in. That there are trends is undeniable. That these trends are easily forecast from factors known at any point in time is an assertion grounded in naïveté. To rely on a bias upward or downward for merely playing the game is to make a risk premium or a characteristic bias the raison d'être of trading. Unfortunately, there is no universal truth about such an assertion. Each trade made with such an assumption must be examined on its own merits and validated meticulously.

The foregoing points up what is perhaps the most important lesson to be learned from the behavior of futures prices. There *has* been serious work done in the field. A bibliography *does* exist, and familiarity with it will pay the trader definable dividends. One of the most rewarding is the ability to think critically about the methodology employed by any one person or institution selling positions in this or that commodity. The methodology at times has a great deal to do with affirming or disclaiming a particular conclusion. The trader should bring a healthy skepticism to the marketplace in the realization that well-trained scholars with a deep and abiding interest in the field do not find it incredibly difficult to disagree with one another. Somehow the vision on the one hand of pockets bulging with easy money and on the other the tip sheet which glibly asserts that sugar is most assuredly on its way up to a 500-point upswing will seem more and more mutually exclusive. To such affirmations the trader aware of the behavior of commodity futures prices will remember to add that even a broken clock is right twice a day and that the capacity of the human mind to resist the intrusion of new knowledge seems close to infinite.

Playing the Game (Trading)

Armed with an understanding of the basics of the game, the trader is ready to become familiar with the decision-making processes. The six chapters in this section attempt to isolate, describe, and analyze several elements of successful trading. Successful traders have discovered the importance of sound money management which is often the least understood and most neglected aspect of trading. For that reason the section begins and ends with considerations that involve the management of funds committed to the commodity futures game.

Chapter 5, "Risk, Reward, and You," supplies the trader with a profile of his own attitudes toward risk and profit at different levels of capital and leads him step by step in constructing his own trading curve. Understanding his personal graph can help fit the trader's personality and value judgments about money with the type of trading he does.

Chapter 6, "The Fundamental Approach," analyzes those factors that constitute what traders call the fundamental approach. Conceptual supply-demand considerations and applied price-quantity relationships are studied. The often blurred distinction between explaining price changes and forecasting them is presented, as are examples of successful explanatory and forecasting models.

Chapter 7, "The Technical Approach," provides a panorama of technical tracking and forecasting methods in a format that underlines the advantages and disadvantages of each approach. Generous footnoting guides the trader to areas of further market research which may be of interest. From the simple arithmetic bar chart the trader is led through various systems of price tracking and forecasting, which include trend-following methods, character of the market approaches, and, finally, strategies that focus on market structure and more esoteric systems such as the Elliott wave theory.

Chapter 8, "Spreads and Options," may be considered by some to represent only a choice of commodity positions, but the subject is far broader than that and deserves separate and more elaborate treatment. Opportunities in these vehicles are flanked by different risks that must be carefully evaluated.

Chapter 9, "The Game Plan," attacks the problem of the trading plan directly by discussing its elements in some detail. The accent in this chapter is on gathering and organizing specific information in a format that is useful, regardless of whether the plan accents a fundamental or technical approach. The roles of stops and objectives as well as mistakes in plan formulation are analyzed.

Chapter 10, "Money Management," concludes the section by wrestling with the critical problem of money management which commodity traders ignore to their enormous peril. Even if the essential behavior of prices is understood and a rational strategy based on fundamental or technical considerations is formulated and the elements of a successful plan are followed, disaster will still strike if basic skills are not developed in the area of capital management.

CHAPTER FIVE

Risk, Reward, and You

> Sometimes the most incredible thing
> in the world is the answer to an
> unasked question . . .
>
> REINHOLD NIEBUHR, *The Nature and Destiny
> of Man*

INTRODUCTION

At this point the reader possesses more information about the basics of the commodity futures game than the majority of the participants now playing. A three-minute interview with a boardroom sample of traders (randomly selected, of course) will confirm that the information imparted in the first four chapters is not the subject of everyday brokerage office banter.

If such information is to be used intelligently, however, the reader must apply it to the decision-making process that leads to taking a position in the markets. Among the first decisions to be made are how to utilize one's capital and how much capital to risk. Treatment of these issues involves personal analysis and the concept of money management.

Money management is concerned essentially with four elements:

1. Objectives or preferences of the individual, including his present attitude toward money.

2. Initial and subsequent dollar capital to be utilized or risked in trading.

3. The expected value of the game.

4. The probability of ruin.

These elements are the fascinating subjects of this chapter and Chapter

10. Those playing the game are reminded that the issues of money management should share top billing with trade selection in the decision process. The first sections of this chapter discuss the concepts of probability as a numerical measure of optimism and of utility as a numerical measure of preference or satisfaction. The *relationship* of probability to utility is used to construct the trader's personal trading curve and to make some useful analysis and interpretations of it.

OPTIMISM AND PROBABILITY

The commodity trader operates in an atmosphere of uncertainty due to randomness. He cannot know with certainty what the outcome of any trade will be, but he can, and usually will, assign probabilities to the various outcomes, based on his relative optimism or pessimism. A probability is merely a number assigned to an outcome to reflect the strength of the assigner's opinion (on a scale from 0 to 1) of the possibility that the outcome will occur; for example, he may feel that the probability of reaching his objective in a trade is .4, whereas the probability of losing is .6. A probability in such a situation can be considered an index of optimism or pessimism. If the probability of reaching his objective were changed to .5 instead of .4, it could be said that he became more optimistic. It does not matter whether his probability came from objective evidence, newsletters, hot tips, brokers' research, or personal intuition. Whatever the source, the numerical probability does measure *his assessment* of the likelihood of various outcomes, and it does help to determine his action and therefore the market price. Analysts and traders often attempt to estimate this probability, or optimism index, for large groups of traders. They may, for example, analyze the actions of large traders or insiders or they may count the proportions of brokers and newsletters that recommend particular positions. These points are discussed in connection with contrary opinion in Chapter 7. If properly interpreted, such collective estimates can be useful. Even more useful and more easily measured, however, are the personal probabilities of the trader himself. Merely asking the right questions often provides useful insight.

PREFERENCES AND UTILITY

Suppose a commodity trader does assign probabilities to the various possible outcomes of a prospective trade. What principles does he use to make the decision whether or not to trade? How much is it worth to him to participate in a particular trade? Some will say that "worth" is the mathematical expectation of the gain or *expected value* or *average payoff* in money.[1] The rationale generally given for using the expected value of money involves

---

[1] The expected value, average payoff, or mathematical expectation is merely the sum of the possible *outcomes*, where each outcome is weighted by its probability; for example, in a trade in which there is a possible gain of $500 with probability .4 versus a possible loss of $200 with probability .6 the *expected value* or *average payoff* is $500 · (.4) − $200 · (.60) = $80.

an argument about what will happen in the long run, that is, when the trade is repeated many times. It is easy to see the merit of such a decision criterion for a gambling house but not for an individual trader. In the first place he trades relatively few times. Even more important, an approach that *would* give him maximum profit in the *long run* will do him no good if it leads to his economic ruin (treated in Chapter 10) in the short run. Some difficulties of choosing a simple criterion with which to make decisions are illustrated in the following examples:

The trader should put himself into each of the following four hypothetical situations and decide for each whether he would accept the bet.

1. He is offered a wager in which he will gain $200 if a (well-balanced) coin falls heads or lose $100 if it falls tails.

2. His entire fortune (which took 50 years to amass) has a cash value of $5 million. He is now offered the opportunity to gain $10 million if a coin falls heads or lose his entire irreplaceable fortune of $5 million if it falls tails.

3. He has been planning a vacation this month in Florida and intends to spend all the cash he has available during that month. Assume that he now has $5,000 available, which is more than ample for that purpose. He is offered a bet that will yield a profit of $5,000 (which he would use for *additional* spending on his vacation) if the coin falls heads or a loss of $5,000 (which would deprive him entirely of his long-planned vacation) if it falls tails.

4. He is desperate to see the next Olympic Games. He has $5,000 available in cash but the total expenses for him and his family will amount to $8,000. He is offered a chance for a profit of $5,000 if the coin falls heads or a loss of $5,000 if it falls tails.

The authors would accept the positions or bets in situations (1) and (4) but would say "no" in situations (2) and (3). What causes them to have different responses in situations (1) and (2)? The two situations are similar in that favorable 2-to-1 money payoffs were offered when it seemed appropriate to offer only even 1-to-1 money. What causes the difference in the authors' preferences? In situation 1, with equal probabilities, twice as much money can be gained as lost. In situation 2, with equal probabilities, it is also true that twice as much money can be gained as lost, but the gain of $10 million would not increase the satisfaction gained compared with the considerable dissatisfaction that would result from the loss of the entire $5 million fortune. Similarly, in situations (3) and (4), even though the money payoffs and probabilities are the same, the responses are different. These reflect the differences in the satisfaction to be gained from the money in the two different circumstances.

This indicates that if such a trade were made many times it sometimes would result in a gain of $500 and sometimes in a loss of $200, but in the *long run* the average gain would be $80 *per trade.*

Apparently, in uncertain situations people do *not* act consistently with respect to their average monetary gain. They do, however, act consistently to maximize their own satisfaction. Much theoretical and experimental work has been done in this area, and useful models have been developed to measure the preferences or satisfaction that individuals exhibit for various bets and outcomes. Just as probability is merely a number (on a scale from 0 to 1) assigned to reflect the degree of optimism, so the *utility* of a bet or of an event is merely a number assigned (on *any* scale) to reflect the degree of preference or satisfaction.

The following material includes a brief discussion of these utilities along with some examples and a step-by-step procedure by which the reader can find his own utilities and construct his own utility curve for commodity trading (subsequently called his trading curve). The construction and interpretation of his personal trading curve will serve as a useful tool in his money management and trading activities.

This chapter should be read with pencil in hand. The reader should make notes or calculations to make sure that the examples are clear to him.

UTILITY PROPERTIES

It can be shown that if a person is "rational" in the sense that he can express his preference between any two events and if he shows some measure of consistency in his preferences, then a numerical value or utility can be assigned to each event that will measure his satisfaction for that event; that is, of any two events, the one preferred will have a larger number (utility) assigned to it. In other words, if a person is guided entirely by his utility values, he will be acting in accord with his own true preferences. Therefore once a person's utility values are found they can be used to help him make rational decisions. In this chapter personal utilities are calculated and graphed in the personal trading curve. It is important to note here that each utility value reflects the preference for the particular event in the particular situation [e.g., see situations (3) and (4)] at the particular time. Attitudes and preferences do change. It should also be pointed out that different people have different tastes and therefore different utility values.

It can also be shown[2] that the utility of any bet or venture to an individual will be equal to the average or expected value of his utilities for the different possible outcomes of that bet. The average or expected value is computed by adding the utilities of the various outcomes, with each utility weighted (multiplied) by the probability of the particular outcome. (As indicated earlier, these probabilities may be personal and reflect one's degree of optimism.) It is interesting to note that for a "rational" individual the utility of a bet is shown to be equal to the expected value of the utilities of the outcomes, without any assumptions or discussion of long run effects

---

[2] John Von Neumann and Oskar Morgenstern, *The Theory of Games and Economic Behavior*, Princeton University Press, Princeton, N.J., 2nd ed., 1947.

or repeated trials. In other words, the relationship holds even if the prospect is to be faced *only once*. Utility, then, can always be computed by using ordinary probabilities and expected values.

COMPUTING PERSONAL UTILITIES

The computation of utilities, or measures of preference, is illustrated in the four examples that follow. Understanding these examples will make it possible for the reader to construct his own trading curve.

Example 5-1   Suppose Mr. Glassford, a famous soybean speculator, has taken a position in the commodity market and has set his objective so that, if it is reached, he will gain $1,500. He also has a stop set so that if the worst happens he will lose $900. Suppose that for Mr. Glassford the utility of $1,500 is 10 (the 10 is arbitrarily chosen) and the utility of $-$900$ is (arbitrarily) -6, that is, $u(\$1,500) = 10$ and $u(-\$900) = -6$. Assume further that Mr. Glassford believes his probability of success is $\frac{1}{2}$. The utility of the trade, therefore, would merely be the average (expected value) of the utilities of the possible outcomes, that is, the sum of the utilities of the outcomes with each utility multiplied by the probability of the particular outcome.

$$u(\text{trade}) = \tfrac{1}{2} \cdot (10) + \tfrac{1}{2} \cdot (-6) = 2,$$

which would be halfway between -6 and 10, the utilities of the outcomes.

If Mr. Glassford's judgment of the probability of success were $\frac{2}{3}$, his utility would become

$$u(\text{trade}) = \tfrac{2}{3} \cdot (10) + \tfrac{1}{3} \cdot (-6) = \tfrac{14}{3} = 4.7,$$

which would be exactly $\frac{2}{3}$ of the distance from -6 to 10.

Similarly, with a probability of success judged to be $\frac{9}{10}$, the utility of the trade would become

$$u(\text{trade}) = \tfrac{9}{10} \cdot (10) + \tfrac{1}{10} \cdot (16) = 8.4,$$

which is $\frac{9}{10}$ of the distance from -6 to 10. Obviously, as the probability of success increases from 0 to 1, the utility increases from -6 (the utility of the worst outcome) to 10 (the utility of the best outcome).

In order to illustrate the difference between the expected *utility* (average of the utilities of the gains and losses) and the *expected gain* (average of the gains and losses themselves), the following example may be used.

Example 5-2   Consider a trade that, if successful, would yield a gain of $600 and, if unsuccessful, a loss of $500, where the probability of gain is .8. If the utility of $600 gain is arbitrarily called 20, and the utility of $500 loss, 10, the *expected utility* (or utility of the trade) is given by

$$u(\text{trade}) = .8 \cdot (20) + .2 \cdot (10) = 18,$$

whereas the expected gain (in money) is given by

$$.8 \cdot (\$600) + .2 \cdot (-\$500) = \$380.$$

Note that the amounts differ and, as illustrated in the four cases in the preference and utility section of this chapter, that expected gains do not necessarily reflect personal preferences as expected utilities do.

Example 5-3   In Example 5-2 the utilities of the best and worst outcomes were arbitrarily chosen to be 20 and 10, respectively. If, instead, other values had been chosen, the computed expected utilities would be just as useful and would reflect the same relative preferences for different bets;[3] for example, if the utilities of the best and worst outcomes had been chosen to be 1 and 0, respectively, the expected utility of the preceding example would have been

$$u(\text{trade}) = .8 \cdot (1) + .2 \cdot (0) = .8.$$

Note that when the highest and lowest utilities chosen are 1 and 0, respectively, the expected utility will always be equal to the probability of the best outcome. Such a choice of values is often made because it simplifies the computation of utility values.

Example 5-4   Utilities are similarly computed in situations in which there are *more* than two outcomes; for example, assume that a certain commodity trade could result in payoffs of $1,000, $800, $500, or $200. Assume that the estimates of probabilities for the respective outcomes are .2, .1, .4, and .3. To calculate the utility of the trade, assuming that the utilities of the outcomes are as follows,

$$u(1000) = 22, \qquad u(800) = 15, \qquad u(500) = 7, \qquad u(200) = 3,$$

one merely calculates the average of the utilities; that is,

$$u(\text{trade}) = .2 \cdot (22) + .1 \cdot (15) + .4 \cdot (7) + .3 \cdot (3) = 9.6.$$

In the following section the computational methods used in examples 5-1 and 5-3 are applied to find the reader's personal trading curve.

THE PERSONAL TRADING CURVE

For the next 60 minutes the prospective trader should pick a spot in which he is unlikely to be interrupted. During that time he is going to construct his own trading curve from questions he will answer during a self-administered trading profile interview (TPI). There are some ground rules that should be clear at the outset of the self-interview:

1. The TPI is *not* a test. One answer is no more correct than another. Rather the TPI *measures* the reader's attitudes about gains and losses and about money at this point in time. The same TPI taken at a later date, especially after a large gain or loss or after a significant change in the trader's capital or income tax bracket, could well reveal a significant change in attitude. Trading curves derived from the TPI can easily measure such changes.

2. The dollar amounts risked, gained, or lost during the interview should be considered by the reader as *real* dollars with *real* purchasing power, which if lost would represent some varying degree of pain. Lost dollars can be replaced by the reader only from his savings or checking accounts, new earnings, or other sources. The pain of replacing $100 is obviously less than that of replacing $1,000, and the reader's feelings should reflect that difference to *him*, in consideration of his total current situation.

---

[3] Two utility values (any two, e.g., for the best and worst outcomes) can be chosen arbitrarily. After they are chosen, however, all the other utility values are determined by the method of computation illustrated.

3. The rewards to the reader should also be considered to be immediate and in cash, so that there will be virtually no lag between the time dollars are risked successfully and the ensuing payoff.

4. Many readers will be content to answer the questions in the TPI subjectively. Others will prefer to have paper and pencil handy. Either approach is satisfactory if the decisions reflect the reader's personal preferences and are not merely the result of some mechanistic computation. The reader should consider each trade and each level of risk capital separately and not relate them to preceding or subsequent questions. Each question should be considered independently and answered carefully.

The personal trading curve is constructed by first choosing two possible outcomes of a trade. These outcomes are called the "best" and "worst" outcomes, and utility values of 1 and 0, respectively, are assigned to them. Then, using trades involving only those best and worst outcomes, other utilities are computed in Table 5-1 and the results plotted as a preliminary personal trading curve in Figure 5-1. For purposes of verification and improved accuracy, and to measure the consistency of the trader's decisions, additional utility values are computed in Tables 5-2 and 5-3. These values use trades with new best and worst outcomes. The results, along with those in Table 5-1, are plotted in Figure 5-2. Then, in the next section of this

TABLE 5-1 COMPUTATION OF FIRST SET OF UTILITIES FOR TRADING CURVE

Utilities of		Probabilities of		Computed utility of trade (col. 5)	Reader's cash equivalent of trade (in dollars) (col. 6)	
best outcome (col. 1)	worst outcome (col. 2)	best outcome (col. 3)	worst outcome (col. 4)			
1	0	1.0	0	1.00	2,000	best outcome
1	0	.95	.05	.95	1,500	
1	0	.9	.1	.90	1,250	
1	0	.8	.2	.80	1,100	
1	0	.7	.3	.70	1,000	
1	0	.6	.4	.60	800	personal choices from TPI
1	0	.5	.5	.50	450	
1	0	.4	.6	.40	0	
1	0	.3	.7	.30	−400	
1	0	.2	.8	.20	−600	
1	0	.1	.9	.10	−800	
1	0	0	1.0	0	−1,000	worst outcome

chapter, the trading curve is extended to include gains and losses that are larger than the initial best and worst outcomes.

Construction of a personal trading curve now proceeds in the form of a trading profile interview:

INTERVIEWER: What are the *largest* amounts you have had regular experience winning and losing on trades or investments?

TRADER: I've often had experience winning as much as $2,000 on a single
venture and I've risked as much as $1,000 on single trades.

The interviewer now fills out the first five of the six columns in Table
5-1. He enters $2,000 and —$1,000 as the best and worst outcomes on the
top and bottom lines of Table 5-1 in column 6. He assigns a utility of 1 to
the best outcome and enters it on every line of column 1. He also assigns 0
to the worst outcome and enters it on every line of column 2. He then fills
out column 3 with a fairly uniformly spaced set of probabilities. These
represent the respective probabilities of winning $2,000 (the best outcome)
for each of the different trades to be considered. Each line of Table 5-1
represents a separate and distinct trade. Column 4 is merely the complement of column 3. It shows the probability of *losing* $1,000 (the worst out-
come) for each of the trades. In column 5 the interviewer computes the
utility of each trade by taking the average of the utilities (1 and 0 in each
case); each utility is weighted (multiplied) by its own probability as in Example 5-3. To illustrate the computation of the utility of .70 on the fifth
line of Table 5-1, column 5, the following computation is made

$$1 \cdot (.7) + 0 \cdot (.3) = .70,$$

which yields the computed utility of the trade.

All that remains to be filled out is column 6, but doing that properly is
the essence of the trading profile interview. The trader must consider each
line (trade) separately and carefully, always remaining cognizant of the
four ground rules stated at the beginning of this section.

INTERVIEWER: (describing the trade indicated by line 2 of Table 5-1):
If you have a trading opportunity wherein you would either gain $2,000
(best outcome) or lose $1,000 (worst outcome) with probabilities .95
and .05, respectively, would you take that trade?

TRADER: Certainly! Who wouldn't?

INTERVIEWER: Obviously the trade has some worth to you. Would you pay
me $800 cash for the opportunity to make that trade?

TRADER: What's going on here? You want me to hand you $800 in cash,
right now, just for the opportunity to make that trade?

INTERVIEWER: If the trade ($2,000 possible gain with probability .95 or
$1,000 possible loss with probability .05) is not worth $800 to you, forget
it. If you think it is, then pay me the $800 now and enter the trade.
Remember, whether you win or lose the trade you don't get the $800
back. It's mine, once you give it to me.

TRADER: The trade is good. I'm *almost* (.95) certain to win the $2,000.
I'll pay the $800 and take the trade.

INTERVIEWER: In other words you feel that the cash value of the trade is
more than $800?

TRADER: Right.

INTERVIEWER: I'm glad that's settled. Now, instead of $800 would you pay me $1,200 to enter the same trade?

TRADER: (after some painful introspection and colorful rhetoric): Yes.

INTERVIEWER: Then you feel that the trade is worth *more* than $1,200 to you. Now, instead of $1,200, would you pay $1,400?

TRADER: That's a tough question; $1,400 is a lot of cash to pay for that opportunity. On the other hand, that trade would yield $2,000 with a very high probability (.95) and *almost* no chance (.05) of the $1,000 loss. O.K. I'll pay $1,400, but not much more.

INTERVIEWER: You have just told me that the trade is worth *more* than $1,400 to you. Would you pay $1,600?

TRADER: Definitely not!

INTERVIEWER: Obviously the trade is worth *less* than $1,600 to you, and in your preceding statement we decided it was worth *more* than $1,400. How about $1,500?

TRADER: (after much introspection): That's difficult to decide. Maybe I would pay $1,500 and maybe not. I'm sort of indifferent at that price.

INTERVIEWER: That's fine. Then the value of that trade to you is approximately the same as the value of $1,500 to you. Therefore your utility for the $1,500 cash is the same as your utility for that trade, already computed on line 2 column 5 as .95.

At this point the interviewer enters $1,500 in column 6 of line 2 in Table 5-1. Note that the $1,500 in column 6 is entered next to its utility .95 in column 5.

By a similar careful and thoughtful process each line of column 6 is filled in. Each line represents a separate and distinct trade, with its own unique probability (column 3) of success. For each distinct trade in the table the best ($2,000) and worst (−$1,000) outcomes remain the same.

To illustrate the computation of utility for a negative amount of money, that portion of the trading profile interview (TPI) applicable to line 9 is also shown.

INTERVIEWER: (now describing the trade indicated by line 9 of Table 5-1): Assume that you have a trading opportunity in which you would gain $2,000 (best outcome) or lose $1,000 (worst outcome) with probabilities .3 and .7, respectively. Would you take that trade?

TRADER: You mean the probability of winning $2,000 is only .3? Why I have more than twice the chance (.7) of losing $1,000. That's not an opportunity. What do you take me for?

INTERVIEWER: Some people might welcome that opportunity. Obviously you have different preferences. For you that trade has a negative cash value. Would you take the trade if I handed you $100 right now? You keep the $100 win or lose, but if you accept the $100 then you must go through with the trade.

TRADER: Keep your $100.

INTERVIEWER: How about $300?

TRADER: That's better but still not enough to induce me to take that risky trade.

INTERVIEWER: Would you take the trade if I give you $400 to keep, whether you win or lose the trade?

TRADER: That's tempting. Maybe I would, but not a penny less than $400.

INTERVIEWER: That's fine. Then you would require a cash payment of at least $400 as inducement to take the trade. That trade has a negative value for you, —$400 cash. Therefore your utility for —$400 cash is the same as your utility for that trade, previously computed on line 9, column 5, as .30.

At this point the interviewer enters the —$400 on line 9 of column 6 in Table 5-1. Note that the —$400 in column 6 is entered next to its utility .30 in column 5.

With the completion of Table 5-1, a preliminary trading curve is constructed by plotting the numbers in column 6 on the horizontal axis versus the numbers in column 5 on the vertical axis. Such a plot from Table 5-1 is shown in Figure 5-1. If a smooth curve were drawn through the points in that figure, it would show some interesting preliminary results. For values of $1,000 to $2,000 the curve is concave downward. The reader can examine Figure 5-1 in that region to see that each added $100 increment of cash adds successively less utility value to the total.

For values of $0 to $1000, on the other hand, the trading curve is concave upward, and in that region, each additional $100 increment adds successively more utility value to the total. The trader has quite different attitudes toward gains and losses in these two regions.

For values of —$400 to —$1,000 the trading curve seems to be linear. In that region successively larger losses decrease the utility proportionately; for example, the decrease in utility going from —$400 to —$600 is the same as the decrease in utility going from —$600 to —$800 or from —$800 to —$1,000. The trader's reactions to possible gains and losses in this region, where the trading curve is linear, will be quite different from his reactions in regions where the trading curve is concave upward or downward. Analysis of these differences are made in the following sections of this chapter.

For purposes of verification and improved accuracy and to measure the consistency of the trader's decisions additional utility values for some of the same dollar amounts are again computed and the results shown in Tables 5-2 and 5-3. The computations are made from trades using new "best" and "worst" outcomes. The new results, along with the prior information from Table 5-1, are plotted in Figure 5-2.

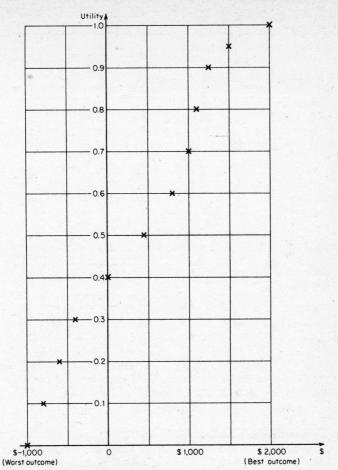

FIG. 5-1 Preliminary trading curve.

To proceed with Table 5-2 the interviewer must first choose new "best" and "worst" outcomes for which the utility is known. Any two values from Column 6 of Table 5-1 will do. Assume he chooses $800 as the new "best" outcome, and —$800 as the "worst." The utility of $800 is shown as .60 in column 5 of Table 5-1. The utility of —$800 is shown as .10. These amounts are then entered in Table 5-2. The utility .60 of the new best outcome is entered in column 1 and the utility .10 of the new worst outcome, in column 2. The outcomes themselves, $800 and —$800, are entered on the first and last lines, respectively, of column 6 in Table 5-2. Then, as before,

TABLE 5-2 COMPUTATION OF SECOND SET OF UTILITIES
FOR TRADING CURVE

Utilities° of		Probabilities† of		Computed utility of trade (col. 5)	Reader's cash equivalent of trade (in dollars) (col. 6)	
best outcome (col. 1)	worst outcome (col. 2)	best outcome (col. 3)	worst outcome (col. 4)			
.60	.10	1.0	0	.60	800	} best outcome
.60	.10	.95	.05	.575	650	
.60	.10	.9	.1	.55	550	
.60	.10	.8	.2	.50	400	
.60	.10	.7	.3	.45	250	
.60	.10	.6	.4	.40	150	personal choices
.60	.10	.5	.5	.35	−100	from TPI
.60	.10	.4	.6	.30	−400	
.60	.10	.3	.7	.25	−450	
.60	.10	.2	.8	.20	−500	
.60	.10	.1	.9	.15	−600	
.60	.10	0	1.0	.10	−800	} worst outcome

°From Table 5-1.
† Same as in Table 5-1.

columns 3 and 4 are filled in with a set (it may be the same as before) of fairly uniformly spaced probabilities. Again, as before, in column 5 the interviewer computes the utility of each trade by taking the average of the utilities (this time .60 and .10 in each case), where each utility is weighted by its respective probability. To illustrate the computation of the utility .55 in the third line of Table 5-2, column 5, the following calculation is made:

$$.60 \cdot (.9) + .10 \cdot (.1) = .55,$$

which yields the computed utility of the trade.

All that remains to be completed is column 6, and this is done by using the trader's profile interview, as before, in which the trader must again separately and carefully consider each line (trade) while remaining cognizant of the four ground rules stated at the beginning of this section. When Table 5-2 is completed in this manner, the results are plotted (column 6 on the horizontal axis versus column 5 on the vertical axis) as "2's" in the trading curve (Figure 5-2). (The results of Table 5-1, which were plotted in Figure 5-1, are plotted as "1's" in Figure 5-2.)

Further verification is achieved by completing Table 5-3 in a similar manner. New best and worst outcomes of $1,500 and −$400 are chosen, again from Table 5-1, with their respective utilities, .95 and .30. [Note that this range of values ($1,500 to −$400) is in the upper part of the original range ($2,000 to −$1,000), whereas the previous range of outcomes

TABLE 5-3 COMPUTATION OF THIRD SET OF UTILITIES
FOR TRADING CURVE

Utilities° of		Probabilities† of		Computed utility of trade (col. 5)	Reader's cash equivalent of trade (in dollars) (col. 6)	
best outcome (col. 1)	worst outcome (col. 2)	best outcome (col. 3)	worst outcome (col. 4)			
						best
.95	.30	1.0	0	.95	1,500 }	outcome
.95	.30	.95	.05	.9175	1,200	
.95	.30	.9	.1	.885	1,150	
.95	.30	.8	.2	.82	1,100	
.95	.30	.7	.3	.755	800	
.95	.30	.6	.4	.69	600	personal choices
.95	.30	.5	.5	.625	500	from TPI
.95	.30	.4	.6	.56	400	
.95	.30	.3	.7	.495	100	
.95	.30	.2	.8	.43	−100	
.95	.30	.1	.9	.365	−200	
.95	.30	0	1.0	.30	−400 }	worst outcome

°From Table 5-1.
† Same as in Table 5-1.

($800 to −$800) was in the lower portion of the original range.] Table 5-3 is then completed, as were the preceding tables, and the results are entered as "3's" in the trading curve (Figure 5-2).

Figure 5-2 represents the completed personal trading curve of the trader for gains and losses between $2,000 and −$1,000. The general shape can be more readily seen by drawing a freehand *smooth* curve, passing "near" most of the points. The next sections include comments on this curve and some analysis and interpretation of personal trading curves in general.

Tables 5-4, 5-5, and 5-6 are provided so that the reader can complete them during his self-administered trading profile interview (TPI). He should be sure to follow the ground rules discussed at the beginning of this section. He should feel free, however, to change the best and worst outcomes to those that represent the relatively large gains and losses that *he* experiences regularly. Whatever his best and worst outcomes are should be entered in Table 5-4 and Figure 5-3. After the tables are completed the results (from all three tables) should be plotted in Figure 5-3 which is provided for that purpose. A smooth curve can then be drawn to pass near most of the points.

In the next section the boundaries of the trading curve are extended beyond the original best and worst outcomes so that the reader can also get a graphic interpretation of his attitudes toward the gains and losses that are larger than those with which he has had regular experience.

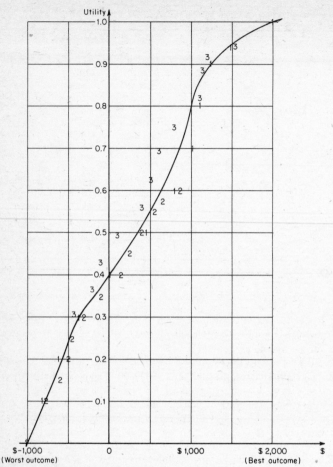

FIG. 5-2   Trading curve.

EXTENDING THE TRADING CURVE FOR
LARGER GAINS AND LOSSES

In this section the trading curve is completed. It not only includes that
portion of the curve illustrated in Figure 5-2 but is extended to include
gains larger than $2,000 and losses larger than $1,000. The interpretation
of the shape and scatter of points for these larger values will yield significant information concerning the sizes and kinds of trades that should be
accepted or avoided. Such information can be invaluable to the trader as
well as to his broker or adviser.

As a first step in extending the curve, Figure 5-4 is prepared with gains

TABLE 5-4 COMPUTATION OF FIRST SET OF UTILITIES
FOR TRADING CURVE TO BE COMPLETED BY READER

Utilities of		Probabilities of		Computed utility of trade (col. 5)	Reader's cash equivalent of trade (in dollars) (col. 6)	
best outcome (col. 1)	worst outcome (col. 2)	best outcome (col. 3)	worst outcome (col. 4)			
1	0	1.0	0	1.00	2,000 }	best outcome
1	0	.95	.05	.95		
1	0	.9	.1	.90		
1	0	.8	.2	.80		
1	0	.7	.3	.70		
1	0	.6	.4	.60		personal choices
1	0	.5	.5	.50		from TPI
1	0	.4	.6	.40		
1	0	.3	.7	.30		
1	0	.2	.8	.20		
1	0	.1	.9	.10		
1	0	0	1.0	0	−1,000 }	worst outcome

and losses ranging from −$3,000 to $5,000 and with the utility scale ranging from −3 to 2. The next step is to plot all of the points from Figure 5-2
(or from Tables 5-1, 5-2, and 5-3 if it is easier) on this new scale of Figure
5-4. Then computations are made in Tables 5-7 and 5-8 to determine utilities for larger gains and losses, also to be plotted in Figure 5-4.

Utilities for larger gains. In Table 5-7 utilities are computed for

TABLE 5-5 COMPUTATION OF SECOND SET OF UTILITIES FOR
TRADING CURVE TO BE COMPLETED BY READER

Utilities of		Probabilities of		Computed utility of trade (col. 5)	Reader's cash equivalent of trade (in dollars) (col. 6)	
best outcome (col. 1)	worst outcome (col. 2)	best outcome (col. 3)	worst outcome (col. 4)			
		1.0	0			best outcome
		.95	.05			
		.9	.1			
		.8	.2			
		.7	.3			
		.6	.4			personal choices
		.5	.5			from TPI
		.4	.6			
		.3	.7			
		.2	.8			
		.1	.9			
		0	1.0			worst outcome

TABLE 5-6 COMPUTATION OF THIRD SET OF UTILITIES FOR TRADING CURVE TO BE COMPLETED BY READER

Utilities of		Probabilities of		Computed utility of trade (col. 5)	Reader's cash equivalent of trade (in dollars) (col. 6)	
best outcome (col. 1)	worst outcome (col. 2)	best outcome (col. 3)	worst outcome (col. 4)			
		1.0	0		}	best outcome
		.95	.05			
		.9	.1			
		.8	.2			
		.7	.3			
		.6	.4		}	personal choices from TPI
		.5	.5			
		.4	.6			
		.3	.7			
		.2	.8			
		.1	.9			
		0	1.0		}	worst· outcome

TABLE 5-7 COMPUTATION OF UTILITIES FOR LARGER GAINS

	Trade				Reader's cash equivalent of trade	
Gain (in dollars) G	Computed[*] utility $u(G)$	Loss (in dollars) L	Utility from Fig. 5-2 $u(L)$	Probability of winning p	Cash (in dollars) C	Utility from Fig. 5-2 $u(C)$
	$\dfrac{u(C) - .4(1 - p)[*]}{p}$					
2,500	.97	0	.40	.70	1,000	.80
3,500	1.08	0	.40	.50	900	.74
5,000	1.15	0	.40	.40	800†	.70
	$\dfrac{u(C) - .3(1 - p)[*]}{p}$					
2,500	1.10	−400	.30	.50	800	.70
3,600	1.30	−400	.30	.50	1,000	.80
5,000	1.75	−400	.30	.40	1,200†	.88
	$\dfrac{u(C)[*]}{p}$					
2,500	1.00	−1,000	0	.40	0	.40
3,500	1.40	−1,000	0	.40	500	.56
5,000	1.33	−1,000	0	.30	0	.40

[*] Utility of gain = $u(G) = \dfrac{u(C) - u(L) \cdot (1 - p)}{p}$, where G, L, p, and C are as indicated in the table headings.

† Example of obviously inconsistent decisions (most inconsistencies are much less obvious).

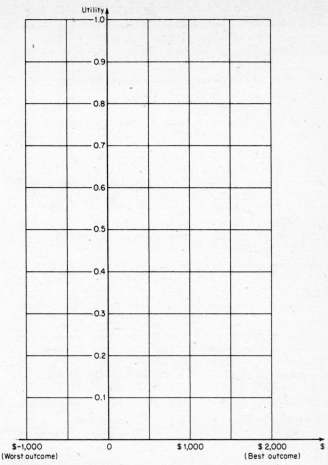

FIG. 5-3 Reader's trading curve.

large *gains* of $2,500, $3,500, and $5,000. Each of these utilities is computed three times in order to give some information about the trader's consistency in making decisions. As in the preceding trader's profile interview (TPI), each of the nine trades in Table 5-7 is to be separately considered by the trader. He must consider the possible GAIN *G*, the possible LOSS *L*, and the PROBABILITY *p* of a winning trade. After sufficient introspection of this information, the trader, as before, decides on an amount of CASH *C* which for him, at this moment, is the equivalent of the trade; for example, in considering the second trade (GAIN $3,500, LOSS $0, PROBABILITY .50) in Table 5-7 the TPI could proceed as follows:

INTERVIEWER: Would you accept a trade in which you would gain $3,500 with probability .50 or lose $0 with probability .50?

TRADER: Certainly I would. There's no risk in that one.

INTERVIEWER: Would you pay me $500 for that trading opportunity?

TRADER: Yes.

INTERVIEWER: Would you pay me $1,000 for that opportunity?

TRADER: Probably not, but maybe a little less.

INTERVIEWER: How about $900?

TRADER: I think I would be indifferent about paying $900 for that trading opportunity. I would not pay $1,000 and I would be willing to pay $800, but I don't know about $900.

The amount of $900 is then recorded in the CASH C column of Table 5-7 for that trade. The utility .74 of $900 is then taken (approximated) from Figure 5-2 and written in the Column $u(C)$ next to the $900. Similarly, the utility .40 of the $0 LOSS is taken from Figure 5-2. The desired utility 1.08 of the $3,500 GAIN is then computed by using the formula in Table 5-7 and its footnote.

The interview and computation should proceed in this manner through each of the other trades in Table 5-7; for example, in the sixth trade the interviewer would begin as always by first asking the trader if he would accept the trade ($5,000 possible GAIN with PROBABILITY .40 versus $400 possible LOSS with probability .60). If the trader accepts, the interviewer proceeds as before to find the largest amount he would be willing to *pay* for that trading opportunity. That amount is then entered in the CASH column and the utilities of the CASH C column and the LOSS L column are estimated from Figure 5-2. The desired utility 1.75 is computed from the formula in Table 5-7.

After all nine utility values $u(G)$ of the large gains are computed in Table 5-7, they are plotted in Figure 5-4 as X's. The trading curve can now be extended to the right to $5,000, and a *smooth* curve can be drawn through the points in Figure 5-4.

Note how these points are spread out at $3,500 and even more at $5,000, especially compared with the small spread at any particular dollar value between the original boundaries ($2,000 and $-$1,000). This spread indicates inconsistencies in the trader's decisions. Most of them are not readily apparent, but two in Table 5-7 are. Pointing these out will give the reasons for large differences in some of the computed utility values. The first inconsistency occurs between the third and sixth trades in Table 5-7. Both offer the same gain of $5,000 with the same probability .4 of winning. The third trade is better than the sixth, however, because the loss is $0 rather than $400, yet the trader has indicated that he is willing to pay more ($1,200) for the sixth trade than ($800) for the third. A similar inconsistency exists between the decisions on the second and fifth trades. Because of his tendency toward inconsistent decisions in trades involving potential gains greater than $2,500, this trader should plan such trades with great care.

Utilities for larger losses. In Table 5-8 utilities are computed for large *losses* of $1,500, $2,000, and $3,000. Each of these losses is computed four times and then plotted in Figure 5-4. As before, each of the 16 trades is treated separately by considering its GAIN G, its LOSS L, and its PROBABILITY p of success. Using that information, the trader (perhaps with the help of an interviewer) decides on an amount of CASH C which, for him, is equivalent to the trade.

Consideration of the ninth trade (GAIN, $1,000, LOSS, $3,000, PROBABILITY, .8) in Table 5-8 begins with the interviewer asking the trader if he will accept the trade. If the trader answers "no," then the interviewer may ask if he will accept the trade if given an inducement of say $500. An affirmative answer would bring forth a lesser offer. The interviewer

TABLE 5-8   COMPUTATION OF UTILITIES FOR LARGER LOSSES

	Trade				Reader's cash equivalent of trade	
Gain (in dollars) G	Utility from Figs. 5-2 and 5-4 $u(G)$	Loss (in dollars) L	Computed° utility $u(L)$	Probability of winning p	Cash (in dollars) C	Utility from Fig. 5-2 $u(C)$
			$-\dfrac{1.25p - u(C)°}{1-p}$			
3,500	1.25	−1,500	− .13	.50	500	.56
3,500	1.25	−2,000	− .37	.50	100	.44
3,500	1.25	−3,000	−1.87	.60	−1,000	0
			$-\dfrac{p - u(C)°}{1-p}$			
2,000	1	−1,500	− .47	.70	500	.56
2,000	1	−2,000	−1.00	.70	0	.40
2,000	1	−3,000	−1.65	.80	200	.47
			$-\dfrac{.75p - u(C)°}{1-p}$			
1,000	.80	−1,500	− .53	.70	0	.40
1,000	.80	−2,000	−1.20	.80	0	.40
1,000	.80	−3,000	−1.60	.80	−200	.32
			$-\dfrac{.56p - u(C)°}{1-p}$			
500	.56	−1,500	− .37	.70	−400	.28
500	.56	−2,000	−1.09	.80	−500	.23
500	.56	−3,000	−2.74	.90	−500	.23

° Utility of loss $= u(L) = -\dfrac{u(G) \cdot p - u(C)}{1-p}$, where G, L, p, and C are as indicated in the table headings.

will proceed in this manner until he finds the smallest amount the trader will accept as an inducement for him to proceed with the trade. In Table 5-8 for the *ninth* trade that amount is —$200. It is then recorded in the CASH C column of Table 5-8 for that trade. The utility .32 of —$200 is taken from Figure 5-2 and written in the column $u(C)$ next to the —$200. Similarly, the utility .75 of the $1,000 gain is taken from Figure 5-2. (For the first three trades in Table 5-8 the utility of the $3,500 gain is approximated from Figure 5-4.) The desired utility —1.40 of the $3,000 LOSS is then computed by using the formula in Table 5-8 and its footnote.

After all 12 utility values $u(L)$ of the large losses are computed in Table 5-8, they are plotted in Figure 5-4 as X's. This extends the trading curve

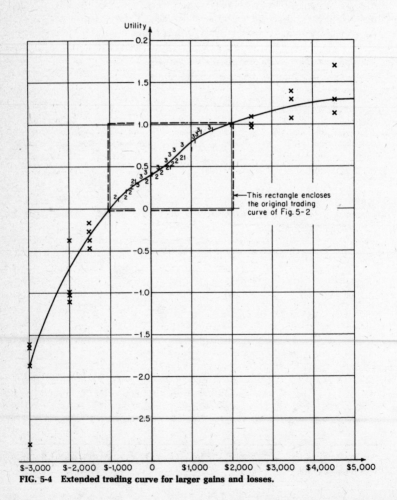

FIG. 5-4 Extended trading curve for larger gains and losses.

to the left to —$3,000, and the smooth curve of Figure 5-4 can also be extended to the left and downward.

Note that the points in Figure 5-4 are slightly spread out at —$1,500, much more spread out at —$2,000, and considerably more at —$3,000. This shows the growing inconsistencies in the trader's decisions as his losses grow large. He would do well to plan carefully when considering trades in which he will risk more than $1,500.

Comments on the extended trading curve. An analysis and interpretation of trading curves follows in the next section of this chapter and in the notes from a trader. It would be useful, however, to comment on the completed trading curve shown in Figure 5-4.

From the aforementioned discussion of inconsistencies and the spread of points on the curve, it can be seen from Figure 5-4 that the trader makes uniformly consistent decisions on trades involving gains as high as $2,500 and losses as large as $1,500. Beyond those values extra care in planning is necessary. As experience is acquired, these boundaries could be expanded considerably. Periodic construction of trading curves will note such expansion.

The general shape of the curve is also of great interest. From small losses of $200 to gains as high as $1,000 the curve is slightly concave upward. This indicates that the trader's utility for gains of those amounts increases at an increasing rate. He therefore has a slight tendency to accept even an unfavorable (negative expected value) trade in those amounts. Those with such tendencies are sometimes called' "risk lovers." Many traders act as risk lovers for small gains and losses.

TABLE 5-9 COMPUTATION OF UTILITIES FOR LARGER GAINS
TO BE COMPLETED BY READER

Trade					Reader's cash equivalent of trade	
Gain (in dollars) G	Computed° utility $u(G)$	Loss (in dollars) L	Utility from Fig. 5-3 $u(L)$	Probability of winning p	Cash (in dollars) C	Utility from Fig. 5-3 $u(C)$
2,500		0		.70		
3,500		0		.50		
5,000		0		.40		
2,500		—400		.50		
3,500		—400		.50		
5,000		—400		.40		
2,500		—1,000		.40		
3,500		—1,000		.40		
5,000		—1,000		.30		

° Utility of gain $= u(G) = \dfrac{u(C) - u(L) \cdot (1 - p)}{p}$, where G, L, p, and C are as indicated in the table headings.

As our trader's *gains* increase beyond $1,000, the shape of his trading curve becomes concave downward, which indicates a decreasing utility for incremental gains. His decisions in regard to larger trades will be more conservative, and he will have a tendency to take only favorable (positive expected value) trades. Such are the actions of a "risk averter." Many traders act that way for large gains and losses.

For *losses* greater than $200 our trader's curve is also concave downward, indicating that, as losses grow, his pain (dissatisfaction) increases at an increasing rate. He abhors large losses and has a tendency to avoid risking much capital on any one trade. If he is convinced that a trade is going badly, he will quickly close the position and take his loss to avoid a larger loss.

Tables 5-9, 5-10, and Figure 5-5 are provided so that the reader can complete his personal trading curve and, by using the information in this and the next section, analyze the results.

ANALYSIS AND INTERPRETATION OF THE TRADING CURVE

Scatter of points and choice of best and worst outcomes. Widely scattered points within the original boundaries of his trading curve reflect inconsistencies in the trader's decisions. These inconsistencies result typically from one of two causes. The first is usually easy to rectify. It comes about

TABLE 5-10   COMPUTATION OF UTILITIES FOR LARGER LOSSES TO BE COMPLETED BY READER

					Reader's cash equivalent of trade	
		Trade				
Gain (in dollars) G	Utility from Figs. 5-3 and 5-5 $u(G)$	Loss (in dollars) L	Computed° utility $u(L)$	Probability of winning p	Cash (in dollars) C	Utility from Fig. 5-3 $u(C)$
3,500		−1,500		.50		
3,500		−2,000		.50		
3,500		−3,000		.60		
2,000		−1,500		.70		
2,000		−2,000		.70		
2,000		−3,000		.80		
1,000		−1,500		.70		
1,000		−2,000		.80		
1,000		−3,000		.80		
500		−1,500		.70		
500		−2,000		.80		
500		−3,000		.90		

° Utility of loss $= u(L) = -\dfrac{u(G) \cdot p - u(C)}{1 - p}$, where G, L, p, and C are as indicated in the table headings.

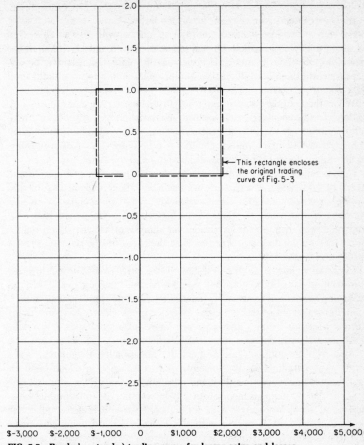

FIG. 5-5   Reader's extended trading curve for larger gains and losses.

because of the superficial evaluation of some of the trading opportunities presented in the table. Correction involves careful reevaluation of some of the trades.

If, after reevaluation, a wide scatter remains, it may be indicative of the second cause of inconsistencies which is related to the boundaries (best and worst outcomes) chosen. The boundaries should be close to the maximum gain or loss *regularly* achieved. If both best gain and worst loss are too small, the trading curve often approximates a straight line and the scatter of points is usually small. In this case the boundaries should be moved farther apart and the tables reevaluated. If the curve is still linear, especially if the points are reasonably spread, it is good evidence that it is the true shape of the curve, not merely the result of improper boundaries.

If either the best gain or worst loss is too large, the points on the trading curve may be widely scattered and not fit any smooth curve. This often results if the subject has had no real experience with gains or losses of the magnitude that he is graphing, in which case bringing the offending boundary in toward the other will enable him to construct a set of points that will fit a smooth curve reasonably well.

When the trading curve is extended to include larger gains and losses, widely scattered points still indicate inconsistent decisions. For these large amounts, however, the scatter pattern yields valuable information. It helps to define upper limits to the trader's risks and objectives if he wants to act rationally and consistently in planning and executing trades.

Curves with excessive scatter may be of value to a broker attempting to evaluate his client's ability to think critically about expected gains and losses. An assessment of the client's attitudes toward gains and losses would supplement the usual questions about his capital, savings, and insurance and yield more complete information. An analysis of the shape and scatter of points would help the broker to advise the client on the size and type of trades and positions to take.

Shape of trading curve. When a smooth (trading) curve is drawn through the computed utilities, different regions of that trading curve can be identified as concave downward, concave upward, or approximately linear. Sometimes the entire trading curve may have one shape, and sometimes different regions within the same curve have different shapes.

A curve that is concave downward indicates that successive constant amounts of gain add smaller and smaller increments to the trader's utility (satisfaction). In the region in which his trading curve has that configuration (a) the trader would prefer to keep his money rather than take fair (or unfavorable) bets [4] and (b), if he were forced to take a fair bet, he would prefer smaller fair bets to larger ones. A person with this attitude toward gains and losses is a risk averter. Most persons are risk averters for large enough sums of money. As indicated above, a risk averter will avoid unfavorable or fair bets. Depending on the degree of risk aversion (concavity of the curve), he may even avoid slightly favorable trades. He will take moderately favorable trades but not large positions, preferring instead to keep some cash or to diversify. Only for extremely favorable bets will the risk averter prefer large positions. The latter temptation should be resisted, however, because of the increased probability of ruin that can accompany increasingly larger positions. This topic is treated in Chapter 10.

[4] A fair bet is one whose average or expected value is zero. An unfavorable bet has a negative expected value. A favorable bet has a positive expected value.

A curve that is concave upward indicates that successive constant amounts of gain add larger and larger increments to the trader's utility (satisfaction). For the amounts of money for which his trading curve has that configuration (a) the trader will prefer fair (or favorable) bets to keeping his money, and (b) he will prefer larger fair bets to smaller ones. A person with this attitude toward gains and losses is a risk lover. Many traders are risk lovers, especially for small amounts of money. The risk lover will take fair or favorable trades and, in fact, will prefer large positions. He may even take them in slightly unfavorable trades. Of course, if a trade is sufficiently unfavorable, the risk lover will keep his cash and not trade. Those two situations express his preferences—all or nothing. He prefers not to diversify and would prefer large positions. A risk lover who trades often and follows his preferences has a high probability of ruin because he will often take large and sometimes unfavorable positions. He should be careful to enter only favorable trades, and the size of his positions should be consistent with a low probability of ultimate ruin. The principles of money management, as discussed in Chapter 10, are most important to the risk lover.

A trading curve that is linear indicates that successive constant amounts of gain add proportional increments to the trader's utility (satisfaction). For the region in which his curve has that configuration the trader will accept favorable trades, decline unfavorable trades, and be indifferent to the size of fair bets. In summary, the person with this trading curve will always prefer to maximize the mathematical expectation of *gain* (because doing so will also maximize his utility). Maximizing the average gain is good in the long run, but even this trader must be aware of the probability of ruin to give him a better chance of reaching the "long run."

Figure 5-6 represents five different risk attitudes in the continuum from one extreme to the other. From left to right the curves are characterized by an increasing preference for risk.

It is important to note that the risk attitudes, and therefore the trading curve, of an individual can change for a number of reasons, including additional experience, gains or losses, changes in capital, changes in personal income tax rate bracket, and loss of income source. This can be shown

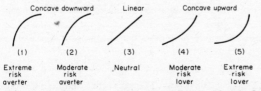

FIG. 5-6 **Trading curves representing different risk attitudes.**

dramatically by comparing trading curves prepared both before and after a large gain or loss or a series of gains and losses. The trader would do well to prepare new trading curves at regular intervals so that they can be compared with previous ones and interpreted. Preparation and interpretation of a trading curve, after the first one, takes little time, and can be an important step toward successful money management in the commodity futures game.

NOTES FROM A TRADER

The concept of utility may appear academic to some, but it actually explains much of what makes one person act differently from others under similar circumstances. Two people may react completely differently, yet each is acting in a manner that is right for him. One may risk an important amount of money trying for an even greater amount, whereas another would not even consider risking what he has. The first is not necessarily bold or irresponsible (depending on whether he wins or loses his big bet) nor is the other wisely cautious or cowardly; they merely have different utilities for gaining or losing money. There are other utilities, not discussed in detail here, that also account for trading decisions. There is utility for time, for example. One person may wish to devote many of his waking hours to making more money, whereas another may feel that his time should better be spent for other activities more important to him. There are different utilities for avoiding pressure, so there are those who would forego making more money because they do not wish to pay the price in sleepless nights and spoiled weekends waiting breathlessly for markets to open.

It is a wise man who makes an honest effort to understand himself well enough to give proper credit for his accomplishments where due and proper blame for his failures as well. Students in school almost invariably say "I got an A" and "He gave me an F." Such a student, later in life, might say "I called that corn market perfectly," and "My broker sure touted me a miserable egg position" or "I wanted to get out and my broker wouldn't let me." Such foolishness may be a little soothing for a trader's morale in the short run, but, unfortunately, it does not help him understand himself, which is the first step to improved trading.

The trader's personal trading curve can give insights to possible biases which, if not overcome, can lead to poor decision making. The trader with biases is not unique. However, the trader who recognizes his biases and controls them with a well-conceived plan to avoid impairing his trading results is a member of a select group.

Some predispositions that the authors have noted following some experience with administering the TPI are:

1. An exceptionally large scatter of points at any dollar level for gains or losses may indicate enough inconsistency to suggest that complete trading plans should be made during periods when the markets are closed to avoid

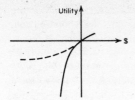

FIG. 5-7

accepting levels of risk and reward incompatible with the trader's feelings (assuming that he understands the game).

2. The trading curve may bend sharply and flatten at an extremely low dollar level. This indicates that increased dollar gains beyond that point do not occupy a high priority in the trader's value system. A person with such a curve might first question whether he should be a trader at all. If he concludes that the curve is shaped as it is because of his own inexperience and he still wants to try his hand at trading, he could begin by trading spread positions or commodities with less than average volatility until his confidence grows enough to change his attitude and his curve so that it does not turn downward so sharply.

3. The shape of the trading curve in the "loss" region is extremely important. In Figure 5-7 the *solid* line showing the curve in the loss area reveals that the person described suffers acute pain even from relatively small losses. He would find it easy to decide on a stop-loss point, enter an order at that point, and feel little or no temptation to change it. On the other hand, the person with the curve indicated by the *dotted* line would feel little pain from even relatively large losses. This might sound good, but pain in trading is like most pain in that it is nature's way of warning that all is not well. Such a person is likely to let losses run, either ignoring them or rationalizing them; he will suffer disaster sooner or later. A broker who notes these tendencies in a client should encourage use of a stop-loss procedure or recommend that the client not make his own trading decisions.

4. The trading curves in Figure 5-8 denote a quality that can best be described as greed. The owner of such a curve may be a rational risk averter or a mild risk lover in the lower dollar values, but he reaches a point (of sharp upward curvature) at which he is seized by a consuming desire to

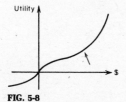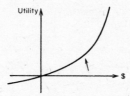

FIG. 5-8

"shoot the works." His type is frequently seen at the casino, where up to a point, say $250, he plays by risking small increments of his total capital. Above that point he is suddenly possessed by a fever that demands higher and higher risks, regardless of the probabilities of success. His counterpart is the trader who chortles happily as he talks about pyramiding his profits into amounts beyond the dreams of avarice. A sensible alternative for a trader so predisposed is to have a managed account (preferably by someone who has studied this book thoroughly) or to trade so lightly that the fun involved in the activity is greater than the cost of playing the game.

CHAPTER SIX

The Fundamental Approach

> ... There's nothing *wrong* with a technician. You
> just wouldn't want your sister to marry one.
>
> A. FUNDAMENTALIST

CONCEPTUAL SUPPLY-DEMAND ANALYSIS

INTRODUCTION

In the long run conventional economic wisdom would conclude that the
price of a commodity must ultimately reflect the equilibrium point of all
the combined forces of supply and demand. Isolating, quantifying, and
evaluating in some reasonable way the respective weight of each supply-
and-demand factor is the job of the fundamentalist.

To grasp the magnitude of such a task the trader must grapple with some
elementary economic theory. At this point the inevitable question arises,
"Why is theory important? Give me the facts!" There are three problems
with facts. First, it is not always easy to say exactly what a fact is. A court
of law provides an excellent illustration of the effort that must be expended
to isolate "facts," especially when two witnesses contradict each other. A
second trouble with facts is that we are simply overwhelmed with them;
for example, the number of facts about soybeans available to the trader is
far beyond his ability to digest them. When the number of unknown facts
about soybeans which can affect price are listed, the result becomes totally
unmanageable. Simplification of "reality" becomes a necessity. The third

trouble with facts is that the individual trader seldom can know in advance the degree to which a particular set of emerging facts has been expected (discounted). Many traders have puzzled over markets that opened lower following news that they believed was bullish and higher following news that they considered bearish.

The proper contrast, then, is not between theory and facts. The successful trader must understand and give meaning to the relevant facts about a commodity. In doing so he theorizes. The proper contrast is between good theory and bad theory, between useful theory and irrelevant theory. Good theory should lead to good practice. If theory does not do this, it is simply not good theory.

It is important for the trader to become familiar with the historical efforts to explain intelligently the supply-demand forces at work in speculative markets like commodity futures.

DEMAND ANALYSIS

A demand schedule like the one presented in Table 6-1, is a list of prices and quantities. At each price the corresponding quantity is the amount of the commodity that would be bought at that price; for example, if the price were $2.45, the quantity bought would be 10,000 bushels. The demand schedule does not indicate what the price is but only what amounts would be bought at different prices. The "law of demand" in economics reflects the fact that the lower the price, the larger the quantity bought.

A demand schedule may be transformed into a demand curve (D_1D_1), as in Figure 6-1. With unimportant exceptions, a demand curve is negatively sloped; that is, it goes downward from left to right. The "slope" of the demand curve refers, roughly speaking, to the degree of its steepness. It is examined in greater detail when the concept of elasticity is analyzed in a subsequent section.

A change in demand is a shift in the entire demand curve, represented by D_2D_2 in Figure 6-1. The quantity opposite each price becomes larger. Such action is not to be confused with an increase in quantity brought about because of a fall in price, illustrated by a given demand schedule in Table 6-1.

A demand curve is an extremely useful tool that may be used to illustrate

TABLE 6-1   A DEMAND SCHEDULE

Price	Quantity in thousands of bushels
$2.50	5,000
2.45	10,000
2.40	15,000
2.35	20,000
2.30	25,000

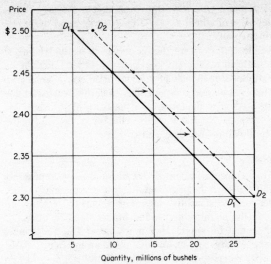

FIG. 6-1   A demand curve and a change in demand.

the meaning of commodity shortages or surpluses, both of which the trader must understand. If wheat is being analyzed in any given crop year, a demand curve may be constructed as in Figure 6-2. Assume that the total supply of wheat available for consumption is OB and the present price for wheat is P_1. At price P_1, however, the demand for wheat is only OA, which is the information transmitted by the demand curve DD. The amount AB, then, is surplus, and unless demand increases so that OB is bought the sellers must store the surplus or lower the price to P_2. On the other hand, suppose that OA is the amount of wheat offered for sale and that the price

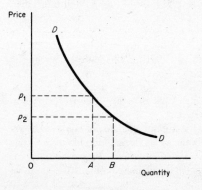

FIG. 6-2   Using a demand curve to illustrate surpluses and shortages.

is P_2. Wheat buyers demand OB, with the result that a shortage AB is generated. Unless the price of wheat is raised to P_1 or demand decreases to OB, a disequilibrium results.

The demand curve illustrates a point that is pervasive in the trading of commodities; prices perform a rationing function. All other things being equal, in the long run a large crop sells at a lower price and a small crop sells at a higher price. All of the complications that may surround the building of a sophisticated price model rest on the truth of the rationing function which price represents. Later in the chapter a specific model will be constructed to illustrate shortages and surpluses.

ELASTICITY OF DEMAND

It is one thing for a trader to understand that a demand curve represents the inverse relationship between the price and quantity of a given commodity. It is quite another to understand the degree of responsiveness that an increase or decrease in the quantity demanded brings about in price. At lower prices more wheat may be bought. How much more? The trader must be aware of the term "elasticity" and its broad application to price analysis.

In economics elasticity refers to the ratio of the relative changes in two quantities. There is substantial literature in the field of economics devoted to the conceptual analysis of elasticity. For trading or forecasting purposes an important concept is the relative change in market demand as the price changes, that is, in the elasticity of demand E_D with respect to price.

$$E_D = \frac{\text{relative (or \%) change in demand}}{\text{relative (or \%) change in price}}$$

Because an increase in market demand will theoretically occur with a decrease in price (and vice versa), the elasticity E_D of demand is negative; for example, suppose the relative change in quantity is $+2$ percent and the relative change in price is -1 percent and that price falls. $E_D = 2\%/-1\% = -2$. If, instead, the price goes up, then quantity demanded by definition, goes down. If the absolute value $|E_D|$ of the elasticity is greater than 1, demand is said to be elastic. If $|E_D|$ is less than 1.00 but more than 0, demand is inelastic. If $|E_D|$ equals 0, demand is considered to be perfectly inelastic.

Elasticity of demand may be understood clearly by referring to Figure 6-3, which portrays demand curves of differing elasticities. The elastic curves are relatively flat; the inelastic curves are relatively steep. The trader can quickly become aware of the important principle of elasticity by considering the changes in quantity that may be brought forth by a decrease in price from P_1 to P_2.

An elastic demand curve exhibits a greater change in quantity in response to a given price change, whereas an inelastic demand curve brings forth a smaller quantity response for a given downward price adjustment. When demand is unit-elastic at all prices, the change in quantity is identical

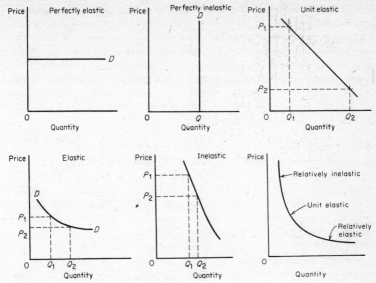

FIG. 6-3   Different elasticities of demand.

to the change in price. Perfect elasticity results when a change in quantity does not affect price at all. The demand for the wheat crop of any one wheat farmer could be considered perfectly elastic. When a demand curve is perfectly inelastic, a price cut does not bring out any increase in demand. Conversely, a price rise does not cut into the quantity demanded. The demand curve for eggs is inelastic over a fairly wide price range. Because eggs are a cheap source of protein, consumers buy them whether they are 35 cents a dozen or 70 cents a dozen. If the price of eggs drops from 70 to 35 cents a dozen, the consumer does not eat four eggs rather than two. Therefore lowering the price in a market that faces a highly inelastic demand curve is not a rewarding strategy for increasing total demand.

The trader should understand that to portray elastic demand curves as relatively flat and inelastic demand curves as relatively steep is accurate enough for most purposes. For some cases, however, the concept of varying elasticities on the same demand curve is relevant; that is, a demand curve may be elastic at high prices and inelastic at low prices. Elasticity of demand also varies with the length of time and the substitutability of one commodity for another. Generally, demand becomes more elastic the longer the period of time because of the substitution factor. The automobile industry might grumble at a substantial rise in copper prices over a two-month period, but it would probably continue to use copper in the short run. If, however, a long strike in the copper industry reduces output significantly so that the long-run price outlook for copper is much higher for an indefinite period of time, the auto industry would in all probability turn to aluminum or other substitutes.

The concept of substitutability is relevant in other areas as well. The retail demand for meat is slightly inelastic in the short run, that is, the year-to-year demand. The long-run retail demand for meat is elastic. If the meat supply were curtailed for longer than one year, prices would first rise, then fall, and consumers would spend less on meat. Generally, the closer the substitutes, the more elastic a commodity's demand curve will be. The importance of substitutability is stressed as the chapter progresses.

SUPPLY ANALYSIS

Supply, like demand, implies a schedule of prices and amounts that would be sold at each price at a given time. However, the analysis of supply is more complex than that of demand because there are so many variables that affect the quantity offered at any point in time. Among these factors are the prices of closely related commodities, the seller's expectation of future prices, weather, and strikes, ad infinitum.

Table 6-2 presents a supply schedule similar in form to the demand schedule shown earlier. At each price the corresponding quantity is the amount of the commodity that would be supplied at that price. The higher the price, the larger the quantity. Figure 6-4 illustrates the supply schedule in Table 6-2 with the curve S_1S_1. Generally speaking, supply curves are positively sloped. A change in supply is a shift in the entire supply curve, as is illustrated by S_2S_2, and results in the quantities opposite each price becoming larger.

ELASTICITY OF SUPPLY

Elasticity E_S of supply has a meaning comparable to elasticity of demand and may be defined as the relative change in market supply divided by the relative change in price, or

$$E_S = \frac{\text{relative change in supply}}{\text{relative change in price}}$$

Because price and quantity theoretically rise and fall together, elasticity E_S of supply is positive.

TABLE 6-2   A SUPPLY SCHEDULE

Price	Quantity in thousands of bushels
$2.50	25,000
2.45	20,000
2.40	15,000
2.35	10,000
2.30	5,000

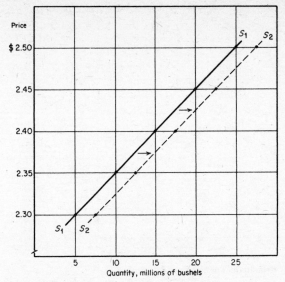

FIG. 6-4   A supply curve and a change in supply.

When supply is elastic, producers should respond to small price changes with significantly greater offerings. A small quantity response by sellers to price changes may signify an inelastic supply curve. Time is more important to elasticity of supply than it is to elasticity of demand. The longer the time period, the more elastic a supply curve is likely to be. The metals are a good illustration of this principle. If the short-run prices for silver or mercury, for example, should rise to high levels, producers might not undertake the production costs of opening new mines unless they were reasonably sure that prices would stay high over the long run. In other words, producers might insist on a shift in the demand curve as the price of increased production, not just a slide upward on the same demand curve.

EQUILIBRIUM ANALYSIS

Figure 6-5 helps the trader to visualize the equilibrium price of the demand and supply schedules discussed so far. The two curves intersect at A, which corresponds to 15 million bushels and $2.40, the equilibrium price. At $2.45 demand is 10 million bushels and supply is 20 million bushels. Excess supply forces prices down. Similarly, at $2.35 the 20-million-bushel demand forces prices up toward A.

It should be noted that this theoretical model of long run equilibrium is as elemental as it is elementary and may be cautiously applied to all but extremely long run situations.

One short run illustration will suffice. Assume that the closing market

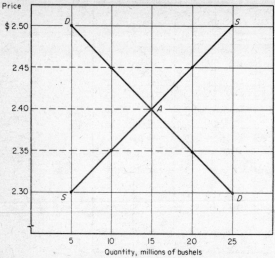

FIG. 6-5 **Market price equilibrium of supply and demand.**

price of a given nearby soybean option is $2.50 a bushel and a trader has a long position. Such a situation is described in Figure 6-6 by point A, where the demand curve D_1D_1 intersects the supply curve S_1S_1. If a sudden shift in the demand for beans occurred, the equilibrium price would tend to shift to B, or $2.55 a bushel. If the free supply of deliverable beans in Chicago was at a historically low level, because of a farmer holding movement, in the short run the trader might face a supply curve like S_2S_2. If demand by crushers or exporters increased suddenly to D_2D_2, the relative inelasticity of the supply curve S_2S_2 means that the equilibrium point might shift to C, or $2.73 a bushel, quite a significant increase. The implications to the trader of the relative elasticities of supply curves $S_1'S_1$ and S_2S_2 are enormous. He may wish to pyramid a long position established at $2.50 and follow the upward move with a trailing stop. He may wish to sell a new-crop position against his long old-crop position, thereby spreading soybeans and lowering his margin and risk requirements while not seriously impairing his potential. The important fact to realize is that, regardless of the intricacies involved, the trader's estimate of future price action is based on an explicit or implicit theoretical base. Such a base must include the dynamics of price equilibrium, which in turn features the various elasticities of both supply and demand curves and the response of each factor to changes in the others.

DISEQUILIBRIUM

It remains to discuss the implication for the trader of those conditions in which disequilibrium exists. Disequilibrium, in fact, is the normal condition

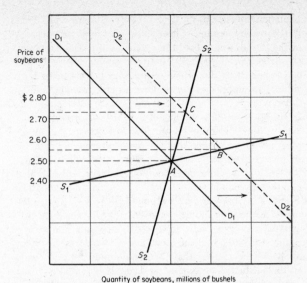

Quantity of soybeans, millions of bushels

FIG. 6-6 An increase in demand with differing elasticities of supply.

of a trading market. This realization does not render the theory of equilibrium useless because equilibrium is a meaningful way of referring to the direction of the long-term forces working on price and quantity changes.

Disequilibrium can easily occur; for example, assume that demand for a particular commodity can change much more quickly than supply. The fact that silver coins can be melted profitably when the price of silver exceeds $1.38 an ounce does not mean that silver futures cannot go higher than that price. Demand for silver may become so pervasive that prices may skyrocket before the supply of silver can be increased effectively in response to the higher prices or before melting in any quantity can take place. Disequilibrium would be the order of the day, in silver especially, because present reserves of the white metal are contained in ores mined chiefly for other metals. Therefore a dramatic immediate increase in production is an improbable response to higher prices.

In many commodities prices and quantities have shown pronounced cyclical movements over long periods of time; for example, much of the cocoa crop is grown by small farmers in Ghana and Nigeria. The price of cocoa for a period of two or three years affects the quantity of beans supplied in the following period. If cocoa prices are high during one period, the farmer will be financially able to expand planting or, equally important, afford insecticides and fertilizers to ensure greater yield of the trees he has. As greater yields come on line, prices drop, expenses are cut, and the cycle is slowly reversed.

A general explanation for some of the cycles that result in disequilibrium is furnished by the "cobweb theorem." This theorem is useful also because it presents one of the simplest models of the dynamics of demand, supply, and price. The model shows the relation between supply, demand, and price in a commodity like cocoa, for which output lags behind price for a given period of time. The supply and demand curves are stationary.

The cobweb theorem has been presented in many models. For simplicity and illustration Figure 6-7 presents the model in which price perpetually oscillates from high to low and output from low to high. In this model equilibrium is never attained. Assume that the average price of cocoa for the first two-year period is 40 cents a pound. During the following two-year period 1,200,000 tons is produced. The demand curve indicates that this production can be sold only at the low price of 20 cents a pound. The price for years 3 and 4 becomes 20 cents a pound. In years 5 and 6 the supply curve and lag assumption indicate that 800,000 tons will be produced. Such a quantity, however, sells at 40 cents a pound. The arrows indicate the perpetual oscillation that the cocoa market would make under such assumptions. It will be noticed that the requirement for such even oscillations is that the elasticities of demand and supply be equal and that buyers of cocoa and producers make the same kind of responses to price changes. If the supply of cocoa in the illustration is less elastic than demand, the result would be that the cocoa farmer in Ghana would respond less to changes in price than the buyers for the Hershey Chocolate Company. This lesser response would cause equilibrium to be reached eventually by the successive diminution of price fluctuation from one 2-year period to the next. The trader can verify the outcomes of different "cobwebs" by varying

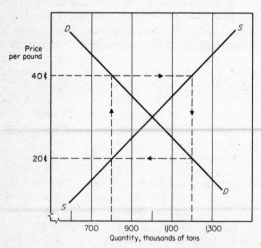

FIG. 6-7 The cobweb theorem: perpetual oscillation.

the slope (elasticity) of the supply curve while leaving the demand curve constant.

APPLIED SUPPLY-DEMAND ANALYSIS

INTRODUCTION

In the real trading world good theory must lead to good practice. Good practice begins with the trader's familiarizing himself with the basic market factors underlying the price movement of any commodity. After isolating and quantifying these factors, a model or simplification of the dynamics of these basic factors must be formulated so that the trader can *explain* satisfactorily a significant amount of the *past* price movements in any commodity. In moving from *explaining* past prices to *forecasting* future commodity prices, what seem to be insuperable difficulties frequently appear. Examples of both explanatory and forecasting models are analyzed. The limits of traditional supply-demand analysis are recognized and additional price-quantity relationships such as price-volume, price-open interest and price-speculation, and hedging are referred to as possible clues in the forecasting process.

BASIC MARKET FACTORS

Total supply and demand balances for most commodities are analyzed on a crop-year, not a calendar-year, basis; for example, the season for wheat and oats begins July 1 and ends the following June 30. Comparable dates for corn and cocoa are October 1 to September 30. In Section 5 crop seasons are given for each commodity when applicable.

Generally total supply includes the old-crop carry-over, new crop production, and imports. Carry-over includes all unused stocks from all earlier seasons. Total demand is domestic consumption plus exports. Domestic usage may be broken down further, as in soybeans, for example, into the demand for the meal and oil, which result from the bean-crushing operation, and seed requirements. In addition, supply and demand factors will include the levels of inventory and various external influences on production and consumption.

If substantial amounts of any commodity are owned by the government, under government loan, or desired by the government, allowance must be made for the possibility of increased or decreased supply or demand at some point in the future. If a substantial amount of any commodity is placed under loan, it is no longer, for practical purposes, part of the "free" supply. Similarly, if the strategic level of stocks of a given commodity by government standards is low, allowance must be made for a possible nonrecurring increase in demand.

For the typical trader the planning horizon is such that most of the variables affecting supply are irrelevant. For some commodities, in some instances, therefore, analysis of supply may be much easier than that of demand. If the dominant short run supply factors are "set in concrete," the number of variables involved in any analysis will be reduced, along with the probability of wrong analysis. The use of many variables enables the trader to explain past data but at the same time increases the probability of error in future analysis.

Basic market factors may result during a given crop year in total-supply shortage, total-supply surplus, free-supply shortage, or free-supply surplus. There are innumerable combinations possible within the components that make up the basic market factors; for example, the trader may well examine the timing and extent of price moves in seasons in which a large crop follows a large crop, a large crop follows a small crop, a small crop follows a large crop, or a small crop follows a small crop. Of no small interest may be the size of the carry-over at the beginning of each season when associated with any of these combinations.

To all these basic factors must be added the critical component of *expectation*. The fundamentalist finds that he is confronted not only with the factual relationships discussed above but with the compound relationships described by the demanding yet gossamer prefix "expected." Hence the multiplicity of relationships increases dramatically. Supply factors double from carry-over, new crop production, and imports to *expected* carry-over, *expected* new crop production, and *expected* imports. Where the fundamentalist was once required to reason as best he could concerning the combinational change that could occur among three dominant variables, there are now six variables, with the ensuing proliferation of possible outcomes. Demand for soybeans explodes from an analysis that includes the demand for oil and meal, the amount of beans crushed, and exports into the *expected* demand for oil, the *expected* demand for meal, the *expected* crush of beans, and the *expected* export figure.

To ensure that the trader will capture the full import of these mind-boggling variations, it is necessary only to add the concept of expectation to the rather simple analysis suggested earlier. The timing and extent of price moves in any season may be visualized by considering the following combinations;

A large crop follows a large crop when either, both, or neither was expected.

A large crop follows a small crop when either, both, or neither was expected.

A small crop follows a large crop when either, both, or neither was expected.

A small crop follows a small crop when either, both, or neither was expected.

A small carry-over or large carry-over precedes any of the foregoing combinations.

It should not be necessary to elaborate on the importance of general basic market factors. In Section 5, many of these historical supply-demand relationships for individual commodities are suggested and may be isolated, quantified, and evaluated at the individual trader's leisure.

MODEL BUILDING

Figure 6-8 is a flow graph of the cocoa industry which illustrates the magnitude of the forces that affect the price of a particular commodity at any

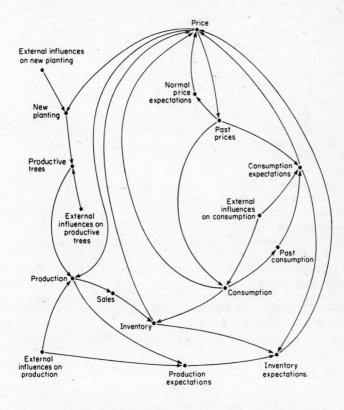

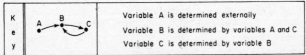

FIG. 6-8 Flow graph of cocoa industry structure. (F. Helmut Weymar, *The Dynamics of the World Cocoa Market*, The M.I.T. Press, Cambridge, Mass., 1968, p. 2.)

point in time. These relationships include hundreds of variables, some of which are quantifiable to some degree. Theoretically, if the flow chart is correct and all the factors that affect the price of cocoa have been included and weighted according to their dominance, a mathematical formula might be produced to explain the average price of cocoa for each crop year.

Because such an exercise would require many years to prepare if it could be done at all, simplification of these relationships appears to be a necessity. This simplification, referred to as model building, attempts to reduce the number of variables from that approaching the infinite to a few dominant factors that retain the power of explanation.

As a simplification of reality, models have limitations recognized by good theory. A serious one is that many factors affecting the price structure must, by definition, be eliminated from consideration. The trader must develop sufficient insight into the supply-demand factors of a given commodity to be able to identify the *dominant* price-making influences at any point in the crop year; for example, with reference to Figure 6-8, the planting of new cocoa trees will certainly have the effect of increasing the production of cocoa in the long run. The lag in such incremental supply, however, is approximately five years. The most sanguine fundamentalist would admit that the price of cocoa futures will reflect many other shorter term influences in the meantime, such as figures that may indicate that cocoa users face a second year of reduced carry-over inventory levels. Therefore caution must be used in the selection of individual elements when models are constructed.

In eliminating so many factors from consideration in the interest of simplification, care should be exercised to ensure that such simplification should not give way to contradiction of reality; for example, a case for sharply higher prices might be made for wheat futures if new-crop production fell below total estimated usage and if a simple two-variable model were constructed. However, assume that wheat futures have fallen. If a less casual study indicated that old crop carry-over had been at a 20-year high, the model for supply would have to be expanded to include carry-over as well as new-crop production to avoid future contradictions.

EXPLAINING VERSUS FORECASTING

Before proceeding to specific examples of explanatory and forecasting models, the trader should be aware of the significant differences between the terms. One of the most insistent myths surrounding fundamental analysis in commodity futures is that explaining price changes is equivalent to *forecasting* price changes. On the contrary, an explanation is seldom equivalent to a prediction. In fact, explanation frequently requires only that the trader be equipped with 20/20 hindsight.

In an explanatory model the variables used to explain a price at a particular time are also measured at the same time and thus must be currently available with the prices they seek to explain; for example, assume that the trader has found that the price of hogs is a function of the quantity of hogs available, the prices of substitutes (beef and veal, lamb and mutton, fish, and poultry), the income position of buyers, and consumer preference and that there are no further variables necessary to explain past prices. Assume further that the proper quantities for all past years are absolutely known for all four of these variables and that they have been weighted properly. As magnificent as such a model of price behavior would be, it would enable the trader only to *understand* past hog prices, not to *predict* future hog prices. The problem of turning explanatory variables into forecasting variables would still remain; for example, one determinant of the price for hogs, the quantity of hogs available, is reported quarterly in December, March, June, and September. Unfortunately no one has yet been able to forecast consistently the quantity of hogs before these reports are issued. If, as already discussed, the behavior of commodity futures prices is based partly on *expectations* and *changes* in expectations, it becomes a formidable task to predict price changes even if the trader were given a perfect preview of the figures to be reported. Unless the trader were also privy to accurate estimates of what figures were *expected*, he might still be unable to forecast the price changes that might follow the input of new information.

On the other hand, there are really only two general ways in which a *forecasting* model can be built. The first approach, using the preceding example, is to forecast the *next* hog quantity from a knowledge of past hog quantities. This simple extrapolative technique would have proven worth only if the explanatory variable, lagged for one 3-month period, were found to have predictive value when estimating the quantity of hogs in the next report; for example, assume for a moment that the trader had access to 10 years of figures reflecting the quantity of hogs available as evidenced by the annual December report. It is now March and the trader wishes to forecast accurately the March quantity-of-hogs figure soon to be released. If his only source of information is the December hog quantity figure, he has an *explanatory* variable lagged by three months. If the pattern of December figures offers a significant clue over the years to the upcoming March figures, the trader can use this lagged explanatory variable to *predict* future variables. The published material to date, however, does not give the trader much encouragement in this regard.

The second method of forecasting isolates a variable that is predictive of hog quantities apart from past hog quantity figures; for example, the trader may find that quarterly changes in hog quantities are related to changes in the price of beef. However, for this information to be of forecasting, rather than explanatory value, the prices of beef in the *present* period would have to correlate highly with the quantity of hogs available in a *future* period. Again research indicates that this approach to forecasting does not easily yield significant results.

BUILDING AN EXPLANATORY MODEL

To date the trader has been exposed to conceptual supply-demand analysis from which he gained an insight into basic economic relationships that can affect the pricing of commodities. The basic market factors intrinsic to each crop year were discussed, and the myriad possibilities that revolve around the factors themselves, as well as the expectations of those factors, were considered. The need to formulate a model that simplifies real-life complications while recognizing the limitations of such simplification leads the trader to recognize the difference between explaining commodity futures prices and forecasting them.

The ability to explain prices in any commodity necessarily precedes the ability to forecast prices. Perhaps the most rewarding way for the fundamentalist to try to explain supply-demand factors is not only to simplify the countless variables into the more dominant factors, as discussed earlier, but to shorten the span of concentration from the entire crop year into segments more easily analyzed.

A particularly interesting area of concentration might be a discussion of the effect of inventory and inventory expectations on the price of cocoa (see Figure 6-8). Many analysts agree that cocoa price levels are highly correlated with carry-over inventory levels.[1]

Table 6-3, Miscellaneous Cocoa Data, provides basic information on supply, demand, and inventory and average price levels for a number of years. Figure 6-9 graphs the yearly relation between the actual carry-over stocks (inventory) as a percentage of the world grind (consumption) and the average price of spot cocoa in New York.

Before examining this specific relationship, the trader should understand why, in general, commodity price levels should show a strong inverse relation to the ratio of carry-over inventories to the recent consumption rate. There are two basic reasons for this phenomenon: (a) the need for prices to ration existing inventories if present levels are low and (b) the need to strike an equilibrium in the longer run between supply and demand.

Inventory rationing. Inventory levels have an immediate impact on the relations between near and deferred contracts of the same commodity. An inverted market, in which the near futures are selling for premiums above deferred contracts, reflects the presence of relatively low levels of inventory. In a situation in which a manufacturer's cocoa bean inventories are

---

[1] For an excellent comprehensive analysis of the economics of cocoa see F. H. Weymar, *The Dynamics of the World Cocoa Market,* The M.I.T. Press, Cambridge, Mass., 1968. In the following discussion the authors draw as well on Dr. Weymar's article "Cocoa, the Effect of Inventories on Price Forecasting," *Commodity Yearbook,* Commodity Research Bureau, 1969, pp. 15–22. The latter was updated through private correspondence.

low he faces real business risks. He may have to change his production mix because he does not have on hand the amount or variety of cocoa beans he needs. His vulnerability to strikes or transportation difficulties increases, and he may not be able to honor his shipping commitments. For these and other reasons there is a convenience yield that attaches to the holding of a minimum cocoa inventory in and of itself. This minimum inventory will be held even though a manufacturer may expect a decline in cash cocoa prices. On the other hand, if the cocoa bean inventory being carried is large in relation to the user's historical needs, any additional inventory will not only have no added value but will not be tolerated unless the costs of carrying excess inventory can be recovered. This recovery can take place either in an increase in the price of cocoa or by short hedging in the futures market at a premium sufficient to cover carrying costs.

Throughout this process it is price that is the rationing instrument. As inventory carry-over levels decrease, all other things remaining constant, nearby contracts increase their premiums over more distant futures, thereby forcing those who hold the inventory to bear an increasing penalty for not selling it in the cash market for a high price and replacing it with a lower

TABLE 6-3   MISCELLANEOUS COCOA DATA

Crop year	World production (before 1% weight loss)	World grind during crop year	World stocks, end of crop year	Ratio, actual carry-over stocks to grind	Crop year average price New York spot Accra
	Thousands of long tons			Years	c/lb
1952/53	798	787	168	0.214	33.6
1953/54	776	770	166	0.216	55.4
1954/55	802	690	269	0.390	43.0
1955/56	843	785	319	0.406	29.3
1956/57	896	895	310	0.346	26.6
1957/58	771	890	183	0.206	42.9
1958/59	908	842	240	0.285	38.4
1959/60	1039	897	371	0.414	30.7
1960/61	1173	999	533	0.534	24.2
1961/62	1124	1089	556	0.511	21.9
1962/63	1158	1149	553	0.481	23.4
1963/64	1216	1158	598	0.516	24.3
1964/65	1482	1274	791	0.620	19.0
1965/66	1205	1378	605	0.439	22.5
1966/67	1333	1364	561	0.411	26.9
1967/68	1333	1387	492	0.354	30.4
1968/69	1225	1348	356	0.264	44.5
1969/70	1413	1335	420	0.315	37.9
1970/71	1479	1372	512	0.373	30.1
1971/72	1548	1499	545	0.364	28.2

SOURCE: As modified from F. H. Weymar, "Cocoa, the Effect of Inventories on Price Forecasting," *Commodity Yearbook*, Commodity Research Bureau, 1969, p. 16.

priced contract for delivery some months later. Conversely, when inventories are excessive, nearby prices will be battered when compared with future contract prices, for potential storers of cocoa must be induced to carry substantial inventories.

Long run equilibrium. Obviously there are many long-term fluctuations in production and consumption that influence massive price changes in the price structure of cocoa. As always, expectations about these changes, both in their timing and impact, play an important part in generating a realistic price level. Yet a glance at Figure 6-9 will confirm that whatever long-term price assessment is made in terms of production and consumption generally appears to be consistent with known current inventory levels. The

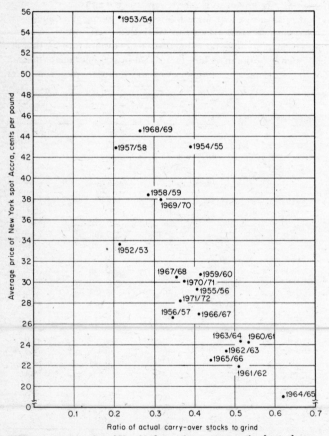

FIG. 6-9   Average price of New York spot Accra versus ratio of actual carry-over stocks to grind (years).

reason for this seems to lie in the fact that following a prolonged period of production surplus current inventories tend to be high, whereas subsequent to a series of short crops inventories fall to quite low levels. Thus, as Weymar notes, "The carry-over ratio alone explains major price movements reasonably well, both because it provides a measure of the near term need to ration or encourage inventory holding, and because it provides a good proxy for the market's assessment of the longer term supply-demand balance."[2]

Inventory expectations. Figure 6-9 confirms the general tendency for cocoa prices to vary in line with the ratio of carry-over inventories to the recent consumption rate. The trader must remember, however, that the price scale is quite large and that each grid on that scale represents 2 cents a pound or $600 a contract. A miss of this dimension can represent as much as a 60 percent loss of a $1,000 margin requirement; for example, the carry-over inventory ratios for the years 1952–1953, 1953–1954, and 1957–1958 crop years were almost the same, and, hypothetically, the trader would have reason to expect that prices would ration supplies in a similar fashion. Yet average price levels for those years were 34, 57, and 44 cents, respectively. Clearly, such excessive scatter is disturbing to the trader trying to explain these price levels.

This result has not been unanticipated. The reader will remember that model building presents disadvantages as well as advantages. The search for simplicity often eliminates factors that turn out to be dominant and that demand recognition if a good explanatory model is to be built. As promising as the explanation is for cocoa prices given in Figure 6-8, a dominant factor is missing. That factor, as might be surmised by now, is the variation in inventory *expectations* which have in many years differed significantly from the *actual* inventory carry-over figures eventually included in statistical records. The market never knows what world production and consumption will be for a given year until that reality is close to fulfillment.

The effect of including the expected carry-over ratio is illustrated in Figure 6-10. The basis of computation is complex[3] but it can be summarized briefly. At the beginning of each crop year estimates of the new crop production and consumption of cocoa are issued by Gill & Duffus, Ltd., in London. Because the carry-over stocks from the preceding year are known, a computation of the expected new crop carry-over ratios can be made at that time. A year later, when the actual carry-over ratio is known, there are frequent mismatches between the expected and actual amounts. Figure 6-10 plots yearly average cocoa prices against the average for each year of the initial expected and *final* actual carry-over ratios. Justification for an averaging process is based on the fact that expectations tend to trend rela-

[2] F. H. Weymar, "Cocoa—The Effect of Inventories on Price Forecasting," *Commodity Year Book,* Commodity Research Bureau, 1969, p. 21.

[3] See Appendix 4A in F. H. Weymar, *The Dynamics of the World Cocoa Market,* The M.I.T. Pres, Cambridge, Mass., 1968, pp. 195–217.

tively smoothly to their actuality at the end of a given crop year. Certainly the trader can appreciate that there is less scatter in Figure 6-10 than in Figure 6-9, which indicates a better fit and therefore a more satisfactory explanation of yearly average cocoa prices.

Toward a general model of prices. Of course, not all commodities are similar to cocoa in that the trader is able to isolate and quantify inventory adjustments as a promising approach to an explanation of price changes. There are futures markets for commodities without continuous inventories. Potatoes, for example, are produced seasonally, but most stocks are disposed of before June 1 each year. Other commodities such as live beef cattle and fresh eggs have no inventories at all in the usual sense. The

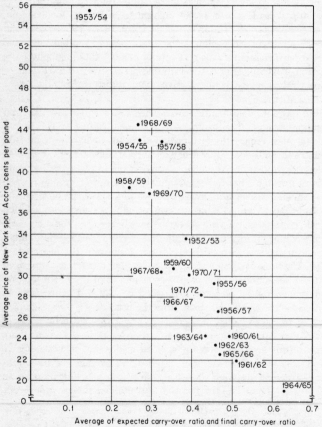

FIG. 6-10 Average price of New York spot Accra versus average of expected carry-over ratio and final carry-over ratio.

trader must approach the basic market factors in these commodities without the help of carry-over analysis.[4]

Lately interest has increased in the attempt to isolate and quantify factors that have a general explanatory effect, no matter what individual commodity is studied. The feasibility of an approach toward constructing a general model is gaining impetus because of the availability of the computer. A recent study, which utilized spectral analysis, of six commodities (soybean oil, cottonseed oil, soybean meal, soybeans, rye, and wheat), used to monthly price changes over a nine-year period concluded that in the long run prices were determined mainly by the prices of substitutable commodities, followed in importance by hedging and speculative activity, supply and demand components, and the business cycle.[5]

BUILDING A FORECASTING MODEL

The bridge from explaining past price changes to forecasting future price changes is not easily crossed. Many traders are sure that someone, somewhere, knows everything, in that this person is knowledgeable enough to list all the sets of supply and demand conditions that would cause *all* bull or bear markets. In reality, traders do extremely well to isolate, quantify, and evaluate any set of conditions *sufficient* to cause a particular bull or bear market, even if viewed retrospectively. The development of a forecasting model requires even more rigor.

There is no requirement that the trader be omniscient in order to make money. It is enough that he isolate and quantify any set of sufficient conditions for bull and bear markets in the commodities he is trading. The trader following this strategy will simply not trade a commodity (regardless of its price fluctuations, all of which are caused by sufficient conditions of which he is unaware) until he sees the sufficient conditions he has previously validated materialize. Then, and only then, will that trader take a position in the market.

Such a strategy is similar to that which might be followed by someone paid to predict fires. He might miss a great many fires caused by, say, chemical combinations of which he was completely unaware, but the specific knowledge that rags soaked with flammable fluids usually combust might be enough to earn him a generous living.

The purpose of the following discussion is to develop a basic understanding of some of the requirements for the construction of a successful forecasting model. To accomplish this the informal process with which the ex-

---

[4] The recent emergence of futures markets for noninventory commodities is discussed by William G. Tomek and Roger W. Gray, "Temporal Relationships Among Prices on Commodity Futures Markets: Their Allocative and Stabilizing Roles," *American Journal of Agricultural Economics*, 52, No. 3 (August 1970), 372–380, and the ensuing "reply," 53, No. 2 (May 1971), 362–66.

[5] Walter Labys and C. W. J. Granger, *Speculation, Hedging, and Commodity Price Forecasts,* D. C. Heath and Co., Lexington, Mass., 1970, Chapter 8.

planatory model dealt must give way to an actual step-by-step statistical process; for example, assume that a commodity analyst is attempting to isolate and quantify a supply-demand relationship in the soybean market which will have predictive value. Because inventory stocks were found to be an integral part in explaining cocoa price changes, the analyst similarly will decide to use the quantity of soybeans crushed and exported as a measure of the demand for a given period and the stocks of soybeans in all positions as an indicator of supply. Stocks in all positions are reported quarterly during the soybean crop year, which, for the purpose of this historical analysis, begins October 1. Crush figures are available monthly and export figures weekly. The earliest practical period, therefore, on which a meaningful comparison of usage and supply may be made is in January of each calendar year. Historically, the date of the "stocks-in-all-positions" report for soybeans has not varied significantly from January 24. At that time annual comparisons may be made between the size of the October–December crush plus exports and the stocks of beans in all positions.

In Figure 6-11 the X axis represents the annual ratio of January 1 stocks of soybeans in all positions, divided by the previous quarter's usage. Since 1952 that ratio has been as low as 2.22 and as high as 3.38. The lower the figure, the higher the October–December usage of soybeans relative to the present supply. Plotted on the Y axis is the highest price reached by the July soybeans future between March 1 and the end of the July contract, measured against the Chicago equivalent of the loan price each year; for example, if the average farm loan price for soybeans in 1966 was $2.50 a bushel, approximately 20 cents would be added to it to equal the Chicago equivalent. If the actual high reached by July soybeans on the Chicago Board of Trade from March 1 to the end of the contract was $3.77¼, it may be said that July soybeans sold as high as $1.07¼ above the Chicago equivalent of the loan price.

If there were a perfect linear relation between the variables X and Y, as shown in Figure 6-11, the yearly dots would fall exactly on the regression line that serves to measure the historical average relation between the variables. The scatter about that regression line measures the "goodness of fit." Given the value of the January supply-demand factors that constitute the variable X, the "best" estimate of the high price in July beans is given by the Y' value of the regression line. This step may be accomplished graphically or by using the predictive equation $Y = 3.99 - 1.213X$,[6] which was computed by using the data from 1952 to 1972. As X becomes available on January 24 each year, the trader has only to solve for Y' to estimate the July high. The coefficient of determination r^2 is .55. This measures the proportion of change in Y that can be attributed to changes in X. The standard deviation $S_{y \cdot x}$ of Y for any given X is 26.7 cents a bushel, which indicates that for any value X that becomes available on January

---

[6] This equation was determined by using the least-squares method, which is illustrated in any elementary statistics text.

24 the July high price will be within 26.7 cents of the Y' value, as shown on the regression line approximately 68 percent of the time.

To date Figure 6-11 has been constructed as a simple two-variable explanatory model that illustrates a principle with which the trader is now familiar: prices tend to vary inversely to the ratio of inventories to the recent consumption rate. However, to achieve a *predictive* value from such a relationship a significant amount of the price rise in July soybeans in any given year must occur *after* January 24.

Certain conclusions are evident in a study of the relationships in Figure 6-11. First, research indicates that the profit potential is poor when X is greater than 2.60. For most of these years the closing price of July soybeans

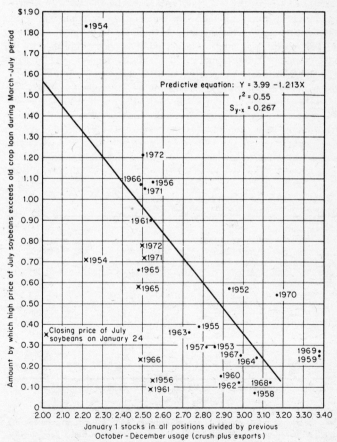

FIG. 6-11 Soybean supply (stocks in all positions, January 1) and demand (October-December crush plus exports (X) versus price highs (Y) in March-July for July soybeans, 1952–1972.

on January 24 was not significantly below the high price reached in the subsequent March–July periods. There is no significant forecasting value to the model in these years. Second, when X is less than 2.60, the probability of a major bull market in soybeans in that crop year becomes high. The years 1954, 1956, 1961, 1965, 1966, 1971, and 1972 produced such a ratio. The trader in these years was faced with the possibility of sufficient conditions for a price rise of extraordinary amplitude. Because the "stocks-in-all-positions" report issued quarterly does not become available until about three weeks after the effective date, January 24 thus becomes the earliest practical date on which the trader may take the position dictated by the predictive equation in Figure 6-11.

Table 6-4 summarizes the results of instituting a long position on January 24 of each soybean crop year when X is less than 2.60. Column 2 gives the price of July soybeans versus the loan on January 24 of each crop year. Column 3 shows the March-to-July expected high price established by the predictive equation. The potential profit is entered in column 4. By referring to Figure 6-11 it may be seen that in each year except 1964–1965 the expected high price in July soybeans was equaled or exceeded in the given period. In the 1953–1954, 1955–1956, 1960–1961, and 1965–1966 seasons, the actual price on January 24 was more than two standard deviations removed from the regression line. For these years the trader could say with an extremely high probability (.95) of being correct that the price of July soybeans in the March-to-July period would be significantly higher than it was on January 24. The crop years 1970–1971, and 1971–1972 reflected

TABLE 6-4   RESULTS OF LONG POSITIONS IN JULY SOYBEANS
INSTITUTED ON JANUARY 24 WHEN X IS LESS THAN 2.60

(1) Crop year	(2) Premium of January 24 price of July soybeans over Chicago equivalent of loan price (to nearest cent)	(3) Predictive equation price ($Y = 3.99 - 1.213X$)	(4) Equation profit potential (3) minus (2)
1953–54	$0.71	$1.30	$0.59
1955–56	0.13	0.90	0.77
1960–61	0.09	0.91	0.82
1964–65	0.58	0.98	0.40
1965–66	0.23	0.97	0.74
1970–71	0.72	0.94	0.22
1971–72	0.78	0.96	0.18
1972–73*	1.98	1.09	− 0.89

*Preliminary data for 1972–1973 present an interesting example of the dilemma faced by every trader using the fundamental approach. Following the January 24, 1973, stocks report, the premium of the price of July soybeans over the Chicago equivalent of the loan price was $0.89 *above* the average price expected by the predictive equation. Clearly, expectations of a bull market had pulled prices very high early in the crop year, and a trader believing that prices could go even higher was faced with establishing a long position over $4.00 a bushel, a level rarely attained historically. The fact that July soybeans exceeded $6.00 a bushel in early March is one more illustration that historical relationships, although of immense help, do not guarantee the trader a clear outline of Camelot.

a ratio of less than 2.60 on January 24, which called for $0.22 and $0.18 increases, respectively, in prices sometime between March and the end of the July contract. These expectations were exceeded in 1971 by $0.10 and in 1972 by $0.25.

LIMITS OF SUPPLY-DEMAND ANALYSIS

Because intrinsic value at any point in time is elusive, disequilibrium can well be the normal condition of commodity futures markets. For this reason the trader must go slowly in applying conventional supply-demand theory to the markets, especially in the short-run. Many traders begin to feel comfortable with traditional supply-demand analysis just in time to lose 85 percent of their capital in one trade because cocoa or soybeans simply "cannot go down." Such traders find out too late that the supply coming into the market does not always decrease when the price falls. In fact, the fear of a further fall in price may be an inducement to offer an even greater supply on the market, thus causing prices to weaken beyond the point indicated by traditional equilibrium analysis. The same possibility exists on the demand side, where the fear of a further price rise may induce tremendous demand in the short-run which can outstrip all economic projections and account for many a tragic tale of getting short "too soon." The inapplicability to the trader of "equilibrium" prices in the short run is reflected by rather substantial totals in the loss column each year.

The implicit possibilities of such a trap were discussed in an early study which argued that, even though a price run, up or down, could not continue indefinitely without regard to basic supply-demand considerations, rather large price movements could occur within broad limits. The area between these limits was defined as the "penumbra."[7] Figure 6-12 illustrates an attempt to explain the relation between bar-charts and supply-demand curves by using this concept.[8]

Instead of assuming that supply and demand can be represented by single lines that intersect to give a single equilibrium price, as in Figure 6-5, the penumbra concept assumes a series of lines that oscillate about an intrinsic value to form price bands. These bands serve as a proxy for the penumbra under conditions of fixed supply-demand (Part A) and fixed supply-increased demand (Part B). In Part A prices reflect a trading range within a broad equilibrium state, whereas Part B illustrates the same trading range with an upward drift that reflects an increase in demand. Unfortunately, for the trader, the concept of a single equilibrium price or a band within which prices move is difficult to test on a rigorous basis.

The analysis of the behavior of commodity futures prices has emphasized that price changes are formed according to *expectations* of changes in supply and demand rather than their known values. Because the behavior of

[7] F. W. Taussig, "Is Market Price Determinate?" *Quarterly Journal of Economics,* 35 (May 1929), 394–411.
[8] L. A. Bernstein. "How Commodity Price Charts Disclose Supply-Demand Shifts," *Commodity Yearbook,* 1958, pp. 33–42, as modified by Labys and Granger, *op. cit.,* p. 113.

traders provides price changes, it is the constant search for significant new information that produces the key to future changes. This new information and its impact is, itself, unpredictable. Therefore the random quality of new information, not actual changes in supply and demand, is responsible for the disequilibrium that is too often the norm in futures prices. The implications of these concepts for the trader include the avoidance of his relying exclusively on conventional supply-demand estimates as the cornerstone of successful trading.

ADDITIONAL PRICE-QUANTITY RELATIONSHIPS

Traditional supply-demand analysis does not generally include price-quantity relations apart from the basic market factors discussed earlier in the chapter. Yet there is merit in the suggestion that prices might be related to quantities other than carry-over, production, imports, exports, and usage. Price-volume, price-open interest, and price-speculation and hedging are examples of intermarket speculative relationships that might be considered in the search for explanatory and predictive variables. These and many other indicators have long been the province of what is known as technical analysis, or the attempt to construct a model of future price changes using past trading statistics as a guide. Chapter 7 discusses the specific advantages and disadvantages of trading utilizing this approach.

NOTES FROM A TRADER

There is little argument against the proposition that, competently and consistently performed, fundamental analysis provides the trader with a powerful tool in his quest for profits in the commodity futures markets. Those who are aware early of changes taking place in dominant factors may initiate positions that ultimately yield handsome profits. Yet there can be several rocky detours along the way.

BASIC DATA

Errors in basic data will obviously lead to errors in forecasts. The trader must realize that every statistic, whether generated by government or private sources, has a band of error about it. There are many problems in specifying what, how, and when to measure the factors that influence prices. Masses of data are meaningless unless they are grouped in some manner; however, there is the problem of the most representative totals or averages for various markets, seasons, or time periods.

No matter how accurate the estimate of a crop size, for example, may be, that estimate is based on a sample. Samples are less than perfect reflections of reality for many reasons, the most important of which is cost. At some point the return in the form of increased accuracy is not so great as the increased cost. The trader should remember that accuracy is also impaired because of revisions to data that are constantly being made. The words "preliminary" and "estimate" liberally dot most factual summaries.

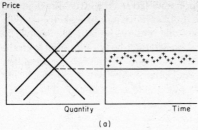

Price

Quantity   Time

(a)

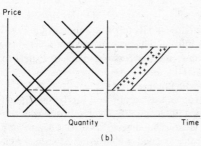

Price

Quantity   Time

(b)

FIG. 6-12 Influence of supply
and demand on futures price
movements. (a) Fixed supply-
fixed demand; (b) fixed supply-
increased demand. (W. C. Labys
and C. W. J. Granger, *Speculation, Hedging and Commodity
Price Forecasts*, D. C. Heath and
Company, Lexington, Mass.,
1970, p. 113, as modified from
L. A. Bernstein, "How Commodity Price Charts Disclose Supply-
Demand Shifts," *Commodity
Year Book*, Commodity Research
Bureau, New York, 1958, pp.
35–36.)

THE ANALYTICAL FRAMEWORK

Even though there are no substitutes for competent statistical tools in the
process of appraising the outlook for prices, the trader must bear in mind
that such tools are not reliable substitutes for judgment. Because judgment
is present continually, it can be extremely difficult to reproduce, on a
quantifiable basis, fundamental studies performed at a particular point
in time. As one study concluded, when referring to the estimation of
certain variables in the pork bellies market, the procedure used "was
not systematic, was not documented, and could not be duplicated."[9]

An important source of error is in the construction of the model itself.
Explanatory models attempt to specify historical price responses to supply-
demand forces which involve a complicated set of varying leads and lags.
Forecasting models bear the additional burden of having to lead actual
price response. Because models are but a simplification of reality, no model
can include all of the relevant factors. A second source of error may be the
choice of equation form. Some relationships are linear, whereas others are
curvilinear and may be more difficult to identify. Some relationships may
best be studied in terms of changes rather than levels. Finally, estimates of
elasticity are subject to a range of error which may arise from inaccurate
basic data or a poorly constructed model.

OPPORTUNITY COST OF CAPITAL

The trader employing the fundamental approach is not concerned so
much with the question *when* prices will move significantly up or down as

he is with the probability *whether* prices will move in a given direction and the possible extent of such a move. If prices move immediately through the objective indicated by his study, the trade presents no hazard. However, if prices move opposite to the trader's expectation, he is confronted with the vexing problem of losses or, at least, foregone alternative opportunities. If such action persists for months and other trades are rejected because capital has been unavailable for commitment, the cost of capital becomes a real consideration.

INCREASED MARKET EFFICIENCY

Implicit in the fundamental approach is the search for the discrepancy between the actual price of a commodity and its intrinsic value, as indicated by the price model formulated. As information systems become more complex and computer capability becomes more accessible, it seems logical to predict a damping effect on the quantity and degree of discrepancy that a given market will allow to remain unexploited.

It will be remembered that the concept of an efficient market is implicit in the random walk model developed in Chapter 4. The implications of this model for the fundamentalist are clear. The closing price of a commodity for any one day or month is generally as good a clue as any fundamental factor to the closing price on the following day, week, or month. If the full import of such a truth dawns on the trader with something less than instant clarity, he may be comforted to learn that a sage observer of futures markets for many years has wryly observed:

> It is remarkable how long a known fact can in effect remain unknown, for lack of sufficient thoughtful attention to it; the near randomness of speculative price movements has long been widely recognized, in the limited form of recognition that no simple method was known for reliable prediction of speculative price movements.[10]

At least one study has documented the fact that commodity futures prices are almost as active when markets are closed as they are during formal market hours[11]; that is, prices vary almost as much overnight and over any weekend as they do during the actual trading period. Such continuation of activity underscores the never-ending search by traders for new information. It seems that expectations never sleep, and prices are pulled inexorably toward events unknown but about to transpire. Indeed, on those plains of expectation bleach the bones of countless traders who insist that in the short run there must be a continual significant correlation between basic market factors and prices.

---

[10] Holbrook Working, "Tests of a Theory Concerning Floor Trading on Commodity Exchanges," *Proceedings of a Symposium on Price Effects of Speculation in Organized Commodity Markets, Food Research Institute Studies, Supplement,* 7 (1967), 14.

[11] Labys and Granger, *op. cit.,* pp. 81–82.

CHAPTER 7

The Technical Approach

> ... There's nothing *wrong* with a fundamentalist. You
> just wouldn't want your sister to marry one.
>
> A. TECHNICIAN

INTRODUCTION

"Technical analysis" refers to a study of the market itself rather than of
the external factors that affect the supply of and demand for a given commodity. The basic assumption underlying all technical analysis is that by
studying statistics generated by the market it is possible to come to meaningful conclusions about future prices; that is, the way the market behaved
yesterday may indicate how prices will behave today. The technician does
not believe that price fluctuations are random and unpredictable. He
believes that if he studies the transactions taking place impending price
movements will tip their hands.

The fundamentalist reasons inductively, seeking to isolate and quantify
dominant factors. By taking into consideration the expected supply and
expected usage of a commodity, which includes such factors as carry-in,
carry-out, production, exports, free supplies, substitutability, and a host
of others, the fundamentalist tries to deduce the intrinsic value of the
commodity. If the current price is substantially above or below this appraisal, appropriate action is taken in the futures market.

The technician contends that this is a futile procedure. The factors the fundamentalist is examining are in many cases estimates subject to important revision. Furthermore, the technician asserts that there are so many fundamental elements in play at any time that an important one can often be overlooked or those being analyzed may be weighted improperly. Even if all relevant supply/demand factors can be estimated with total accuracy, the technical analyst still believes that the result would be of only limited value in appraising prices. As two advocates of the technical school declare:[1]

> Of course, the statistics which the fundamentalists study play a part in the supply/demand equation—that is freely admitted. But there are many other factors affecting it. The marketplace reflects not only the differing value opinions of many orthodox (commodity) appraisers, but also all of the hopes and fears and guesses and moods, rational and irrational, of hundreds of potential buyers and sellers, as well as their needs and resources—in total, factors which defy analysis and for which no statistics are obtainable—In brief, the going price as established by the market itself comprehends all the fundamental information which the statistical analysts can hope to learn (plus some which is perhaps secret from him, known only to a few insiders) and much else besides of equal or even greater importance.

Even a cursory look explains why the technical approach to commodity trading has had little trouble gathering followers. Only three series of data are required: price, volume, and open interest. These data are easy to get and to store and are available with almost no time lag. The models that the technician constructs with this statistical information are relatively simple and straightforward, applicable to anything that can be traded on a free market, anywhere, at any time. One noted technical analyst has stated, "The technician of 1900 would be completely at home in the markets today."[2] The same certainly could not be said of the turn-of-the-century fundamentalist.

These considerations have appeared to be especially attractive to many traders searching for a better and easier way to make decisions. In the last several decades a vast amount of work has been done to erect a maze of technical tools—all with the aim of anticipating future prices from trading statistics.

Every technical approach, from the simplest to the most complex and esoteric, falls into one of four broad areas of technical analysis: patterns on price charts, trend-following methods, character of market analysis, and structural theories. Volumes could be—and have been—written about many of the methods contained in these four basic areas. To go into great detail on any one method would be beyond the scope of this book, but a comprehensive survey is presented, with ample references for further study of the key methods within each area.

[1] Robert D. Edwards and John Magee, *Technical Analysis of Stock Trends*, John Magee, Inc., Springfield, Mass., 1948.

[2] John Magee, *The Stock Advisory Service*, John Magee, Inc., Springfield, Mass., 1964.

PATTERNS ON PRICE CHARTS

The use of patterns of movement on price charts is one of the oldest methods of market analysis known. The approach is said to have gained great popularity in 1901 when William Peter Hamilton, then editor of *The Wall Street Journal*, stunned his readers by recounting in detail precisely what James R. Keene was doing when he successfully promoted the first public offering of stock in U.S. Steel. Hamilton was said to have had an informant in Keene's inner circle, and Keene himself believed this. *The Wall Street Journal* readers were amazed to learn that all of Hamilton's deductions were made by simply tabulating—and shrewdly analyzing— the price and volume action of U.S. Steel stock on the market.[3]

Although Hamilton used only common sense in analyzing the price movement of U.S. Steel, it was not long before many other researchers attempted to catalog and codify any number of price patterns with supposed forecasting value. At first it was said that the "pools" (secret groups of wealthy speculators who manipulated stock prices) revealed their actions to the trader who charted prices and volume. In later years, when the pools were banished by legislative fiat, the charts were supposed to show "changes in psychology." Whatever one believes is being measured, this entire approach rests on the assumption that certain repetitive patterns of price and volume action will often occur before significant price movement.

BAR CHARTS

The most popular method of storing price and volume history in searching for these repetitive patterns is the bar chart. In standard procedure each day (week, month, or year) is represented by one vertical bar on a graph. The bar is drawn to cover the range between the extreme high and low price of the day and a "tick mark" indicates the close. This is illustrated in Figure 7-1, which shows three consecutive days of price action for wheat. Each day is plotted to the right of all preceding days until a record of prices is compiled. Below each price plot on the graph another bar could be drawn to indicate volume of trading for that day.

A number of variations are possible on this standard procedure. Some technicians will graph the close only. A "midrange" price can be entered on the graph, which consists of the high plus the low divided by 2. The opening price can be shown as well. All of these procedures have advantages and disadvantages and each technician must decide which he considers most useful.

As a trader records daily (or weekly) price action, he will begin to observe those patterns that the chartists assume are of a recurring vari-

[3] William Peter Hamilton, *The Stock Market Barometer*, Harper & Brothers, New York, 1922. Hamilton explained in some detail the kind of reasoning he used in his deductions. Hamilton's exposition of the basic premises employed in technical analysis remains one of the best available, even after more than half a century.

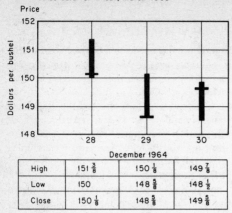

Price data for wheat, March 1965

	December 1964		
High	$151\frac{3}{8}$	$150\frac{1}{8}$	$149\frac{7}{8}$
Low	150	$148\frac{5}{8}$	$148\frac{1}{2}$
Close	$150\frac{1}{8}$	$148\frac{5}{8}$	$149\frac{5}{8}$

FIG. 7-1 Constructing a bar chart. (*Guide to Commodity Price Forecasting*, Commodity Research Bureau, New York, 1965.)

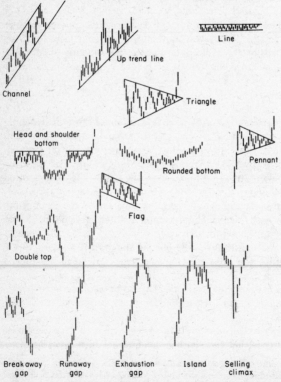

FIG. 7-2 Typical chart patterns. The mirror image of most of these patterns has an opposite implication.

ety.[4,5] Figure 7-2 illustrates a number of patterns that have been well publicized. The price action of May soybeans in Figure 7-3 reveals how these and other popular patterns may be noted and used by a trader. A, B, and C may be said to form a "head-and-shoulders" top, which is completed during the first week of December. Following classical lore, measuring from the head B to D on the "neckline" indicates a minimum objective of 10 cents below the "breakout" at E, or $2.14. F illustrates an "exhaustion gap" and H shows the "resistance" met by the 10-cent rally from G as prices "pull back" into the "left shoulder" (A) area. I represents a "double bottom" which takes 11 weeks to form before supporting a 7-cent rally to J. Throughout this entire time "trendline" T1/T2 is drawn across three important tops and is used as a benchmark to indicate the development of the downtrend, as well as possibly helping to time its ending.[6]

It should be clear from this brief discussion that the field of bar charting could be discussed in great detail. Because of a multitude of alleged patterns, quite an extensive vocabulary has been developed to describe all manner of price-action phenomena.

POINT AND FIGURE CHARTS

The point and figure chartist makes two assumptions that the bar chartist does not. First, he views the volume of trading as unimportant, a mere side-effect of price action with no predictive significance. Second, he dismisses the importance of how much time has elapsed as price moves from one level to another. Only one thing matters and that is the direction of price change. Point and figure charts are constructed to show the direction of price change and nothing else.

Figure 7-4 illustrates a typical point and figure chart for cocoa. The chartist had decided in advance that he wants to characterize every fluctuation of 20 points or more and has scaled the chart accordingly. Each box on the graph equals 20 points.

If the price of cocoa rises by 20 points, an "X" is used to indicate the price change. As long as the price of cocoa continues to rise, new "Xs" will

[4] Edwards and Magee, loc cit. This work is the definitive source of information on chart patterns and their analysis. Another work is William Jiler, How Charts Can Help You in the Stock Market, Commodity Research Publications Corp., New York, 1961.

[5] Two out-of-print works which detail methods of technical analysis using price charts are Richard W. Schabacker, Technical Analysis and Stock Market Profits, B. C. Forbes Publishing Co., New York, 1934, and Robert Rhea, The Dow Theory, Vail-Ballou Press, Binghamton, N.Y., 1932. Both books can be found in many big-city libraries. More modern publications will overlap all or most of their content, but these books are based on original research.

[6] A strong exponent of using charts to trade commodities, and one who believes in paying special attention to "measuring implications" of price patterns, is Houston Cox, A Common Sense Approach to Commodity Trading, Reynolds & Co., New York, 1968. A slightly revised edition of this book, Concepts on Profits in Commodities, was published in 1972.

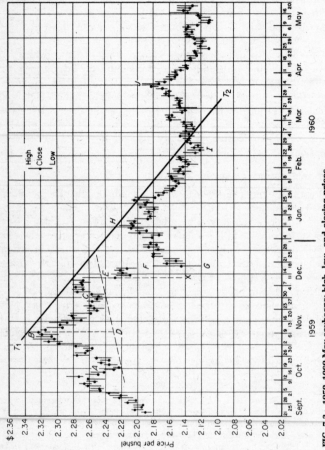

FIG. 7-3 1959–1960 May soybeans: high, low, and closing prices.

be entered on top of those preceding, one for each 20 points of rise. If the price of cocoa rises 3 cents (300 points) with no interruption of as many as 20 points, 15 "Xs" would be placed on top of one another in the same column. This would continue until the price drops by the minimum amount decided on previously, in this case 20 points. Once this happens, an "O"[7] is placed in the column to the right. Each additional 20-point drop causes an "O" to be placed below the preceding "O" as long as the price continues down with no 20-point interruption. When a 20-point rise finally occurs, an "X" is placed in the next column to the right, and the sequence continues as changes in the prices dictate.

The P & F chart is a record of price reversals with no reference to time. For comparison purposes a weekly chart of cocoa for the same period is shown in the lower half of Figure 7-4. The closing price each week is blacked in on the chart to make the comparison easier. Clearly, the more often cocoa reverses direction by 20 points, the more vertical columns are used up.[8]

Any amount of price fluctuation can be shown on a point and figure chart. A chartist with an extremely short-term orientation could, if he had access to successive prices during the day, construct a chart to show reversals of the minimum fluctuation of 1 point. A single day's action might use up scores of columns. On the other hand, another trader interested in a long-run view of cocoa, might construct a chart to show reversals of no less than 300 points. With such a large unit of reversal, a considerable history of price fluctuation could be compacted onto a small chart.

Despite their unique construction, point and figure charts are used much like bar charts.[9, 10] Figure 7-5 illustrates many of the popular bar-chart patterns in a point and figure format. The most important difference in claims made for these two methods of charting, and perhaps the only substantive difference, is that many chartists believe that the *extent* of future price moves can be predicted by using point and figure charts. This is accomplished by a consideration of what is known as "the count."

In its simplest form the count is the number of squares across an area of lateral movement on a point and figure chart. Chartists who use the count believe that a direct relation exists between how many squares are used up during a lateral movement and the size of a subsequent rise or fall out of

[7] Some technicians will use an "X" in both up and down columns of price movement.

[8] The two standard works on the interpretation of point and figure charts are Alexander Wheelan, *Study Helps in Point and Figure Technique,* Morgan, Rogers and Roberts, New York, 1962, and A. W. Cohen, *The Chartcraft Method of Point & Figure Trading,* Chartcraft, Larchmont, N.Y., 1960.

[9] The first published work on point and figure charts is Victor DeVillers, *The Point & Figure Method of Anticipating Stock Price Movements,* printed by Traders Press, New York, 1972. This book shows how importantly DeVillers was influenced by the Dow theory and other classical technical concepts.

[10] An exceptionally intricate theoretical rationale of the use of point and figure charting is presented in John W. Schulz, *The Intelligent Chartist,* WRSM Financial Service Corp., New York, 1962.

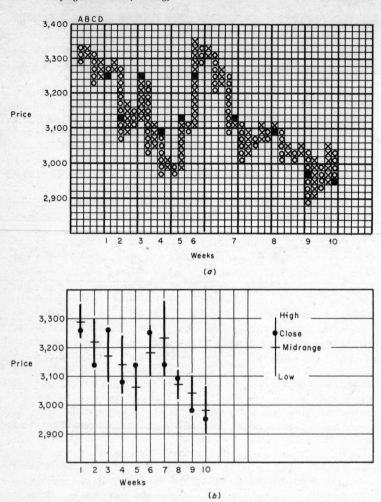

FIG. 7-4   Point-and-figure chart versus bar chart. (a) Point-and-figure chart for a 10-week period in cocoa: each X or O represents a change of 20 points; (b) bar chart for cocoa covering the same 10 weeks as (a).

this congestion area. There are several variations on precisely how to use the count to project the extent of the future move.[11]

---

[11] Wheelan, *loc. cit.*, Cohen, *loc. cit.*, and Schulz, *loc. cit.*, all present several variations of "the count" in point and figure charts. An ardent point and figure chartist who believes the projection of price targets to be a worthless pastime is James Dines, *How the Average Investor Can Use Technical Analysis for Stock Profits*, Dines Chart Corp., New York, 1972. Dine's book contains several variations on basic point and figure techniques.

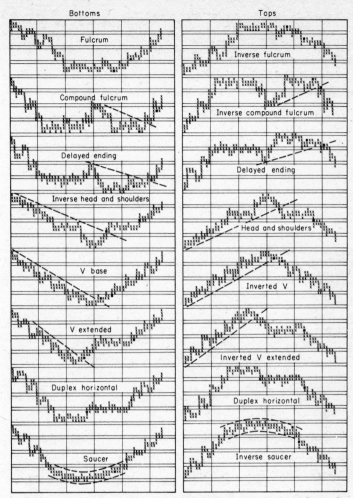

FIG. 7-5 Examples of patterns of point-and-figure charts. (*Guide to Commodity Price Forecasting,* Commodity Research Bureau, New York, 1965.)

OLD-TIME PRICE PATTERNS

In many old books and courses considerable space is devoted to the observations of "veteran traders" who have detailed simple price patterns that allegedly have predictive significance. Although these principles of chart reading fell into obscurity for many years, a recent flood of reprints of these old works has led to renewed interest.[12] Possibly the reason these patterns are largely ignored in modern publications is that invariably they are presented with no accompanying rationale and are described as being short-term in nature.

An example will illustrate one bit of market folklore: the "stair-step" principle. To put this principle into operation the following elements must be present:

1. A rise in price of at least three upward waves and two downward waves, working steadily higher.

2. The bottom of each downward wave is below the top of the preceding upward wave.

3. When the bottom of the last downward wave is penetrated, the principle says, "when the last step is broken, all will be broken."

Figure 7-6, which shows a daily chart of May soybeans, is a real-world example.

It is worth noting that many of these old-time patterns are described in far more objective and explicit terms than their modern counterparts.

STRIKING THE BALANCE—ADVANTAGES AND DISADVANTAGES OF USING PRICE PATTERNS IN TRADING

The advantages. (a) The trader does not even have to prepare charts. Many services sell up-to-date charts for modest prices, and some brokerage houses will even supply them gratis. (b) It cannot be denied that successful analysts, past and present, have used price-pattern concepts successfully. Although studies[13] on the accuracy of chartists' forecasting have yielded disappointing results, they have also unearthed the occasional practitioner who has achieved substantially nonrandom results over a long period of time. Individuals making successful forecasts from this kind of analysis are not unknown, though they are, admittedly, few. (c) Even if the use of any specific price patterns for forecasting purposes is considered unacceptable, it is nevertheless true that a study of price charts can reveal information about market action that may assist the trader in making a decision; for instance, a trader contemplating purchase of two different commodities might well use a different operating plan in a commodity whose chart showed a steady descent to ever lower levels, as opposed to another whose chart showed prices soaring to record highs.

The disadvantages. (a) The use of most chart patterns has been widely publicized in the last several years. Many traders are quite familiar with these patterns and often act on them in concert. This creates a "self-ful-

[12] Some extensive and detailed old works with interesting technical methods are the several courses written by Mark and Jared Pickell, Ralph Ainsworth, Burton Pugh, and W. D. Gann. These courses have long been out of print and can be picked up only occasionally through such specialty dealers as Allan C. Davis, 1617 Linner Road, Wayzata, Minn. 55391, and James Fraser, 283 S. Union Street, Burlington, Vt., who maintain sizable inventories of books and courses on speculation.

[13] Alfred W. Cowles, "Can Stock Market Forecasters Forecast?," *Econometrica*, 1 (1933), 309–324, and Daniel Seligman, "The Mystique of Point & Figure," *Fortune* (March 1962). These studies do not increase the prestige of chartists or price forecasters in general.

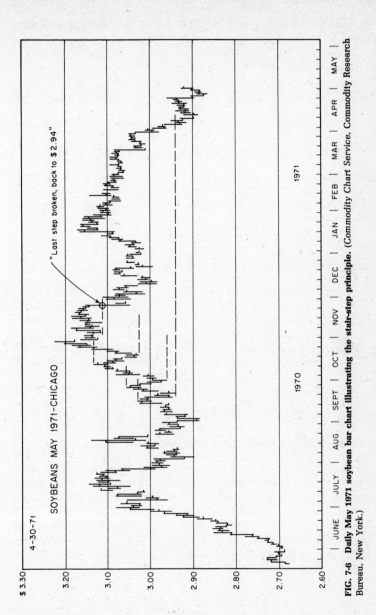

FIG. 7-6 Daily May 1971 soybean bar chart illustrating the stair-step principle. *(Commodity Chart Service, Commodity Research Bureau, New York.)*

filling prophecy," as waves of buying or selling are created in response to "bullish" or "bearish" patterns. After this chartist buying or selling is exhausted prices will very often reverse direction to create vicious "chart traps." Just as positive or negative fundamental information can be discounted in the prices, so can positive or negative technical information be discounted. (b) Chart patterns are almost completely subjective. No study has yet succeeded in mathematically quantifying any of them. They are literally in the mind of the beholder. This subjective element makes it impossible to put any of them to an objective test to see how they have worked in the past. (c) The few analyses done to date of the records of the chartists themselves have not been encouraging. Chart-oriented advisers have, in almost all cases, given advice that was no better than random. Even with the few who have distinguished themselves, there is no evidence their success rests solely in chart reading. It is safe to assume that whatever predictive value there may be in price patterns is not easily comprehended.[14]

TREND-FOLLOWING METHODS

Isaac Newton can be given credit for probably the best-known assumption on which most technicians operate: "A price trend once established is more likely to continue than to reverse." This is simply a restatement of Newton's first law of motion, applied to price action. If this concept is accepted as true, then a successful trading strategy can be built on the simple principle of buying strength and selling weakness. The only problem remaining is the optimum way in which to carry it out.

MOVING AVERAGES

An average is defined as "the quotient of any sum divided by the number of its terms." Thus a 10-day average of soybean closing prices is the sum of the last 10 days' closings divided by 10. A moving average of prices is a progressive average in which the divisor number of items remains the same, but at periodic intervals (usually daily or weekly) a new item is added to the end of the series as, simultaneously, an item is dropped from the beginning.

If one is constructing a 10-day moving average of soybean closes, the average on the tenth day is the sum of days 1 through 10 divided by 10. On the eleventh day the eleventh day's close is added to the total and the close of day 1 is subtracted. This new sum is then divided by 10. On day 12 the close of that day is added to the total and the close of day 2 is subtracted. This total is divided by 10 and so on. Table 7-1 illustrates the com-

---

[14] *Ibid.* Seligman's study unearthed one point and figure chartist whose results over a long period were exceptionally good and much better than chance alone would indicate. Nonetheless, it was obvious that this chartist used many other factors than charts in achieving this result. For a cynical view of any successful trader see Fred Schwed, Jr., *Where Are the Customers' Yachts*, John Magee, Inc., Springfield, Mass., 1955, Space Age Edition, in the chapter entitled, "A Brief Excursion into Probabilities."

TABLE 7-1   COMPUTATION OF A 10-DAY
MOVING AVERAGE FOR A TYPICAL MAY
SOYBEANS CONTRACT

Date	Close (in cents)	10-day net change°	10-day total†	10-day average‡
3/15	290.000			
16	291.500			
17	294.000			
3/20	290.500			
21	291.500			
22	300.500			
23	304.000			
24	204.500			
3/27	301.250			
28	305.250	. . . .	2973.000	297.30
29	297.750	+7.750	2980.750	298.08
30	300.250	+8.750	2989.500	298.95
4/3	300.500	+6.500	2996.000	299.60
4	299.750	+9.250	3005.250	300.53
5	302.250	+10.750	3016.000	301.60

° Difference (plus or minus) between latest close and the
tenth close, counting back.
† Sum of 10 latest closes.
‡ The 10-day-total column divided by 10. These figures in
sequence make up the moving average.

putation of a 10-day moving average based on the closing prices of May
1961 soybeans.

Figure 7-7 shows a 10-week moving average of soybean closes. An examination of this chart will point out the important properties of moving
averages. The 10-week moving average smooths out the erratic week-to-
week changes in actual prices and thereby indicates the underlying trend.
Further, the moving average lags behind prices and crosses the current
price only when a new direction is established. These same properties are
characteristic of moving averages calculated for any time span.

Shown on the chart are "buy" and "sell" signals, given when price penetrates the 10-week moving average. The technician acting on this signal is
following the strategy of buying strength and selling weakness. He hopes
that the prevailing trend, like the buy signal of late 1953, will continue
long enough—and powerfully enough—to compensate adequately for the
kind of whipsaw losses that resulted from the first two signals of 1952.

There are countless systems that use moving averages,[15,16] but all are
based on variations of just two factors:

[15] A number of moving average systems are presented in the following works: C. W. Kelt-
ner, *How to Make Money In Commodities,* Keltner Statistical Service, Kansas City, Mo., 1960;
Garfield Drew, *New Methods for Profit In The Stock Market,* Metcalf Press, Boston, Mass.,
1955; Curtiss Dahl, *Consistent Profits In The Commodity Futures Market,* Tri-State Offset
Co., Cincinnati, Ohio, 1960, with 1961 addendum; Irving Levine, *Successful Commodity
Speculation,* Levro Press, Newark, N.J., 1965; Robert Joel Taylor, "The Major Price Trend
Directional Indicator," *Commodities Magazine* (April 1972). Dunn & Hargitt, P.O. Box

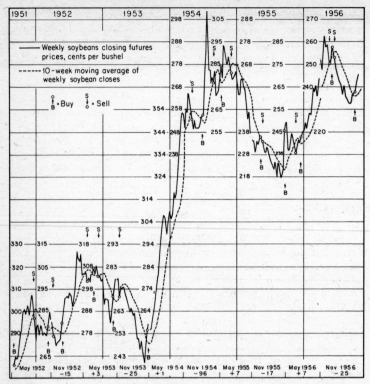

FIG. 7-7 Weekly May and November soybeans, weekly closing price versus 10-week moving average. Prices of contracts adjusted to each other for continuity. (*Guide to Commodity Price Forecasting*, Commodity Research Bureau, New York, 1965.)

1. The length of time used in computing the moving average. It is here that an important trade-off is involved. The shorter the length of time, the more sensitive the moving average will be to any change in trend. New trends will be acted on earlier and do not need much time to establish themselves. The trader pays for this sensitivity because the shorter the moving average's length, the greater the number of trades that will be made. This means greater commissions and a larger number of whipsaw losses. A longer period of time used to calculate the moving average will

---

101, Lafayette, Ind., 47902, sell a computerized study of hypothetical trading in several commodities for a number of years in which most of the best-known moving average trading systems are used.

[16] An increasingly popular form of moving average is one that has been "exponentially smoothed." It is doubtful if exponential smoothing is an important improvement on the standard calculation of moving averages. One source on this as well as other smoothing methods is Robert Brown, *Smoothing, Forecasting & Prediction of Discrete Time Series*, Prentice-Hall, Englewood Cliffs, N.J., 1963. Brown's book particularly stresses the "how-to" aspect of smoothing procedures.

reduce the number of trades and the number of whipsaw losses but will signal new trends much later—often so late that the trend will be closer to completion than initiation.

2. The kind and amount of penetration required. In an effort to reduce false signals, many technicians demand more than just a simple penetration of the moving average; for instance, having the price in Figure 7-7 penetrate the moving average by 5 cents before acting on any signal would eliminate several whipsaws. This strategy, however, is subject to the same limitations described above. Too small an amount of penetration does little to reduce whipsaws and excess trades. Too large a penetration has the effect of cutting down profits on successful signals. The trader is referred to Chapter 4, in which many competent academic studies using several moving-average decision rules are discussed in some detail.

SWING CHARTS

Swing charts provide many of the trend-following properties of moving averages but they are usually easier to calculate. Swing charts are similar to point and figure charts because the trader is interested in price movements of a certain minimum amount. Figure 7-8 is a chart of July 1971 platinum constructed by drawing in only those swings of 300 points or more. The key difference between the swing chart and a point and figure chart covering the same time period is that the swing chart shows the precise highs and lows and a point and figure chart is likely to show them to the nearest 20 or 50 points.

To carry out the basic trend-following strategy of buying strength and selling weakness the trader buys when the top of a previous swing is penetrated on the upside and sells when the bottom of a previous swing is penetrated on the downside. These signals are shown on the chart.

The theory behind swing charting is that tops and bottoms in price become "important" if they are terminations of swings of some minimum amount. If they are later penetrated, a new trend is presumed to be in force. The trader who employs swing charts is following the age-old dictum to "take positions along the line of least resistance."

Any swing-charting method[17] is composed of just two elements: (a) The amount of the minimum swing to be charted and (b) The amount and type of penetration required when price penetrates a previous top or bottom. The same trade-off occurs here that occurs with moving average methods. The smaller the amount of penetration required, the more quickly new trends are signaled and the more whipsaws that result. A larger required price penetration reduces whipsaws, but also puts the trader in later on the more successful signals. The choice of the amount of minimum price

---

[17]Keltner, loc. cit.; Wm. Dunnigan, New Blueprints For Gains In Stocks and Grains, privately published, San Francisco, Calif., 1956 (out-of-print but available from various specialty dealers), and Richard Donchian, "Trend Following Methods in Commodity Price Analysis" in Guide To Commodity Price Forecasting, Commodity Research Bureau, New York, 1965, are comprehensive sources of information on swing charting, as well as moving average and other trend following techniques.

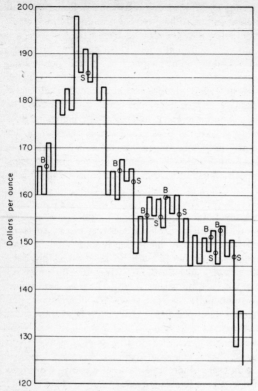

FIG. 7-8   July 1971 platinum, 300-point swing chart. Buy and sell signals shown for February–October 1971.

swing charted is analogous to the choice of the number of days used for a moving average.

Some technicians have constructed swing charts based not on price but on time.[18] Tops or bottoms that hold for some arbitrary number of days (or weeks) are defined as important. When they are penetrated, "buy" or "sell" signals are generated. The choice of the length of time during which a top or bottom must stand, and the amount and type of penetration required, makes this kind of chart subject to the same limitations of standard swing charts.

[18] W. D. Gann, *How To Make Profits Trading In Commodities*, Lambert-Gann Publishing Co., Miami, Fla., 1951, revised edition (out-of-print but found in many big-city libraries) was probably the originator of this kind of swing chart. Gann covers the subject in more detail in many of his commodity trading courses cited elsewhere. A time factor is also used by many moving average devotees; instead of requiring price to penetrate the moving average by a certain amount, the trader requires price to penetrate and then stay beyond the moving average by a certain number of days.

A mathematical technique highly analogous to swing charting is the use of "filters." This approach was discussed in detail in Chapter 4, where the results of several studies based on various filter rules were presented.

STRIKING THE BALANCE—ADVANTAGES AND DISADVANTAGES OF USING TREND-FOLLOWING METHODS

The advantages. (a) A trend-following technique is, by definition, objective. All the elements must be clearly defined before it can be put into practice. This means that a trader can, if he has the facilities, determine how well any technique has worked in the past and define its important characteristics. Any number of variations can be back-checked in an attempt to optimize results. (b) Any trend-following method provides the trader with a sizable part of his operating plan, with all of the attendant benefits in terms of results and peace of mind. Because his action points are so clearly defined, the trader is not so likely to be beset by uncertainties. (c) The trend follower believes, along with many famous traders, that "the big swing makes the big money." By employing any trend-following method it is impossible for a big move to occur without his participating in it.

The disadvantages. (a) The trader who uses a trend-following method begins with two counts against him. First, whipsaws are inevitable. One technician, himself an ardent trend-following advocate, indicates that 50 percent of all trades entered into by any such method will result in whipsaw losses.[19] Second, all signals acted on are late by definition. To compensate for these two liabilities, the trader must realize substantial profits on the successful signals, and even during a normally active market this may be difficult to achieve. (b) A commodity moving within a trading range will provide the trend follower with seemingly endless losses until a major trend is initiated. As long as there is no pronounced bias to the up or the down side, long positions will be taken on strength near the top of the range and short positions will be assumed on weakness near the bottom. Some cursory studies have indicated that commodity prices are without important trending characteristics as much as 85 percent of the time.[20] If true, this consideration may present a formidable obstacle. (c) Optimum rules established for a trend-following method during one period of time may result in a poor performance during another; for example, appropriate rules for a moving average system for trading 1960 world sugar, which had a range for the entire year of less than 100 points, would certainly not have been appropriate for that same commodity three years

[19] Donchian, *loc. cit.*

[20] This statement is made by John R. Hill in his course *Technical and Mathematical Analysis of the Commodity and Stock Markets,* Commodity Research Institute, 141 West Jackson, Room 855, Chicago, Ill. 60604, 1971. Most of the course is concerned with the presentation of graphical trading methods which assume that futures prices are usually without important trending characteristics. Such methods are antithetical to those used by a trend follower.

later. In 1963 world sugar had a range of more than 900 points, and often had a two-day range exceeding 100 points. To be used at all successfully, the elements of any trend-following method must be adjusted to both current and predicted volatility. The trader must be certain that his rules are not out of date for each commodity he is following.[21]

CHARACTER-OF-MARKET ANALYSIS

The trader using character-of-market methods operates on premises completely different from those of the chartist or trend follower, both of whom have constructed a number of techniques based on the interpretation of price action. Those technicians who employ a character-of-market approach believe that a deceptive veneer has been painted over the true picture of supply and demand.

The character-of-market analyst seeks statistical measurements of supply and demand that are independent of price or at least uses price information much more subtly than the chartist or trend follower. The important question asked by those traders who use this approach to technical analysis is, "What is the *quality* of a given move in price?" The trader then tries to commit his capital in line with price movements of good quality and to avoid, or even take an opposite position to, movements of poor quality.

As noted before, the technician has only three series of trading data to work with: price, volume, and open interest. Nevertheless, so many combinations and permutations of these data have been employed in character-of-market methods that it is possible here to touch only on the most illustrative and basic.

OSCILLATORS

The term "oscillator" is given to a family of technical indicators based on measurement of price changes rather than price levels. The simplest type of oscillator is based upon the distance the price of a commodity has traveled over a given period of time; for example, a 10-day oscillator is constructed by taking the price on the latest day and subtracting the price of the tenth trading day previous. The number obtained is either positive or negative, depending on whether the commodity has risen or fallen in the last 10 days. The same procedure is followed during subsequent trading days.

The calculation of oscillators has often been carried to surprising complexity.[22] Some oscillators are specially smoothed, some are weighted,

---

[21] Cox, *loc. cit.*, presents a moving average method that to some extent does adjust to current price volatility. A simpler, but similar, procedure is presented by Levine, *loc. cit.* Taylor, *loc. cit.*, adjusts the length of the moving average in relation to current volatility.

[22] A potpourri of oscillator calculation and interpretation is to be found in the following: many special studies in the "Indicator Digest" Advisory Service, Palisades Park, N.J. 07650, have appeared over the last several years; Drew, *loc. cit.*; Carl W. Floss, *Market Rhythm,* In-

and some are modified in conjunction with one or more additional factors (such as volume). Sometimes all of these options are used. Time periods employed for constructing oscillators can range from two or three days (or even less if the trader has access to intraday data) to several weeks or longer. The use of *any* oscillator, however, rests on one or both of these contentions:

1. A price rise or price decline can become overextended if it gathers too much velocity. If the price of any commodity enjoys an unusual gain that is compacted into a short time span, the presumption is that buying is temporarily exhausted and part of all of the gain will be retraced. Such a market is said to be "overbought." The opposite kind of price action would lead to an "oversold" market. By constructing an oscillator the technician seeks to monitor excessive rates of price change that could lead to exhaustion and subsequent price reversals.

2. A price trend can simply peter out as it steadily loses momentum. In this case a price trend continues but generates less and less energy until it dies. A top is signaled when, for instance, the price continues to make new highs for the move but the oscillator moves from large positive numbers to small positive numbers. The reverse is true for a bottom. Used in this way, an oscillator is a tool for measuring the exhaustion of a price trend.

These two concepts are not mutually exclusive. Figure 7-9 shows the daily action of November 1970 eggs against a 20-day price change oscillator. For this period levels in the oscillator above +300 (meaning that price had advanced more than 300 points in the preceding 20 days) spotlighted markets that were overextended on the upside. Similarly, levels in the oscillator below —300 indicated that price had become oversold.

During this period the penetration of "trendlines," drawn across key tops or bottoms in the oscillator, indicated, exhaustion in the current price trend. In line with this concept of exhaustion, it will also be noted that the oscillator can peak or bottom ahead of price in many instances, thus signaling possible reversal.

STRIKING THE BALANCE—ADVANTAGES AND DISADVANTAGES OF USING THE OSCILLATOR

The advantages. (a) Overbought/oversold signals generated from oscillators will usually work well in trading markets, which occur more frequently than trending markets. If there is no dominant trend, points of upside and downside exhaustion can, in theory at least, be identified with a fair degree of accuracy. (b) Signals of an overbought or oversold market can act as a valuable check on a trader's emotions. No matter how bullish

---

vestors Publishing Co., Detroit, 1955 (out-of-print but available from specialty dealers); James Waters and Larry Williams, "Measuring Market Momentum", *Commodities Magazine* (October 1972), H. M. Gartley, *Profits in the Stock Market,* H. M. Gartley, Inc., New York, 1935 (out-of-print but available from specialty dealers), gives highly detailed instructions on trading with price oscillators and discusses a number of possible predictive relationships mentioned by no other source.

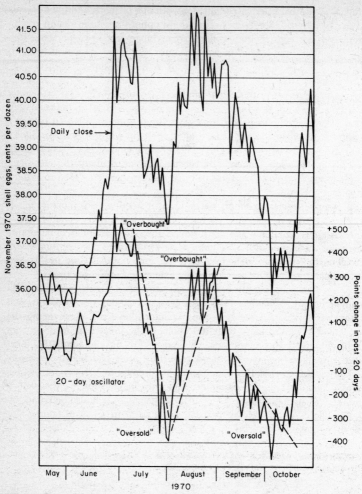

FIG. 7-9 **November 1970 shell eggs daily close versus 20-day net change oscillator for May–October 1970.**

a situation may appear, a high positive reading on the oscillator at the same time could be a sobering influence. The reverse is also true. (c) History is replete with examples of price trends that peaked or troughed, whereas accompanying rate-of-change oscillators showed a clear loss of momentum well in advance.

The disadvantages. (a) Acting on overbought/oversold oscillator signals will lead to financial disaster in any market with a dominant price trend. During a powerful bull or bear swing an oscillator will repeatedly move into "overextended" territory and will often stay there for a long time. This danger cannot be avoided because a trader who could consistently anticipate dominant price trends in advance would not be using an oscillator as a trading device. (b) Zones that represent overbought or oversold markets must be decided on the basis of history. If the commodity being followed suddenly becomes either more or less volatile, whether still in a trading range or not, previously determined zones will be worthless. All commodities do change their volatility over time. (c) Loss of momentum before key tops and bottoms are reached is well documented, but this phenomenon is much easier to see in retrospect. In Figure 7-9 trendlines are drawn on the oscillator itself to determine loss of momentum. These trendlines could have been drawn in many other ways, and several of them would not have yielded satisfactory results. In practice, declining momentum will indicate a pause in the price trend or a reversal, and there is no way to tell which. Using this technique, the analyst can often explain past price action, but he cannot easily predict future price changes.

TRADITIONAL VOLUME AND OPEN-INTEREST METHODS

"Volume" refers simply to the aggregate number of contracts or bushels of commodity futures traded in a given period; it is a measure of the combined futures market supply and demand for that period. "Open interest" is the total purchase or sale commitments outstanding. At any time, the purchase commitments or number of contracts "long" are equal to the sale commitments or number of contracts "short." The different types of trades and their effects on the open interest are listed below. "Old" buyers are those who have outstanding long positions, whereas "old" sellers have outstanding short positions in the market. "New" buyers or sellers are those who are just entering the market to take a long or short position.

Transaction	Effect on open interest
Purchases by old sellers from old buyers	Reduced
Purchases by old sellers from new sellers	Unchanged
Purchases by new buyers from old buyers	Unchanged
Purchases by new buyers from new sellers	Increased
Sales by old buyers to new buyers	Unchanged
Sales by old buyers to old sellers	Reduced
Sales by new sellers to old sellers	Unchanged
Sales by new sellers to new buyers	Increased

The open interest increases only when new purchases are offset by new sales. Decreases in open interest occur only when previous purchases are sold and are offset by the buying in of previously sold contracts. Since it is the effect on open interest that is reported and not the type of transaction, the technician interested in this aspect of market behavior must infer the latter from the former.

Volume and open-interest data are reported daily in newspapers and wire services. They are also printed and distributed at different intervals by the CEA and by various advisory services.[23] Most technicians use the totals for both the volume and open interest of a given commodity rather than the figures for individual contract months.

Significant changes in volume and open interest generally last over a period of a few days to a month. These changes must be related to their respective seasonal patterns before a meaningful analysis may be undertaken. The seasonal changes are substantial for open interest, whereas seasonal changes in volume are not so wide or significant. Illustrations of the seasonal changes in both volume and open interest are presented in Section 5 for several specific commodities.

To illustrate the relevance of seasonal adjustments consider the following example. Suppose the total open interest in all soybean contracts amounts to 125 million bushels on October 15, when the May contract is selling at $2.75 a bushel. By November 15 May soybeans have risen to $2.86 and the open interest for all soybean contracts has increased to 137,500,000 bushels. A quick judgment may conclude that prices have risen 4 percent in the same period that open interest has increased 10 percent. Inspection of the soybean seasonal open interest and volume chart on page 356 indicates that the seasonal rise from October 15 to November 15 is 14 percent (from 118 to 132 percent). Although actual open interest increased 10 percent, on a seasonally adjusted basis it has really *decreased* for the period being examined. In order for a net increase of 10 percent to occur, open interest would have had to increase to 155 million bushels by November 15.

Because there is no measurable seasonal pattern for volume, technicians generally compare it to that of the immediate past; for example, if total soybean volume has hovered around 50 million bushels a day and suddenly increases over a period of a week to 75 million bushels, a significant change may be occurring in the psychology of the market.

General rules have been formulated to indicate how significant net changes in open-interest and volume figures may be analyzed in conjunction with price analysis.[24]

The tendencies for volume alone may be summarized as follows:

1. When a major price advance is under way, volume tends to increase on rallies and to decrease on reactions.

2. Conversely, during a major price decline, volume tends to increase on down moves and decrease on rallies.

[23] Edward B. Gotthelf, *The Commodex System,* Commodity Futures Forecast, 90 West Broadway, New York, N. Y. 10007, presents a completely mechanized system that converts traditional price/volume/open interest relationships into daily index numbers interpreted with objective rules. Hamilton, *loc. cit.*; Rhea, *loc. cit.*; Edwards and Magee, *loc. cit.*; Hill, *loc. cit.*, are all sources of interpretation of price/volume relations and generally follow the "Classical" rules of divination. Two more involved procedures for using volume data are "Quinn's Moving Volume Curve", found in Drew, *loc. cit.*, and the *Relative Volume Index* published by Trend Way Advisory Service, P. O. Box 7184, Louisville, Ky. 40207. All but one of these sources refer to analysis of stocks, but the identical principles can be applied to commodities.

[24] An advisory service that places much stress on analysis of open interest and presents rules of interpretation to its readers is John K. Hart, *Commodity Trend Service,* 518 Empire Building, Columbus, Ga. 31901.

3. Volume expands sharply as bottoms and tops are approached.

Open interest, when compared with price action, tends to act in the following ways:

1. If prices advance and open interest advances more sharply than a seasonal analysis would suggest, aggressive new buying would seem to have taken place.

2. If prices advance and seasonally adjusted open interest declines, the advance has been fueled by short covering and might be regarded as technically weak.

3. If prices decline and aggressive new selling is taking place, the market may be considered to be technically weak.

4. If prices decline and open interest decreases beyond seasonal expectations, the decline has been fed by discouraged longs who have liquidated their unprofitable positions, leaving the market relatively strong technically.

A perhaps oversimplified form of some of the relations among volume, open interest and price is sometimes given as follows:

If prices are up and   (a) volume and open interest are up—the market is strong;

(b) volume and open interest are down—the market is weak.

If prices are down and (a) volume and open interest are up—the market is weak;

(b) volume and open interest are down—the market is strong.

The confidence level of such observations has not been statistically measured. One cursory study[24a] found the following:

1. There was some forecasting value in blow-off action at major tops where prices advance sharply on high volume and a sharp drop in open interest.

2. Similarly, after a long decline when prices drop sharply on heavy volume and a sharp drop in open interest, a major bottom is possible.

3. Price moves away from consolidations tend to be greater if the consolidations period was marked by a sharply higher than seasonal buildup in open interest.

STRIKING THE BALANCE—ADVANTAGES AND DISADVANTAGES OF USING TRADITIONAL VOLUME AND OPEN-INTEREST METHODS

The advantages. (a) The basic principles of interpreting volume and open interest appear quite logical. It seems reasonable that the expansion and contraction of volume and open interest compared with price action should yield worthwhile clues to the balance of supply and demand in the market.

[24a] William Jiler, "Volume and Open Interest Analysis as an Aid to Price Forecasting," *Guide to Commodity Price Forecasting,* Commodity Research Bureau, Inc., New York, 1965, pp. 63-64.

(b) The trader following volume and open-interest principles uses a three-dimensional model rather than one of single dimension found in other technical approaches. There are many other ways in which price action can be viewed, and many more shadings can be used to describe bullish or bearish behavior. (c) If the forecasting ability of volume and open interest is denied, there is still a significant amount of information to be obtained by simply monitoring such data. The trader knows which contracts are most active, the size of the market in which he is dealing, and any important properties of trading activity.

The disadvantages. (a) This type of analysis is replete with a number of ill-defined terms: "low volume," "increase in open interest," "decline of greater than seasonal expectation," and several others. To make use of this approach the technician must quantify his terms to avoid meaningless generalities. (b) General rules for volume and open-interest interpretation are well publicized. Application of these classical principles leads to the problem of the "self-fulfilling prophecy" discussed among the disadvantages of using price patterns. Volume and open-interest behavior which is clearly bullish or bearish can be discounted in the present price level as easily as other more familiar supply-demand factors. (c) The validity of these standard principles rests on unproved assertion. No publicly available studies that use volume and open-interest decision rules confirm their value in actual trading.

ON BALANCE VOLUME

The bulk of character-of-market analysis originates from the belief that "big-moneyed" traders consistently take positions prior to substantial price moves in any commodity. The "big money" is seen, for instance, as surreptitiously acquiring sizable long positions before price advances, well ahead of the "ignorant masses." This quiet buying is known as "accumulation." When these same interests are selling their longs and going short at the top of a rise, before a large decline, their activity is called "distribution." Tracking the supposed clandestine flow of accumulation and distribution has led to the growth of countless technical methods over the years.

An old approach to measuring accumulation and distribution by the action of price and volume, which has enjoyed a popular renaissance since the early 1960s[25] is currently known as "on balance volume," or OBV. Easily calculated and graphed, OBV attempts to provide information on the quality of price movements by yielding a volume curve that can be compared directly with the price curve.

Table 7-2 illustrates a hypothetical OBV calculation. Each day's closing price is compared with the closing price of the preceding day. If the latest day has a higher closing price, *all* the volume of trading that day is assigned

[25] Joseph Granville, *Granville's New Key to Stock Market Profits,* Prentice-Hall, Englewood Cliffs, N.J., 1963, has popularized this approach in recent years.

TABLE 7-2   COMPUTATION OF ON-BALANCE VOLUME

Date	May cocoa daily closing price	Volume (number of contracts)	OBV (cumulative volume)
March 1	27.09	—	—
2	27.15	+3,000	+3,000
3	27.22	+2,500	+5,500
4	27.07	− 800	+4,700
5	26.85	−1,200	+3,500
8	27.01	+2,500	+6,000

a plus sign. If the latest day's close is lower than that of the preceding day, all the volume is assigned a minus sign. These daily plus
and minus volume figures are added to a cumulative running total.
This cumulative total is the OBV. The absolute level of the OBV
curve is of no significance; the technician is interested only in the
contour of this curve when it is compared with the contour of price,
either graphically or in tabulated form.

The dominant theory behind OBV, as previously noted, assumes that
large-scale accumulation or distribution can take place in the market. Because this activity would have to be done quietly, it is further assumed that
worthwhile accumulation or distribution is carried out under cover of small
net or deceptive price changes. The OBV curve is believed to illustrate the
true state of affairs by showing whether volume of trading is highest during
periods of rising or falling prices. When the bias in volume deviates significantly from the price curve, unusual activity is presumed to be taking
place.

Under normal circumstances the OBV curve will move parallel to the
price of the commodity under surveillance. As long as this relationship remains the trader using OBV will have no particular interest. However,
when the OBV curve begins to diverge from price, notice is taken because
many analysts believe that such divergence indicates accumulation or distribution. In Table 7-2, for instance, the price of cocoa dropped a nominal
eight points between March 1 and March 8. Yet the OBV record shows
that 6,000 more contracts changed hands on days of rising price than of
falling price. If this kind of behavior continued for a significant period of
time, the technician would conclude that cocoa was being intensively accumulated. Moneyed interests would be presumed to be buying heavily,
putting prices up for a day or so before quietly allowing them to drop on
low activity until they moved again into a satisfactory buying area. In
theory, this process would continue until accumulation was completed.
Prices would then move much higher as the "big money's" analysis was
proved correct and the "crowd" began to act on the now favorable news
developments affecting cocoa.

Figure 7-10 illustrates an actual example in which a daily OBV analysis
spotlighted an impending break in pork bellies. During the period labeled
"1" in late May 1967 prices moved to their final high above 43 cents while

several thousand more contracts changed hands at lower prices than changed hands at higher prices. The OBV curve peaked 16 days before the price. Again in late June during the period labeled "2" a 300-point rally hoisted prices well above the early June highs but left the OBV seriously lagging. These two marked divergences, presumably showing strong distribution, were followed by a sharp and sustained break in the market.

There are more sophisticated, and complicated, ways to calculate and use OBV,[26] but the basic principle of interpretation remains the same.

STRIKING THE BALANCE—ADVANTAGES AND DISADVANTAGES OF USING OBV

The advantages. (a) If there is, in fact, important money from intelligent sources that quietly assumes positions in advance of large price moves or if such substantial buying or selling takes place for any reason, it cannot help but leave a record in daily transactions. OBV pinpoints periods in which a substantial excess of volume takes place at higher or lower prices, thus giving the technician a "lead" for further study. (b) Whatever interpretation is used, OBV gives the analyst information with which to quantify the volume of any price move. Even if the trader is not looking for "signals" per se, the knowledge that the largest volume occurs on rising or falling prices, and how it compares with price, can be helpful in appraising market action.

The disadvantages. (a) Research to date indicates that the profit-making ability of the large trader is impressive.[27] These studies have shown that large traders succeed mainly by trading *short-run* price fluctuations. Such conclusions do not support the relatively longer term accumulation/distribution thesis on which much of OBV analysis rests. (b) No objective rules of interpretation have ever been presented by advocates of OBV,[28] thus ensuring the impossibility of performing any tests that would determine whether the use of OBV would lead to nonrandom trading results. (c) On theoretical grounds the calculation of the most commonly used form of OBV is open to serious question. Each day's price change is determined by transactions on both the buying and selling side, and it does not seem reasonable to assign *all* the volume to the plus or minus side simply because the close one day is higher or lower than the close of the preceding day. If pork bellies, for example, were up 130 points during the day but closed down 5 points,

[26] David L. Markstein, *How To Chart Your Way to Stock Market Profits*, Parker Publishing Co., West Nyack, N.Y., 1966, advocates multiplying the amount of price change by the volume of trading. R. F. Martel, *Charting Supply and Demand for Stock Analysis*, Martel & Co., 1505 Old Mill Road, Reading, Pa. 19610, presented a system in 1972 that also attempts to quantify price/volume activity by means of a highly modified OBV curve.

[27] C. S. Rockwell, "Normal Backwardation, Forecasting, and the Returns to Speculators," *Food Research Institute Studies*, Supplement, 7 (1967), 107–130.

[28] Granville, *loc. cit.*, presented many objective collateral OBV calculations but failed to present a completely quantifiable set of decision-making rules.

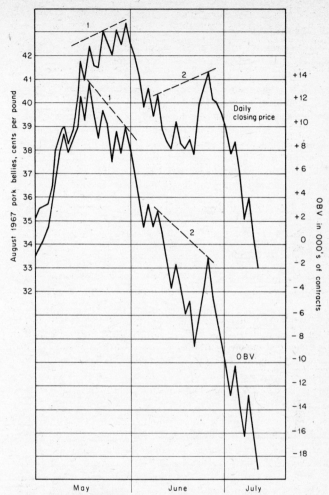

FIG. 7-10   August 1967 pork bellies daily close versus daily on-balance volume (OBV) for May–July 1967.

it would not seem proper to assign all of the volume that day to the minus side. Calculation of basic OBV may be too simplistic.[29]

[29] Two attempts to weight OBV more precisely in accordance with intraday price activity are David Bostian, *Intra-Day Intensity Index,* privately printed, Fort Benjamin Harrison, Indiana, 1967, and Larry Williams, *The Secret of Selecting Stocks for Immediate and Substantial Gains,* Conceptual Management, Carmel Valley, Calif., 1973. These two variations are also open to criticism on theoretical grounds.

ARMCHAIR TAPE READING

In the late 19th century, when "pools" manipulated the stock and commodity markets, tape readers attempted to monitor the flow of "inside money." They would watch every transaction on the tape and note the price and volume. If the tape reader were shrewd enough, he might be able to deduce the action being taken by the pool and follow its lead.[30]

An important element of tape reading consisted of paying special attention to large blocks that appeared on the tape, as these were presumed to be the actual transactions of the pool. In later years, with the pools but a memory, the analysis of large transactions is still an integral part of tape reading. The tape-reading technician believes that large transactions, by their very nature, represent important and far-seeing money.

Some years ago a method was published[31] that enables a trader to "read the tape by proxy." It was designed solely to indicate when large transactions are appearing on the tape and thereby to provide a lead for further study. It is not presented here as a complete or proved indicator.

Each day the trader calculates a "resistance index" in the following way:

$$\frac{(\text{number of contracts traded})}{(\text{high price})-(\text{low price})}$$

This ratio measures the number of contracts that changed hands in relation to the range for the day. When the ratio is unusually large, it may be presumed that unusually large transactions are crossing the tape. High ratios do not occur often, but they do stand out as "spikes" on the chart.

Figure 7-11 shows the daily closing prices of June 1971 live hogs graphed with a daily resistance index. The three figures greater than 60 (meaning that 60 or more contracts changed hands per point of range in price) are numbered 1, 2, and 3. All three of these high index days came close to advantageous buying or selling areas. Whether these days with unusually large tape transactions actually saw informed money taking a position in the market before a price reversal is an open question.

There is no question, however, that this technique can only be subjective and could not be used effectively without information from other sources or methods. Furthermore, price action and volume varies greatly over time. A large resistance index during one period may not be significant in another span of time, thus adding yet another interpretative problem.

[30] Humphrey Neill, *Tape Reading and Market Tactics,* reprinted by Fraser Publishing Co., Wells, Vt., 1960, and Richard Wyckoff, *Studies in Tape Reading,* reprinted by Traders Press, New York, 1972, are sources of detailed instruction on tape reading. Edwin LeFevre, *Reminiscences of a Stock Operator,* reprinted by the American Research Council, New York, 1964, provides a number of absorbing insights into tape reading from the legendary Jesse Livermore.

[31] Edwin H. Tomkins, *Systematic Stock Trading,* The Moore Guide, P. O. Box 42, Riverside, Ill. 60546, contains a complete discussion of his "resistance index." The author also discusses tape reading and short-term trading techniques.

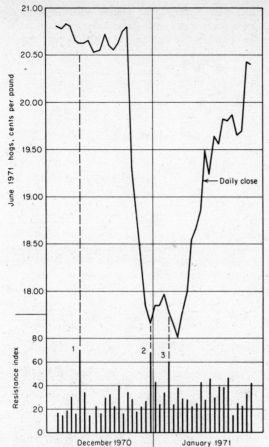

FIG. 7-11   June 1971 live hogs daily close versus daily resistance
index for December 1970–January 1971.

ANALYSIS OF OPEN INTEREST TO DETERMINE
ACTIVITIES OF LARGE AND SMALL TRADERS

Another way to measure accumulation and distribution is the proposal
made by many technical analysts to differentiate between "smart money"
and "stupid money." Those making this differentiation believe that there
are, essentially, two categories of traders: winners and losers; for example, in the stock market, exchange specialists have often been identified as a winning group and odd-lotters as a losing group. Techniques

long in use with these and other series can be applied to commodities as well.[32] This approach attempts to focus on data showing the activities of winning and losing groups of traders and then suggests the following action:

1. Initiate positions opposite those of the losing group when it shows a strong preference for one side of the market.

2. Initiate positions in line with those of the winning group when it shows a strong preference for one side of the market.

Twice monthly the U.S. Government[33] provides a breakdown of the open interest in all regulated commodities. Both long and short positions are tabulated for three groups: bona fide hedgers, large traders with legally reportable positions, and the remaining portion of open interest which consists of small traders with less than a reportable position. If it can be assumed that generally large traders are winners and small traders are losers over a reasonable period of time, it is possible to construct a number of technical indicators that might delineate the actions of these groups.[34]

Figure 7-12 illustrates one of many gauges that could be constructed to measure the activity of large traders. The closing prices of December 1969 cattle are plotted at two-week intervals against a ratio that measures large trader short positions as a percentage of the total open interest. When large trader short positions are "low," on this chart below 6 percent, it might be assumed that they are strongly biased to the bullish side of the market and prices therefore should rise. When they are "high," 9 percent or higher on this chart, an important degree of pessimism would be indicated and lower prices expected to follow.

It is surprising that although similar procedures have long been used to analyze stock prices and regular breakdowns of open interest have been supplied since 1923 this area of technical analysis has attracted almost no attention in the commodity field.

Because the total open interest is divided into six constituent parts, a great number of ratios and/or oscillators can be derived between these

---

[32] In-depth discussions of techniques for handling odd-lot trading data are found in Drew, *loc. cit.*; Garfield Drew, "A Clarification of the Odd-Lot Theory," *Financial Analysts Journal* (September–October 1967); Thomas J. Kewley and R. A. Stevenson, "The Odd-Lot Theory-A Reply," *Financial Analysts Journal* (January–February 1969); Stanley Kaish, "Odd Lot Profit and Loss Performance," *Financial Analysts Journal* (September–October 1969). Expositions of techniques for handling both specialist and odd-lot data are found in Indicator Digest, *loc. cit.*; Walter Heiby, *Stock Market Profits Through Dynamic Synthesis,* Institute of Dynamic Synthesis, Chicago, Ill., 1965 (a supplement to this book, explaining new techniques, "The New Dynamic Synthesis," was published in 1967); William X. Scheinman, *Why Most Investors Are Mostly Wrong Most of The Time,* Lancer Books, New York, 1970.

[33] Periodic report on open interest are available from the Commodity Futures Trading Commission. Different regional offices publish separate reports for commodities directly under their supervision. The CFTC, 2033 K Street, N.W., Washington, D.C. 20036, will furnish information on all reports available and how to obtain them.

[34] Chapter 13 discusses in detail estimated rates of return for the large speculator, small trader, and hedger.

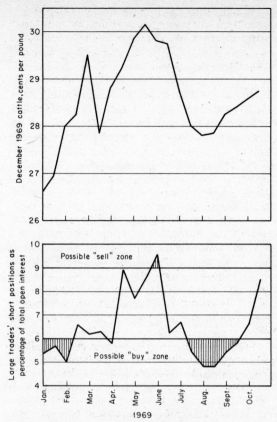

FIG. 7-12   December 1969 live beef cattle bimonthly closing price versus bimonthly large traders' short positions as percentage of total open interest for January–October 1969.

available series. It is also possible to play the large traders off against the small traders and isolate marked dichotomies of opinion; for example, a ratio of various large trader positions to comparable small trader positions would clearly pinpoint times of sharp disagreement between the two groups.[35]

[35] Roy E. Christian, *New Methods for Long Term Stock Market Forecasting*, Physician's Market Letter, 1691 Wilshire Drive, Aptos, Calif. 95003, 1966 (there is also a supplement, *Long Term Study*, and several back letters) has discussed numerous means of using odd-lot, specialist, and other data that specifically employ the technique of measuring marked divergences of opinion between two groups of traders. The Physicians Market Letter is defunct but many of these studies are still available.

STRIKING THE BALANCE—ADVANTAGES AND DISADVANTAGES OF USING OPEN INTEREST TO REVEAL THE ACTIVITIES OF LARGE AND SMALL TRADERS

The advantages. (a) Similar techniques have been used with some success in the stock market for many years. The breakdown of open interest available on regulated commodities yields series of data that are highly analogous to those used in stock market analysis. (b) Whether or not the trader constructs operative technical indicators from the open-interest breakdown, knowledge of the current interplay between hedgers, large traders, and small traders can be helpful in explaining market action in any commodity. (c) This kind of analysis can become exceptionally intriguing when it is realized that little research has been published in this area. The six series of data available regularly have the potential of yielding large numbers of permutations and combinations in the form of ratios, rate-of-change oscillators, and other indices. Interesting new territory is offered the inquiring technical analyst.

The disadvantages. (a) The work that has been done on the behavior of large and small traders argues against the value of open-interest breakdowns. Small traders, rather than acting consistently on the wrong side of the market, are better described as trading haphazardly. Large traders are consistent winners but are short-term oriented as a group.[36] It might be concluded that there is no available information on "stupid money," and that "smart money" data are available but come too late and too infrequently to be helpful. (b) The biweekly report on open interest is available to the public with a time lag of two weeks or more, thereby reducing the effectiveness of using this information. (c) The fact that technical analysts have done so little work here is not because this area is obscure. Most commodity traders with even a rudimentary background in the stock market would see the possible relevance of open-interest data. Rather this neglect might well indicate how arid the field is.

CONTRARY OPINION

> . . . the supposedly stolid Dutch were overcome by the Tulip Craze, the volatile French had their Mississippi Bubble, while the sturdy English had their South Sea Bubble.

> As I read the account of these madnesses, I was tempted to shout, 'This cannot have happened'. Yet within my own lifetime I have seen similar deliriums in the Florida land boom of the 1920's and the stock market speculation that led to the 1929 crash. Something of the same crowd madness may have been at least partially responsible for Hitler's rise to power in Germany.

> These crowd madnesses recur so frequently in human history that they must reflect some deeply rooted trait of human nature . . . if his book showed how baseless are man's moods of wild hope, it also showed that man's moods of

---

[36] Rockwell, *loc. cit.*

black despair are equally unfounded. Always in the past, no matter how black the outlook, things got better . . . Whatever men attempt, they seem driven to try to overdo.[37]

With these words, Bernard Baruch explained how he related an account of the "madness of crowds"[38] written in 1841 with the extremes of psychology that he had observed in his own experience. His astute decision to sell his holdings in 1929 has been credited to his reading this book at an opportune time. Baruch apparently never attempted to utilize the lessons of history contained in McKay's book in any systematic way, but a stock market analyst named Humphrey Neill did ponder on the implications of swings in mass psychology. The result was a new way of thinking called "contrary opinion."[39]

Neill's contention was that crowd madness did not have to go to the point of making history before it could be detected and used to advantage. His belief was that any crowd, such as stock or commodity traders, could frequently be carried to extremes of action and opinion. The astute observer could recognize these extremes and act opposite to the prevailing psychology to his own advantage. In other words, he would adopt a "contrary opinion." Neill attempted in his book to demonstrate that this phenomenon extends far beyond trading stocks or commodities.[40] However, only its use in practical commodity trading is considered here.

In market letters and boardroom talk the term "contrary opinion" appears frequently. Apparently most traders have come to believe that the contrarian takes positions opposite the prevailing opinion almost as a reflex action. This popular notion is far too simple; the true contrarian does more than merely lean against the current state of thinking.[41]

Before money is committed to a trade the contrarian insists that certain basic elements be present. First there must be a strong consensus about the

[37] Bernard Baruch, *Baruch: My Own Story,* Henry Holt & Co., New York, 1957, p. 219.

[38] Charles Mackay, *Extraordinary Popular Delusions and the Madness of Crowds,* L. C. Page & Co., London, 1932, reprinted from the 1841 edition. Several reprints of this book have since been published; it documents scores of historical occurrences in which people lost all semblance of reason and were dominated by mass psychology.

[39] Humphrey Neill, *The Art of Contrary Thinking,* The Caxton Printers, Caldwell, Ohio, 1960, is the definitive source of information on contrary opinion. Transcripts of various "Contrary Opinion Foliage Forums" held over the years are also available from Fraser Publishing Co., *loc. cit.*

[40] Neill, *loc. cit.,* contains an addendum in which he notes that popular expectations at the time of major world events were directly opposite of what actually occurred.

[41] Other excellent sources of information on singular aspects that might be related to contrary opinion are Gustave Le Bon, *The Crowd,* The Viking Press, New York, 1960, which delineates the difference between a solitary individual and an individual in a crowd; James Dines, *loc. cit.,* discusses myriad psychological aspects related to trading and is a prolific source of still more highly specialized references on subjects relating to psychology and contrary opinion; Hadley Cantril, *The Invasion From Mars,* reprinted by Harper & Row, New York, 1966, contains one section of interest to traders that centers on *how* a fantastic rumor (in this case, the celebrated 1938 radio broadcast by Orson Welles) can gain wide acceptance.

future price or behavior of a commodity. This opinion must be almost unanimous—virtually taken for granted—before there is any chance that mass psychology has been carried to extremes. Examples of widely held opinions that would interest a contrarian would be: "Beans are going much higher", "July cotton will go off the board weak", "February bellies will gain on the May", "Cocoa will take its lead from next month's purchase figures and not do much until then", and so on. Any of these opinions unfulfilled could represent a trading opportunity. Note that the opinion need not be only one of price direction. A normally popular commodity that has been unusually neglected is one example of a consensus that could provide a contrarian with much food for thought.

A second and equally important prerequisite is that the strong bias of opinion be supported by "weak" reasons. In determining how strong or weak these supporting reasons are, the contrarian differs sharply from the fundamentalist. The trader using contrary opinion is not interested in how important the facts are or even if they are true. The reasons behind an opinion are judged strong or weak only according to the manner in which they have been disseminated and the reaction they have produced.

To the contrarian supporting reasons are weak if they have one or both of these characteristics:

1. The facts have been widely publicized and well known for some time.

The presumption here is that any such facts are already discounted in the current price; for example, suppose that the great majority of traders are bearish on wheat. If such a position is popular because a coming bumper crop has been apparent for several weeks and prices have already dropped substantially, the question how much risk remains on the downside may well be raised. If news of the impending record crop has generated most of the selling it warrants, any favorable developments will be a surprise to most traders.

This kind of well-publicized fact is especially weak if its realization is far in the future. If, for example, the expected bumper crop is many months away from being harvested, a great many things could happen in the meantime (including the discovery that the crop is not nearly so large as the earlier estimates) to change the present bearish psychology sharply.

2. The facts of the situation are not known but only supposed.

This sort of situation can occur anywhere but is more common in those international commodities that are unregulated, such as sugar, cocoa, copper, silver, and coffee. Opinion is formed on the basis of preliminary indications that have all been in agreement but for which no hard evidence is yet available. Cocoa may be regarded as an exceptionally bullish situation on the basis of preliminary crop estimates long before any solid facts are in on the crop size. Even if the crop is small, such expectations may already have been discounted in the current price. Other than extravagantly bullish news could find the market vulnerable to decline following the first factual reports.

If the trader who uses contrary opinion can find a situation in which there is a near-unanimous opinion supported by weak reasons, he has, at least in theory, found a trade with high potential and low risk. The low risk comes from the probability that the factors that caused the consensus have been discounted. The high potential comes from the element of surprise that can be a dominating influence when mass psychology carries to extremes and only one-sided news is expected. If the reason behind the crowd's opinion turns out to be entirely invalid, which has happened frequently in the past, the contrarian gains a bonus.

STRIKING THE BALANCE—ADVANTAGES AND DISADVANTAGES OF USING CONTRARY OPINION

The advantages. (a) More than almost any other technical approach, the premises behind contrary opinion are solidly logical. When strong feelings prevail toward a particular commodity, it is indisputable that conditions in that market are abnormal. Most known facts are likely to have been discounted completely or partly, offering little potential to the trader who is following the lead of the majority. Of equal importance, such a market is extremely vulnerable to unexpected developments not in line with current thinking. (b) Even if a contrary opinion approach is not used to signal trades, it can be valuable to the trader who wants to keep emotions in check. Watching for weak reasons behind strongly held opinions will keep the trader from being carried away by the arguments of the moment and losing his perspective. (c) A contrary approach can often turn up important facts for both technician and fundamentalist. Contrary opinion is more than a means of generating signals. It is a way of thinking that can be conceptually and practically useful. In the final analysis the success of contrary opinion depends completely on neglected facts coming to the fore. By directing attention away from popular thought patterns contrary opinion is one method whose primary purpose is to enable the trader to think for himself and possibly to unearth key factors on which trades may be based.

The disadvantages. (a) Collecting an accurate sample of opinions can be most difficult. Myriad sources must be consulted to determine whether there is a strong consensus toward any commodity. Newspapers, brokerage house letters, private advisory letters, brokers themselves, their clients, and the "signals" currently being given by popular trading methods are only a few of the inputs needed to monitor a consensus situation that may be shaping up. It can be an arduous sometimes almost impossible task to uncover the prevailing psychology, even given a strong consensus. (b) Even if the state of prevailing opinion is known, the depth of that opinion may be hard to evaluate. One group of traders expecting plywood to "consolidate and retrace recent large gains during the next few weeks" is certainly not so bearish as others who expect a major collapse. Weighting these and other shades of opinion can be a perplexing problem.[42] (c) Although contrary opinion can provide the trader with numerous psychological advantages, it can spawn at least one large psychological disadvantage. Used heavily, it can breed arrogance. (d) Points of extreme mass psychology in any commodity are quite infrequent. Even the most adept contrarian may have to wait a long time between trades. (e) The approach is not as precisely quantitative as is generally believed. Because of this, contrary opinion has not yet been put to an objective historical test to determine its validity and characteristics, as some other technical methods have. (f) It is much easier to initiate trades by following a contrary opinion method than to know when or where to close them. In closing a trade, the contrarian must rely heavily on other methods or personal judgment.

STRUCTURAL THEORIES

The final quadrant of technical analysis is as controversial as it is varied. Structural theories include one eminently respectable approach (seasonals) that is possibly the most widely accepted of any technical method used to trade commodities. Another approach in the same category, also well known, is an excursion into the bizarre and the occult. Some structural theories require an exotic brand of thinking; others are far more mundane.

The technician who uses structural theories does not construct indices for predictive purposes as is the case in character of market analysis, nor does he rely on trend following to assist in making decisions. The structural theorist believes, rather, that an intense study of historical performance will reveal understandable and repeating price patterns in the market itself.

This approach is radically different from that discussed earlier of looking for price patterns on charts. Price patterns are expected to occur at irregular intervals, consume a limited amount of time, and predict prices for a limited time in the future. Their form is only general and can assume many variations. The use of structual theories is generally far more comprehensively based. Prices are seen as "following a blueprint" that can provide guidance at all times. When this "blueprint" is understood, the trader should know where prices stand within the structure and what is going to happen next.

SEASONAL PRICE MOVEMENTS

The most respected structural blueprint attempts to define times of the year when commodity prices have a high probability of moving in one direction or the other. These seasonal price trends are usually due to the particular way a commodity is produced and/or distributed. In grains, for instance, the sudden increase in supply at harvest time should lead to lower

---

[42] One advisory service, Market Vane Commodity Letter, 431 E. Green Street, Pasadena, Calif. 91101, attempts to weight the composite opinion of a number of brokerage house letters and to apply the results of this tabulated sample by suggesting positions opposite strong consensuses.

prices. Later in the season, as supplies are used, prices could be expected to rise. Indeed, the desire to stabilize seasonal price fluctuations was one of the most important reasons leading to the birth of the Chicago Board of Trade.[43] It was believed, and subsequently confirmed, that a futures market could at least moderate the violent seasonal price tendencies in grains.[44]

The trader using seasonals believes that although futures trading has moderated formerly marked price tendencies they have not been entirely eliminated. He contends that there are specific times in various commodities that remain significant each year and during which opportune sales or purchases can be made.

Because, ultimately, any seasonal price pattern is produced by the interplay, however subtle, of production and/or consumption factors in a commodity, it is clear that this approach can be classed as fundamental rather than technical. Chapter 4 discusses seasonal price patterns in detail that are of a fundamental nature. For the purposes of this chapter seasonals are defined as repeating patterns of price action that can be discovered and measured from observations alone, with no thought to the factors underlying production or consumption. There will, of course, be considerable overlap in these two "types" of seasonals.

Table 7-3 is a good example of a seasonal tendency that a technician might be interested in exploiting. It was uncovered solely from studies of

[43] See Chapters 1 and 2.
[44] See Chapter 4.

TABLE 7-3   A SEASONAL TENDENCY IN MARCH SOYBEAN MEAL

Years	Long Oct. 5	Close Out Feb. 5	Net Change in Points
1957–58	45.50	45.10	−40
1958–59	48.90	56.40	+750
1959–60	54.70	58.15	+345
1960–61	53.90	61.25	+735
1961–62	50.55	53.85	+330
1962–63	61.95	68.95	+700
1963–64	73.90	71.15	−275
1964–65	68.60	69.20	+60
1965–66	61.10	68.80	+770
1966–67	74.40	75.25	+85
1967–68	72.35	74.35	+200
1968–69	73.75	72.20	−155
1969–70	69.90	78.50	+860
1970–71	79.60	77.80	−180
1971–72	81.40	85.50	+410

SUMMARY: 11 years profitable = 74% of all years.
4 years unprofitable = 26% of all years
Total points gained = 5,245.
Total points lost = 650.
Average points gained in all 15 periods = + 306

SOURCE: Commodity Research Bureau's Futures Market Service Publication.

past price action.[45] A trader interested in this approach would.attempt to develop a "calendar portfolio" of seasonals which would indicate the action to take in a number of different commodities at various times of the year.[46]

Table 7-4 presents a summary of allegedly important seasonal tendencies in a variety of commodities. There are many other sources of seasonal patterns in commodity prices.[47]

Seasonal "blueprints" of price action can be expressed in several ways. The two most common forms are in Tables 7-3 and 7-4. Either a particular period during the year is selected as likely to see rising or falling prices or a

[45] This example, and several others, is taken from various publications of The Commodity Research Bureau, 140 Broadway, New York, N.Y. 10005, an organization that has performed research into seasonal price action of futures. Their weekly "Futures Market Service" and their "Commodity Yearbook" are sources of information on seasonal price action.

[46] The trader interested in developing such a "portfolio" is referred to the "X-11 Procedure" used by the Bureau of the Census, Washington, D.C. 20233, which not only mathematically identifies seasonal tendencies in data but also generates a "stability factor" that measures the consistency of such tendencies.

[47] Gann, *loc. cit.*; Hill, *loc. cit.*; Pickell, *loc. cit.* All sources also mention the famous "Voice from the Tomb" grain seasonals.

TABLE 7-4 SEASONAL PATTERN OF SPOT COMMODITY PRICES °

Commodity	High	Low
Barley	May	June
Cocoa	January–March	June, December (double bottom)
Coffee†	January–February	April, November (double bottom)
Corn	August	November–December
Cotton	July	October–December
Cottonseed meal†	March	December
Cottonseed oil†	June	October
Eggs	November	March–April
Flaxseed	May	October–November
Hides	August, October	March
Oats	(January) May‡	August
Potatoes	June–July	October
Rubber	September	March
Rye	February	July–August
Soybeans	(January) May‡	October
Soybean oil	July	October
Soybean meal†	April	December
Sugar (world)†	September	March
Wheat	(January) May‡	August–September
Wool	December	June

° Some commodities such as the metals do not have clearly defined seasonal price patterns.

† More than the usual number of exceptions to the seasonal pattern.

‡ These grains have often been subject to sharp reactions in February (known as the February break) after which a good rally sometimes has occurred.

SOURCE: Commodity Research Bureau.

particular month is selected as most likely to encompass a key high or low for the entire year.

Another form of seasonal analysis widely used could be called a "conditional seasonal."[48] This concept suggests that a price move will occur provided that some previous condition has been met. Examples of well-known allegations of this kind include, "Potatoes can advance into January if they make a new high in November"; "Eggs can decline sharply in August if cash prices are flat or soft"; "January soybeans can gain on deferreds if Chicago stocks are low in November."

Data on seasonals were presented in Chapter 4, and additional information on alleged seasonal tendencies is included in the later chapters on individual commodities.

STRIKING THE BALANCE—ADVANTAGES AND DISADVANTAGES OF USING SEASONALS

The advantages. (a) If any clear, repeating seasonal tendency has been isolated,[49] the trader can usually then determine the dominant reason for its existence. As long as that reason exists in succeeding years, the presumption is that prices will probably repeat their performance. (b) Seasonal information can be used to argue for or against trades accepted in any other form of analysis. The trader who wishes, for example, to short orange juice during the last half of October is made aware of a strong tendency for prices to rise at that time of year. When any commitment is made, seasonal information may help in appraising the risks. (c) If nothing else, careful analysis of seasonals can help the trader to achieve a better understanding of the basic forces affecting the balance of supply and demand in any single commodity.

The disadvantages. (a) The means by which commodities are produced and consumed are always in a state of flux. For this reason the life-span of the best validated seasonal tendency can prove to be quite limited. (b) Any seasonal tendency that becomes well known is almost certain to be totally smoothed out as more and more traders act on it. Chapter 17 describes how this has occurred in corn, to note just one instance. Seasonal forces can be discounted in the price, as can other fundamental and technical facts previously discussed. (c) Although seasonal trading is unique in that both an entry and exit date are usually indicated in advance, little is said about what can be termed "interim risk." In holding a commitment for one, two, or more months, the trader is exposed to the chance of considerable loss while waiting for the presumed gain. Referring to Table 7-3, for example, the average seasonal profit on March soybean meal is approximately 300 points. Yet between the starting and ending date of this trade meal often showed

---

[48] This approach is particularly favored by many brokerage houses that deal exclusively in commodities.

[49] The tendency should be validated by sound statistical techniques.

300 points or more adversity before the ultimate profit occurred. How is the trader to control losses in this or any other seasonal trade? The answer is not clear. Seasonal analysis, as usually presented, provides little information on "interim risk." Much judgment must be employed to determine if a seasonal trade is on course and how to deal with real and possible interim losses.

TIME CYCLES

Seasonals, no matter how derived, deal with repeating annual phenomena. For at least the last century, however, a great many investigators have concluded that there is a longer term structure in commodity prices.[50] Even longer term cycles have been isolated and documented. In 1875 Samuel Benner wrote a short book[51] wherein, among other things, the prices of pig iron and corn were predicted for the next several decades. Had a hypothetical trader, with the required money, warehouses, and other resources, bought and sold pig iron during the years indicated, dollar gains would have exceeded losses by a ratio of 31 to 1.[52] Benner's predictions on corn were less spectacular, but gains still shaded losses by a margin of $3\frac{1}{4}$ to l, and the average annual gain trading in cash corn would have exceeded 7 percent compounded.[53] Results like these, achieved over a span of more than 80 years, strongly suggest that Benner's success might have been correlated with underlying cyclical phenomena.

The technician who uses time cycles to forecast prices employs a unique *modus operandi.* He believes that back records of prices contain evidence within themselves of at least one and usually several time cycles during which prices are carried up or down. Whether a computer or a paper and pencil is used, the trader attempts to isolate and quantify the important cycles in any commodity. These cycles are then combined to yield a prediction of the dates of future high and low prices. The trader then takes action accordingly.

Although the concept of time cycles can be spun into elaborate complexity, most cycles fall into three categories, no matter how sophisticated the mathematics.

1. Important highs and lows are spaced by distinct, repeating intervals. Table 7-5 shows a regular $67\frac{1}{3}$-month cycle in cash corn prices. The pre-

[50] Perhaps the first person to investigate time cycles in a scholarly way was Hyde Clark, who alleged an 11-year cycle in speculation and famine in 1838. Influenced by Clark, William Stanley Jevons published, *The Periodicity of Commercial Crises and Its Physical Explanation* and *The Solar Period and the Price of Corn* at the University of Manchester in 1875. Jevon's thesis was that repetitive cycles in sunspots affected crop yields, and therefore prices, on a predictable basis.

[51] Samuel Benner, *Benner's Prophecies of Ups and Downs in Prices,* privately printed, Cincinnati, Ohio, 1875 (reprinted by The Foundation for the Study of Cycles, 124 South Highland Avenue, Pittsburgh, Pa. 15206).

[52] Edward R. Dewey, "The $5\frac{1}{2}$ year Cycle in Corn Prices" and "Samuel Turner Benner" in *Cycles Magazine* (February and March, 1955).

[53] *Ibid.*

TABLE 7-5   IMAGINARY PURCHASE AND SALE OF CORN ON
THE BASIS OF A 67½-MONTH CYCLE (CASH NO. 3 YELLOW
AT CHICAGO)

Date	Buy	Sell	Short	Cover	Gain in cents		Percent gain	
					Long	Short	Long	Short
May 1899	33							
Mar. 1902		59	59		26		78.8	
Jan. 1905	42			42		17		28.8
Oct. 1907		65	65		23		54.8	
Aug. 1910	64			64		1		1.5
Jun. 1913		60	60		−4		−6.3	
Mar. 1916	73			73		−13		−21.7
Jan. 1919		143	143		70		95.9	
Nov. 1921	47.4			47.4		95.6		66.9
Aug. 1924		117.3	117.3		69.9		147.5	
Jun. 1927	98.9			98.9		18.4		15.7
Apr. 1930		82.0	82.0		−16.9		−17.1	
Jan. 1933	23.6			23.6		58.4		71.2
Nov. 1935		62.1	62.1		38.5		163.1	
Sep. 1938	52.7			52.7		9.4		15.1
Jun. 1941		73.7	73.7		21.0		39.8	
Apr. 1944	114.5			114.5		−40.8		55.4
Feb. 1947		141.9	141.9		27.4		23.9	
Nov. 1949	116			116		25.9		18.3
Sep. 1952		176	176		60		51.7	
Jun. 1955	147			147		29		−16.5
Apr. 1958		129	129		−18		−12.2	
Feb. 1961	113			113		16		12.4
Dec. 1963		119	119		6		5.3	
Sep. 1966	144			144		−25		−21.0
Jun. 1969		130	130		−14		−9.7	
Mar. 1972	118			118		12		9.2

Total cents gained long	=	341.8	% Gained long = 660.8
Total cents lost long	=	52.9	% Lost long = 45.3
Net cents gained long	=	288.9	Net % gained long = 615.5
Total cents gained short	=	282.7	% gained short = 294.5
Total cents lost short	=	78.8	% lost short = 59.2
Net cents gained short	=	203.9	Net gained short = 235.3

SOURCE: Cycles Magazine (February 1955).

dicted highs are 67⅓ months apart from one another, as are the lows. This cyclical analysis is common among technicians who use time cycles to predict commodity prices.[54]

2. "Kick in the pants" cycles. A certain span of time carries prices strongly up or down and this action repeats at regular intervals. Figure 7-13 shows a monthly chart of world sugar prices in which a brief but powerful

[54] Gann, loc. cit., is a typical exponent of this analysis. His book contains extensive historical price tables for a wide variety of commodities.

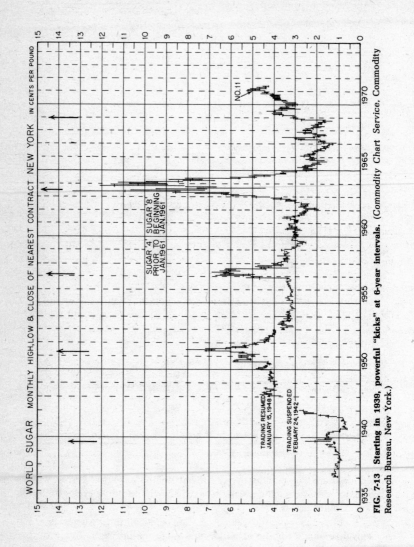

FIG. 7-13 Starting in 1939, powerful "kicks" at 6-year intervals. (Commodity Chart Service, Commodity Research Bureau, New York.)

upward "kick" is seen at roughly six-year intervals. This form of analysis is also common.[55]

3. Complex and sophisticated mathematical models. Many organizations have developed models of considerable depth which are designed to define precisely the timing, shape, amplitude, and other characteristics of time cycles being investigated.[56]

Although virtually any trader can do research by using a record of commodity prices[57] in an effort to discover profitable time cycles, this approach has never been popular.[58] Occasional waves of interest in cyclical forecasting have always subsided, leaving those using these techniques in the backwater of technical analysis.

STRIKING THE BALANCE—ADVANTAGES AND DISADVANTAGES OF USING TIME CYCLES

The advantages. (a) Hard evidence has been presented that time cycles are probably a real phenomenon, not a statistical fantasy. A mathematical test has been developed to calculate the probabilities that any observed cycle is due to chance.[59] Because commodity prices possess a structure that is at least partly ordered by time, trading on the basis of cycles is theoretically possible. (b) Even if time cycles are not used to signal commitments, such research can be valuable in helping to appraise the risks behind any trade. The trader becomes aware if his contemplated actions agree or disagree with the underlying cyclical background.

The disadvantages. (a) Not all the evidence indicates that cycles are a real phenomenon. Extremely sophisticated mathematical techniques[60] have not

---

[55] Again the best source is Gann, *loc. cit.* A short interesting article on the subject is Edward R. Dewey, "Kick In the Pants Cycles", *Cycles Magazine* (August 1961). An imaginative use of cycle types 1 and 2 is George Lindsay, "A Timing Method For Traders", in *The Encyclopaedia of Stock Market Techniques* published by Investor's Intelligence, 1965 rev. ed.

[56] One organization that appears to be heavily influenced by members interested in investment and speculation is The Society for Investigation of Recurring Events, P.O. Box 174, Bowling Green Station, New York, N.Y. 10004. The pre-eminent force in this field is the Foundation for the Study of Cycles, 124 South Highland Ave., Pittsburgh, Pa. 15206. A not-for-profit, tax-exempt foundation, it has carried on research into cyclical phenomena found in virtually every available time series. *Cycles Magazine* and the now defunct *Journal of Cycle Research,* both published by the Foundation, can be found in many big-city libraries. Written on a scientific level, these publications are an extensive repository of facts and theories on cyclical phenomena.

[57] This can be done by hand or on a grander scale. The Foundation for the Study of Cycles has published several computer programs for isolating and measuring cycles in statistical data.

[58] Only two books that attempt a comprehensive discussion and evaluation of repetitive time cycles in statistical data have been written: Edwin R. Dewey, *Cycles, The Science of Prediction,* Henry Holt & Co., New York, 1949, and Edwin R. Dewey and Og Mandino, *Cycles: Mysterious Forces that Trigger Events,* Hawthorne Books, New York, 1971.

[59] This is the Bartels Test of Significance. See Charles E. Armstrong, "Testing Cycles for Statistical Significance", *Journal of Cycle Research* (October 1961).

[60] See Walter C. Labys and C. W. J. Granger, *Speculation, Hedging and Commodity Price Forecasts,* Chapter 3, D. C. Heath & Co., Lexington, Mass., 1970. Paul Cootner, Ed., *The Ran-*

supported the contention that repeating time cycles of any length are present in commodity prices. (b) Even if cycles are accepted as a real phenomenon, there is still a great deal about them that is not known. It is impossible to know for any particular commodity what causes observed cycles, how many cycles are currently operating, or even the curvature of a cycle. That there is nothing approaching a complete cycle model is a major obstacle to the technician attempting to use cyclical data. Any time cycle the trader has isolated may prove to be useless as hidden properties of the cycle become apparent or other undetected cycles nullify or override it. (c) Almost all published serious work in commodity price cycles has been conducted with cash prices, not futures prices. The corn forecast in Table 7-5, although accurate for several years, would have been of little value to the futures trader at that time. The cash and futures markets do not always move in tandem. Also, the fact that futures have a limited life and can represent different crops makes it far more difficult to analyze prices in any meaningful way. (d) Even with complete cycle knowledge the trader has only part of the picture. Important current developments can ruin the clearest cyclical indications, with prices getting back "on track" too late to help the trader.

THE ELLIOTT WAVE THEORY

As must be common to all who publish investment services, I received frequent letters from individuals who had developed "infallible" methods or systems for forecasting the stock market. My usual reply was that the individual go on record with me over a market cycle after which I would determine whether I cared to investigate the matter in detail. In most instances, at some point in the cycle the system went haywire and correspondence died on the vine.

Elliott was one of three notable exceptions. He wrote me from California in late 1934 that a bull market had begun and would carry for some distance. . . . In March 1935 the Dow Rail average crashed under its 1934 low, accompanied by an eleven percent break in the industrial average. Having recent memories of 1929–32, this development scared the lights out of the investing public. On the bottom day for the industrial average, the Rails having leveled off four days previously, I received a late evening telegram from Elliott in which, as was always his way, he *dogmatically* affirmed that the break was over and that another leg of the bull market was beginning. This break, looking back, was Primary Wave No. 2 of the Cycle movement then under way under Elliott's Wave Principle although, at the time, I had no idea as to his method."[61]

It was in this way that the Elliott wave principle, possibly the most unusual technical theory ever conceived, first became known to Mr. Charles Collins and then to an ever-wider audience. If Elliott's forecasts were spec-

---

dom Character of Stock Market Prices, The M.I.T. Press, Cambridge, Mass., 1964, discusses periodic time cycles related to stock prices in Chapters 6, 8, and 9.

[61] Hamilton Bolton and Charles Collins, "The Elliott Wave Principle – 1966 Supplement", *The Bank Credit Analyst,* 1245 Sherbrooke Street West, Montreal 109, Quebec, Canada.

tacular, so were the basic tenets underlying his theory. In brief, Elliott believed in "counting" waves of advance or decline in stock prices. These waves, he felt, fell into patterns so complete and so comprehensive that one could know at any time where prices stood in their development, how much potential they had on the upside or downside, and roughly how much longer a trend would persist.

Elliott's basic theory was that prices move in a five-wave sequence in line with the direction of the main trend and in a three-wave sequence during "corrective" movements against the main trend. Figure 7-14 illustrates how these main trend and corrective movements are formed. One of many fascinating aspects of Elliott's theory is that each wave is broken up into subwaves of its own (either three or five waves) and that these waves, in turn, break down into smaller subwaves, and so on. In principle, Elliott waves can be carried down to the level of each individual trade. The theory can also be extended to a larger scale, in which each wave is a subwave of a larger wave which in turn is part of a still larger wave. Elliott actually believed that some waves in prices were centuries long. His system of labeling waves is extremely complicated, and references should be consulted to study Elliott in proper detail.[62]

Given this all-inclusive system of categorization, it is theoretically possible for the trader to know where prices stand at all times. Figure 7-15 shows an Elliott wave analysis of Chicago rye, plotted on a monthly scale. The major bull market that began in 1942 may be visualized as a sequence of five waves which carried prices up into 1948. The trader who thought Elliott would pinpoint the top would begin counting after wave 4[63] was clearly over, expecting the fifth and final wave to break down into five subwaves (not shown on the chart). Once the "fifth wave of the fifth wave" became apparent, possibly on a weekly chart, the trader would use more detailed data to determine the fifth wave of *that* fifth wave.

Following the major bull move, a three-wave, or "A-B-C," correction

---

[62] The most comprehensive single work on the wave principle is Hamilton Bolton, *The Elliott Wave Principle — A Critical Appraisal*, Bolton, Tremblay & Co., Montreal, 1960. Bolton, Tremblay & Co.'s *Bank Credit Analyst* has also published a number of supplements for irregular years, starting with 1961, that seek to up-date Bolton's original work and provide current interpretations. Cox, *loc. cit.*, is a strong advocate of using Elliott's principles for commodity trading. William O'Connor, *Stocks, Wheat & Pharaohs*, Weiner Books Co., New York, 1961, is an offbeat source of information on Elliott applied to futures prices. The book is out of print but available in many big-city libraries. O'Connor not only uses unique principles of interpretation but is the only source that places great stress on daily charts for identifying Elliott waves in the very short run. Elliott's two monographs are long out of print and almost impossible to obtain, as are past issues of his advisory letters. R. N. Elliott, "The Wave Principle", *Financial World* (1939), reprented by BCA Distributors, Ltd., Montreal, 1963, consisting of a series of articles that appeared in *Financial World Magazine*, is his only work still readily available.

[63] Bolton, Collins, and O'Connor are the *only* practicioners of the Elliott wave theory who adhere to the vital rule laid down by Elliott that wave 4 must not, under any circumstances, overlap wave 1. Every other Elliott theorist in print at the time of this writing has ignored this rule with no word of explanation.

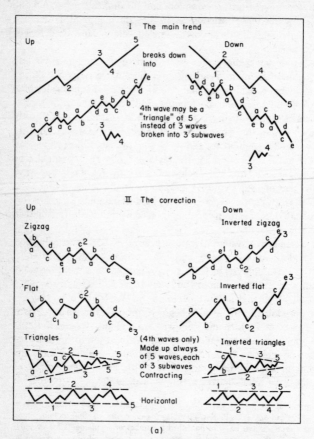

FIG. 7-14 (a) Basic Elliott wave sequences. (Hamilton Bolton, **The Elliott Wave Principle**—A Critical Appraisal, Bolton, Tremblay and Co., Montreal, 1960. **(b) Corrective patterns and triangles.** (*Financial World*, 1939.)

would be expected, and this broke into the "zig-zag" 3-3-5 corrective pattern shown in Figure 7-14. Following the final wave of the A-B-C correction in 1954, no new Elliott pattern appears to have taken place.

This approach, which is increasingly popular in technical analysis of commodity prices, certainly is most unusual, and results in some bizarre considerations when the advantages and disadvantages of using this method are discussed.

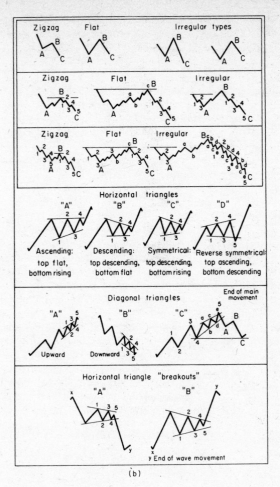

(b)

STRIKING THE BALANCE—ADVANTAGES AND DISADVANTAGES OF USING THE ELLIOTT WAVE THEORY

The advantages. (a) During the time that Elliott was using his method he compiled a spectacular record of forecasting stock prices. Following in his footsteps, both Collins and Bolton continued to make surprisingly

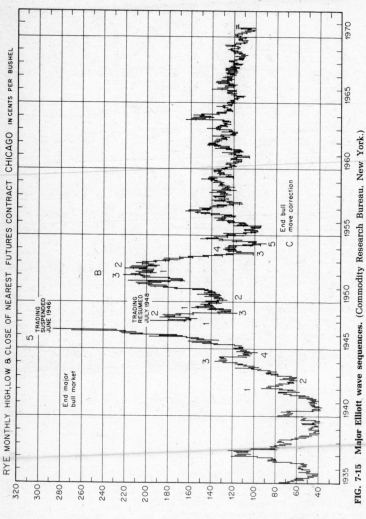

FIG. 7-15 Major Elliott wave sequences. (Commodity Research Bureau, New York.)

accurate predictions of the stock market averages.[64] Using a "side-effect" of Elliott's concepts, Bolton was able to forecast the level of a key stock market top with an accuracy of 99.6 percent.[65] These accomplishments argue strongly for some viability in the wave principle. (b) Elliott's wave counts are based on the "Fibonacci Summation Series," a number series with interesting properties. It has been affirmed that both living and inanimate objects obey a number of laws that revolve around the mathematical properties of this series. Using a Fibonacci summation (1-2-3-5-8-13-21-34-55-89-144-233-etc.) it is possible for scientists to predict how populations of animals will multiply, how plants will grow, how crystalline structures will form naturally, and a great many other things.[66] This series also yields the "golden mean" that is used in architecture. Although detailed discussion of Fibonacci is beyond the scope of this book, it is evident that study of this series discloses mathematical relationships that hold in real-life situations. It has been hypothesized that these relationships are so all-inclusive that they extend into the psychological arena as well, with price fluctuations reflecting their subtle but all-pervasive influence.

The disadvantages. (a) Elliott never hinted that his "law" might apply to commodity prices. His forecasting work centered almost exclusively on the Dow Jones Averages. Even in individual stocks research performed indicates that application of Elliott's principle is quite intricate and possible only in selected instances.[67] (b) The entire concept of the Elliott wave theory rests on counting "waves." Yet it is impossible to answer objectively the question, "What *is* a wave?" Elliott himself gave no answer to this question.[68] This means that the technician is forced to use highly subjective judgment to label a wave on the chart and also to identify the time scale which the wave fits. Figure 7-15 illustrates the problem. The last wave of the major bull move seems to break up into many more than five subwaves. Either the theory is wrong or some of the subwaves should not be counted for some unknown reason. This problem occurs quite frequently in Elliott's

---

[64] The Bank Credit Analysts' annual Elliott Supplements, *loc. cit.*, especially those written by Bolton, give explicit forecasts of general stock market action. Several important major bull and bear markets were correctly forecasted. Charles Collins, "Market Ebb Tide," *Barrons* (March 1970), contains an accurate prediction relating to the Dow Jones Averages.

[65] Bolton, "The Elliott Wave Principle—A Critical Appraisal," predicted in 1960 that the "super cycle" high for the Dow Jones Industrial Average would theoretically be 999. The actual level of Elliott's "super cycle" peak was 995, reached in January 1966.

[66] *Ibid.* Bolton, discusses several mathematical properties of the Fibonacci Summation Series. The "1968 Elliott Supplement", *loc. cit.*, presents a technical analysis of the Fibonacci Series by W. E. White. A brief article for the layman is "The Fibonacci Numbers", *Time* (April 1969), which also contains further references.

[67] In Elliott's series of articles in *Financial World* in 1939, *loc. cit.*, he gave brief examples of forecasting prices for individual stocks. The "1964 Elliott Supplement" devoted some space to the problem of adapting Elliott waves to individual stock prices and came to disappointing conclusions.

[68] The "1967 Elliott Supplement," written by A. J. Frost, posed the question. Though a devoted Elliott practitioner, Frost stated the question could not be answered.

analysis. (c) The theory is so flexible that it is possible to get several radically different wave counts by using the same price data, and leading Elliott interpreters are in almost constant disagreement.[69] A particularly disturbing corollary to all of this is that the more back data the trader has accumulated, the greater the number of possible counts. In most endeavors additional information usually clarifies; with Elliott, additional information can just as easily add to the confusion. (d) One flexible aspect of the theory is the fluid concept of "extensions"; for example, a five-wave move can, under Elliott's rules, extend itself without warning into nine-waves. These and other features of the theory make it difficult to come to any decisions at any given moment and easy to see the correct count (and decision) after the fact. (e) Elliott, beyond question, intended that his wave principle mold current prices into a comprehensive structure that would provide guidance at all times, but virtually any commodity chart will show long "blank" spots in which it is impossible to get any sort of wave count. Because one of the fundamental tenets of the theory is that *all* waves can be categorized, the existence of these blank spots means either that the premise is invalid or that the count at these times is subtle enough to escape all observers. (f) It is not generally realized that Elliott was a mystic who also believed in numerology. In his monograph,[70] published in 1948, he discussed how mathematical relationships in the Great Pyramid of Gizeh not only predicted future world events but tied in with his own wave theory as well! Although the trader should keep an open mind in regard to the claims of technical analysis, a trading method that is in agreement with pyramid numerology should, indeed, be cautiously evaluated.

NOTES FROM A TRADER

Isolating, quantifying, and successfully trading nonrandom elements in commodity futures trading data requires unusual determination and discipline. The efficient market is a worthy adversary and, in attempting to forecast, the technician must beware of trying to get more out of an experience than is in it to begin with. As Mark Twain warned, "The cat, having sat upon a hot stove lid, will not sit upon a hot stove lid again. Nor upon a cold stove lid." Consistent profits are earned only when commitments are made on the basis of analysis which is far from obvious to the majority of other traders at a given point in time.

There seems to be an overwhelming urge among most technicians to develop a simple, totally mechanical system that works with near-perfect accuracy. The professional trader quickly becomes aware that the search for a

---

[69] The "1963 Elliott Supplement" gives several different interpretations from various analysts and includes a discussion on this problem.

[70] R. N. Elliott, *Nature's Law—The Secret Of The Universe,* privately published, New York, 1946. Long out of print. The title perhaps indicates Elliott's view of the importance of his methodology.

foolproof trading system in which all observations promptly find their pre-ordained place has the same large challenge and the same small promise as any all-encompassing system in any other discipline, be it medicine, philosophy or law. The mature trader recognizes that although judgment can be reduced it can never be eliminated and that many losing trades will mar even the best trading results.

At least two important lessons can be retrieved from technical analysis. First, almost all methods generate useful *information,* which if used for nothing more than uncovering and organizing facts about market behavior will increase the trader's understanding of the markets. Second, the trader is made painfully aware that technical competence does not ensure competent trading. Speculators who lose money do so not always because of bad analysis but because of the inability to transform their analysis into sound practice. Bridging the vital gap between analysis and action requires overcoming the threat of greed, hope, and fear. It means controlling impatience and the desire to stray away from a sound method to "something new" during times of temporary adversity. It means having the discipline to "believe what you see" and to follow the indications from sound methods, even though they contradict what everyone else is saying or what "seems" to be the correct course of action.

The rewards are great and they are attainable. As one astute observer of the markets remarked,

> . . . commodity price developments are watched by relatively few traders, most of them quite set in their ways; even in the most active futures markets, the volume of serious research by participants seems to be quite small. It is therefore possible that systematic patterns will remain largely unknown for a very long time. [71]

---

[71] Hendrick Houthakker, "Systematic and Random Elements in Short Term Price Movements," *American Economic Review,* 51 (1961).

CHAPTER EIGHT

Spreads and Options

Why worry about realized losses?
They are more than overcome by potential profits.

INTRODUCTION

Spreads and options may be considered by some to represent only a choice in a type of commodity position, but the subject is far broader than that and deserves separate and more elaborate treatment.

Most unsophisticated commodity traders are converted security traders who bring their habits with them. They are much more likely to be long the market than short and know little or nothing about spreads and options. The professional trader is at least as conversant with the short as the long side of the market and knows considerably more about spreads and the concept of option trading.

SPREADS

Spreads may represent a significant percentage of the open interest of a commodity and may be entered for reasons that may be either technical or fundamental in nature. The word "spread" has several meanings to commodity traders but all imply a price difference. The word in its most general sense applies to the difference between the cash and futures price of the same commodity. In a more restricted sense it refers to the difference in the prices of two contract months.

A spread also describes the actual position taken by a trader who is simultaneously long one commodity contract and short another. He may hold equal but opposite positions in two different contracts of the same commodity, such as long 10,000 bushels of March wheat and short 10,000 bushels of May wheat. He might also have equal but opposite positions in two different but related commodities and still hold a spread position; for example, he could be long 10,000 bushels of corn and short 10,000 bushels of wheat or long 25,000 bushels of oats and short 25,000 bushels of corn. Opposite positions in unrelated commodities are not considered spreads. A trader may be long copper and short sugar, but these would merely be considered separate positions because there is little or no basic price relation between copper and sugar.

Historically, the terms "spread" and "straddle" had some shades of difference, but they have since become interchangeable among commodity traders, and in practice the word "spread" is now more commonly used in the futures markets. There was once some tendency for traders to speak of spreads in connection with grain positions and straddles in connection with other commodities, such as cotton. The terms "spread position" and "hedge" are used interchangeably but incorrectly by some traders. A hedge refers to the concurrent holding of two opposite commodity positions, one in the cash, or spot, market and the other in the futures market. A spread position also refers to two concurrent and opposite positions, but both are in the futures markets. In its more general sense spread describes the price difference between the cash and futures markets in a hedged position. "Arbitrage" is a word related broadly to the others described herein, but it generally suggests two positions entered simultaneously, or virtually so, one long and the other short, "locking in" a price difference so great that a profit is virtually assured. In the commodity markets this condition exists when a distant contract exceeds the price of the nearby by an amount exceeding the carrying charge, as in the example on page 218. Such opportunities also exist in the security markets by trading the same security on two different markets at two different prices or the same security in two forms such as common stock against bonds or preferred stock convertible into the same common. Some also are able to take advantage of the price discrepancies that exist in foreign exchange.

SIGNIFICANCE OF PRICE DIFFERENCES

Most of the following discussion centers about the taking of a spread position, but it is worth noting how important the spread differences among the prices of various contract months are to the intelligent establishment of a position. Suppose that it is August and that a trader believes that the price of wheat is likely to go up. He decides to establish a position of 10,000 bushels to take advantage of the expected price rise. He is aware that wheat is then trading for delivery in September, December, March, May, and July. How does he decide which to buy?

There are several factors to consider. One is the crop year which he believes presents the greater opportunity. The crop year for wheat begins on July 1. If he wants to take his position in the forthcoming new crop, he has little choice because the only new-crop contract trading in August is the July of the following year. If he believes the greater opportunity is offered in the current, or old, crop, he must choose among the September, December, March, and May contracts. One factor affecting this decision is the amount of time believed needed for the expected upward price move to develop and when it is expected to begin. If he expects something to happen within a few days because of some near-term development, such as important export business, he could buy any of the old-crop contracts. He would probably lean toward the September delivery because there is less time available for the tightness in wheat to be alleviated and it would best reflect a tight cash market.

If he expects to retain his position for some months, there is no point in considering September and no great attraction in the December contract. He can gain considerably more time by acquiring the March or May contracts. He has also gained the advantage of a possible long-term capital gain on his tax return if he should happen to hold the position more than six months, which would not have been possible had he bought the September or December contracts. In addition, he saves the commission that would be incurred if he bought an early contract and later "rolled forward" into a later one.

The choice between the March and May contracts must still be made. Too many traders make this decision with little or no thought at all or, worse, for the wrong reasons. They may choose the March merely because they or their brokers have been keeping a chart of that contract and they have not followed the May, or they may buy the May because that contract happens to be on the quote boards in the broker's office and the action on the March contract has not been followed. The decision would better be made logically on the current price difference, or spread, between the March and May prices.

To clarify this point assume that the carrying charge on a bushel of wheat is $2\frac{1}{4}$ cents a month. That would be the actual cost of handling, storing, insuring, and financing one bushel for one month. The cost of carrying a bushel of wheat from the March contract into the May delivery would therefore be $4\frac{1}{2}$ cents for the two-month period. It would be virtually impossible for May wheat to sell for significantly more than $4\frac{1}{2}$ cents over the March delivery for any length of time. If it were to do so, it would become profitable for somebody to buy the March and sell the May at the unusually wide price difference. This activity is sometimes called "arbitrage" and anyone engaged in it an "arbitrager." He would be prepared, if necessary, to take delivery of his March wheat, hold his short May position as a hedge, and then deliver his cash wheat against the May contract during the month of

May. More likely, the abnormal spread difference would dissolve sooner or later, and the arbitrager would take off both sides of his spread position and realize his profit. In either case he would be certain of a gain approximating at least the difference between the $4\frac{1}{2}$-cent normal carrying charge and the wider spread difference at which he had taken his position, unless there was a material short-run change in the carrying charge.

Because opportunities like this are so obvious to professional traders and profits in the real world are not so easily attained, the spread difference between March and May would almost certainly stop short of the $4\frac{1}{2}$-cent full carrying-charge difference. Yet if the spread difference was near the full carrying charge it would be of considerable help to a net position trader trying to make an intelligent decision. At near the full carrying charge he would probably place his long position in the March rather than the May contract. Both contracts might go up equally and he would realize the same gain in either one. Both might go down equally and he would suffer the same loss in either one. If the spread difference changed, however, it would almost certainly do so either because March went up more than May or down less, and in both cases the trader would find the March contract the better alternative. March could not lose materially on May, but there is no limit to the amount it could gain on May in a strong market. It could not only sell for more than May, but there is no $4\frac{1}{2}$-cent barrier to its premium. Because clocks run only one way, nobody has yet found a way to buy the May contract of a commodity, take delivery, and then redeliver it against the previous March contract. Premiums of nearby contracts over distant ones can get quite large in strong markets. When nearby contracts sell for more than distant contracts, the market is called "inverted." Traders must remember that risks in carrying-charge market spreads are limited; inverted market spreads are not.

If, with wheat at near a full carrying charge, the trader believed that wheat was going to go down rather than up and he wanted to go short either March or May, his decision would be just as obvious. He would certainly go short the May contract rather than the March. Here again, the only way the spread difference would change materially would be for May to lose on March because March could not lose on May. With May providing the added attraction of two additional months for the trade to work profitably, the choice of March would be a poor one indeed.

There is a third type of trader who is alert to these price differences and who hopes to take advantage of them. This is the position spreader.

SPREAD POSITIONS

A position spreader is less interested in the direction of price than in the difference between two prices. Rather than decide that a given contract price is too high or too low, he is interested in taking advantage of price differences that he considers abnormal. The possible positions open to this trader are intracommodity (or intercontract or interdelivery spreads), inter-commodity spreads, intermarket spreads, or a combination of them. The logic of those taking such positions is best made clear by example.

INTRACOMMODITY SPREADS

An intracommodity spreader tries to take advantage of price differences that he believes are too wide or too narrow in the same commodity in the same market at the same time. He might note that May corn is selling for 4 cents over March and expect a strong market in corn to develop soon. If this should happen, he believes that not only would the general price level of corn go up but that the March contract would gain on the May. If he is right, there is no limit to the amount that March could gain because it could not only close the prevailing discount but could sell for more than May by a substantial amount. If he is wrong, there is little to lose because here, again, March cannot sell below the May for long by much more than the full carry-ing charge. The spread trader would take advantage of this opportunity by buying the March contract and selling an equal amount of the May against it. The position could be entered either by putting on both sides at the same time or by entering one at a time in order to try to establish a still more favorable difference. The latter takes unusual skill and sometimes results in losing the opportunity observed in the first place.

When the spread has been established, the spreader merely has to wait for March to gain on May as much as he thinks it is going to and then take off (lift) his position. He does this by selling out his March contract and buy-ing in his May. The removal of a spread position is often called "unwinding" or "backspreading." Here, again, he can take off both sides simultaneously by instructing his broker to remove the spread at the current market differ-ence or at a difference of a fixed number of cents. He could also take off (lift) one side (leg) at a time and hope to improve his total profit by doing so. Like entering a spread one side at a time, removing it by lifting one leg at a time is not a good practice. Most traders seem to develop a peculiar knack for taking off the wrong side of their spreads first and then watching a profit achieved over a period of weeks dissolve in a few days or hours.

One of the most frequent questions asked by inexperienced traders is, "Why spread in the first place?" If a trader like the one described above thinks corn is going to go up, why not just buy the March? If the spreader is correct in his analysis, he will make a profit on his March contract, lose on his May, and show a net profit on the difference because the March profit will exceed the May loss. It is obvious that he would have had a greater profit per contract if he had just bought the March. His action in taking the spread, however, is not quite so foolish as it may appear. By taking the spread position he has reduced his investment. The margin on one contract, 5,000 bushels of March corn long against a short position of 5,000 May, may be only $500 for the entire position, compared with a margin requirement of $1,500 required for long March corn alone. If the price of March corn rises 15 cents and that of May, 9 cents, the return on investment is greater on the spread than it would have been on the net position. The profit on the net March would have been $750 on a $1,500 investment, or 50 percent. The spread position results in a profit of $750 on the March and a loss of $450 on the May, but this represents a net gain of $300 on a $500 investment, or 60 percent. If he chooses to be more aggressive, he can carry 15,000 bushels in a spread position for the same margin as a net position of 5,000 bushels.

It should also be noted that the analysis of the corn situation may have been wrong in the first place and that corn might go down and not up. In this case a net position in March corn could have been costly or even ruinous, whereas the spread position could hardly prove painful at all because March could not lose significantly on May. The cost of this insurance is not great because the commission on a 5,000-bushel spread position is only $36 versus $30 for a 5,000-bushel net position and, as it has been seen, the funds needed to margin the position are much less. The spread trader has therefore increased his potential profit and reduced both his risk and his investment. It is even possible that the spreader could be completely wrong in his analysis and still make money just because he spread. The price of corn could fall drastically, and the price level of May could lose on March simply because more net traders choose to sell it or have to sell it because of pressure to liquidate. March, of course, still could not lose significantly on May because of the ever-present watchfulness of the arbitrager.

There is hardly any limit to the number of combinations open to the intracommodity spreader, but certain spreads do tend to be relatively popular, such as May potatoes against November, July soybeans against November, July cocoa against December, July flax against October, May wheat against July, and July sugar against October.

INTERCOMMODITY SPREADS

Some commodities are used for the same general purposes as others and therefore are interchangeable to a degree. The easier it is to substitute one for the other, the closer the relationship of their prices. Oats and corn are a case in point, as are hogs and cattle. If a spreader believes that the price relation between two commodities is unrealistic, he can sell the higher priced, buy the lower priced, wait for the relative price levels to approach normality, and then take his profit. The advantages of trading in this manner are similar to intracommodity spreads. The margin on cattle against hogs is usually about the same as it would be for either hogs or cattle taken alone. This is greater than in the case of the intracommodity spread, in which the margin on the spread is considerably less than it would be on one side alone. Unlike the intracommodity spread, however, there is seldom a commission reduction for spreads involving more than one commodity.

Because drastic changes in the price levels of both commodities are likely to be similar, the risk of ruinous losses is considerably reduced at the cost of the opportunity to achieve windfall profits.

Among the more popular spreads of this kind are those involving soybeans and the products produced from the soybeans, namely, soybean oil and soybean meal. A spreader usually assumes that a crusher will find either oil or meal more profitable at a given time and that one of the product prices will be the stronger. If the current prices do not reflect the strength of one of the products adequately, the spreader can buy the product that he feels should be the stronger and sell the other against it. If he believes that the value of the two products combined is too low relative to the beans, he can sell one contract of beans and buy one contract each of soybean oil and soybean meal. This position is usually called a "reverse crush" because it is opposite to the position taken by the soybean crusher, who is typically long beans, which he crushes in order to be able to sell the products. A contract of oil plus one of meal does not exactly equal the amount of oil and meal that could actually be produced from the contract of 5,000 bushels of beans, but it is usually close enough to yield a profit if the beans prove to be selling too high on the products. If the trader thinks that beans will gain on the combined products, he can buy the beans and sell the products, just as a crusher does. The establishment of such a position is sometimes called "putting on running time."

Popular intercommodity spreads include wheat versus corn, hogs versus bellies, domestic versus foreign sugar contracts, and oats versus corn. In the latter case, traders frequently spread one contract of corn against two contracts of oats because they consider a contract of oats to be worth only about 56 percent of a contract of corn.

INTERMARKET SPREADS

Many commodities are traded on more than one market. Wheat is traded on the Chicago Board of Trade, the Kansas City Board of Trade, and the Minneapolis Grain Exchange. Chicago trades basically Soft Red winter wheat, Kansas City, Hard Red winter wheat, and Minneapolis, spring wheat. There is, however, a close relation among all these types, which are interchangeable for many purposes. In some cases the type trading on one exchange is actually deliverable against the type trading on another. All three basic types of wheat are deliverable on the Chicago Board of Trade. In this case the important limiting factors include the cost of transportation between cities, as well as differences in the characteristics of the different types of wheat. If a speculator believes that price differences are out of line between commodities trading in two cities, he sells the higher priced contract and buys the lower priced. In spreads of this kind there is no commission advantage and seldom much, if any, margin advantage.

Popular positions include Winnipeg oats versus Chicago oats, New York cocoa or sugar against London cocoa or sugar, and Chicago versus Kansas City or Minneapolis wheat.

COMBINATIONS

The fact that a trader decides that Winnipeg oats are low on Chicago oats does not mean that he should be long December Winnipeg oats and short December Chicago oats. If he thinks that oats are too high on corn, it does not mean that he should be long March corn and short March oats. The fact that he chose both contracts in the same delivery month may indicate that he has not thought enough about his spread position. More often than not the nearby contract will gain on the distant in strong markets because of the influence of strong cash markets on the nearby futures contracts, and carrying charges will decrease or inversion will increase. In weak markets nearby contracts tend to lose on the distant, and carrying charges will increase or inversion will decrease. The long side of a spread trade should probably be the contract that is lowest priced in terms of the prevailing spread differences in the commodity, and the short side should probably be the contract that appears highest priced at that time. For the best logical choice of both sides to be in the same delivery month would be sheer coincidence, yet this is the choice all too often made by spreaders who have given their positions only superficial thought.

LOW-RISK SPREADS

Many traders contemplating speculation in commodity futures markets are in great fear of the risk involved. In order to reduce fear, many writers and speakers interested in attracting new commodity speculators are fond of discussing the "no-risk spread." The usual example given is an intracommodity spread trading at full carrying charge so that a trader could buy the nearby contract and sell the distant with virtually no risk at all except for a material change in the carrying charges. Actually, attractive opportunities of this kind are quite rare. Other traders will take spread positions before the contracts reach full carrying-charge difference, with the result that the spreads may never get there. The closer the actual prices approach the apparent ideal, the more likely it is that there is such extreme weakness in the nearby lower priced contract that there is no reason for it to gain on the distant contract. The low-risk trade, therefore, may involve little risk but will have little potential. Traders who wait for full carrying-charge situations involving real potential may spend a long time waiting for a trade that will never be made successfully.

TAX SPREADS

There are some who advocate entering spread positions to achieve some tax advantage rather than to realize a profit. Purported advantages include the postponement of gains to another year or the conversion of short-term to long-term gains. The possibility is even advanced of converting a short-term gain in one year to a long-term gain in another.

Trading for tax advantages is a complex process and probably should not be attempted by traders acting without skilled professional advice. It is not only quite difficult to accomplish the objective economically, but there is always the uncertainty that the government will allow the trade to be used for the purpose for which it was intended. Taxes were discussed briefly in Chapter 3, but a really detailed coverage of the subject is beyond the scope of this book and probably beyond that of some brokers and others who are sometimes too generous with advice in this complex and hazardous field.

MISTAKES

The most frequent mistake made by those who trade spread positions is establishing them for all the wrong reasons. A common example is the net position trader who has an open loss that continues to get worse until he receives a margin call. He could, of course, solve his immediate problem by reducing or eliminating his position, but for some reason he regards a realized loss as something so much worse than an equity loss that he will do anything to avoid it. This error is so widespread and usually so disastrous that it is worth examining in some detail.

Presume that a cocoa trader is convinced that the price of May cocoa at 31 cents a pound is such a bargain that it is worth the full use of his available trading capital of $5,000. The margin requirement for a contract of 30,000 pounds of cocoa at the brokerage house of his choice is $1,200. He thereupon buys four contracts of May cocoa at 31 cents a pound and waits for great wealth to come his way. Unfortunately the news items concerning cocoa become unfavorable. Ghana announces that its crop looks better than had been expected. Holland and Germany speak of decreased consumption, and suddenly May cocoa is 29 cents and "not acting well." The trader is convinced that this adversity is temporary, that the forthcoming rise will be bigger than ever, and wishes that he could buy the cocoa now instead of when he did. Nevertheless, his broker's margin clerk, concerned only with numbers, points out that the open loss is $2,400 and that there is insufficient margin remaining to support four cocoa contracts.

The trader now has several choices. First, he could deposit additional funds, but he has none available for this purpose. Second, he could sell two cocoa contracts and keep the other two, but he does not like the prospect of having to make 400 points on each of two contracts to compensate for the 200 points he lost on each of the four. Third, he could admit that he was wrong about the cocoa market and get out of all four. This he finds impossible to do because he would now have a realized loss of about $2,000 in addition to the necessity of admitting to himself, his wife, his broker, and his accountant that he is not a particularly good trader. So he seeks a way to postpone the inevitable by buying time. Accordingly, he orders his broker to sell four contracts of July cocoa at its present price of 29.30 cents a pound.

The margin requirement on a cocoa spread is only $400 compared with the $1,200 on a net long or short position, so his total margin requirement is reduced from $4,800 to $1,600. The equity in the account was reduced from $5,000 to $2,600 by the decline in May cocoa and so the margin call is satisfied.

On close examination it should be apparent that the trader has not really improved his position and may have made it worse. He has reduced his margin requirement from $4,800 to $1,600 but would have had no requirement at all if he had simply sold his May cocoa. His new plan, if he has one, is probably to cover his short July position after cocoa stops going down and take his "profit." It should be clear, however, that his position will be no better than if he had just taken off his May cocoa and reinstated it. It is probable that the May will drop just as much as July if July goes down, and therefore his July closed profit will be equaled by an additional May open loss. The commission expense of trading the four July contracts is just the same as that incurred in taking off the four May. The moment the July short position is lifted, the margin requirement reverts to $4,800 and the trader has the same problem he had before because there has been no equity improvement. A common procedure for such people would be to take off July early one day and hope that May would rise enough by the close to overcome the margin call—which, of course, might happen. Because the trend of cocoa has been down, however, it is at least as likely that cocoa will go down during the day and make matters worse. In the end he might trade his July cocoa several times, paying commissions of about $200 every time he does until he has a margin call even on the spread position and his situation has become hopeless. At this point he will probably blame the cocoa exchange, his broker, or his bad luck, when actually he was guilty of overtrading, failing to take a loss quickly, and spreading for the wrong reasons. Aside from a rally in the May futures on the day he covers his July position, the only other way out of his predicament is an improvement in the spread itself resulting from May gaining materially on July, but in a bear market the reverse is more likely. The chances of spreading a bad position and then recovering by day trading one side of the spread or by improvement of the spread itself are extremely slim ones.

A second serious error common among spreaders is choosing a spread in preference to a net position primarily to reduce margin and then putting on such a large spread position, just because the margin is low, that they ultimately take more risk and pay more in commissions than they would have paid with a net position. Such traders fail to realize that a spread provides some but not complete protection. A spreader might consider a price difference warped and thereby offering an opportunity, but it might well become even more warped and result in a loss before it returns to normal, that is, assuming it was warped in the first place and did not merely reflect some condition overlooked by the spreader.

A corn trader, for example, may consider May corn cheap at $1.22 and consider the purchase of 5,000 bushels for an anticipated 6-cent gain, for which he would risk a 2-cent loss. The gain would give him a profit of $300 at the risk of a $100 loss. The required margin might be $400 and the round-turn commission $30. The $300 profit would be almost 75 percent of the margin deposited, but the trader concludes that he would do even better spreading because his broker will carry 5,000 May corn long against 5,000 December corn short for only $100. He believes that the expected 6-cent gain in May corn will result in its gaining 3 cents on December corn during the same time, which would represent a potential profit of $150 on the $100 margin, or a rate twice the 75 percent on the net position. The commission on the spread position would be $36 a contract compared with $30 on the net position, so the rate of net profit would still be materially higher.

This seems so attractive to the trader that he is reluctant to leave idle the remainder of the $400 margin that the net corn position would have required. He thereupon decides to utilize the same capital for the spread and puts on four of the spreads, or 20,000 long May corn against 20,000 short December. If his trade succeeds, he will realize a gross profit of $600 less the total commission of $144 or $456 on his $400 margin. What he fails to consider is the possible adversity. It is unrealistic to assume that one could be prepared for a possible loss of less than 1 cent on a spread of this kind, which means that an unplanned loss caused by some unexpected event like a change in the corn loan could easily cause a loss of 2 cents or even more. A 2-cent loss on the spread would be $400 plus the $144 commission, which would more than wipe out the trader's capital. This is a far greater loss than could reasonably have been suffered on a net position. As a result the apparently safer position with a smaller investment has become a far greater risk with an equal investment and a larger commission.

There is sometimes a temptation to establish a spread one leg at a time or to remove it one leg at a time. This has at least one clear disadvantage and usually two. The spread commission is lost. Instead of a corn spread, for example, costing the spread commission of $36, the customer must pay the full $30 for each side, or $60. Second, most traders have an uncanny ability to put on the wrong leg first or take off the wrong one first. This is so probably because most of them try to choose the exact moment that a market will turn, which is almost impossible to do; for example, suppose that the corn spread previously discussed has worked favorably and that May corn has gained the planned 3 cents on December. The trader could take off the spread at the prevailing difference and realize his profit. He could also cover his December short and allow the May to continue to rise. Instead, he will more often yield to the temptation to take off the May because it is the profitable side and stay short December, hoping that it will go down, overcome its paper loss, and allow him to show a profit on both legs of the spread. Actually, what seems to happen all too often is that the May side is taken off on a day when corn is strong, which very strength caused the spread to succeed. It is also taken off early in the day because the trader wants as much time as possible for December to react. So corn continues strong and the 3-cent profit that was realized over a period of months is lost in hours.

A mistake that is not quite so serious, but quite common, is the haphazard choosing of contract months. The trader could have timed his transaction by watching a chart indicating the difference between May and December corn, but at the moment of entry July might be a better choice than May or March better than December. The choice should be based on all pertinent factors, not on the casual choice of contracts on a spread chart or a broker's quotation board.

OPTIONS

Like so many words in the financial field, "option" is used in more than one way in the commodity futures area. One, really a popular misnomer, applies to a designated futures month such as "the July option" for soybeans. Another, and more nearly correct form, has to do with the purchase of the right to buy or sell a commodity at a designated price during a designated future period. This is similar to the same procedure used in stock, real estate, and personal services.

There are three basic forms of option applicable to the commodity markets. One is a "call," which is an option to buy a specified commodity at a specified price (the "striking price") for a designated period of time. The payment for this call is determined by market conditions such as the price level of the commodity, its expected price volatility, and the supply and demand conditions for the calls themselves. The payment is designated as the "premium." To profit by a position the price of the commodity must move up enough to cover the cost of the premium rather than merely the round-turn commission. The option trader nevertheless gains some advantages. His loss is absolutely limited to the cost of his premium. The trader in the futures markets could enter a stop to limit his possible loss, but there is no assurance that the market will not sell through his stop or that he will not remove the stop as is so often the case. More important, the option trader need not fear interim adversity. Regardless of adversity, he receives no margin calls and need only hope that he will achieve a satisfactory profit sooner or later during the period he has bought with his option.

A second popular form of option is the "put," which operates much as the call, with the same advantages and similar costs, except that the buyer of a put has the right to sell a commodity contract at a set price over a specified period of time. He expects and hopes that the price will decline.

The third type is a "straddle" or "double option." This gives the buyer the right to buy or sell the commodity at a fixed price over a specified period of time or even both if the price moves over a range wide enough to yield him a profit on the upside and downside. The straddle amounts to nothing more than a combination of a call and a put and, logically enough, costs approximately the same as a call and put combined would cost.

Usually the only options available are those that are written by underwriters in the London markets on sugar, copper, silver, or rubber. Intermittently, however, options written in the United States have been popular.

Trading in options (often called "privileges" in the past) was carried on from time to time between the early 1860s and middle 1930s. There were many efforts by the exchanges and the state and Federal governments to stop trading but early rules and laws were largely ignored by those who were supposed to obey them and by those who should have enforced them largely because the violations were so widespread that enforcement would have disrupted the entire commodity business.

The Commodity Exchange Authority finally stopped trading in options on regulated commodities after 1936. The government was concerned about many aspects of options trading but especially by the artificial price movements caused by option traders attempting to protect the options they had bought or sold. The volume of options traded became so large that it disrupted regular commodity trading on the exchanges, especially at the close of the markets, and was uncomfortably closer to a gambling practice rather than a speculative activity.[1]

One flaw in the law prohibiting options proved to be its limitation to regulated commodities. About 1970 several firms took advantage of this loophole to begin trading in popular unregulated commodities such as silver, platinum, copper, silver coins, cocoa, sugar, and plywood. About the same time the prices of many of these commodities became extremely volatile which permitted option buyers to recover their premiums in unusually short times. Buyers of straddles could hardly lose and found themselves making important amounts of money within a few weeks or even days. Bernard Baruch's two and two still made four, however, and with everyone winning losers had to be found. As long as new buyers of options entered the field faster than old ones left it there was no problem. In fact, the old ones were more anxious to reinvest in new options than they were to withdraw even their profits, much less their capital. From a short-term cash-flow point of view there was no immediate problem, but in 1973, as throughout history, the piper had to be paid. When regulatory bodies stopped trading "temporarily" and most of the public lost their confidence, liquidations equaled and finally exceeded new purchases of options, and the option companies could raise sufficient capital only by speculating successfully with the cash received for options quickly enough to pay off their underwriting obligations. The amount needed to be earned proved too great and the time available to earn it proved too short, and widespread failures of commodity option firms resulted.

The London options, which are written against actual cash commodities, underwritten by substantially capitalized companies, and realistically priced, remain popular among a small group of sophisticated traders. From time to time some American exchanges, particularly those in New York, move toward initiating option trading similar to that available in London. The Chicago Board of Trade began trading in stock options in April 1973, but theirs was more of an effort to attract business from the over-the-counter dealer's market in such options than an emulation of the old and largely discredited privilege markets.

NOTES FROM A TRADER

Spread trading is not so simple as taking net long or net short positions in a commodity. The advantages are sometimes so great, however, that it is well worth the necessary time and energy needed to master them. Most spread positions involve less risk than net positions and frequently less investment. The extra commissions incurred are usually a small consideration compared with the advantages. The avoidance of catastrophic losses is one of the greatest advantages of spread trading. Commodity markets sometimes have sudden violent price movements. When one of these movements is in favor of a trader, he realizes a welcome windfall profit, but when one is against him he is no longer a commodity trader. Many speculators with experience in trading are happy to forgo the opportunity for such windfall profits if the equal chance for a disastrous loss can be avoided. Spreads accomplish this reduction of risk because what is lost on one side in an unusually large adverse move is frequently matched by an approximately equal gain on the other side. The cost of this insurance against disaster is quite low. For a new trader spreads provide an opportunity to enter the commodity markets with minimum capital and risk.

If unregulated option trading revives, buyers should be as concerned with the financial integrity of the underwriters as with the volatility of the underlying commodities relative to their price.

CHAPTER NINE

The Game Plan

"Would you tell me, please,
which way I ought to go from
here?"
"That depends a good deal on
where you want to get to."
LEWIS CARROLL, *Alice in Wonderland*

INTRODUCTION

Many traders find themselves in a position similar to that of the German
High Command as it faced its adversary across the Channel during World
War II. The invasion of Britain was planned but never executed, whereas
the Battle of Britain was executed but never planned. Similarly, many commodity futures traders seem to go through life planning trades they never
execute and executing trades they never plan. The preceding chapters
in this section have dealt with various elements of the decision-making
process of futures trading. The objectives of the individual trader and the
size of his initial capital commitment were analyzed in Chapter 5 which
deals with risk and rewards, and the trade selection process was thoroughly
discussed from the fundamental and technical approaches. The tasks that
remain are to synthesize specific information into a game plan that will
provide for any eventuality in a trade and to complete the consideration of
the elements of money management begun in Chapter 5.

Bernard Baruch, who was no mean trader in his own right, knew the
danger of arguing with numbers. He was fond of pointing out that two and
two equal four. Once he said that "two and two make four and no one has
ever invented a way of getting something for nothing."

Many speculators less intelligent than Baruch, and much less prosperous, seem to go through life unaware of this simple truth. They take positions based on impulse instead of reason and then wait to get lucky. They have not learned that even the best speculators consider themselves fortunate to be right on most trades or even to make significant profits during most years. Some traders find that their trading has resulted in more losses than profits, that the size of their average loss exceeds the size of their average profit, and execution costs and commissions must be added to their losses and subtracted from their profits. Such traders eventually learn that two and two equal four.

The speculator has no more hope of winning on every trade than the gambler has of winning on every roll of the dice or every turn of the cards. The gambler learns to use words like "maybe," "usually," and "perhaps," and the speculator should learn the same. He can no more know all the contingencies of determining price change than a card player can know the makeup of every hand before the cards are dealt.

If the speculator will plan his trades properly, he can possibly have the odds on his side in the long run, which is something few gamblers can achieve. Over a long period of time the skilled speculator who follows a carefully thought out plan in a disciplined manner should expect to have favorable results. The gambler can win in the short run, but in the long run the odds prevail and most will lose. No reasonable person would expect good luck to prevail forever or expect skill to fail forever. At least, not so long as two and two still make four.

If there is one consistency among successful traders, it is the disciplined use of a good plan. In the following pages the manner of developing a plan and the elements it should contain will receive careful consideration. Mistakes in formulating as well as implementing such a plan will be noted so that losing tactics may be avoided. It should be evident, however, that no chapter in this book or any other, no tract, nor any lecture can make successful commodity traders out of everyone. There is a considerable amount of art, and perhaps luck, that affects results so that no simple set of rules can ever guarantee profits. Furthermore, if every trader became successful, there would be no losers to provide the profits acquired by the winners.

THE BROAD PLAN

Reduced to its most basic elements, the trading plan provides the reasons for logically entering and getting out of any position, whether or not it proves ultimately profitable. Once a position is taken in the markets a price level can do nothing but rise, fall, or remain unchanged, and a trading plan must provide a blueprint for entering a trade and establishing the action to be taken by the trader in *any* of the *three* eventualities.

Although there are several key elements of a game plan to be considered, the core of a plan must indicate, unequivocally, how the trader is to exit from trades that have been entered. Such an approach consists of not one exit plan but three. There must be a plan for accepting losses if a position shows adversity, a plan for accepting profits, and a plan for getting out of a trade if the price change over a significant period of time is negligible.

There is usually only one valid procedure for exiting from a trade that shows a loss, and that is by means of a stop-loss order. Before entering any trade the trader must decide how much adversity—for whatever reason —he is willing to accept and then place a stop-loss order at that point. An exit plan that does not involve the use of stops to close out losing positions will almost certainly be a disaster.

If a trade shows a profit, the guidelines to the trader who is composing a game plan are not nearly so clear-cut. Several possibilities exist, and a case can be made for all of them. Depending on the method of trade selection used, one obvious procedure is to decide, on entering a trade, at what price profits will be taken. Trading by price objectives may not, however, suit a trader who uses other methods of trade selection. A trader need not be a trend follower to believe in letting profits run until some gauge, technical or fundamental, gives a "signal" for opposite action. In this case the exit plan might read, "sell at the stop-loss point or when Indicator X gives a sell signal, whichever comes first."

Other methods of trading may call for holding a position until a certain amount of time has passed and then accepting whatever profit (or loss) exists. Whatever plan for accepting profits is used, the important thing is that the trader recognize that accepting profits is ultimately the name of the game. Unless he plans to rely on luck, he should have in mind one or more clear conditions that will tell him to close out his trade and take whatever profits there are. Many successful traders have found that "It is easier to make money than to keep it," and the trader who ignores the part of his plan that calls for realizing profits will ultimately learn the painful truth behind this saying.

The problem caused by a trade that does virtually nothing after it is entered is not nearly so serious. If it happens often, the trader may find that he is not trading the proper commodities; thinly traded commodities may trade at approximately the same price for years. For the occasional trade that "goes dead" there are two possible solutions. Either an arbitrary time limit can be placed on the trade (closing it out if little net change has occurred at the end of this alloted time) or it can be held until the delivery month approaches. The method of trade selection will determine which concept is followed.

The trader with well-conceived exit plans not only has completed a large part of his total trading plan but will find that in the heat of actual trading he now has important peace of mind. Knowing exactly where and why to exit a trade is the best medicine for maintaining calm nerves in the commodity futures trading game. The alternative to such planning probably causes a trader to make his greatest mistake, namely "watching the market" and making decisions based on impulsive reactions to random price moves or to margin calls. Watching the market does not alter the basic price directions that are possible once a position has been entered, that is, up, down, and sideways. The dangers of watching a market include the often overwhelming temptations to cut profits quickly, ride losses, or overstay positions going nowhere which tend to tie up capital, waste energy, and confuse and demoralize the trader.

KEY ELEMENTS OF THE PLAN

CAPITAL

Basically, any plan worthy of the name contains certain key elements. One of the first decisions to be made by any speculator who has decided to trade commodities is the amount of capital that he is willing to devote to this trading. The extremes that limit this decision are clearly definable. The minimum is the margin on the books of the broker offering the most liberal terms. The maximum is the net worth of the trader plus all he can borrow. In practical terms, neither of these extremes would be considered by a reasonable person, although there is little doubt that both routes have been followed more than once.

The actual amount of the trader's net worth to be utilized for commodity trading depends on many considerations. These were discussed at length in Chapter 5, but some should be noted here because they influence construction of the trading plan. One is the motivation of the trader. If commodity trading is to be only a stimulating avocation, it might serve its purpose just as well if done on a small scale. Another consideration is the personal aggressiveness of the trader expressed by his desire to make money in relation to his willingness to risk losing what he already has. Some traders might be willing to risk a substantial proportion of their net worth in an effort to increase the total by an important amount. Others might be willing to risk only a comparatively small amount of capital because of fear of loss, the difficulty of replacing what might be lost, or personal responsibilities. These considerations in turn may be based on the age of the trader, the effort that was expended to accumulate the capital that must be risked, the size of his family, his health, the type of job he holds, the attitude of his family toward his trading, and his nerve. Basically, a trader should not take a risk disproportionate to the importance to himself of the potential profit. Traders vary in their reactions to different types of trade which helps explain why one trader will enter a trade rejected by others and reject others that somebody else may find appealing. Sooner or later each trader should become familiar with his own trading curve and select trades partly in accordance with it.

In formulating a plan, a trader is faced with a major question of the types of technical and/or fundamental data on which to base his trade selections. Before he embarks on the all-important trade-selection process, however, he should probably consider the related problems of learning where the data are to be found and how to obtain them regularly with the expenditure of reasonable time, effort, and cost; for example, one might use a point and figure chart based on a ¼-cent reversal in an active soybean market only to learn that the difficulty of scanning miles of ticker tape searching for the ¼-cent reversals is impracticable and that buying such data might cost too much or take too long to be of any use.

If a trader must study data to make intelligent decisions, he must have a place to do his studying and the time in which to do it. Part-time trading is difficult, and haphazard preparation under adverse conditions makes satisfactory results highly unlikely. The trader must know what types of order he prefers, hopefully for carefully considered reasons, and how to communicate his instructions to his broker without missing markets. These last items may seem mechanical and routine, but they may prove more difficult to resolve satisfactorily than they first appear, and they *must* be resolved satisfactorily.

TRADE SELECTION AND EVALUATION

No rational person would undertake trading in commodities unless he felt that he possessed some method of selecting profitable trades. Recommending any single trade-selection method is not the province of this book. In-depth surveys have been presented of technical and fundamental trading methods so that the reader will be aware of many lines of inquiry. These possibilities are expanded in Section 5 for 29 active commodities. The purpose of this discussion is to illuminate some of the vital factors that must be considered when a trader chooses a particular method of trade selection and to present some general guidelines on how the method chosen may be evaluated.

Choosing a trade-selection method. The would-be trader is bombarded constantly with advertisements and claims. He is informed of methods by private advisory services, brokerage houses, and acquaintances. Few of these methods are worth serious study and some can produce dangerous errors in thinking. Because most methods are alleged to be wildly profitable, choosing a method by the sole criterion of having produced the largest past profits is probably an exercise in futility. Instead careful consideration should be given to other important characteristics that should mark any method of trade selection.

At some point in time the trader must make a general determination of the factors that will cause him to enter into a market position. He may follow the guidance of some other person or a service or he may gather sufficient fundamental and technical data of his own to justify a position. Some traders engage primarily in technical research. Others rely on basic fundamental research and seek out situations they believe to be undervalued or overvalued. Still others rely on their own feelings which may be designated a "judgment," "the touch," or "a hunch," depending on how much dignity one wishes to lend to this usually fatal approach. The type of research preceding the trade entry will help to determine a trader's strategy; that is, whether he will lean toward short-term trades or positions held for extended periods, prefer the long or short side of the market, or search out net positions, spreads, or options. If he considers being against the speculative crowd as of great importance, he might have to prefer the short side. If small margins and the elimination of drastic adverse moves are sought, spread positions may be preferred.

A popular opinion holds that "fundamentals will give the main direction of prices, and technical factors will provide the timing." Although it is true that most fundamental methods are concerned with long-term factors, one has only to consult a commodity calendar to realize that daily fundamental factors are available for a number of commodities, and there is no logical base for assuming that short-term methods of trade selections based on such information could not be devised. Moreover, a valid technical method can easily be long-term as well as short-term oriented. The authors cannot conceive of a technical method that indicates when to take action but gives no clue to the anticipated direction of price. The trader should realize that fundamental and technical methods are probably independent means of analyzing markets and as such are not necessarily complementary or contradictory.

Apart from the basic approach, other factors may be considered. Does the trader wish to follow a well-publicized method or a more obscure method which has been purchased or is based on the trader's own research? Advantages and disadvantages may be noted for both approaches. In the first instance the trader may feel that one or more popular methods of trade selection embody valuable truths and that discipline is the one missing element needed to trade them profitably. An analogy has been made that there are hundreds of thousands of pianos in the United States but only a handful of virtuosos. A disadvantage in trading many popular methods, however, is that large numbers of traders may act on such signals. This may result in poor executions because signals from these methods may be efficiently discounted. Even worse, such methods have often caught the public fancy because they rely on axioms of market behavior that appear to be logical but have no basis in fact. They are testimony to a saying often attributed to Jesse Livermore, "With ease, human beings believe what it pleases them to believe."

Perhaps scores of obscure trading methods, some mechanically complicated, are privately printed and sold to limited numbers of people for prices ranging from $10 to several thousand. An advantage to procuring one of these methods may be that the approach to markets may be viable but the seller may not have the discipline or the desire to trade himself. If this is the case, the quality of the seller's research is not necessarily low. Another reason for buying a method may be that the method of trade selection is sound but that the trading plan is incomplete, with no allowance made, for example, for money management considerations. In this case both the inventor and his clients may have experienced losses due to poor planning and not because trade selection was inherently poor. Because the importance of a complete plan is usually overlooked, the chances are that any valid private method of trade selection that the trader does locate will become available to him because of this reason. The disadvantages of securing private methods are clear and are probably applicable most of the time. That these methods are available calls into question their efficacy. Assuming that their originators are economically motivated, if the trading methods were successful, there would be little need to broadcast their availability to others.

It is possible that the trader may conclude that most, if not all, methods of trade selection available to him are of little use and may wish to do research of his own. If this is the case, he must overcome the almost insuperable obstacle of fooling himself. To avoid self-deceit the trader should vow to be as conservative as possible in validating his method and even then to add an extra margin for error. Results in the real world are seldom as good as they look on paper, using hindsight. Worse than this, frequently some overlooked problem in the method of trade selection is apparent only after the trader's capital has been lost. The number of handwritten worksheets and computer printouts detailing methods of trade selection, all with "excellent" results, must approach infinity.

The frequency of trades should be considered. Some traders may feel comfortable trading every day, whereas others may prefer only a handful of trades every year. Two factors will have an influence on how many trades are made over any time span. The first is the number of commodities followed. If a trader follows many commodities, he will trade more actively over a significant period of time. The second depends on whether the method used is designed to select trades for long-term or short-term price changes. As a general rule a long-term method will select fewer trades than a short-term method.

Whatever method of trade selection is chosen, the trader must have enough confidence in it and be comfortable enough with it to build it into his trading plan. Once a method of trade selection has been integrated into the total plan it should not be changed or substituted while trades are being contemplated or made. If, after unhurried consideration, a better method of trade selection appears or an improvement on the existing method seems feasible the entire trading plan should be redrawn, with the new method of trade selection inserted.

Because of the time factor, the trader may feel that he prefers to use the trade selection method of a broker, an advisory service, or some other organization. If so, he has saved himself considerable work in this area, but a crucial problem remains. Whether a trade selection procedure is based on his own or someone else's work, it *must* be validated by the trader himself.

Evaluating a trade-selection method. Trading commodities with a trade-selection method that has not been validated makes a mockery of the rest of the trading plan. There are few methods of trade selection available to the trader that will not bear the claim that they have been exhaustively validated. The trader is best advised to ignore such claims and validate the method himself. If he does so, two important advantages will accrue. First, he will have certain knowledge of how the method has performed to date without having to rely on the claims of others who are more likely to have a vested interest in displaying impressive results. Second, validating a method of trade selection makes the trader more aware of its properties in a way that cannot be duplicated. This information can lead to valuable peace of mind during the periods of adversity inevitably encountered by even the most successful traders.

A number of considerations must distinguish all worthwhile trade-selection methods or the generation of "buy" and "sell" signals. These are:

1. The method must rest on a solid, logical theory. If the basic concept doesn't make a modicum of sense, the trader would do well to leave the pioneering stages to others.

2. The method must have a back record with the following properties: (a) The back record must be in real time, not hypothetical time. If a trader is employing a signaling method and "tests" the signals over some period *in the past,* such a test is in hypothetical time. If a trader compiles a record of signals *before the fact,* the test is in real time. Although considerable back testing must be done, a significant portion of the back record must be in real time. Almost any literate person can invent a system that will produce vast hypothetical profits over any past period. Few methods will work under real-time conditions when interpretative principles cannot be modified by hindsight. (b) The real-time record of signals must include many different types of markets. Some methods work quite well when prices are in a relatively narrow trading range; others succeed in dynamic trending markets. Still other methods are most profitable when price action is somewhere between these two extremes. It may require a considerable amount of time to produce a back record that is extensive enough for purposes of evaluation. If the trader is too impatient to obtain a back record or is falsely persuaded by others that his requirements are not reasonable, he runs a serious risk of evaluating the method by using what is known as a "biased sample." This approach would be equivalent to a poll taker determining national attitudes toward taxation by polling only those people who work on Wall Street.

3. The signals themselves must have the following properties: (a) The entry and exit prices at which the method suggests action should be realistic. Wheat, for example, might give a buy signal at $2.40, calculated

on Tuesday night. If it opens on Wednesday at $2.45 and then rises from there, the entry price must be considered as $2.45 or the trade must be abandoned. It is surprising how many back signal records use the closing price of the signal day rather than a realistic price on the day the trader would act. The same point can be made about exit prices. If the method suggested a stop-loss price of 38.50 cents a pound on a short pork bellies trade and the price rallied 100 points in the last minute of trading to close at 39.00, the exit price should be figured at 39.00. Not only must the most conservative entry and exit prices be used in compiling the record of any method, but it is sound practice to make an extra allowance for "execution costs" in compiling a back record. Adding an extra commission on each trade is one possible procedure. Almost all professional traders will insist that they have never seen a method that made adequate allowance for execution costs. (b) Results should be consistent; a number of methods will fail badly when tested in this way. The question the trader should ask is, "To what extent does *each* profitable trade support the overall result?" A method that "would have" transformed $10,000 into $20,000 over a span of 100 trades is not deserving of confidence if the entire gain was achieved by five spectacular winning trades plus 48 nominal losses. A method that made less cumulative profit but had its gains evenly distributed among the successful signals might be much more deserving of confidence. (c) The signals must be validated by using sound statistical principles. It can then be determined how worthwhile any signaling method is likely to be and what the probability is that observed results could have been duplicated by chance alone. Chapter 10, Money Management, covers this important point in more detail.

A hypothetical method with a logical theory behind it, a three-year back record that includes 20 active commodities with 600 real-time signals, of which 450 were profitable, does not require lengthy calculations to suggest that it may be worth trying for the next several months. Hopefully, a great deal of realistic research on the trader's part will simplify this evaluative step. Nonetheless, it must be done. Jumping to false conclusions about the validity of a method from a sample of observed trades that is too small is probably one of the most common errors of the speculating public.

4. The method must provide for a realistic stop-loss order on every trade. Stops must not be placed at obvious points suggested by books that explain how to get rich in the commodity markets. But stops must be entered. Without them, the question is not *whether* the trader will lose all of his trading capital but only *when* that event will occur.

NUMBER OF COMMODITIES TO FOLLOW

An important element of the game plan mentioned briefly to date has to do with the number of commodities to be followed and, of that number, how many to trade actively at a given time. The trader who speculates only as an avocation and who relies on detailed analysis of fundamental information or elaborate technical analysis may find it difficult to follow all active commodities without making significant errors. The margin of difference between success and failure in commodity speculation is narrow enough without having to deal with opportunities that were inadvertently overlooked or losses that were taken on trades that should not have been entered in the first place. Concentrating on only a few markets permits the accumulation of a larger amount of valuable fundamental knowledge and gives a better feel for the technical action of a particular market. The limitation of such concentration is that many markets may present opportunities for a time but then trade within narrow limits for extended periods while new or previously inactive markets become active. Willingness to trade in any market that becomes active provides an adequate number of opportunities, but it is possible to be tempted into too many positions or to know too little about a situation to justify taking the necessary risks. Because concentration in selected areas provides fewer opportunities, there may be a tendency to compensate by plunging heavily into riskier positions that will result in large profits if right and large losses if wrong.

TIME HORIZON

The expected life-span of a trade deserves some thought. The overall objective is to realize the greatest possible return on the capital commensurate with risk which has been made available for commodity trading. As in any risk venture, "return" is a function of the time required, not just the number of dollars returned. A small profit attained in two or three days may justify the time expended and the capital risked, whereas a small profit that takes months to realize may be worth little even if the chance of attaining it is quite high because of the unavailability of the capital tied up in margin while the trade is open. The trader who makes a quick paper interim profit on the way to what may be a significantly greater objective must give considerable thought to his wisest course of action. Exhibit 9-1 may help to clarify this problem.

EXHIBIT 9-1   Alternative Price Objectives.

If a trader has bought pork bellies for a 4-cent (400 points) gain over a one-month period, he may be willing to accept a 100-point profit the first day or a 200-point profit during the remainder of the first week. Any point significantly over the line connecting the entry price with the price objective may be considered attractive at any time. Some traders may even wish to enter orders each day to liquidate their positions at a point significantly over the line but within a reasonable day's range. Any order taken alone is unlikely to be filled, but over a lifetime of trading a large number will be.

Considering such alternative price objectives allows the trader to avoid the problem of casting aside a well-conceived plan to take a small profit impulsively which may be as sure a road to ultimate ruin as any. Most traders willing to seize the opportunity to realize a quick small profit are much less willing to liquidate a position when faced with a quick small loss. Replacing possible large profits with small ones but leaving large losses because stop-loss points are considered inflexible produces a series of small profits and large losses and this requires a ratio of gains to losses far too favorable for most traders to achieve.

ADDING TO POSITIONS

The simplest type of plan might provide only for entering a position and liquidating it, but some traders prefer something more elaborate. A trader might intend, for example, to add to an initial position after the price has moved in a direction favorable to him. He is averaging *with the market*. Having bought a contract of sugar at 5.65 cents a pound, he could average by buying an additional contract at 5.80 cents, or, having sold short a contract of copper at 55.50 cents a pound, he could average by selling another at 53.50 cents. The logic of this procedure is that the new price level offers the opportunity to increase the potential profit but that the open profit already achieved allows the possible loss on the expanded position to be little or no greater than it was on the original position. It might even be less if the paper profit was large enough when the new units were added. The sugar trader was willing to risk 15 points from the current price, so that when he bought his first contract of sugar at 5.65 cents his 15-point risk would have come out of his working capital if the market had gone against him. When he added his second unit at 5.80, the market continued to rise, but if it had reacted 15 points and he got out he would have lost 15 points on the second unit but nothing on the first except his paper profit. If he had added a third unit, or line, at 5.95 cents, he would no longer have lost any of his capital on a 15-point reaction because he already had a 45-point open profit to act as a buffer. The disadvantage of trading in this manner is that each new unit offers less potential and more risk than those previously added because the market is closer to its ultimate objective by the amount of the price change that has already taken place. The result of poorly timed additions might well be the loss of profits already achieved in order to try to gain even larger profits. The trader who regards equity as the ultimate measure of his financial strength does not consider the loss of paper profit very different from the loss of any other kind of capital, and this might well be the most logical attitude.

Averaging *against the market* is the alternative to averaging with it, which provides for the addition of new lines after the initial position shows a loss. Use of this averaging technique against the market assures the trader of making more money than the trader who averages with the market when he proves to be right in his selection of a position and his timing. It also means that his worst positions will be his largest because so much adversity has provided him with the "opportunity" to add so much. His best positions will be his smallest because they provide no opportunity to add to the original line. Eventually the averager against the market is likely to find himself in a position that deteriorates so far that he can no longer support it, much less add to it. It has been said that sooner or later all that an averager will have left is averages.

Both types of averager face the problem of how many units to add to their initial position and when to add them. Adding a number of units at the new level greater than the number originally established is a technique too aggressive for most traders to accept. The trader, for example, who buys one contract of cotton, adds two more on strength, three more on still more strength, and continues to add in this way eventually risks buying such a large number of units near the top of the price move that even a relatively slight reversal quickly eliminates all of the paper profit that was gained on the smaller number of units acquired at lower price levels.

STOPS

The trader must estimate the amount of loss that might have to be suffered in the event that the trade proves unsuccessful. This amount may be determined from a price level indicated by chart analysis or a percentage of some dollar figure deemed to provide a valid guide, such as a percentage of the margin or of the current price level of the commodity. It may also be nothing more elaborate than the monetary loss the trader is willing to take before abandoning the trade. The potential profit may then be compared with the potential loss. Many traders erroneously believe that the potential profit must be at least twice the potential loss before a position is justified, whereas others are willing to vary the ratio according to what they regard as the *probability* of achieving the profit. They may feel, for example, that a potential profit of a given amount is worth seeking even at the risk of a loss of an equal or even greater amount if the chance of achieving the gain is materially greater than that of suffering the loss. The opportunity for even a small profit can be quite attractive if the risk of losing a small amount is minimal. This concept is discussed in detail in Chapter 10. Regardless of the favorability of the ratio of expected profit to expected loss, some trades must be passed just because the dollar amount of loss that must be risked is too great for the trader's capital to bear. Erosion of his capital by the attrition of one bad (or unlucky) trade after another is a hazard that no trader can eliminate, but to risk consistently so much of his capital in trades that "can't miss" that recovery is not reasonably likely is a certain road to ruin. For some perverse reason the trades that cannot miss are always the ones that seem to.

There is some difference of opinion concerning the relative wisdom of actually placing orders to liquidate a position at predetermined points and liquidating when the market touches one of them. Generally it is difficult to justify failure to enter an order when the objectives and stop points have been determined. Actually entering the orders assures that a carefully prepared plan will not be replaced by impulse during the heat of a trading session. A satisfactory profit that was expected, achieved, and then lost in the effort to try for more can be completely demoralizing. A reasonably small planned loss that is replaced by an unreasonably large unplanned loss can be more than demoralizing; it can be ruinous. To spend an important amount of time watching short-term ripples in a market in order to avoid entering orders in advance is usually a useless expenditure of time and energy.

Some traders are reluctant to enter stop-loss orders because of some vague feeling that somebody will force the price toward their stop price until their position is lost, after which the market will promptly go the other way. As often as not, this is an excuse to avoid putting in the stop.

A trader who decides not to use stops should at least consider their use carefully before he rejects them. If the market does not move to the stop point, no harm has been done. If the stop is elected and the price moves well beyond that point, the trader may have been saved from complete disaster. If the price moves just a little beyond the stop point, the trader often has time to reconsider without the bias of having to defend a position he is presently holding. If he wants to reinstate, he may do so, and the only cost to him is the added commission which the market may have saved for him anyhow by going far enough past his stop.[1] The only really painful course that the market could take would be to elect the stop and reverse almost immediately. If this happens to a trader often, he is probably placing stops at rather obvious points, such as just below recent lows or above recent highs. Moving markets have a tendency to reverse temporarily and clean out stops before continuing their moves, and traders should take this into consideration before using stops. Difficulties in this area result not from the use of stops but from their improper use.

Few traders are sufficiently well disciplined to be able to dispose of a position showing a loss quickly. Those who are might not be able to reach

---

[1] Some exchanges grant reduced commissions for day trades, which make the total cost of liquidating and then reinstating a position quite minor.

their brokers quickly enough to act before a small loss becomes large. Even those who have both the necessary discipline and good communications with their brokers seldom gain by not having the orders entered in advance.

THE PLAN IN ACTION

FORM OF THE PLAN

Plans may be mental or written, but written plans are preferable for most traders because they are more likely to be complete and to be followed conscientiously. Each trader may develop a plan form of his own to complement his own style of trading. Exhibit 9-2, although not exhaustive, probably contains most elements that most traders will wish to consider for each position entered but it is best for the trader to devise the form that he finds most useful. Some may wish to add or delete items or leave more or less room than is provided in the illustration for specific items. Errors are more likely to result from a plan that is too sparse than one that is too elaborate. The time and energy spent in thinking through a plan is doubtless worth the money saved through trading haphazardly. A brief explanation of the purpose and use of most items in the plan exhibited follows.

The first item, "commodity position," can be completed by indicating the commodity chosen and the contract month after either "long" or "short." If a spread position is to be entered, both blanks could be filled in or a third blank marked "spread" could be added. If a trader keeps his plan forms filed together, he will be kept aware of his overall position. Considering each trade on its own merits may result in the trader's having a number of positions all long or all short. Certain events, such as war or currency devaluation, may cause many seemingly unrelated commodities to move sharply in the same direction and leave the trader with a greater loss than he was prepared to take. This should be considered when adding new positions.

The margin for any new position, whether long, short, or spread, should be considered before a trade is entered, not after. Margins can be changed by exchanges or individual brokers and sometimes by considerable amounts. If the trader had expected to be called for an amount materially smaller than is actually required, he may find himself faced with an unexpected shortage of margin immediately after a trade is entered.

The commission per contract must be considered in order to make certain that the possible profit compared with the possible loss is adequate to justify the trade. The trader who decides to scalp 25 points in cocoa only to realize that this would represent a $75 gross profit, which must be reduced by a commission of perhaps $60, finds that he is trading for the benefit of a cocoa broker rather than for himself.

The "type of plan" may depend on the nature of the opportunity or the personality of the trader. Some people prefer to trade in one consistent

EXHIBIT 9-2 Trading Plan Summary.

1. Commodity position: Long _____ Short _____ Per contract or per spread: Margin ____ Commission ____ Trade # _____

2. Type of plan: ☐Scalp ☐Full move ☐Averaging with position ☐Averaging against position ☐Other

3. Entry plan:

Line number	Conditions necessary for entry of lines			Quantity	Cumulative quantity	Average price
	Date	Price	Other			

4. Actual entries:

Line number	Date	Quantity	Price	Cumulative quantity	Average price

5. Liquidation plan:

Line number	Conditions for liquidation of line			Quantity	Remaining quantity	Final objective	Interim objective	Initial stop	Adjusted stop	Final date
	Date	Price	Conditions							

(A) Net dollar gain to final objective _____ X Probability of achieving objective _____ = $ _____

(B) Maximum dollar risk _____ X Probability of reaching stop point _____ = $ _____

(C) Expected dollar value, (A) minus (B) = $ _____

6. Actual liquidation:

Line number	Reason for liquidation (check one)				Other	Date	Quantity	Price	Gross dollar gain or loss	Commission	Net gain	Net loss
	Planned date	Final date	Objective reached	Stop elected								

Summary·Actual dollars gained _____ Actual dollars lost _____

7. Other factors (where applicable)

Technical comments _____
_____
_____

Seasonal _____
Historical price level _____ High _____ Neutral _____ Low _____ Consensus _____ Government loan equivalent _____
Price nearest option month _____ Carrying charge _____ Cash price _____
Crop year supply-demand comments _____
_____
Near term supply-demand comments _____
_____
Landmarks necessary to indicate trade on course (include dates where applicable)_____
_____
Perils (include dates where applicable)_____

Comparable years

Year	Results	Comments
19__		
19__		
19__		

_____
_____
_____
_____
_____
_____
_____
_____

8. Trade evaluation:

Entry plan versus actual entry   Liquidation plan versus actual liquidation
☐ Good   ☐ Fair   ☐ Poor   ☐ Good   ☐ Fair   ☐ Poor
Mistakes committed:
Entry _____
Liquidation_____

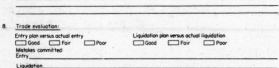

manner, whereas others believe themselves flexible enough to trade in different ways at different times or at the same time in different trades. If additional lines are not to be added to the initial position, a quick profit, or scalp, may be expected or perhaps a major change in price level over a relatively long period of time would be possible, in which case the trader may hold his position for a full move. If additional lines are to be added, they may be made when the market has moved favorably for or against the trader. In either case he must determine what factors, if any, will cause him to add a second, third, or more lines. Additions may be made at fixed intervals, as predetermined price levels are reached, or based on some other factor that seems important to the trader, such as a reaction after a rise in price. Adding new lines by utilizing paper profits is called "pyramiding."

The "actual entries" may differ from the "entry plans" because of the manner in which orders are filled; for example, a trader may have planned to enter a position in platinum on the opening of the market at a price of about $139 an ounce only to be surprised by an opening at $145 because of some unexpected news. If differences between the planned entries and actual entries are so great and so material that they affect trading results to any great degree, a change in the method used to enter trades is indicated.

The "liquidation plan" is the heart of any plan form. In providing for an exit from a trade that covers any eventuality, the trader avoids the demoralizing experience of riding losses or taking profits impulsively. It is also important that such a plan forces a trader to think through the expected dollar value of a trade before he enters, not afterward. The "expected value" concept is covered in detail in Chapters 5 and 10, but the computational aspects are not difficult and may be introduced at this time.

Assume that the trader believes he has isolated, quantified, and validated a nonrandom technical device that results in profits in 65 percent of the indicated trades over a reasonable period of time. Further assume that the technical device has signaled a particular trade that, if successful, should result in a profit of $780, whereas the execution of a stop would mean a $600 loss. Multiplying the profit $780 by the probability .65 of achieving the profit gives $507. Similarly, if the dollar risk on the trade $600 is multiplied by the probability .35 of losing, the result is $210. The expected dollar value of the trade, $297, is computed by subtracting $210 from $507. Obviously the expected value of a trade should be positive or the trade should be rejected.

The summary following the section "actual liquidation" refers to the *actual* dollars gained or lost on the trade. The trader should check his record of closed profits and losses frequently to ensure that results generally parallel expectations, both in the number of profits and losses and the average dollar amount of profits and losses.

The section headed "Other Factors" can be adapted by each trader to summarize the factors he considers important. "Technical comments" may include chart formations, volume, open interest, or response to news.

The "seasonal" item is noted because some traders think that many commodities have seasonal trends. There is nothing wrong with sometimes attempting to take advantage of a contraseasonal move, but the trader should at least be aware that he is doing it.[2]

Noting the "historical price level" makes certain that the trader knows whether he is trading at prices that have been proved unusually high or low in the past. This might not dissuade him from buying at historically high prices or selling at historically low prices, but it guarantees that he is doing it knowingly rather than inadvertently.

The "consensus," particularly of brokers and services that influence a number of traders, helps to determine whether a contemplated position is with or against the crowd. This factor, again, may not be considered critical, but it does help one to avoid being the last to buy or sell.

The "government loan equivalent" (where it applies) should be considered with the historical price level to help determine whether the current price of a future is too high or too low. If the price seems historically high but the loan level has been increased drastically, the market price may appear to be not nearly high enough rather than too high.

The relation of the cash price to the near-term option often is a clear indicator of near-term strength or weakness. A change in the relationship may provide an early indication of a change in price direction of the futures market.

"Landmarks" point out events that can reasonably be expected to happen if the trade is to be considered on course; for example, the results of a government report which is scheduled to be released on a given date should generally be in line with expectations of what the report will indicate.

"Perils" are closely related to landmarks because a report that contains statistics unfavorable to the trader's position may prove to be a peril instead of a landmark. Some perils, of course, such as a late freeze in Florida when a trader is short orange juice or a large unexpected release from the government stockpile of copper when he is long copper futures, cannot be definitely dated.

The "comparable years" section simply indicates past years in which conditions were similar to those in the current year. If the direction of price or timing in those years is not consistent with the trader's intended position, he should have some reason to believe that there are conditions existing in the present year different enough from the past to justify his position. Because the list of "other factors" may be wide and deep, additional space should be provided for their notation.

---

[2] Seasonal movements, like most apparent consistencies in the commodity markets, have a natural tendency to disappear or become distorted when they become well known. If a trader believes he has discovered a consistency, he would do well to keep it to himself.

The "trade evaluation" section of the plan is a control of the trader's discipline. Sooner or later price movement must have elected a stop or an objective or time must have run out. In any case, the result of most trades should be in accordance with the objectives and risks covered in the plan. The trader should eventually have a plan form complete enough and a discipline strong enough so that there is seldom a significant variation within his control between the possible results, good or bad, and the actual results.

A SPECIFIC PLAN

A plan is so basic to successful trading that it is worth pausing to explore in depth some of the thought that goes into its construction. Assume that a speculator has decided to enter the commodity markets and will risk $10,000 for this purpose. He has selected a brokerage house and a registered representative, opened an account, and deposited his money. He has also decided to limit his trading to wheat on the Chicago Board of Trade until he becomes knowledgeable enough to enter other markets.

It is October, the recently harvested wheat crop was a large one, and current prices are low. The trader has decided that the current price level adequately reflects the size of the crop and that there is no logical reason for it to go much lower. He also concludes that potential foreign and domestic demand, as well as anticipated commercial hedge lifting, should result in a price rise. The chart he keeps also indicates that the decline in price has stopped, and he interprets this as a signal that bullish forces are about to become dominant and that a rise is probable. He therefore decides to enter a long wheat position.

Having decided to buy wheat, a rational choice must be made among the various markets where wheat trades. This decision will be based on the estimated location and time of the greatest demand for wheat and the type of wheat that will be in the shortest supply. If the trader decides that the anticipated demand will reflect in Soft Red more than Hard Red and in winter more than in spring wheat, he will probably take his position on the Chicago Board of Trade rather than on the Kansas City or Minneapolis exchanges. He will then have to determine which contract will best reflect the expected tightness. He can do this either by making a fundamental judgment or by looking at wheat charts from other years with similar fundamentals and noting what happened then. He may also consult charts of other commodities in an effort to find similar patterns. It appears to the trader that the December contract does not provide him with enough time before having to risk taking delivery, but believing that a rising market will cause inversion he prefers nearby contracts to those more distant. He therefore compromises by selecting the March contract. He notes that in recent years during which wheat prices have risen, March gains on May, and May gains on July. Therefore a spread position in which March is bought against a short position in July might be profitable. Because the trader has adequate capital available for margin and because he believes that the risk of a net long position is reasonable, he decides merely to buy the March wheat, which is selling at $2.54½ a bushel.

Analysis of the recent market, as well as of those in years with similar characteristics, indicates that a gross profit of 8 cents a bushel has a .55 probability of being achieved by December 15, whereas a decline to $2.47 a bushel would indicate that the market is not "acting right" and that the trade should be abandoned. The probability of the latter is judged to be .45. If the price were to rise 18 cents, the gross profit on a contract of 5,000 bushels would be $900, which would leave a net profit of $870 after deduction of the round-turn commission of $30. If the trade had to be closed out unfavorably at $2.47, the decline of 7½ cents a bushel would represent a loss of $375, plus the $30 commission, or a total of $405. Considering that the expected value of a profit is worth $478.50 ($870 times .55) and the possible loss estimated at only $168.75 ($375 times .45), the trader decides to enter the trade.

Because he thinks the ratio of profit to loss is small and because so much time may be needed for the position to reach its potential, he decides not to tie up much available capital in this trade. The modest objective and close stop-loss level preclude any additions to the original position on either strength or weakness. The speculator decides that the most he is willing to lose on this trade if it proves to be unsuccessful is 5 percent of his trading capital, or $500. Note that he is concerned more with the amount of his trading capital he might lose than with the percentage of his margin or the change in the price of the wheat itself. Accordingly, he buys 5,000 bushels of wheat at $2.54½ and immediately enters another order to sell the 5,000 bushels at $2.72½ or at $2.47 stop O.C.O. (one cancels the other). A reminder is written on the trading plan to liquidate the position at the close of the market on December 15 if neither the objective nor the stop-loss points have been reached by that time. The amount of thinking and planning represented by a plan even as simple as this is probably considerably more than is done by many traders, which may be why so many people lose money trading.

A refinement of the plan outlined here is a provision for accepting something less than an 18-cent profit before December 15 in order to consider the time needed to make a profit as well as its amount. As an extreme example, a rise of 17 cents on the very same day that the position was taken would leave the trader in the position of possibly waiting for at least two months or more to make one more cent at the risk of losing back the 17 cents plus the other 7½ cents to the stop point. It may appear to be logical to accept the 17 cents because the additional gain is too small to justify the possible loss from the new price level. By the same token, it is never possible to make 18 cents in a position if a profit is always taken at 17 cents. One possible solution is to wait for the other cent in accordance with the plan. Another is to have the plan provide for such possibilities by allowing partial profits to be taken if achieved quickly; for example, it may provide a profit of 14 cents be taken during the first week, 16 cents during the next two weeks, and 18 cents thereafter. It is important, however, to work these possibilities into the plan rather than to modify the plan in accordance with impulses.

MISTAKES

As in most activities requiring skill, success or failure in trading commodities is largely a matter of how many mistakes are made. Most of them occur in the area of planning, but the greatest is not having a plan at all because no plan, no matter how poorly constructed, will allow for the loss of a trader's entire trading capital. A plan should give him a chance to try again. The alternative to planning is "watching the market," which usually results in trades being made in response to haphazard impulses triggered by random news items or hunches. It also results in considerable time being wasted watching a tape or a quotation board, time that could be used more productively by doing almost anything else. Boardroom traders too often take a small profit as quickly as possible and then rationalize by saying, "You never go broke taking a profit," or they ride a loss and say "I'm locked in."

It should be remembered that the primary advantages of planned trading include the limitation of losses in relation to available capital and a formula for getting out of a trade, regardless of the direction taken by price. If a trader devises a plan that permits him to risk all of his trading capital or does not allow him to get out of a trade unless it goes in only one direction, he had better spend some time thinking about plans before he does much trading.

Aside from not having a plan at all, the greatest possible mistake probably is to have one and not follow it. The temptations to make errors when a plan is not followed may be overwhelming. When the profit objective has been reached, the market has obviously been "acting well," and the trader must beware of "waiting for a while" to see what happens next. If still more profit is made, he can put in a new stop at the level of his original objective and make more money. The danger, however, is a reaction just after the initial objective is reached and before a stop can be inserted at a favorable point. If reasonable profits are attained and then lost back, the chance of success in the long run becomes remote. Even worse is making excuses not to take a loss when the stop point is reached. Every trader is able to rationalize riding losses by convincing himself that recovery is virtually certain from the new level, that if he were not already in the trade he would certainly enter it now, that further adversity is simply impossible, or that it is the wrong day or wrong time of the day to take the loss. The fact remains that the risk level influenced the size of the position being carried, and this in turn influenced the amount of capital being risked, which was the maximum considered reasonable. Any further loss therefore becomes unreasonable by definition. The solution to this problem is to remove temptation by putting in the stop order to liquidate the position immediately after the position is taken and leaving it in regardless of current news, time of the day, or anything else. Unfortunately the alternative to a planned loss is an unplanned loss, and the trader who habitually receipts for unplanned losses is firmly embarked on the road to ruin.

Perhaps the most stultifying mistake that can befall a trader is the assumption that success is virtually certain if he adopts a rational trade selection strategy and intelligently follows the elements of a successful plan as developed in this chapter. Unfortunately there is a final obstacle to success — money management — which is the proper concern of the closing chapter of this section for those who play the game.

NOTES FROM A TRADER

The most important aspect of planning is to *have* a plan. The second most important point is to follow it. A plan not followed is like an automobile seat belt not buckled. A plan should be kept to oneself. When other people are looking over the trader's shoulder, things start to go wrong, because he begins to attach some importance to their reactions to what he does, when they really should not affect what he does at all.

There is always some apparent reason for trying for still more profit or not taking a loss. If the trader lacks the discipline to set objectives and risk limits and to act when either is reached, he should not trade commodities.

The trailing stop seems to be an infallible method of taking advantage of big moves with modest risk. For reasons developed thoroughly in Chapter 4, this device rarely works.

Plans may be difficult to devise and adapt to one's own trading preferences and even a carefully conceived plan may not work. Markets may act in a way in which they have never acted before, and all the work that went into a plan's preparation may appear to have been wasted. Discouragement from time to time is part of the game and famines have a way of following feasts. Despite any apparent disadvantages, there can be no doubt that trading with a game plan is far better than trading without one.

CHAPTER TEN

Money Management

> It is remarkable that a science which
> began with the consideration of games
> of chance should become the most
> important object of human knowledge. . . .
> The most important questions of life
> are, for the most part, really only
> problems of probability.
>   PIERRE SIMON DE LAPLACE, *Théorie Analytique*
>   *des Probabilités, 1812*

INTRODUCTION

Games of speculation are different from gambling games in both the economic and legal senses, but to the typical speculator the similarities of the two activities greatly exceed the differences. His reasons for engaging in either one are the same; profit, excitement, diversion, compulsion, or some of their combinations. Most important, many of the rules are quite similar, and therefore the extensive thought applied to gambling games is quite applicable to the commodity trading game as well.

The trader, like the gambler, will find it far more difficult to handle his money in a logical and disciplined manner than to learn the rules of the game. Anyone, for example, can learn to play draw poker—the ranking of possible hands and local interpretations of the rules and procedures—in an hour or so. Many people, however, have played the game for years and have lost consistently because of poor money management. Most of these losers bemoan their bad luck, just as losing commodity traders tend to blame their brokers, unexpected events, or bad luck for their own errors in money management.

It is impossible to develop a set of rules in this chapter to serve as a guide for all traders under all conditions. Trading is an individual decision-making process and each trader brings his own unique intellectual and behavioral background to bear on the problem of approaching commodity trading most profitably. Traders have different goals in the markets, different attitudes toward their profits and losses, and different preferences in their styles of trading, to say nothing of a host of other differences such as time available, tax considerations, and financial and psychological strength. The trader who hopes to succeed in the long run must be able to recognize and develop his behavioral skills in order to determine a set of objectives most logical for his concept of maximum advantage. To employ a money management system effectively a trader must consider its four basic elements:

1. Initial capital.
2. Objectives.
3. The expectation of the game being played.
4. The probability of ruin.

The first two were discussed in preceding chapters. The remaining two are considered in the pages that follow. The discussion here does not consider subjective motivations in great detail because it would require an extensive foray into psychology involving a wide range of personal drives such as a guilt-ridden risk-lover's desire to lose his money.

EXPECTATION OF THE GAME PLAYED

Probability. A game, as discussed here, may consist of one or more trials which a gambler would call bets and a speculator would call trades. The expectation, or average payoff, of the game being played indicates whether it consisted primarily of fair bets (those with zero expectation), good bets (those with a positive expectation), or bad bets (those with a negative expectation). If the game consisted of only one trial, the expectation of the game and the trial would be the same. A basic element of expectation is the long run relative frequency of an event occurring. This element is probability, expressed as a number ranging from a low of zero to a high of one.

An example is provided by a game centering on the flipping of a coin. The probability of "heads" is .5 and the probability of "tails" is .5. Another example is provided by the draw poker player who is holding four spades and draws one card to his hand hoping to find a fifth spade to make a flush and, hopefully, winning the pot. The probability of drawing that fifth spade from a deck of cards without a joker is .191; the probability of not drawing it is .809.

It should be noted that the gambler or player of a social card game has a decided advantage over the speculator in the commodity or stock market in that the gambler is able to determine the precise probabilities inherent in his game and to act accordingly. (This is not to say, of course, that the player will actually use his advantage or that knowing his probabilities will enable him to profit from playing the game.) A roulette player may be interested in betting on red versus black or odd versus even. He can readily determine that the wheel has 36 numbers, half odd, half even, half on a red background, and half on black. In addition, most American roulette wheels have a "0" and "00" on a green background, on both of which the casino wins all red, black, odd, and even bets. The player knows, therefore, that he has 18 chances to win and 20 chances to lose, regardless of how he bets. The probability of winning is .4737 ($\frac{18}{38}$) and the probability of losing is .5263 ($\frac{20}{38}$).

Unlike the coin flipper who knows that after many flips approximately half will have resulted in heads, the commodity trader who concludes that sugar is going to increase in price is far less certain of measuring the probability of this event occurring before an unreasonably large adverse move. He may believe that the chance of an adequate rise in price before a substantial drop is .7, but this probability is subjective. Regardless of the thoroughness of his fundamental or technical research, the commodity trader is applying his knowledge of the past to make his evaluation of the future. But in an area as dynamic as the commodity futures markets conditions as well as probabilities change frequently. Even a huge number of samples to serve as a guide cannot lead to certain determination of the probabilities of success or failure because of the complex and fluid nature of the game and the rules under which it must be played.

Payoff. One who plays a game or trades a market normally hopes to get more out of it than he puts into it. The emphasis here is placed on money payoff rather than psychic costs and income (most people seem to get more satisfaction out of winning than losing, anyway). The money payoff of a game (gambling or trading) can be used to measure what may be won versus what may be lost, modified sometimes by an admission charge to a casino or a commission charged by a broker. A player may be in a position, for example, to win $1,000 if he wins or to lose $500 if he loses. In this case his "money odds" may be said to be 2 to 1 of winning.

It should be clear that the mathematical *expectation* of a game depends on the probabilities and payoffs. Specifically, it is the sum of the possible payoffs with each payoff weighted (multiplied) by its respective probability. The player who stands to win $1,000 or lose $500 with a probability of winning of .5 has a mathematical expectation or average payoff of $1,000 $\times$ .5 − $500 $\times$ .5 = $250, and obviously might consider playing the game because in the long run he will average $250 gain per play of the game. Suppose, however, that a player stands to win only $500 if he wins or lose $1,000 if he loses. He might be tempted to reject the game out of hand, but what if the probability of winning were .9 and the probability of losing only .1? The expectation of the game would be $500 $\times$ .9 − $1,000 $\times$ .1 = $350, still a positive value. On the basis of monetary expectation, the second game is even more favorable than the first, for which reason the often-given advice to take a position in the stock or commodity markets only if the trader will make two or three times or more what he may lose is ordinarily so foolish. Those giving such advice rarely speak of the *probability* of winning or losing, and without it the expected monetary value of taking the position cannot be determined. A game in which the player may win twice as many dollars as he stands to lose is no different in expectation from a game in which he may lose twice as many dollars as he may win if his probability of winning the first game is .33 and the second game, .67. Expectation, in short, is nothing more than the average payoff which is derived by modifying the payoff of an event by its probability of occurring.

Depending on the combination of probability and payoff, a game may be said to be favorable if its expectation is more than zero or unfavorable, if less. Returning to the roulette player discussed above, it will be recalled that the probability of his winning was .4737 and of losing, .5263. In the usual casino the player will be offered a money return equal to the money that he risks; that is, a player who bets a dollar on red, black, odd, or even will lose the dollar if he loses and win a dollar if wins. Usually there is no admission charge to a casino, so the payoff to the player is even (or the odds may be said to be 50-50). The mathematical expectation of the game to the player betting on one of the four items listed would therefore be 47.37 cents of each dollar bet and the expectation of the casino would be the other 52.63 cents. The house "take" or "advantage" is the difference of 5.26 cents on a one-dollar bet or 5.26 percent of all bets. The player may be said to be making a bad bet, and because the house has the other side of all players' bets it may be said to be making all good bets, each by the same margin.

The commodity trader who tries to discover whether he is in a better or worse position than the roulette player finds his analysis difficult. He is aware precisely of only one aspect of his expectation of winning and that is some part of his payoff. He can probably determine the commission that he will have to pay and estimate the opportunity cost on the capital that he utilizes for margin. The remaining element of the payoff, that is, how much he will win or lose because of market action, is far more difficult to determine accurately. A disciplined trader can, of course, determine the points at which he intends to liquidate his position, win or lose. He may even be sufficiently disciplined to enter orders at the two points he has determined —one intended to take his profit at the objective and the other to stop his loss when he has all the adversity he cares to suffer on a trade. If he sets his objective at a definite limit and leaves an open order in at that point, the chance of his getting exactly his price on a *successful* trade is quite high. He obviously cannot get less and only infrequently will a market act so favorably for him that he will be filled at a price even better than he has asked. On a losing trade, however, the outcome is far less certain. If he enters a stop-loss order which is elected, that order can be filled at his stop price, but also at better or worse. A fill at a better price than the stop specified is even rarer than a fill at a price better than a limit on the order at a trader's objective, but a fill at a price worse than that specified on a stop-loss order is quite common and sometimes the fill is *much* worse. On balance, therefore, if he wins, the trader's objective will usually be exactly as planned, but if he loses the loss will frequently be greater than expected. (This is one of the major reasons why trading in the real world seldom turns out to be so profitable as one's paper trading has indicated that it should be). The sophisticated trader must learn eventually to take this into consideration and plan in advance for the "execution costs" of his trades to include not only commissions but also some extra adversity on his losing trades. He may well have learned that the cost of extra adversity over a long period of trading may approach the far more obvious cost of commissions.

Despite his problems of probability and payoff, the trader must reach a conclusion concerning his chance of being ahead after making one or a series of trades, determine how much he expects to be ahead if he wins, how much he expects to lose if he loses, and use this knowledge to help plan how to play the game. He may, of course, also decide not to play at all after completing an evaluation of his expectation.

Fair bets. It is obvious that if a game consisted of one or more fair bets it would involve a zero expectation and be an even game. It might be concluded that participants in such a game must be playing basically for fun and that no one has the right to expect to win in the long run. This, however, is not the case. Although the amount of money a person has does not affect the expectation on a single play of the game (whether the flip of a coin or a trade in plywood), the capital available to the players can be of tremendous importance in determining their eventual financial outcome.

If two players are betting on coin flips and one has significantly more capital than the other, that player's chance of eventually winning all the other's money, hence ruining him, is considerable. The greater the difference in relative capital and the more of his capital the poorer of the two players bets, the greater the probability that the richer will ruin the poorer and the faster it will happen. Even though the coins will work toward 50 percent heads and 50 percent tails, the probability of "runs" of heads or tails also increases as the game progresses. The probability, for example, of a series of 10 heads being flipped consecutively in 10 trials is not great, but if one continued to flip a coin for days at a time the probability of 10 heads appearing in a row *sooner or later* actually will become rather high. If this event should be favorable to the poorer player, he will increase his capital and the richer player will be somewhat impaired, but if the series favors the richer player, the poorer can well be ruined. The richer player can expect to have his run sooner or later. That is why a gambling casino competing against small players does not even need its favorable probability to win on balance from a high proportion of its small opponents. This also helps the large commodity trader to win even more from smaller traders as time goes on. In commodity trading, as in so many other areas of financial endeavor, the nature of the game favors the rich getting richer.

Good bets. The player making a good bet, which may be referred to as favorable or positive, has in his favor a mathematical expectation of winning money each time he makes it. A game consisting of one such bet or a preponderance of them is a favorable game. (Some consider each bet a game and a series of bets would then be a series of favorable games, but the difference in semantics is of more interest to game theorists than to commodity traders.) Positive expectation merely requires some combinations of probability and payoff (including cost of playing the game) that makes the bet or game financially favorable to the player. The coin flipper, for example, may be betting even money that he can flip one head before his opponent flips two, or he may be betting that he will flip a head before his opponent flips a tail, but he will win a dollar if he wins and lose 50 cents if he loses. He may need to flip one head to win a dollar at the risk of losing one dollar if his opponent flips a tail, but he gets paid a dime for playing the game. Better still for the fortunate player such as a racetrack which has a positive expectation of winning a high proportion of wagers placed but still charges its patrons for the opportunity of entering the premises, to say nothing of collecting fees for allowing them to park their cars outside, is some combination of these favorable terms.

Bad bets. One might ask why a person would make a bad bet, that is, one in which he has a negative expectation when probability and payoffs are considered. One reason, of course, is that some players do not realize that their bets are bad or how bad they are. Others choose to play in negative games, knowing they are unfavorable, because they have motivations explained by psychological drives rather than logically based financial factors. Presumably some people find a masochistic pleasure in losing or pride themselves on their courage in playing David to the bookmaker's Goliath. Some maintain that they enjoy playing the game enough to warrant the inevitable cost of playing, but here again the subjective world of individual psychological makeup (or mixup) would have to be examined. This chapter assumes that the reader is interested in making good bets and playing favorable games.

In passing, it might be noted that there can be a high probability of eventually winning a game by ruining your opponent, even in a game in which each bet is bad, provided that it is not *too* bad and that the player making the bad bets has capital materially exceeding that of his opponent and that bets are large. This happy circumstance, however, can never accrue to a commodity trader who is trading badly because he is always small in relation to the combined size of his opponents. The large trader who tried to overcome an unfavorable approach to commodity trading would almost certainly find himself among the small traders within a reasonably short time.

Strategy for a favorable game. The commodity trader typically has, or thinks he has, a positive expected payoff, and it is that kind of game that is examined in more detail for a logical approach to ultimate victory. The reader should not treat this subject lightly. The *manner* in which he plays the commodity futures trading game is far more likely to cause his ultimate success or failure than is any other aspect of his trading, including his method of selecting trades.

It would be of considerable value if a money-management strategy applicable to all traders could be offered here. This is impossible, however. The number of possible variables in the solution of all possible trading strategy problems would extend this book into at least a five-foot shelf. Factors that would have to be considered include not only differences in personal attitudes toward profits and losses but also the specific probabilities that traders believe are inherent in the trades they select. The varying differences in probabilities of success and various ratios of profit to loss, differences in commissions, and different possible combinations of "good trades," "better trades," and "best trades" make for a huge number of possible variations. A single trader with an elaborate system of selecting trades may enter positions with wide variations in probabilities, payoffs, temporary adversity possibilities, commissions, required capital commitments, and time requirements. Too, there may be times when certain completely unexpected events create biases that were not taken into consideration and unexpectedly cause many simultaneous positions to have good or bad results at the same time. A trader, for example, may have long positions in four commodities presumed to be reacting to different forces, with all four trade entries based on apparently independent technical signals. An event may occur that will prove to be bearish on *all* commodities, and the trader will suffer four losses. Had he been short, he would have had four profits.

An individual trader facing this problem must consider the data he has available that apply to his own methods of trade selection and, even recognizing some of the subjectivity in money management and determination of probabilities, at least do his best to solve his problem logically. This is considerably better than making decisions haphazardly and hoping that everything will turn out well. The numbers that might apply to a mythical trader and what they mean to him should be a useful subject for detailed examination.

Assume that a trader has initial trading capital of $10,000. He has developed a technical trading method he believes will indicate trade opportunities that will offer a profit opportunity equal in dollars to the risk of loss when commissions and other execution costs are considered. Based on his research or experience, the trader believes that his chance for a profit on any given trade is .55 and his chance for a loss, therefore, .45. His mathematical advantage on each trade is .10. (He may feel that some trades will give him more advantage than that, but he has learned to temporize optimism and always take the conservative approach to any of his trading decisions.) It is also assumed that the trader plans to trade indefinitely rather than aim for some specific objective, no change is expected in his presumed probabilities based on his continuing research, and that his attitudes toward his gains and losses will remain unchanged as his fortunes ebb and flow. If he is successful, his gains could range between reasonably satisfactory and huge, depending on the frequency of his trades. As he proceeds from his research into real-time trading, the trader should be alert to bench marks to make sure that he is on course.

Real-time validation. As has been indicated, life in the real world has a way of being more difficult than paper trading has shown it should be. The trader implementing his untested plans should make some effort to be sure that he is "on course." The statistics will vary with the plan being used, results expected, and degrees of variation from the expected acceptable to the trader, but at some point a method counted on to yield a given number of profits should begin yielding them.

The trader who anticipates a 10 percent advantage could make use of the figures in Table 10-1. This table can help to show him how many losses he should have suffered in a given number of trades. Suppose, for example, that he has taken three losses in his first five trades and is concerned because he believes he should have had only two. The first line of Table 10-1 indicates that he has a probability of .9497 of more than zero loses, .7438 of more than one, .4069 of more than 2, .1312 of more than three, and .0185 of losing on all five. Three losses in five trades represent more than 40 percent, and in the column headed by "40" he will note that the chance of three or more losses was .4069. Three losses in five trades, there-

TABLE 10-1   PROBABILITY OR MORE THAN p PERCENT
UNSUCCESSFUL TRADES WITH A PROBABILITY .55 OF
WINNING (10 PERCENT ADVANTAGE)*

No. of trades \ P→	0	10	20	30	40	50	60	70	80	90	100
5	.9497		.7438		.4069		.1312		.0185		.0000
10	.9975	.9767	.9004	.7340	.4956	.2616	.1020	.0274	.0045	.0003	.0000
20	1.0000	.9991	.9811	.8701	.5857	.2493	.0580	.0064	.0003	.0000	.0000
30	1.0000	1.0000	.9960	.9306	.6408	.2309	.0334	.0016	.0000	.0000	.0000
40	1.0000	1.0000	.9993	.9717	.7376	.2624	.0283	.0007	.0000	.0000	.0000
50	1.0000	1.0000	.9998	.9835	.7615	.2385	.0165	.0002	.0000	.0000	.0000
60	1.0000	1.0000	.9999	.9903	.7820	.2180	.0097	.0001	.0000	.0000	.0000
70	1.0000	1.0000	1.0000	.9942	.7998	.2002	.0058	.0000	.0000	.0000	.0000
80	1.0000	1.0000	1.0000	.9965	.8156	.1844	.0035	.0000	.0000	.0000	.0000
90	1.0000	1.0000	1.0000	.9979	.8294	.1706	.0021	.0000	.0000	.0000	.0000
100	1.0000	1.0000	1.0000	.9987	.8426	.1574	.0013	.0000	.0000	.0000	.0000
150	1.0000	1.0000	1.0000	.9999	.8909	.1091	.0001	.0000	.0000	.0000	.0000
200	1.0000	1.0000	1.0000	1.0000	.9209	.0791	.0000	.0000	.0000	.0000	.0000
250	1.0000	1.0000	1.0000	1.0000	.9440	.0560	.0000	.0000	.0000	.0000	.0000
300	1.0000	1.0000	1.0000	1.0000	.9592	.0408	.0000	.0000	.0000	.0000	.0000
400	1.0000	1.0000	1.0000	1.0000	.9778	.0222	.0000	.0000	.0000	.0000	.0000
500	1.0000	1.0000	1.0000	1.0000	.9877	.0123	.0000	.0000	.0000	.0000	.0000

* In this table and in Tables 10-2 and 10-3 probabilities shown for trades 5 through 30 were derived from binomial distributions; for 40 through 500 they were derived from normal distributions that approximate binomial distributions.

fore, should come as no great shock. By the same token, if he had lost on all five of his first five trades he should also note carefully that there was a chance of only .0185 of this happening if in fact his probability of winning had been .55. Some traders might go back to their paper trading for a while, even at this early juncture, but others might go on trading despite the uncomfortable odds of more than 50–1 that the real world is not doing what their paper worlds said it should. If after 30 trades such a trader has had more than 18 losses (more than .60, hence $P = 60$) he will know that he is still in an unpleasant area with only a .0334 chance of being right, and if he has had more than 21 losses the chance of his being on a satisfactory course is an almost ridiculous .0016. As he approaches his hundredth trade, his percentage of losses should be clearly closing in on the expected .45. The chance of anything over .50 losses at this level is only .1574, over .60, only .0013, and over .70, statistically approaches the impossible.

Tables 10-2 and 10-3 provide the same information for traders who believe that they have probability advantages of .20 (.60–.40) or .30 (.65–.35). Traders with greater advantages have an inkling much sooner than those with smaller advantages whether they are on course, and at each level the chance of their judging correctly whether they are on course is higher than those with smaller advantages at the same level. A trader with a .30 advantage, for example, who has traded 100 times and who has had more than 50 losses knows that there are only eight chances in 1,000 that his real-world trading is in line with his researched expectations.

A trader following his program has two tasks in the area of validation.

TABLE 10-2   PROBABILITY OF MORE THAN p PERCENT UNSUCCESSFUL TRADES WITH A PROBABILITY .60 OF WINNING (20 PERCENT ADVANTAGE)

No. of trades	P→ 0	10	20	30	40	50	60	70	80	90	100
5	.9222		.6630		.3174		.0870		.0102		.0000
10	.9940	.9537	.8328	.6178	.3670	.1663	.0548	.0123	.0017	.0001	.0000
20	1.0000	.9964	.9491	.7501	.4045	.1277	.0222	.0017	.0001	.0000	.0000
30	1.0000	.9997	.9829	.8238	.4216	.0972	.0083	.0002	.0000	.0000	.0000
40	1.0000	.9999	.9951	.9017	.5000	.0983	.0049	.0001	.0000	.0000	.0000
50	1.0000	1.0000	.9981	.9256	.5000	.0744	.0019	.0000	.0000	.0000	.0000
60	1.0000	1.0000	.9992	.9430	.5000	.0570	.0008	.0000	.0000	.0000	.0000
70	1.0000	1.0000	.9997	.9561	.5000	.0439	.0003	.0000	.0000	.0000	.0000
80	1.0000	1.0000	.9999	.9661	.5000	.0339	.0001	.0000	.0000	.0000	.0000
90	1.0000	1.0000	.9999	.9736	.5000	.0264	.0001	.0000	.0000	.0000	.0000
100	1.0000	1.0000	1.0000	.9794	.5000	.0206	.0000	.0000	.0000	.0000	.0000
150	1.0000	1.0000	1.0000	.9938	.5000	.0062	.0000	.0000	.0000	.0000	.0000
200	1.0000	1.0000	1.0000	.9981	.5000	.0019	.0000	.0000	.0000	.0000	.0000
250	1.0000	1.0000	1.0000	.9994	.5000	.0006	.0000	.0000	.0000	.0000	.0000
300	1.0000	1.0000	1.0000	.9998	.5000	.0002	.0000	.0000	.0000	.0000	.0000
400	1.0000	1.0000	1.0000	1.0000	.5000	.0000	.0000	.0000	.0000	.0000	.0000
500	1.0000	1.0000	1.0000	1.0000	.5000	.0000	.0000	.0000	.0000	.0000	.0000

TABLE 10-3 PROBABILITY OF MORE THAN p PERCENT
UNSUCCESSFUL TRADES WITH A PROBABILITY .65 OF
WINNING (30 PERCENT ADVANTAGE)

No. of trades \ P →	0	10	20	30	40	50	60	70	80	90	100
5	.8840		.5716		.2352		.0540		.0053		.0000
10	.9865	.9140	.7384	.4862	.2485	.0949	.0262	.0048	.0005	.0000	.0000
20	.9998	.9879	.8818	.5834	.2376	.0532	.0060	.0031	.0000	.0000	.0000
30	1.0000	.9981	.9414	.6425	.2198	.0301	.0014	.0000	.0000	.0000	.0000
40	1.0000	.9995	.9766	.7463	.2537	.0234	.0005	.0000	.0000	.0000	.0000
50	1.0000	.9999	.9869	.7707	.2293	.0131	.0001	.0000	.0000	.0000	.0000
60	1.0000	1.0000	.9926	.7938	.2062	.0074	.0000	.0000	.0000	.0000	.0000
70	1.0000	1.0000	.9957	.8098	.1902	.0043	.0000	.0000	.0000	.0000	.0000
80	1.0000	1.0000	.9975	.8258	.1742	.0025	.0000	.0000	.0000	.0000	.0000
90	1.0000	1.0000	.9986	.8401	.1599	.0014	.0000	.0000	.0000	.0000	.0000
100	1.0000	1.0000	.9992	.8527	.1473	.0008	.0000	.0000	.0000	.0000	.0000
150	1.0000	1.0000	.9999	.9003	.0997	.0001	.0000	.0000	.0000	.0000	.0000
200	1.0000	1.0000	1.0000	.9309	.0691	.0000	.0000	.0000	.0000	.0000	.0000
250	1.0000	1.0000	1.0000	.9512	.0488	.0000	.0000	.0000	.0000	.0000	.0000
300	1.0000	1.0000	1.0000	.9653	.0347	.0000	.0000	.0000	.0000	.0000	.0000
400	1.0000	1.0000	1.0000	.9819	.0181	.0000	.0000	.0000	.0000	.0000	.0000
500	1.0000	1.0000	1.0000	.9905	.0095	.0000	.0000	.0000	.0000	.0000	.0000

One is determining statistically or by excellent judgment whether his results are approaching his expectations at various levels of real-time trading. The other is deciding on the level that will cause him to abandon this method if results are less than favorable. One trader with losses indicating only a .20 chance of his being right may continue trading, whereas a second may go back and do more research, and a third may throw up his hands in disgust and buy U.S. Treasury bills.

PROBABILITY OF RUIN

Conceptual foundation. Success presents few problems to most traders; it is the loss of trading capital, or ruin, that must be considered primary. Consideration of ruin demands an early and one of the most critical decisions in the area of money management. The risk of ruin in favorable games increases directly as more of the available trading capital is utilized for each trade. Increasingly conservative approaches also result in less profit potential, either because less will be gained on each winning trade or because there will be fewer trades. An intelligent median must be chosen.

Assume that the trader decides to use $2,500, or one-fourth of his $10,000 capital, for each trade and plans to continue making $2,500 commitments indefinitely. His risk of ruin is heavily concentrated in the early stages of his trading program. If he loses on his first two or three trades, he is in serious trouble, and if he loses on his first four trades he is out of the trading business. The chance of his losing on his first trade is .45. His chance of losing on all four of his first four trades is only $(.45)^4$, or .04.

If he is ahead after the first four trades and finds himself with trading capital five or six times the size of his $2,500 commitments, four losses (consecutive or net) can no longer ruin him, but then he also faces an increasingly high probability of more than four net losses as he continues his trading over time. The probability R of his eventual ruin is given by the formula

$$R = \left(\frac{1 - A}{1 + A}\right)^C,$$

where A is the trader's advantage in his trades expressed in decimal form and C is the number of trading units with which he begins.[1] If a trader is willing to risk one-third of his capital in a trade, he has three initial trading units. If he risks $\frac{1}{20}$, he has 20 trading units. The trader being considered here will risk $2,500 of his $10,000 on each trade and so has four trading units when his trading begins. His chance of eventual ruin is $[(1 - .1)/(1 + .1)]^4$, or .45. He may find this number uncomfortably high and may examine his chance of succeeding if he risked only one-tenth of his capital on each trade rather than one-fourth. The trader may consider survival more important than maximizing expected profits as fast as possible but having to accept more risk to do so. Some traders, of course, may choose maximization and accept the added risk that goes with it. The risk of only $1,000 of the trader's $10,000 capital on each trade provides a dramatic example of the virtue of taking small risks if survival is the major motivation. The chance of losing all of the $10,000 capital in the first 10 trades drops to $(.45)^{10}$, or less than one chance in 3,000. Even if he continued to trade indefinitely, risking $1,000 on every trade in order to gain $1,000, his chance of ruin would be only .1341. The probability of success on any given trade has remained unchanged, but the trader's chance of survival has increased from .55 to .87 merely by his trading on a more conservative scale.

One of the most difficult and important decisions to be made by the trader is what to do if his account grows on schedule, thereby further indicating that his favorable research projections were correct. If his original capital of $10,000 has grown to $20,000, his chance of being ruined if he continues trading on a scale of $1,000 has become much smaller than the original .1341 because it would now take 20 net losses rather than 10 to ruin him. The probability of this happening is only .018. The chance of his continuing to add to his capital over time becomes more and more certain as it builds in size if he does not greatly increase his scale of trading. Having reached $20,000, the chance of reaching $30,000 is even greater, and having reached $70,000, say, the chance of then reaching $80,000

[1] William Feller, *An Introduction to Probability Theory and its Applications,* John Wiley & Sons, New York, 1957. A good source of basic probability theory is Samuel Goldberg, *Probability: An Introduction,* Prentice-Hall, Englewood Cliffs, N.J., 1960.

is even greater still. On the other hand, when the trader reached $20,000, he could have become more aggressive. He could have begun trading $20,000 with the same degree of probability of reaching $40,000 as he originally had of reaching $20,000 from $10,000. The chance R of being ruined before reaching a higher specified level from any given starting point is provided by the formula

$$R = \frac{\left[(1 + A)/(1 - A)\right]^{W} - 1}{\left[(1 + A)/(1 - A)\right]^{C + W} - 1},$$

where A is the trader's advantage, C is the original trading capital expressed in trading units, and W is the number of those same sized units he hopes to accumulate.[2] In the case of the trader being considered in detail here, his original capital is $10,000, which represents 10 trading units. With his .10 advantage his chance of getting to $20,000 successfully is .8815. If he arrives at the $20,000 level and chooses to try for $40,000 by using $2,000 units of trading, his chance of arriving at $40,000 is again .8815. Each time he doubles his money, he will have the same chance of doubling it again by doubling his trading units. This assumes that he will not eventually find himself trading on a scale that will raise market liquidity problems, thereby decreasing his assumed .10 advantage, or that he will pass his "stress point" and damage his judgment. Such a program may seem quite exciting because a trader has to double his original $10,000 only seven times to accumulate $1,280,000. Before he is too quick to give up his virtual certainty of continuing to accumulate money (if he never raises his scale of trading) he should realize that if he doubles his scale of trading his overall risk of ruin will increase considerably. The chance of success in seven successive series with a chance of .8815 of winning each series is $(.8815)^7$ and the chance of ruin is $1 - (.8815)^7$ or an uncomfortable .5866. Even this may be exaggerating the real chance of success because (a) the presumed .10 advantage may have some high hopes mixed in with the research; (b) independence of results often does not exist, which makes runs of "bad luck" more likely than the computed probabilities would indicate; and (c) the growth of execution costs and market liquidity problems, as capital grows, becomes increasingly likely.

A trader must work out his own probabilities, given his own facts, judgments, and attitudes, but it may be of interest to note in Table 10-4 the probabilities faced by traders with advantages of 10, 20, and 30 percent in their favor on each trade, including all costs, with payoffs equaling losses. The effects of different sizes of commitments and the length of time during which trading is planned to continue become quite clear; for example, if a trader has an assumed 10 percent advantage, capital of $10,000, and a plan to risk $2,000 (one-fifth of his capital; hence his capital represents five original trading units), with payoff and dollar risk also $2,000, and expects

[2] *Ibid.*

TABLE 10-4   TRADER'S CHANCE OF RUIN WHEN HE HAS A
.10, .20, OR .30 ADVANTAGE ATTEMPTING EITHER TO
DOUBLE HIS INITIAL CAPITAL OR TRADE INDEFINITELY

C	W	.10 advantage probability of		.20 advantage probability of		.30 advantage probability of	
		success	ruin	success	ruin	success	ruin
1	1	55	45	60	40	65	35
1	∞	18.2	81.8	33.3	66.7	46.2	53.8
2	2	59.9	40.1	69.2	30.8	77.5	22.5
2	∞	33.1	66.9	55.6	44.4	71.0	29.0
3	3	64.6	35.4	77.1	22.9	86.5	13.5
3	∞	45.2	54.8	70.4	29.6	84.4	15.6
4	4	69.1	30.9	83.5	16.5	92.2	7.8
4	∞	55.2	44.8	80.2	19.8	91.6	8.4
5	5	73.2	26.8	88.4	11.6	95.7	4.3
5	∞	63.3	36.7	86.8	13.2	95.5	4.5
6	6	76.9	23.1	91.9	8.1	97.6	2.4
6	∞	70.0	30.0	91.2	8.8	97.6	2.4
7	7	80.3	19.7	94.5	5.5	98.7	1.3
7	∞	75.5	24.5	94.2	5.8	98.7	1.3
8	8	83.3	16.7	96.2	3.8	99.3	.7
8	∞	79.9	20.1	96.1	3.9	99.3	.7
9	9	85.9	14.1	97.5	2.5	99.6	.4
9	∞	83.6	16.4	97.4	2.6	99.6	.4
10	10	88.1	11.9	98.3	1.7	99.8	.2
10	∞	86.6	13.4	98.3	1.7	99.8	.2
11	11	90.1	9.9	98.9	1.1	99.9	.1
11	∞	89.0	11.0	98.9	1.1	99.9	.1
12	12	91.7	8.3	99.2	.8	99.9	.1
12	∞	91.0	9.0	99.2	.8	99.9	.1

Key: C, trader's initial capital in units; W, the number of additional units
the trader is attempting to gain; the symbol "∞" indicates that the trader
expects to trade indefinitely. Format of this table was derived from Edward
O. Thorp, *Beat the Dealer*, Random House, 1962, p. 63.

to trade indefinitely, his chance of success would be .633 and his chance of
ruin .367. If he reduced his exposure and objective on each trade to $1,000,
his chance of long-term success would increase to .866 and his chance of
ruin would drop to .134. If a trader thought that his advantage was .30
(.65 — .35) his chance of ruin, risking only one-tenth of this capital and
trading indefinitely without increasing his scale of trading, if successful,
would be a minuscule .002. It should be obvious that a greater advantage
vastly increases the chance of success in trading, just as it does in gambling,
but it should now also be obvious that a trader with less probability of success but trading conservatively can actually have a better chance of long-
term success (winning the game) than a trader with a higher probability of
success who chooses to trade more aggressively. The trader with .30 advantage, using one-fourth of his initial capital on each trade, faces a chance
of ruin of a little more than .08. The trader with only a .10 advantage,

however, can achieve about the same low risk merely by trading in units of one-twelfth of his capital. The outlook for the time that it would take for each to make important profits, assuming success, would vary considerably.

Multiple positions. The problem of how much of a trader's available capital should be committed to one trade is compounded when he decides to add lines to an original position. This may occur when he follows a program of averaging or when he believes that he has a new reason for taking a position beyond that already existing. This might happen, for example, when a chartist is following various signals and notes a second signal which indicates that he should enter a position when he already has a similar one based on a previous chart signal. He might conclude that these signals should be treated separately and distinctly or even that the second signal will reinforce the first and make its favorable outcome more certain. This situation deserves some thoughtful consideration before it is carried too far. No reason for adding units to an open trade makes a favorable outcome certain. A large number of signals all followed will eventually cause a trader to hold a position so large that an unfavorable outcome will ruin him.

To deal with this situation, which results in great opportunity accompanied as usual by great risk, the trader should consider a protective policy. One such policy might be a limitation on the number of multiple lines to be accepted. This, in turn, will depend on how large his trading capital is and how great a risk he thinks each unit entails. A trader who risks only 2 percent of his capital on each line will still be risking only about 8 percent on four lines of the same commodity. An 8 percent loss is painful but not disastrous. A trader who risks 15 percent on a line, however, would find himself with a loss of about 60 percent if all four lines failed.

Stop-loss points. When the trader has determined how much risk he is willing to face in a trade, he has a starting point from which he will determine his stop-loss level and, hopefully, place an actual stop-loss order. If he believes that a logical stop loss can be placed at a point involving less than his acceptable maximum risk, the closer stop, is, of course, to be preferred. Placing stops may involve many criteria, some of which are regarded as important by some traders but not by others. It would appear that there are two considerations that cannot be ignored by any trader. First is the amount of money that would be lost if the stop were violated. Second is the current price volatility of the commodity being traded. In regard to the first of these points, whether the stop points themselves are based on the current market price of a commodity, the margin required, a chart point, or the day of the month multiplied by the phase of the moon, the number of dollars of loss, including execution costs, can easily be expressed as a percentage of the trader's capital. The trader should also have an informed idea of the maximum number of net losses he may reasonably have to suffer, based on his experience or research. If he risks so much that reasonable adversity will ruin him, his route is suicidal. It should be reiterated that ruin does not consist of a series of losses but rather a series in which the number of losses exceeds the number of profits by enough to cause ruin, regardless of their order; for example, if a trader with $4,000 risks a total of $1,000 on each trade, he will be ruined if he loses four times in a row. He will be just as ruined, however, by a bad period during which he has four patterns of one profit followed by two losses. He will have four profits, eight losses, and no money, even though he never had more than two losses in a row. Because an adverse series becomes increasingly likely as trading is carried on over time, it is obvious why trading too large a position is so deadly.

The second point that must be considered by any trader determining his stop points is the degree of volatility in the markets he is trading. Traders who base their stops on current prices or chart patterns must take into consideration how logical stop-loss points may change drastically as commodities trade at higher or lower levels or current volatility becomes greater or less. Stop-loss levels should be adjusted to recent volatility, but even this must be defined by the trader on a logical and validated basis. Is "current" defined as the range of prices for the last week, month, six months, or something else? Of course, next week may prove to be greatly different from last week, but this is an unavoidable risk that always accompanies speculation. Volatility, like most of the vital data in commodity trading, is fluid and nonstationary, unlike the more stable mass of data to be considered by coin flippers, poker players, and dice shooters. The importance of stop-loss strategy cannot be overestimated. This element of strategy will affect the trader's mathematical expectation in the following manner. If the stop loss is placed far from the current price, the probability of losing will be small but the amount of the loss may be large. If the stop loss is placed close to the current price, the probability of losing will be greater but the amount of the loss will be small. Consistently placing stops too close and getting stopped out in "noise" areas or placing stops so far away that the inevitable losses will be unreasonably large will lead to almost certain ruin.

Strategy following significant success. When an account has grown impressively, a trader has a difficult decision to make, but it cannot be avoided. If a $10,000 account has grown, on schedule, to $20,000, which was the objective hoped for when trading in commodity futures was started, the action to be taken is obvious. A check is requested, deposited in a convenient Savings and Loan institution, and the commodity account is closed. If, however, the trader is thinking in terms of acquiring a chateau in France, a chauffeured limousine, and a cellar of Rothschild wines, he must prepare for the next phase of his trading. Again, no definitive course of action acceptable by all traders can be marked out here, but the alternatives are clear. The trader can leave well enough alone and continue trading in the same way and on the same scale as he had before. Now that he has

$20,000, however, he may be concerned that if he trades on the same scale as he did when he had only $10,000 half of his new level of capital will appear to be idle. If he chooses instead to double his scale of trading, he can achieve his ultimate goals faster, if he reaches them at all, but with the usual added risk and stress. If he doubles his commitments to each trade in his effort to reach $40,000 from $20,000 as rapidly as he reached $20,000 from $10,000, he risks finding himself back at $10,000 in only half that time. After all, it took 10 net successful trades, each yielding a $1,000 gain to reach $20,000, but it would take only five net trades, each resulting in a $2,000 loss, to bring his trading capital back down to $10,000. A delicate balance of probabilities and personal feelings must be considered by each trader at critical points such as these and decisions made according to his own mix of knowledge and emotions.

Strategy following significant adversity. Even presuming that a trader's basic method is viable, if adversity precedes success, he would find his position difficult. The fact that failure came first does not ensure that success is inevitable after that point. All that is completely certain is that his capital is impaired. If he continues to take risks similar to those he has already taken, the chance of ruin becomes ever greater. Most traders would choose to employ a defensive strategy, but here again there is a price to pay.

A defensive strategy can consist basically of one of two courses of action. One is the elimination of trades, for the time being, that have the least chance of success. The other is the elimination of any trades that require the risk of too many dollars in relation to the lower level of the account. Of the two the second would appear to be the better. Regardless of the quality of a trade, the probability of success is never 1 and therefore there is always some chance of loss. Furthermore, trades with knowingly poor ratios of success to failure would never be utilized, regardless of the condition of the account. The range between the most acceptable and least acceptable trades for the typical trader is not wide, considering all the uncertainties of trading. It is unlikely that any trade can ever have much more than a .8 probability of success, and it is also unlikely that a trader would be willing to accept knowingly a trade below about .65 (assuming in both cases an even money payoff). This practical range of only about .15 does not provide much room to maneuver.

If there is a limit on dollar risk in relation to the total number of dollars in the account in a given trade, then trades exceeding this risk can of course be eliminated, but this will reduce the number of trades available to recover the dollars lost, and recovering money lost may take longer than losing it in the first place. If the trades with smaller risks also have smaller profit potentials, as is likely, the trader must again face an ugly statistic. He might have lost half his money by having a series of trades yield 10 net losses and have followed with a new series yielding 10 net profits only to find that he was only halfway back to his original level of capital because his profits were smaller than his losses. A loss of 60 percent from a given level requires a profit of 150 percent merely to get even. Profits of 150 percent are not easy to achieve, getting even is not the most exciting goal, and, of course, the trades entered to attempt recovery would themselves entail the risk of further loss.

Systems. The trader, like the gambler, should learn early the fruitlessness of wasting his time and money trying to profit from a game with a negative expectation by the use of some clever strategy. It is to be hoped that a trader's research has resulted in some method of selecting trades that will yield better results than random selections. The mathematical expectation of a game is not affected by the strategy of varying the size of individual bets. If a trader has a valid method that yields on the average 65 wins for 35 losses in a series of independent trials, he will have the same ratio of wins to losses, regardless of his betting strategy, and no system of risking more or less, depending on the result of his recent trades, will change the ratio. If a game is fair, it will remain fair; if it has a positive expectation, it will remain positive, and, if negative, it will remain negative, and the latter two will maintain their biases with no change in degree.[3] No mechanical system can change probabilities one iota.

Money management "systems" designed to overcome a negative expectation in any game, whether trading or gambling, are usually based on some common misconceptions about the statistical law of large numbers, itself frequently incorrectly called the "law of averages." The designers of systems almost invariably depend on some theory that numbers will average out in time to yield profits. A coin having fallen tails a number of times owes some heads, and so one should bet on heads to take advantage of the certainty that the average number of heads flipped will approach 50 percent of all flips sooner or later. A coin, however, has neither a memory nor a conscience, and one may overlook the significance of the difference between percentages and absolute numbers. Certainly, as the coin is flipped longer and longer, the percentage of heads or tails flipped will inevitably approach 50, but not because a short-term series of tails will be immediately followed by a series of heads. Rather, in the long run, the law of large numbers declares that a large number of subsequent trials will overwhelm any apparent aberrations in any part of the series. In a word, as a game is played longer and longer, the *percentage* of wins and losses will inevitably approach the statistical expectation, but seemingly unusual differences will occur just as inevitably. A pattern of 100 flips of a coin alternating precisely from heads to tails would be almost as miraculous as a consecutive series of 100 heads or 100 tails. This means that streaks of luck (both good and bad) are expectations, not aberrations.

Although variation in the sizes of bets will not change the statistical chance of ultimately winning or losing the game (if the size of bets is varied),

[3] Richard A. Epstein, *The Theory of Gambling and Statistical Logic,* Academic Press, 1967, p. VII. Some of the conclusions that follow were drawn in part from this same scholarly reference, especially in its section entitled, "The Basic Theorems," pp. 58–93.

the ultimate amount of money won or lost and the time it will take to win or lose could be affected. This, however, results entirely from the different average level of capital involved in the game, not a change in the probability of winning or losing on each game or trade. A betting system intended to overcome the disadvantage of a basically bad bet is sometimes called the "gambler's fallacy," and it could be called the "commodity trader's fallacy" just as well. The number of commodity traders who have spent good money for systems and who have lost money following them is legion, as is the number of gamblers who have followed the same ruinous path.

Betting and trading systems are sought with more zeal than are quests for perpetual motion machines and sources of everlasting youth. The chance of finding a reasonably simple system that will consistently "beat the odds" is no greater than satisfying a craving for any other delusion, but the idea refuses to be laid peacefully to rest. There will probably always be men who believe that the coin being flipped, having yielded a series of heads, is due for tails, the clear fallacy of the "maturity of the chances" notwith-standing.[4] A series of bad trades having been suffered just as clearly will indicate to many that a series of good trades is due. Bad luck indicates that good luck is coming and vice versa as surely as a pendulum will retrace its path. This idea of retribution or symmetry permeates philosophical thinking throughout history, back to the ancient Chinese, and will probably influence the actions of gamblers and traders as long as dice roll and people trade in securities and commodities.

All systems, regardless of their complexity, are based on wagering or trading that depends on the outcome of previous trials. Some of these systems, which involve multiplicative, additive, or linear betting, can be-come extremely complex, but the basic premise remains the same. Linear systems have a fixed additive constant. Additive systems increase stakes at an arithmetic rate. Multiplicative systems increase bets geometrically, depending on the immediately preceding result. One of the best known geometric systems is the "Martingale." The Martingale system has many proponents because many people who have used the system have won games and credit the system with the win, whereas actually all it has done is offer a high probability of small gains and a small probability of a large loss. If the system is used for a long period of time, however, the chance of suffering a large loss becomes greater. If the game is continued indefi-nitely, the large loss becomes certain. The basic idea behind Martingale (or any other progression system) is that bet sizes will be increased each

[4] The "maturity of the chances" is a doctrine that, in effect, attempts to assign dependence to basically independent events by attributing to them a memory that they lack by definition. A roulette player may, for example, bet on black after four consecutive reds have come up because a black "is due." The poker player, having failed to complete the last few straights and flushes that he tried for, believes that the next one will be achieved almost with certainty. The horse player may play the favorite each time three favorites in a row have lost because, after all, most of them should win each afternoon.

time a bet is lost until a win covers the most recent string of losses and leaves the player even or ahead; for example, a player who loses one unit can follow by betting two. Therefore, if he wins, he is ahead one unit, and if he loses he will be behind three. If he wins, he will bet one unit and start a new series. If he loses he will bet four units. If he wins, he will be ahead a total of one unit and start a new series. If he loses, he will be behind seven units and will bet eight. Sooner or later he will win, and when he does, he will be ahead one unit for his series. He therefore figures to win one unit for each series, although some series will be longer than others.

The Martingale player soon finds out, however, that he is caught between two bet (or trade) limitations; the lower and the upper. If the least he can bet or use as margin is reasonably close to the upper limit, it will not take many progressive increases of his bets following losses to equal or exceed the upper limit. In gambling the lower and upper limits are determined by the casino. In trading the lower limit is determined by the margin requirement and the upper by the capital or stress point of the trader or liquidity problems in markets; hence good results as bets become larger become increasingly unlikely. The time required for a progression to become unreasonable in trading is undoubtedly shorter than in gambling and the time available even in gambling is too short in itself for long-term success to be expected. The gambler forced to double his $1 bet in a series of 20 losses would have to risk more than a million dollars to have the opportunity of winning his series on the twenty-first bet. This is ludicrous enough even without considering that minimum bets must often exceed $1 and that a house limit often restricts the maximum to about $500. The ninth loss of a geometrically increased $2 bet would carry the player past a $500 house limit. The player might argue that nine losses in a row are highly unlikely. This is true for any particular series of nine bets, but the player who continues playing for a long period will almost certainly have nine losses in a row sooner or later, as will the commodity trader.

The system player would do well to test his system against a random number table. If ostensibly it can, say, double his capital before he loses it with a high degree of probability in a game involving many independent events, merely by "betting smart" he should be able to beat the random number table in a paper game by doubling his capital three or four times in long games before he is ruined. (A person who did this and published his results would have the first such publication in history.[5])

Size of commitments. Despite the fact that varying the size of commitments will not change probabilities, it could well change an outcome by ending the game sooner or later than might otherwise be the case. The trader, as well as the gambler, must be vitally concerned with loss of the

---

[5] An elaborate discussion of systems may be found in Allen N. Wilson, *The Casino Gambler's Guide,* Harper and Row, 1970, pp. 234–258. The mathematics of system fallacies is covered in Epstein, *loc. cit.*

money he has available for trading because its loss eliminates any chance of winning or even trading unless he can later replace his capital. In a word, ruin precludes success and must be avoided if at all possible. Sizing of commitments according to the nature of the game has a vital effect on the possibility of ruin. The correct guiding principles may surprise many traders and gamblers. For fair or unfavorable games, the strategy of betting should be aggressive, and for favorable games the approach should be conservative.

If a commodity trader who regarded commodity trading as a basically losing game intended to take only one position and had a specific money objective in mind, his best strategy would be precisely the same as that of a gambler facing the same problem. If the expectation of a profit is negative or zero, but the game is still to be played for some reason, the best chance available to reach the objective is obtained by making a large commitment and playing the game only once. Of course, the capital might be lost and the objective not reached, but the probability of reaching the objective is less for any other strategy. As one decreases the size of one's commitments in an unfavorable game, the chance of eventually reaching one's objective becomes ever smaller and the chance of ruin greater.

The informed commodity trader, unlike the gambler who competes against a casino's odds, is presumed to be playing a favorable game against a far better capitalized adversary (the market) and should wager accordingly. His wisest policy is simple. *He should trade on a small scale.* The specific amounts risked, of course, depend on the size of his capital, his objectives, and how long he expects to continue his trading. If he intends to trade indefinitely, his positions should be modest in relation to his capital, and errors should be made on the conservative side. Because the probabilities favor his winning in the long run, his primary objective in the management of his capital is to make every effort to *reach* the long run. The best way to defeat himself is to risk so much that he cannot realistically recover from adversity on one trade or a series of bad trades. Regardless of how good the odds are, there is some chance of losing, and there is a certainty of periods of severe adversity even when the system used is valid and the expectation favorable. The longer a game is played, the more inevitable such periods of adversity become. Adverse runs should not be surprising. They are to be expected and should be planned for. The best way is to expose so little capital that ruin will not be the result when nothing seems to go right.

The trader who maintains that his research is valid and that he has a positive expectation on every trade may argue that he could afford to risk one-fourth of his capital on every trade because the chance of his losing four times in a row is quite small. He would be correct in making this assertion, but he should think further before engaging in such an aggressive course. The chance of losing four times in a row, even with favorable probabilities, becomes quite high after several series and after a long series is virtually certain. Even worse is the fact that the trader does not need four losses in a row to be ruined, but only one point in his series of trades at which he has lost on four trades *on balance*. Even with a high expectation of success on any given trade, his chance of surviving a long game without being net loser by four trades at any given time would be poor. If the capital risked were reduced from one-fourth to one-tenth, the chance of being ruined on any series of 10 trades would be infinitesimal and his chance of surviving a long series of trades would become high. In any case, the trader must determine the size of his commitments by his probability estimates, the payoffs, and his own degree of optimism of what his trading talent is worth.

In summary, frequent small commitments in a favorable game will almost certainly yield an ultimate profit, whereas continued large percentage commitments will almost certainly cause ruin. In an unfavorable game large commitments made over a short duration provide the only chance of winning and the best expectation (or rather the least bad expectation) results from playing once. One who is ahead in a game with a negative expectation may be said to be losing at a negative rate. If one with a dollar to risk insists on playing a slot machine, his best strategy is to bet his entire dollar in a one-dollar machine and then quit, win or lose, rather than put 20 nickels in a nickel machine.

The inviting, but usually fatal, temptation to bet too heavily in favorable games is probably what leads so often to the most usual type of overtrading; that is, risking too much of one's capital on any one trade. The other types of overtrading, which include trading too many positions at the same time or trading too often, may also cause severe damage, but trading on too large a scale is probably worst of all.

NOTES FROM A TRADER

If money management now appears to be an area that requires considerable thought, full of dilemmas and contradiction, and generally quite frustrating to the reader, he has made real progress. The first step in solving this problem, like most others, is to recognize its existence and face up to it. Ignoring it merely because its solution is difficult and indefinite and relying instead on blind luck is hardly an intelligent alternative.

Money management principles contain so many decisions that must be determined by each trader for himself that no specific program adequate for all traders can ever be devised. This does not mean, however, that some basic principles that are useful for all cannot be suggested. Some poker players like to bluff frequently and others seldom or never. There are winners to be found among those belonging to either school, most of whom think that those who do not agree do not know how to play poker. Those holding either conviction, however, cannot possibly make money by consistently drawing to bad hands and paying more for the privilege than the hand is worth. There are rules that must be followed by all traders and gamblers if they are to live long enough in the world of games to reach the long run while still solvent. Most of these rules for basic survival are to be found in the area of money management, in which few traders are especially interested, rather than in the area of trade selection, which is the basic interest of most of them.

A wise principle of money management is to make mistakes on the side of the too conservative. It is better to accumulate money too slowly than to lose one's trading capital quickly. If debating whether to buy one unit or two, buy one. If debating whether to take a position, pass it by. As an account grows, consider withdrawing some or all of the profits. If aggressiveness is desired, the number of dollars risked can increase as the account grows, but the percentage risk can be held unchanged or even reduced at the same time. The unexpected always seems to be costly rather than profitable. A trader who assumes that he will be right 65 times out of every 100 trades he makes each year assumes that he can look forward to about 30 winning trades net in the next year (65—35). Somehow a considerable number of things will go wrong. If he has a hundred trades and the number of net wins is not 30, it will almost certainly be smaller. He might find himself with only 20 net profitable trades instead of 30. Execution costs will be higher than expected, especially because bad trades will go further through his stops that he thought reasonable, but the less frequent windfall profits that should logically compensate seem rarely to arrive on time, and then they are smaller or more infrequent than had been anticipated. Errors will almost always impair results and rarely improve them. Oversleeping and missing the opening of the market will not cause one to miss a position that opens unfavorably, but a market that opens within a satisfactory range and then moves toward the trader's objective without any retracement is likely to result in an opportunity lost forever. If the market opens sharply in the anticipated direction, even the trader who wakes up on time may be inclined to wait and try to enter it at a more favorable level. If the market provides the hoped-for adversity, the trader will enter some trades that will work and some that will not. If adversity never comes, however, only the good trades can be missed, not the bad ones. With all this the trader might consider himself lucky to find himself with only about 10 net good trades remaining to make his year profitable. Even the most favorable "trading system" will depend for its ultimate favorable results on a surprisingly few net good trades. It does not take many errors (bad luck) to miss them. Furthermore, 65 correct decisions in a hundred was probably an overly optimistic estimate in the first place.

It is interesting to observe the way most commodity traders play the commodity trading game in relation to the possible ways that money games can be played:

1. The most effective approach to the objective of maximizing results is to play a favorable game on a small scale.

2. Less desirable, but still providing a reasonable chance of success, is playing a favorable game on a large scale with enough profits coming early in the game to avoid ruin.

3. A basically unfavorable game may yield profitable results (presuming that one insists on playing unfavorable games) if one plays seldom and bets heavily.

4. The only road that leads inevitably to disaster is playing an unfavorable game continuously.

The trader who trades on impulse or some other invalid method of making trading decisions is following the fourth route—which is crowded with bumper-to-bumper traffic.

Some of Finagle's laws as applied to speculators and market researchers are especially valuable to traders concerned with money management[6]:

1. If anything can go wrong with a research project, it will.

2. No matter what the result, there is always someone willing to fake a better one.

3. No matter what the result, there is always someone eager to misinterpret it.

4. No matter what occurs, there is always someone who believes it happened according to his pet theory.

5. In any collection of data the figure that is most obviously correct— beyond all need of checking—is the mistake.

6. Even if it is impossible to derive a wrong number, still a way will be found to do it.

In the area of money management, as in no other, the trader should beware of self-deceit. The successful trader does not lie to himself. He does not substitute hope for facts. Fagin's cynical comment in the musical production of "Oliver" is quite appropriate for consideration by an economically motivated trader attempting to evaluate the money management program he has been using. "In this world, one thing counts; in the bank, large amounts."

---

[6] Compiled in the original form by John W. Campbell, Jr., late editor of *Analog Science Fiction Magazine.*

Losers and Winners

*In every game there are winners and losers. The scorecard
in the commodity futures game, which is brutally simple, consists merely of a credit or debit in a trading account over a
period of time long enough to exclude luck, either good or
bad, from playing a prominent role. Because more speculators
lose than win, the section title makes allowance for that
sobering fact by reversing the consideration of the outcomes.*

*Chapter 11, "The Commodity School for Losers," creates
satirical composites of the classic losers. Habits that reinforce
unsuccessful trading results are examined with tongue in
cheek in the hope that familiarity will breed a determination
to avoid the losers' line-up.*

*Chapter 12, "Maxims: Good and Bad," subjects the conven-
tional wisdom of market lore to critical analysis. That there
are platitudes to reinforce any position the trader desires
to take should not surprise the reader. Rather, the study of
market maxims underlines the innate desire of many traders
to avoid coming to grips with the actual behavior of commodity futures prices and the implications of that behavior
for their own.*

*Chapter 13 "Who Wins? Who Loses? Why?" concludes the
section by focusing for careful study on the returns to the
players of the commodity futures game. Hedgers, large speculators, and small traders reflect varying trading results in
the long run. Studies are examined to shed light on the question of the distribution of profits and losses and the skills
employed by the winners. These skills involve behavioral as
well as analytical competence, and one systematic approach
to understanding the role of feelings and thoughts is presented.*

CHAPTER ELEVEN

The Commodity School
for Losers

The capacity of the human mind to resist the
intrusion of new knowledge is infinite.

INTRODUCTION

Some commodity traders learn their lessons at the School of Experience
early and well. They go on to realize profits and enjoy the exciting dynamics
to be found in the world of commodities. Others never learn much of anything and spend their lives at the Commodity School for Losers repeating
the same mistakes or happily discovering minor variations. This school
has campuses in most areas of the world and traces its beginnings to the
seekers of lodestones and to Dutch traders of tulip bulbs. It might help
future commodity traders who wish to avoid attending the school to interview members of the present student body who have been attempting to
graduate, unsuccessfully, for many years.

THE STUDENT BODY

Herbert Hoyle has had more friends, relatives, and counterparts at the
school than anyone else. Herbert himself enrolled as a student more than
40 years ago just after averaging up his security holdings on a 20 percent
margin, starting in August 1929. He has spent all the years since trying
to develop a simple set of mechanical rules (secret, of course) that will
help him to achieve a substantial profit each year at a constant rate while
using a small amount of capital and entailing virtually no risk. Herbert
became seriously interested in his project some years ago when he noticed

that his rules worked spectacularly, particularly when applied carefully to the body of historical data from which the rules had been developed.

"I noticed," says Herbert, his eyes narrowed, "that December Wheat sold at a significantly higher price on September 8 than it had on July 20 throughout the entire period covered by my records at the time (four years). On the July 20 following the completion of my research, I quietly bought all the December Wheat that I could afford (5,000 bushels) but unfortunately a recent reduction in the government loan price had not been fully discounted, and I lost 14 cents a bushel. I decided that henceforth wheat should be bought only in years when there was no adjustment in the loan price, and I changed my rules accordingly.

"The following year I bought wheat again on July 20 but lost 19 cents a bushel by September 8. I noticed too late that the difference in price between wheat and corn was wider than it had been for the last five years and I had failed to consider the importance of this in my earlier conclusions. There was no point in abandoning my work because, of the six observations I now had, four had worked successfully and the other two could be easily filtered out. The following year I was a little unlucky. There was no change in the loan price, but the spread between wheat and corn prices was even wider than it had been the year before, so I naturally did not buy the wheat. In fact, utilizing the information I had gained, I sold it short instead. When it rose 47 cents a bushel by September 8 with no reaction greater than $\frac{1}{4}$ cent a bushel, I was a little disappointed, of course, but then I suddenly realized the significance of the late Lenten season which obviously cancels out the effect of the wheat-corn spread. Of my seven observations, actually five had worked, although I did not benefit by the latest one and two were filtered out. The eighth year was really quite upsetting. I again bought the wheat on July 20 and it was 4 cents higher on September 8, just as I had expected in light of the narrow wheat-corn spread and early Lent. Because of some rumor of heavy French exports in August, wheat prices dropped more than 50 cents and before they could rally back my margin was gone and my broker sold me out $\frac{3}{8}$ cent off the bottom. My record, however, really is six wins in eight years with the other two years filtered out. Now I am sure that I have all the important factors, and if I can get $500 together before July 20 I expect to make some really important money in the wheat market from now on, unless my creditors attach my account again before the realizing move takes place."

Herbert's rules, including the filters and exceptions, now fill 37 typewritten pages (single-spaced) which Herbert keeps in a padlocked drawer for security reasons along with instructions to pass the notes along to his children in the event of his passing or being committed to an institution.

Gary Gullible finds Herbert Hoyle's scholarly fundamental approach far too complicated and believes the soundest approach to trading is a basically simple one. Gary initially tried to achieve wealth at the horse races after buying a book suggesting that the proper approach was to bet on the favorites to show on the last race each day early in the season. The theory held that the winning betters would all have gone home by the last race and that the handicappers had not yet had time to evaluate sufficient data to weight the horses properly. Gary became discouraged when he realized that his profits did not equal the cost of his racetrack admissions, his parking, hotdogs, and cleaning bills for his checked sportcoat. Neither did they exceed his losses.

Gary next tried to make some money playing blackjack at Nevada gaming palaces after reading a book suggesting that it was necessary only to keep track of picture cards and fives and always double down on two nines. Unfortunately, when Gary finally screwed up enough courage to take a bus to Las Vegas, his results were not nearly so good as they had been when he dealt himself several thousand hands on his dining room table. He encountered a flinty-eyed dealer who worked with five decks of cards and dealt them from a card shoe so rapidly that Gary could not keep count. It was then that Gary turned to commodity trading.

"There is no point examining the fundamentals," Gary tells us, "because everything is reflected in prices anyhow. The most important thing is to trade only consistently with the basic trend. Never trade against the trend! When it is up, only be long. When it is down, only be short. The basic trend may be easily determined in many ways, but one of the best is with a line chart. Just draw a line along recent bottoms in a rising market or recent tops in a falling market and you have a clear picture of a market's direction and its rate of movement.

"The best way of all, though, involves the proper use of moving averages which requires some intelligence (I.Q. exceeding 55) and some knowledge of mathematics (addition and subtraction). I have discovered something really remarkable," continues Gary in a confidential tone of voice. "When you use moving averages of different time spans, like 3 days and 10 days, in markets that are moving around at all and plot these averages as lines on a chart, the 3-day line will cross the 10-day line from time to time, although I am not certain what causes this." Gary leans back in his chair to give the listener time to absorb the implications of his revelations. "In order to make the lines clear during periods of narrow price fluctuations I find it best to use colored pencils. It is wise to use chartreuse for the 3-day average and turquoise for the 10-day average. When the chartreuse line is below the turquoise line, I sell short and when it goes above I cover and go long. Of course, I get whipsawed once in a while, but at least when there is a major trend I am in the market the right way and I stay with the move until it has run its course." Unfortunately, while Gary was trading there proved to be more narrow trading markets than trending markets (which was also true before Gary began trading as well as after) so Gary has been whipped and sawed rather thoroughly. He is currently working to improve his system either by requiring sharper crossing of the lines (as measured by a plastic protractor) or by waiting for some period of time to elapse after a crossing before considering a position to be worth taking. So far the ideal period to wait has proved historically to vary from one to 254 days, but Gary believes that the key is on the chart somewhere and needs merely to be discovered. Currently he is unable to trade anyhow because he has lost two-thirds of his capital trading unsuccessfully and spent the other third on chart paper, colored pencils, and the protractor.

Fred Fantasy turned to commodity trading many years ago after suffering grievous losses trading Czarist bonds. He has become a recognized expert in the art of spreading positions to avoid realizing losses. Fred is especially pleased with his results so far this year during which he has not had a single closed loss. He believes that he is finally about to overcome the misfortunes he has borne during the last 26 years, having lost money in 25 of them. (He broke even one year when he was too busy dealing with his divorce and bankruptcy proceedings to trade). Fred has told everyone who will listen of his market successes this year during which he has had six consecutive profits. He has taken particular pains to keep three board-room acquaintances informed because he is currently trying to induce them to allow him to trade their accounts in return for 3 percent a month of their invested capital plus one-half of all closed profits unadjusted by open losses.

"In January I bought December silver," relates Fred, "because of the continuing imbalance of supply and demand, the outlook for more use of film because of the recent invention of a new type of camera, and substantial sales of a series of medals portraying famous Indian chiefs by a private mint. I was a little early, and December silver dropped 600 points, and I thought I had better buy time, so I sold March against my long December. The market dropped another 300 points, just as I thought it would, so I took my profit in the March. To take advantage of the short-term irrational weakness in the market and to protect my December position I sold a May contract. Sure enough, the market continued down and I was able to take a $200 profit in the May and managed to sell July after a further drop of only 50 points. This market has been like a money machine. I have now taken six straight profits on the short side, and now I have a no-risk position short September and still long that original December which will probably yield the greatest profit of all."

Fred proudly displays his six confirmations showing the $1,470 profits on the short-side transactions which he carries with him at all times to help him sell his managed-account program which he has recently had copyrighted as "The Fred Fantasy Infallo Program." Unfortunately the market rallied a little after Fred's seventh short sale and he now has a $150 open loss on the short September silver as well as the open loss of $2,375 on the original purchase of the December silver, but this does not dishearten Fred. He has a plan. "When the market takes its next dip, I'll cover September and stay with the December. This will give me seven profits in a row, so even if December doesn't recover I'll still have seven profits out of eight, and the random walk boys can't laugh that off." A visitor has some questions to ask Fred about some aspects of his logic as well as how he will provide the margin required to support his December position after he liquidates the September, but Fred has been led away for his daily tranquilizer injection.

William Wilde really wanted to be a gladiator but was born in the wrong place at the wrong time. Unable to realize his primary ambition, he turned to commodity trading. "This whole business is kill or be killed," says William, holding up his clenched fist and facing the emperor. "The way to beat this thing is to probe for the big one and then milk it dry." William accomplishes this by waiting until he sees what he believes to be a great opportunity and then moving in with all his resources. "The way to determine the size of an initial position is to divide your credit balance by the margin deposit required and buy all you can. When the market goes your way even a little, your base is big enough so that even the small move will create enough additional capital to pyramid quickly, and then you keep on pyramiding until you have all the money that you can carry home."

William is quite confident at the moment that he is about to achieve a great victory because he has just succeeded in replacing the $2,000 he lost by holding seven pork bellies two days too long with money he borrowed from the Credit Union and is hoping that the 25,000 bushels of wheat he intends to buy in the morning will rise quickly enough for him to repay the loan before his wife learns of it and orders him out of the house again. William's ultraconservative friend, Long E. Bonds, asks what he is going to do if wheat goes down and he finds himself in debt to the Credit Union without the means to pay back the obligation. "When the going gets tough" replies William, "the tough get going." "But," Long persists, "isn't it true that in any game in which probabilities are involved the longer you play the more certain it becomes that a series of losses will occur? And isn't it also true that you are never even prepared for the first loss, much less a series of them?" Utilizing all of his keen reasoning power, William replies, "If you can't stand the heat, stay out of the kitchen."

Marcus Mule once read in a booklet that cash and futures prices have a tendency to meet during the delivery month sooner or later. This made a tremendous impression on Marcus who ranks the importance of this bit of information somewhat above the Bill of Rights. He is currently long one contract of October live cattle which is selling 4 cents a pound below the cash price of cattle as quoted on the newswire in the brokerage office. "Someone is going to make that 4-cent difference," brays Marcus, "and it might as well be me." When Marcus placed the order with his broker, his registered representative volunteered to check with the research department in Chicago for an opinion on the potential in Marcus' trade. Although the research department was about to leave for a hamburger and a milk shake for lunch, he did take the time to reply and the broker, Tradum Offen, called Marcus back with the bad news. "In order to be sure of making the 4-cent difference," Tradum said, "You must have considered such things as location of the cattle, differences in grade, and possible problems with certification for delivery by the exchange. Also, presuming that the 4-cent difference is made up before futures trading stops in October and not after, it could be met just as well by the cash price dropping to meet the futures prices as by the futures price rising to meet the cash, in which case, you would make no money. As a matter of fact, the cash price could drop 8 cents and the futures 4 cents and you could lose." His sharp mind functioning in its usual manner, Marcus replied, "Have you a late quote on November potatoes?" "The futures business is one thing and the cash is another" continued Tradum after telling Marcus that November potatoes are limit up (Marcus is short), "It is not wise to play another man's game." "I have to move my car", replied Marcus shrewdly, "It's in a loading zone."

By the time he returned from moving his car, he had received delivery of the contract of cattle. Only then did he learn that it was the last day of trading and the cattle cannot be redelivered. Shortly thereafter one of Marcus' cattle died and two others are not looking well. Marcus still has the remainder of his contract of cattle and has spent a busy morning writing letters to the Commodity Exchange Authority, the Chicago Mercantile Exchange, Dow-Jones, and the State Consumer Frauds Division bitterly complaining of the false and misleading cash prices reported on the newswires by an incompetent wire operator and questioning how any honest trader could possibly beat a game with such unfair rules. Nothing worse has happened to Marcus since he took delivery of a carload of onions only to learn that trading had ended in that commodity forever and his onions were sprouting through the bags in which they were delivered. He did succeed in selling some of the bags to a dealer in secondhand burlap for almost as much as it cost him to have the bags deodorized. Marcus would like to tell of some other of his experiences, but he has to leave for court to fight the ticket unjustifiably placed on his car for parking in the loading zone.

Ivan Bentaken has had trouble all his life with unreasonable people. In school, whenever he was prepared for "Show and Tell" he never got called on, but when unprepared his name was invariably called. In the Little League he was called out on every play. Policemen herd him out of traffic to give him tickets, although everyone else is clearly going faster. Now he trades commodities. He recently opened his third commodity account to replace the one he has just closed with another broker whom he is suing for recommending the purchase of corn which went down 9 cents a bushel following a surprisingly bearish crop report issued two weeks after the purchase. "My broker obviously knew of the report and got me to buy the corn so he or his firm's partners could bail out," declares Ivan, his eyes blazing. "Even if he did not know it, he is derelict in his fiduciary relationship to me because he should have known it. After all, his firm claims to have a Research Department in Chicago right in the Board of Trade Building."

Having calmed down enough to discuss his trading philosophy, Ivan talks of objectives. "A $1,000 account really ought to provide an average return of several hundred dollars each month and sometimes $1,000 or more. After all, it would yield 5 percent in a Savings and Loan with no risk at all (to say nothing of the use of a notary public at no charge). If you don't get a chance for greater reward, it's foolish to take the extra risk.

"You have to be especially careful of brokers," he continues. "They are always foisting advice on you like urging you to use stops and objectives to make sure that you are always getting out of your position one way or the other. I had a big profit a few months ago, took the profit and went into another position which also resulted in a profit, but I would have made more just staying with the first position. My broker did not make a single move to stop me from switching the position. I am still waiting for the CEA to do something about it, but they won't answer my letters anymore. Three or four years ago I doubled my money in the first six months of the year, and my broker thought that was a big deal, but I had a friend who tripled his money during the same period across the street. My friend's broker is quite conservative and told me that he really only expected an annual yield of 80 percent. I figured if he only did half that well, I was certain of 40 percent so I opened an account. In spite of his virtual guarantee, I lost my money on my first two trades in only a week, so I am having my lawyer file a suit based on material misrepresentation, lack of suitability, and churning."

Eric Von Director believes acting is everything, so he bases all his trading decisions on the manner in which markets are acting during the infrequent periods when he knows what is happening. When his broker calls him with a trading suggestion, Eric checks his charts and then follows the suggestions that have acted well recently (gone in the direction of the broker's suggestion for a least one day). When he is advised to take a loss, Eric usually replies that "the market is acting as if a reversal is about to occur." When advised to take a profit, Eric studies his charts and proclaims that "it is premature to liquidate the position because the market is acting well." Because any position that shows a profit has had to act well, Eric has great difficulty in liquidating positions at a profit. Eric once read in a book that prices tend to act best just before they collapse and worst just before they rally so Eric sold the book.

A friend once suggested that Eric determine objectives and stops in advance and place orders at those points in the market, but Eric prefers to use his judgment and make decisions at points at which market action indicates he should take action. He is not disturbed by the fact that the moment he usually takes action is always one during which he happens to be in the brokerage office or on the telephone to his registered representative. "You should never place stops," intones Eric, "because they will invariably drive the market just to your stop, knock you out of your position, and then run the market just to where you thought it would go in the first place!" When asked whether his problem might not be the placement of his stops, and just who buys or sells the hundreds of contracts necessary to touch off his stops on his one or two contracts, Eric says "You just don't understand the Commodity Futures Markets." He says this with the same haughty air that his ancient ancestor, a Carthaginian general, assumed when explaining the strategy he planned to use against the approaching Romans.

Deposit N. Withdrawal believes in following a strategy of observing statistical runs. Knowing his own trading limitations, which are legion, Deposit follows the advice of his broker who is always sincere and occasionally lucky. Whenever Deposit has a series of successes with small positions, he adds money to his account and takes large positions just in time for the inevitable series of losses. Following this, he withdraws most of his capital in order to trade a minimum amount until his broker recovers his touch. "I couldn't believe it," sobs Deposit. "I no sooner withdrew part of my remaining funds than he was right nine times in a row. I had to pass up four of his suggestions and take positions in the other five only about half as big as I had taken on the way down. On one of those five, I couldn't take the adversity necessary to achieve the profit so I had a loss. The broker claims to be ahead for the year but it certainly doesn't show in my account. He claims it has something to do with money management, but I think he is misrepresenting his results." Following the advice of Ivan Bentaken, Deposit is about to make a claim against the broker for the difference between the results in his account and those he believes he should have had according to the broker's record.

Oscar Ostrich believes that all adversity is temporary. When all is going his way, Oscar can be found telling of his successes to the small group of gray men in gray suits with gravy on their ties who spend all day in the boardroom because their wives drive them from their homes. When markets go against him, however, Oscar is not there. Sometimes he can be seen walking slowly around the block, his lips moving in silent prayer, hoping to find a miraculous recovery in his positions by the time he completes the circuit. More frequently he cannot be found at all.

"If I didn't have bad luck, I would have no luck at all," he tells all who will listen. "I was doing all right until I got into those 12 contracts of May potatoes. I am usually in the boardroom or keep in constant touch with my broker so I know at all times where I am. However, I got busy and I had no time to call or even read a paper for nine days. By the time I was informed, news that the crop was 72 percent greater than expected had become known to everyone but me, and the market sold down so far that I got sold out." Someone suggests that if Oscar had placed a stop in the market, he would have suffered little, but he is busily digging a hole in the school's sandbox in order to plunge his head into it.

Wheeler Bandini is known to every registered representative in the brokerage business except the youngest and least experienced, and they will undoubtedly meet him soon. He can always be recognized by the nature of his proposals which involve unorthodox transactions, huge amounts, and considerable time, effort, and cost to the broker (all wasted). "I have access to 8,000,000 pounds of Mexican coffee which I can place anywhere you want within twenty-four hours" he confides, "if there is some way we can place a hedge against it and cinch the big difference between the present futures market and my cash coffee. Of course, I would expect no margin on the short futures position because this is a bona fide hedge." Or, "I am in touch with a shipload of nonquota sugar being brought in by some Cuban refugees and if we can dispose of it through your cash department I would be glad to split the profit with you." Or, "I handle the financial affairs of a group of 220 brain surgeons who won't make a move without my say-so. If I open a commodity account with $3,000,000, how might we both benefit a little from it?"

Wheeler is not a major menace except to himself when attempting to cross the street unaided and to unsophisticated brokers so anxious to build a profitable clientele that they accept his hallucinations at face value. This has happened twice. In each case an account was opened and an order actually placed against Wheeler's cash positions only to have him disappear into the night leaving behind a disconnected telephone and an "address unknown." A fellow student attempts to ask Wheeler why he does what he does, but Wheeler is furtively slinking down the corridor, eating strange-looking mushrooms, and muttering something about getting the exclusive right to market the entire Russian output of platinum through a holding company he is about to form.

Barry Brass is known to every broker in the country, although he invariably does business elsewhere. He is always the first to mail in the coupon that appears with a firm's advertisement. When the registered representative begins calling prospective clients, he always reaches Barry first. "Put me on your market letter list for a few months," demands Barry, "and send me daily charts on price, open interest, and volume covering mercury, broilers, and rapeseed for the last few years. Also, would you have your research department take a look at the spread relationship between April potatoes and February propane during the third quarter of leap years and let me know what they have to say? I can be reached evenings after 10:30."

Once this initial contact has been made, the broker need have no concern about Barry remaining in touch, especially when reports are due. "When is the cold storage report on bellies coming out and what does the floor expect it to say?" asks Barry on line one while the broker's best client is waiting on hold on line two to place an order for 400 shares of stock at the market. Within one minute after the report is issued Barry will be certain to call back to learn the figures and ask for the reaction on the floor and some estimate of where the market will open in the morning. He would call his own broker, of course, but does not wish to disturb him, especially because Barry has no position in bellies anyhow.

Barry is most in evidence at workshops and seminars presented as business-building devices by brokerage firms. He can be easily recognized by the dogeared notebook and charts he is carrying and by the holes in his shoes. Just as the broker pauses for breath before making his major point about the enormous opportunity in the cocoa market because Ghana and Nigeria have invaded one another, Barry raises his hand and asks, "How much wheat is transported into Kansas City by barge relative to rail and how much does each barge hold? Also, when does it get too cold for barge traffic and what historical implications has this had for the Chicago-Kansas City wheat spread?" While the speaker tries to answer Barry's questions without admitting that he has no knowledge whatever of the Kansas City freight structure, the well-dressed man sitting near the door who was about to ask how to open a $10,000 account looks at his watch, puts his checkbook back into his pocket, and leaves.

During the refreshment period following the speech, Barry has the speaker backed into a corner asking him why the tomato paste market did not have more volume, considering all the pizzas that are sold in the United States. By the time the broker escapes from the corner and cleans the coffee off his suitcoat that Barry has spilled on it, the entire audience has left. Barry picks up four copies each of all the literature, takes all of the remaining cookies and doughnuts, gets his parking ticket validated, and leaves muttering something about the unproductivity of the evening.

Benjamin Franklin Bartlett believes that there is a wisdom in maxims that covers any contingency likely to be faced by a trader. Benjamin has had two articles published, one of which attempts to reconcile "Absence makes the heart grow fonder" with "Out of sight, out of mind" and the other explaining why "Birds of a feather flock together" is completely compatible with "Eagles don't flock." His "Thoughts on Maxims as Applied to Trading" is the definitive work on the subject and has formed the basis for the chapter that follows.

CHAPTER TWELVE

Maxims: Good and Bad

> If, could, should, might;
> Weasel words are always right.   CANDY TREAT

INTRODUCTION

Although the bulk of the work done by Benjamin Franklin Bartlett is presented in this chapter, the reader should be aware that some of Bartlett's conclusions have been attacked by an unfriendly reviewer whose work should be noted, partly because it is quite stimulating and partly because he has made a considerable fortune trading commodities, unlike Bartlett who is currently in charge of french fried potatoes at a small hamburger stand. The reviewer, Orin Thevault, believes that success in trading commodities requires more than the judicious choice and observation of old saws. Some may present a real danger to novices or undisciplined traders, in some cases because they accept them and in others because they do not. There is some old saying that will justify almost any action or lack of action. Many people are not disturbed by the fact that equally plausible maxims might appear to justify diametrically opposed actions. They just blithely choose the one that encourages their doing what they want to do anyhow. Sociologists have named this phenomenon "selective perception." The most favored alibis comfort the trader when he has taken a loss or a smaller profit than he should have. There is real danger in confusing alibis with wisdom, and it might help to provide a small part of Orin Thevault's master list of alibis at this point:

1. I should have entered a stop.
2. I should have taken the profit.
3. I should have let the profit run.
4. I should have had a bigger position.
5. I should have had a smaller position.
6. I should have entered a stop.
7. I should have averaged up.
8. I should not have averaged up.
9. I should have averaged down.
10. I should not have averaged down.
11. I should have bought time by spreading against my position.
12. I should have just got out—the first loss is the best loss.
13. I should have entered a stop.
14. I should have listened to my broker.
15. I should know better than to listen to my broker.
16. I should never trade on the close.
17. I should never trade on the opening.
18. I should have got out before the report.
19. I should just ignore the report and stay in the market.
20. I should have entered a stop.
21. I should have taken the seasonal into consideration.
22. I should know that seasonals are too simplistic an approach.
23. I should have met the margin call and gone just two days more.
24. I should never meet a margin call.
25. I should have entered a stop.

Orin concludes that no list of maxims can replace the time and effort that must go into a carefully prepared trading plan. In fact he derides maxims as conventional wisdom that are overly general, have no predictive value, and belong more in an explanation of the random walk theory than in a trading plan. It is best left to the reader to study some of Bartlett's work on maxims and judge for himself whether they are a consistent and adequate tool for skilled, experienced traders. The following summary of Bartlett's work on maxims has been rather thoroughly edited by Orin Thevault who could not resist editorializing from time to time. In fact, he has even taken the liberty of inserting maxims of his own choosing from time to time which lead to conclusions sharply contrasting with those of Bartlett's. The first group of maxims deals with the selection of a trade.

SELECTION

One of the first decisions to be made by any trader is whether the wiser policy is concentration or diversification of positions. The trader who chooses diversification has widely quoted the maxim. "Don't put all your eggs in one basket," to justify his choice. The more aggressive speculator who chooses to concentrate in order to achieve more potential in a given position can retort with, "It is much easier to watch a few than many," or "Put all your eggs in one basket and watch the basket."

In reality, either of these two broad policies may be correct for people with different objectives or different styles of trading, or for the degree of aggressiveness they might choose to select in their pursuit of profit. The relatively conservative traders can always say, "Patience is a virtue," whereas another who is willing to accept greater risks might answer, "There are two ways to get to the top of an oak tree: climb it, or sit on an acorn."

The choice of specific trades may be made even more difficult by trying to reconcile such conflicting popular advice as "Never sell after a big decline" with the equally popular "Never buy after a long decline." Under given conditions either of these may prove correct; but if both are correct a commodity cannot logically be either bought or sold after a long decline.

A trader may not be too badly injured by heeding the advice to "Buy what will not go down in a bear market." The implication is that such a choice will probably lead the next rise, which is possible, but it also may be out of favor with many traders because it is not considered to have much potential and, although it might not go down, it might not go up either. Similarly, one might heed the advice "never buy something that won't go up in a bull market," only to discover that he has been persuaded not to buy something that merely has not gone up yet and is just about to do so.

The potential buyer who wants a rule that will allow him to do anything that he really wants to can turn to "When a bear market turns to bull, buy what has gone down the most and also what has gone down the least." This sounds plausible, but the security buyer who buys a high-grade preferred stock because it has gone down the least might also find that it will also go up the least. If he hedges by buying what has gone down most, he may find that he has bought stock in a company whose stock is discounting its impending bankruptcy, at which point it will continue down to zero. He learns the truth of the warning, "Many a healthy reaction has proved fatal."

Whatever the reason for which the choice of a purchase is made, it should be because of the opportunity inherent in the trade, not because the buyer wants to acquire a given amount of money for an automobile, a trip, or a new suit. There is considerable validity in the warning, "Never speculate for a specific need," as any poker player can attest if he has played for his supper and subsequently gone hungry. The potential in a trade is proved by the trade itself and not by the desires of the buyer or seller.

The potential seller of a position finds his choices no easier than those of the buyers. He is told on the one hand, "Sell what has gone up the most because it will react the most," but at the same time, "Sell what has gone up the least because what could not go up must come down." If he observes the former, he could find himself short in a market rising most rapidly; if he chooses the second alternative, he might find himself short in a market so completely demoralized that the only real possibility is an ultimate move higher or little move at all for a long period of time. One of the near certainties in speculation is that when everyone is bearish a market must go up because there are no sellers left, just as when everyone is bullish a market must go down because there are no buyers left. The reasons to justify these seemingly unlikely moves will appear after the moves have taken place.

There are those who argue, with considerable logic, that it is best to sell something before it goes down rather than after. Those who warn "Never sell something because it seems high priced" leave the trader in a position of selling positions only if they seem to be low priced. This is difficult to reconcile with the successful trader's ability to buy low and sell high, which appears to be an infallible route to success.

Both a trader who prefers selling on rallies and another who would rather sell something that could not go up might prove to be correct at one time or another. The first can maintain that "The warrior who is first to weaken in battle is often seen as the leader of a retreat," whereas the other can insist that it is wise to "Sell short what will not go up in a bull market."

OPINIONS

The trader who finds it difficult to select positions for himself might choose the seemingly easy course of accepting the advice of others whom he considers to have superior judgment or better sources of information. To do so, of course, he must ignore the admonition, "Don't rely on the advice of insiders." He must also disregard the comment of a highly regarded successful trader who said, "Given time, I believe that inside information can break the Bank of England or the United States Treasury."[1] For some reason he has discounted the elaborate survey that indicated that people who work in the grain trade have managed to lose their own money about as fast as anyone else and that farmers frequently manage to lose even faster than most.[2]

It would appear that brokers would be interested in giving traders good advice in the interest of keeping their business, building their capital, and receiving referral business, but the results obtained by those who slavishly follow the suggestions of registered representatives of brokerage houses have been something less than outstanding. Many customers eventually come to accept the remark of a cynical trader to the effect that "The only sure tip from your broker is a margin call." Another said, "Few people ever make money on tips. Beware of inside information. If there was any easy money lying around, no one would be forcing it into your pocket." One would probably be well advised to "Beware of one who has nothing to lose," because "Markets are never wrong; opinons often are" and "Opinions are worthless; facts are priceless."

If a trader does have enough faith in someone else to accept his judg-

[1] Bernard Baruch, *Baruch: My Own Story,* Holt, Rinehart and Winston, New York, 1957, p. 123.

[2] Blair Stewart, *An Analysis of Speculative Trading in Grain Futures,* Technical Bulletin No. 1001, U.S. Department of Agriculture, Commodity Exchange Authority, October, 1949, pp. 67 and 68.

ment, he would probably be well advised to follow it through to the conclusion of the trade. There are many speculators who have suffered a large loss in a position suggested by someone else only to find that his adviser had seen the error of his selection quickly and liquidated with a much smaller loss or even a profit. This is why one successful speculator advised a friend, "If you get in on Smith's tip, get out on Smith's tip."

Contrary-opinion advocates suggest that one ascertain the prevalent opinion of the trading public in some way and then take the opposite position on the basis that "The public is always wrong." At least, it tends to be wrong at critical junctures. This assumes, of course, that the trader can take note of the same facts available to the remainder of the trading public and be able to accept an opposite position. It is well and good to advise sagely, "Buy when others sell and sell when others buy," but how could everybody follow the advice without making it meaningless?

TIMING

Most successful traders are convinced that timing represents the ultimate difference between profit and loss in trading. "When to buy and sell is more important than what to buy and sell" would be accepted as sound advice by virtually all experienced traders. Most would also agree that "A bull can make money, and a bear can make money, but a hog never can," including Baron Rothschild, who gave as a major reason for his success his rule, "I never buy at the bottom and I always sell too soon."

When to take profits can cause endless problems if one chooses not to develop and follow a plan. Hardly anyone would quarrel with the basic admonition to "Cut losses and let profits run." Just when to cut the losses or how far to let the profits run is difficult to determine. One might agree with such thoughts as "The real money made in speculation has been in commitments showing a profit right from the start." Those who follow this advice probably provide the fuel for the relatively common phenomenon of the false breakout.

"Sell when the good news is out" probably has a better reputation for validity than it deserves. Some markets discount news to a far greater degree than others. Accordingly, the first response to news might reflect all the change in price that there is going to be, but in other cases it might be only the beginning of a major change in the price level. In the latter case buying when the good news is out rather than selling might prove to be far the better alternative. "Never sell on strike news" is in the same category. Some strikes are anticipated and some are not. Some end quickly and present a welcome opportunity to work off surplus inventory, whereas others last for extended periods and result in temporary or even permanent loss of markets, in which case selling on strike news might prove wise.

"Sell on the first margin call" appears to be valid because it really suggests that a position be abandoned before all of the trader's capital has been lost. Much would depend, of course, on the amount of loss that took place before the margin call was received. In most cases considerable attrition must already have taken place, which might imply that a well-constructed plan would not have allowed the position to have been held long enough for the margin call to have been received at all. Margin calls usually indicate that a speculator has either been overtrading or has not cut losses soon enough.

It is debatable whether an attractive trading opportunity always exists. Accordingly, some traders maintain that "There is no need to be always in the market" because they are convinced that money cannot consistently be made by trading every day or even every week. Most speculators agree that overtrading is one of the worst possible errors that can be made and accordingly they advise, "Trade too often and be the broker's good friend, trade less often to be your own true friend."

Others, however, may be going too far when they say, "When in doubt, do nothing." This might lead to considerable trouble. If one is out of the market and in doubt, he might do nothing and miss a profitable opportunity. Even worse, he might be in a market with a losing position and be in doubt. Accordingly, he might do nothing but watch his small loss become a large one. A trader could take the opposite course and listen to those who suggest, "When in doubt do something" and "If you would not buy, sell." Most experienced traders find themselves consistently beset by doubts, and they could hardly react by consistently doing nothing or always doing something. If their doubts become too disturbing when they have an important position, they might well observe the old adage to "Sell down to a sleeping point."

The best way to resolve such problems is to have a carefully prepared trading plan and do one's best to suppress doubts while the plan has time to work. This probably would provide more profitable results than a program based on impulse. Impulse usually results in entering positions at high prices and selling them at low prices because commodities and stocks "Look best at the top of a bull market and worst at the bottom of a bear market." It is only human to want to buy when the market looks good and to sell when it looks bad, which is why it has been said that "The human side of every person is the greatest enemy of the average investor or speculator." The trader might be well advised when he is told, "Trust your own opinion and back your judgments only when the action of the market itself confirms your opinion."

Even when a plan has been devised, it is not always easy to follow it logically if any credence is given to popular maxims; for example, it is often said, "Don't try to get the last eighth." On the same point it has been written that "One of the most helpful things that anybody can learn is to give up trying to catch the last eighth—or the first. These two are the most expensive eighths in the world. They have cost stock traders, in the aggregate, enough millions of dollars to build a concrete highway across the continent."[3] These sound quite logical but if one never tries to reach the last eighth of the entry point or objective specified in his trading plan, how does he ever reach either? A trader might bid 71⅜ for 10,000 bushels of oats when the market is 72½. If the market hesitates at 71¾, he might be tempted to raise his bid to be sure not to miss the market. If his objective was 73 and the price met resistance at 72½, he might sell at the market in order to be sure to get out. If his order is filled at 72¼, he has barely covered his commissions. Those last eighths he failed to gain represented his entire potential profit. When the market turns just short of an entry or liquidation point, it can be highly annoying, but if more flexibility is needed, the plan should provide for it. There are times when a market order is the best way to take or liquidate a position, but there are other times when a limit order is wiser. In the latter case the trader has little choice but to wait for the last eighth.

CHARACTER OF THE MARKET

Some maxims provide some general advice to traders concerning the nature of the market itself. As in the other areas, however, some of them sound logical, but there is frequently a maxim that sounds just as logical but suggests an opposing course of action. One might hear one sage maintain that "The market has no past," only to hear another say that "Nothing new ever occurs in the business of speculation or investing in securities or commodities," which implies that much can be learned from the past. Most traders and all technicians would agree with the latter, although in trading, as in most ventures, there are any number of people who will not or cannot learn from history, as well as some who cannot learn from anything.

There are those who believe, often with good reason, that one should "Never quarrel with the tape." They believe that the current price of something is all that really counts, and if it is not in line with what was expected the wise course is to "Quit while the quitting is good." They feel that it is not productive to be too curious about all the reasons behind all the price movements because so much time might be spent learning about the factors that could influence a trade no trade would ever be made; or that so much effort might be used to justify retaining a position when the tape says it should not be retained severe losses would result. That is why "Wishful thinking must be banished."

Those who believe that inactive markets should be avoided are fond of asserting, "If money cannot be made out of leaders, it will not be made out of the market as a whole." They must contend with the equally popular and probably more accurate assertion that "the leaders of today may not be the

---

[3] Edwin Lefevre, *Reminiscences of a Stock Operator,* George H. Doran Co., New York, 1923, p. 65.

leaders of tomorrow." Trading in today's leaders may result only in trading where there is no longer any opportunity and not trading where there is. Those who are unable to agree with either view can take the middle road by accepting the proposition, "All stocks and commodities move more or less with the general market, but value will tell in the long run." Just how much move indicates a genuine move toward economic value is not so easy to determine. One must remember that "value has little to do with temporary fluctuations in prices" and that this problem will always be with us because "The market will continue to fluctuate."

Some traders even personify a market. They believe that you can "Plot the pattern of a bull market and you will have also plotted the pattern followed by nature for most living things; a slow start and gradual acceleration in growth that terminates at maturity." Most bull markets actually do appear to follow this sort of pattern.

NOTES FROM A TRADER

There is hardly a maxim that someone could not find fault with. There are one or two, however, that most traders believe sooner or later. Many of those who believe them later would have done better to believe them sooner. One of these is, "Put half your profits in a safety deposit box." Although it should be possible to find an investment wiser than cash in a safety deposit box, it hardly seems necessary to utilize any profits gained to take larger and larger positions with the ever-increasing risks that accompany them. Although it may not seem logical, it is probably true that money is easier to make than it is to keep.

Adversity is part and parcel of trading. The only benefits that come from adversity are the knowledge and strength gained. It detracts nothing from the truth to acknowledge it with such seemingly inane statements as, "Winners never quit and quitters never win," or one more profound like "God grant me the serenity to accept the things I cannot change, the courage to change the things I can, and the wisdom to know the difference." The point of both is equally valid. The simple truth is that most successful speculators have been bloodied at least once before achieving success, but all have tried again. Hopefully, one need not accept the cynical proposition that "A speculator who dies rich has died before his time."

CHAPTER THIRTEEN

Who Wins? Who Loses? Why?

Who Wins?

The race is not always to the swift nor the battle to
the strong—but that's the way to bet.

DAMON RUNYON

Who Loses?

The greatest tragedy in all history is the murder of a
beautiful theory by a gang of brutal facts.

ANONYMOUS

Why?

I contradict myself. I am large, I contain multitudes.

WALT WHITMAN

INTRODUCTION

The purpose of this concluding chapter of the trading section is to focus on
the results, however limited, of those who play the commodity futures trading game and to suggest reasons for the outcomes. A discerning trader might
take the position that such an inquiry should *precede* the trading section,
not succeed it, for if commodity futures trading is a zero sum game in which
total profits and losses must be equal it is possible, theoretically at least, for
the participants to cannibalize in a kind of suicidal rotation in which no one
wins in the long run. In such a dismal activity a continual advantage could
be held only by the broker who charged each participant an entry fee in the
form of a commission. Under these conditions the potential trader might
conclude that the game is suited only to those hardy souls who might be
characterized as gladiators who look on each trade as an exercise in "kill
or be killed." Unless the shape of his trading curve indicates an exceptionally active greed factor, the potential trader may find such a game totally
unsuitable. Fortunately there are some facts about the outcomes of futures
trading that square well with hypotheses that are not quite so bleak.

DISTRIBUTION OF PROFITS AND LOSSES

THE BLAIR STEWART STUDY

Probably the best known analysis of the trading record of speculators is that by Blair Stewart, as a consulting economist for the Commodity Exchange Authority.[1] The complete trading records of 8,922 customers of a Chicago commission firm which went bankrupt in the 1930s were turned over to the CEA for analysis. The study is restricted to results in grain futures (wheat, corn, oats, and rye) for a nine-year period from 1924 to 1932.

Futures market participants were divided into two broad classifications — hedgers and speculators. Three broad groups were distinguished among the speculators: scalpers, who were defined as buying and selling on small fluctuations in prices and closing the day with near even positions; spreaders, who were long and short positions of equal amounts; other speculators, who represented all remaining traders. The Stewart study focused on the results of the last group:

Commodity	Profit traders			Loss traders		
	Number	Total net profits	Average profit per trader	Number	Total net losses	Average loss per trader
Wheat	2,045	$1,508,407	$738	5,496	$ 9,411,620	$1,712
Corn	1,525	$1,183,993	$776	2,403	$ 2,222,602	$ 925
Oats	589	$ 124,038	$211	997	$ 772,132	$ 774
Rye	497	$ 293,042	$590	816	$ 825,838	$1,012
All grains°	2,184	$2,064,800	$945	6,598	$11,958,200	$1,812

° The "all grains" figures are not equal to the totals of the figures for the individual grains because some traders made profits in one or more grains but lost on their futures transactions in one or more of the other grains.

The overwhelming conclusion from the general summary is that the vast majority (75 percent) of the speculators (other than scalpers and spreaders) lost money. There were 6,598 speculators in the sample with net losses compared with 2,184 with net profits, or three times as many loss traders as profit traders. Net dollar speculator losses of approximately $12,000,000 overwhelmed net dollar profits of nearly $2,000,000 by sixfold. Speculators were not discriminating — they lost in every commodity, consistently and impressively.

The distribution of profits and losses indicated that for most traders the results indicated that the game was not played for high stakes. Eighty-four percent of the winners during the nine-year period won less than $1,000. Stewart's sample of traders who held reportable positions did not indicate that large speculators were any more successful than small traders, although the sample was too small to warrant any such generalization.

[1] Blair Stewart, "An Analysis of Speculative Trading in Grain Futures," USDA, Technical Bulletin No. 1001, October 1949, p. 57.

Other significant points included the following:

1. Speculators showed a clear tendency to cut their profits short while letting their losses run.

2. The speculator is more likely to be long than short.

3. The entire period was one in which prices declined, and speculators receipted for a disproportionate share of the total losses during the last three years when the price decline accelerated.

4. No occupational group was able to claim results that differed from the general conclusion in regard to aggregate profits and losses. Managers in the grain business were somewhat more successful than other groups, yet they could produce aggregate profits in dollars that were only 28 percent of aggregate losses.

5. There was a clear tendency of long speculators to buy on days of price declines and for shorts to sell on price rises. This action indicates that traders were predominantly price level rather than price movement traders.

The study also presented two case studies which isolated in detail the trades of the largest winner and loser. The loser traded virtually throughout the nine-year period and his losses were more than $400,000 in wheat futures. In the spring of 1928 he had amassed a moderate profit, which he was to give back and follow with heavy losses resulting from a seasonal strategy, beginning in 1928, of buying wheat heavily at harvest time and selling it in the subsequent spring. The most successful trader struck quickly in 1924 by being long corn, wheat, and rye, staying with his position until October of that year, and then fading away with profits of almost $300,000. He did not trade again during the nine-year period.

THE HIERONYMUS STUDY [2]

Hieronymus was able to secure the summary records of closed trades for a commission house for the calendar year 1969. Even though conclusions derived from a one-year inquiry must of necessity be tentative, it is instructive to compare recent results, however selective, against Stewart's observations 35 years earlier. The aggregate results for three major metropolitan offices of the firm are as follows:

Number of accounts	462
Number of accounts with profits	164
Total profits (dollars)	$462,413
Profit per account (dollars)	$2,819
Number of accounts with losses	298
Total losses (dollars)	$1,127,355
Losses per account (dollars)	$3,783
Average result (loss) (dollars)	$1,439
Net loss, all accounts (dollars)	$664,942
Commissions paid (dollars)	$406,344
Put to clearing house (dollars)	$258,598

[2] Thomas A. Hieronymus, *Economics of Futures Trading*, Commodity Research Bureau, New York, 1971, pp. 252–258.

Thirty-five percent of the firm's customers (versus 25 percent in the Stewart study) closed 1969 with a profit. A total of $1,589,768 changing hands between winners and losers and involving 462 people is an *average* of $3,441, a game that cannot qualify as representing staggering sums. This is confirmed by a frequency distribution which indicates that half the winners and losers won or lost less than $1,000 and 84 percent won or lost less than $5,000. Except for a few big losers (16 over $15,000) and fewer big winners (6 over $15,000), the clients of the commission house tended to pass money back and forth, paying commissions in the shuffle. It is interesting to note that a large number (170) of accounts were traded only once or a few times at most. This group, although constituting 37 percent of the total number of accounts, contributed 64 percent of the total losses. Regular traders (those who won or lost at least $500 and contributed $250 in commissions during the year) did better as a group and their net profits were nearly enough to offset their net losses. Regular traders (42 percent) paid $364,647 of the total $406,344 commissions, or almost 90 percent, which strongly suggests that the regular traders relieved the one-time traders of their money and then deposited it with the firm in the form of commissions.

ADDITIONAL EVIDENCE

The authors have been able to confirm that the average expectation of a trader making net profits in any given year will be one in four. The records of one respected brokerage firm indicated that for 10 years, beginning in 1962, the percentage of traders concluding the year with net profits ranged from a low of 14 percent to a high of 42 percent, with an average of 26 percent. In 1969, 23 percent of the accounts made money, compared with 35 percent in the Hieronymus sample of 462, which was approximately 10 percent of the size of the firm the authors examined. At any rate, the three estimates do not seem to be mutually exclusive in their implications for any given year. As the rates of return for the CEA trader classifications are examined, however, it will be seen that there is a significant difference between making profits in any *one* year and making *consistent* profits over a period of many years.

THE ROCKWELL STUDY [3]

The Rockwell Study, based on Houthakker's earlier method of analysis,[4] makes use of more than 7,900 semimonthly observations covering 25 CEA

[3] Charles Rockwell, "Normal Backwardation, Forecasting, and the Returns to Commodity Futures Traders," *Proceedings of a Symposium of Speculation in Organized Commodity Markets, Food Research Institute Studies,* Supplement, 7 (1967), 115. Portions of this study have been referred to in Chapters 2 and 4. Before proceeding, the trader should review the breakdown of the percentage of the value of the open interest by participant in Table 2-2.

[4] Hendrik Houthakker, "Can Speculators Forecast Prices?" *The Review of Economics and Statistics* (May 1957).

regulated markets for 18 years, beginning in 1947, as described in Table 13-1. The study does not include the markets such as pork bellies, cocoa, and sugar, which at that time were unregulated and which constitute a significant percentage of futures trading in more recent periods. Three different market aggregations were used; "All Markets," covering 25 markets, "Large Markets," including only Chicago wheat, New York cotton, and soybeans, and "Small Markets," which included the remaining 22 markets. A reasonably stable general price level occurred from the beginning of the period to the end, as shown in Table 13-1.

For the 18-year period in all markets there is a positive total return of about $750 million on the long open interest, as illustrated in Table 13-2. About 40 percent of the return to the long open interest goes to the small speculator and the remainder is divided fairly equally among the large speculator, the hedger, and spreader.

If, in all markets, those holding long positions account for about $750 million in profits, there must be an offsetting $750 million loss to those holding short positions. Again the small speculator bears approximately 40 percent of this loss.

The large speculator again makes a profit, albeit a small one ($25 million) when compared with his gains on the long side. It is important to note that the large speculators are the *only* group that has an aggregate profit on the short side for All Markets. The short hedger bears 40 percent of the short side losses in All Markets, about equal to those of the small speculator. The hedger, however, does not offset his short losses with long profits because his long side gains account for only 20 percent of the long profits.

In the Small Markets small speculators lose money on their long positions. Their long losses are offset by large speculators and long hedgers, so that the total dollar returns to those holding long positions in the Small Markets is virtually zero. On the short side only the large speculator makes money and he achieves these profits mainly at the expense of the short hedger.

In the Large Markets the small speculator makes almost 50 percent of the long side profits. On the short side the large speculators make a little money, but the short hedgers lose more than twice the amount of their gains on the long side. The total returns on the long open interest in the Large Markets ($751.4 million) contrast markedly with the insignificant returns on the long open interest in the Small Markets.

A summary follows of the significance of the net returns to each group for the 18-year period, as presented in the last three rows of Table 13-2. It should be noted that the profit flow in the three Large Markets determines to a great extent the behavior of the All Market aggregate.

1. When the short-side losses of small traders are compared with their long-side profits, the group shows a small net loss for All Markets.

2. Large speculators win consistently (though unevenly) in Small and Large Markets, and their total winnings ($178.8 million) come almost entirely at the expense of hedgers in the Large Markets.

3. In the Small Markets hedgers do much better ($6.5 million) than they

TABLE 13-1 DESCRIPTION OF DATA AND PRICE LEVELS

Commodity and markets*	Period of observation from	Period of observation to	Number of semimonthly observations	Change in price level of nearby contract† (dollars) start	end	Annual percentage price change from start to end	between maturity years
Wheat, Chicago Board of Trade	7/47	6/65	432	2.39375	1.42250	-2.3	-2.2
Wheat, Kansas City Board of Trade	7/50	6/65	360	2.30375	1.43500	-2.3	-1.6
Wheat, Minneapolis Grain Exchange	7/50	6/65	360	2.36125	1.59750	-2.2	-2.5
Corn, Chicago Board of Trade	7/47	6/65	432	2.30375	1.32250	-2.2	+1.4
Oats, Chicago Board of Trade	7/47	6/65	432	1.02000	.67750	-1.9	-5.1
Rye, Chicago Board of Trade	7/47	6/65	432	2.52000	1.15750	-3.0	-1.6
Soybeans, Chicago Board of Trade	7/47	6/65	432	2.78000	2.96000	+0.36	-0.7
Soybean meal‡, Chicago Board of Trade	7/47	6/65	432	87.50	71.10	-1.0	-12.0
Soybean oil,§ Chicago Board of Trade	7/50	6/65	360	0.1245	0.1008	-1.3	-3.1
Cotton, New York Cotton Exchange	7/47	6/64	408	0.3898	0.3328	-0.9	-2.8
Cotton, New Orleans Cotton Exchange	7/50	6/60	240	0.3569	0.3278	-0.8	-4.3
Cottonseed meal, Memphis Merchants Exchange Clearing Association	7/47	6/60	312	79.90	54.00	-2.5	-9.4
Cottonseed oil, New York Produce Exchange	7/47	6/65	432	0.2350	0.1232	-2.6	-0.6
Lard, Chicago Board of Trade	7/47	6/62	360	0.1960	0.0870	-3.7	-1.6
Flaxseed, Minneapolis Grain Exchange	7/50	6/62	288	3.7150	3.1900	-1.2	+2.0
Shell eggs, Chicago Mercantile Exchange	7/47	6/65	432	0.5282	0.3490	-1.9	-0.1
Frozen eggs, Chicago Mercantile Exchange	7/61	6/65	96	0.2635	0.2687	+0.5	-4.6
Potatoes, New York Mercantile Exchange	7/47	6/65	432	2.96	2.58	-0.7	+5.0
Wool tops, Wool Association of the New York Cotton Exchange	7/47	6/62	360	1.570	1.666	+0.4	-4.7
Grease wool, Wool Association of the New York Cotton Exchange	5/54	6/63	257	1.413	1.190	-1.7	-0.2

Bran, Kansas City Board of Trade	7/47	6/56	216	58.50	33.20	−4.8	−7.8
Shorts, Kansas City Board of Trade	7/47	6/56	216	60.00	38.90	−3.9	−9.8
Middlings, Kansas City Board of Trade	7/55	6/56	24	37.00	35.15	−5.0	−8.4
Onions, Chicago Mercantile Exchange	9/55	6/59	91	2.10	1.30	−9.5	−1.0
Butter, Chicago Mercantile Exchange	7/47	6/53	144	0.6775	0.6120	−1.6	−2.4

• "Large markets" are wheat at Chicago, cotton at New York, and soybeans.

† The nearby contract is the first contract that expires after the first observation; generally it is July.

‡ Soybean meal is for the Memphis Merchants Exchange Association until July 1953.

§ Soybean oil is for the New York Produce Exchange until July 1950.

SOURCE: Rockwell, *op. cit.*, 115.

TABLE 13-2   AGGREGATE PROFITS BY TRADING GROUPS: LONG,
SHORT, AND NET (MILLION DOLLARS)

Trading group	Large Markets		Small Markets		All Markets°	
	Long	Short	Long	Short	Long	Short
Small traders	369.7	−303.6	−68.1	−1.4	301.6	−305.0
Reporting speculators	114.8	3.1	38.8	22.2	153.5	25.3
Reporting spreaders†	159.0	−159.6	5.5	−3.4	164.5	−163.1
Reporting hedgers	108.1	−291.2	25.4	−18.8	133.5	−310.1
Total long open interest°	751.4		1.5		752.9	
Small traders, net	66.1		−69.5		−3.4	
Reporting speculators, net	117.8		61.0		178.8	
Reporting hedgers, net	−183.2		6.5		−176.6	

° Because of rounding, totals are not necessarily exact sums of the components shown.

† This category is included only for balance purposes. The sum of the net positions is not zero because of its omission.

SOURCE: Rockwell, *op. cit.,* 119.

do in the large markets, and the profits of the large speculator ($61 million) are made at the expense of the small speculator.

4. The losses of hedgers in the three Large Markets provide the profits to large speculators and almost enough profits to small speculators to offset their losses in the 23 Small Markets.

Even more instructive is the yearly presentation in Table 13-3 of the an-

TABLE 13-3   ANNUAL PROFITS FOR ALL
MARKETS (MILLION DOLLARS)

Year	Small traders, net	Large speculators, net	Hedgers, net	Total
1947/48	16.2	19.5	−34.2	115.9
1948/49	−13.5	− 0.5	13.8	− 48.2
1949/50	7.9	17.0	−24.9	153.3
1950/51	47.5	28.9	−76.11	229.5
1951/52	−10.5	7.8	2.7	126.2
1952/53	−44.3	− 4.3	46.4	−171.9
1953/54	12.8	16.3	−29.7	113.4
1954/55	−17.0	5.1	12.0	− 27.7
1955/56	2.5	12.7	−15.5	73.9
1956/57	− 6.4	6.5	− 0.1	5.8
1957/58	− 9.4	0.9	8.4	− 27.4
1958/59	− 3.6	1.4	2.5	− 3.7
1959/60	−14.6	4.5	10.2	− 38.3
1960/61	63.3	35.2	−98.6	217.8
1961/62	−19.4	− 5.4	24.8	− 95.9
1962/63	− 3.6	2.1	1.6	50.5
1963/64	−24.1	10.0	14.1	− 75.0
1964/65	13.0	21.2	−34.1	155.0
Total	− 3.4	178.8	−176.6	752.9

SOURCE: Rockwell, *op. cit.,* 120.

nual profits in All Markets for all participants. The small speculator loses in 11 of the 18 years. His average loss is $15.1 million and his average profit, $23.7 million. If the largest profit years are removed (1950–1951 and 1960–1961), the average profit drops to $10.5 million, well below the average loss. There is little consolation to the small speculator in the realization that 68 percent of his profits for the 18-year period may be attributed to only two years.

The large speculator, on the other hand, shows a profit in 15 of the 18 years. His average yearly profit is almost $13 million, even though he accounts for perhaps less than 2 percent of the total value of the open interest, whereas his average annual loss is only $3.4 million. If the two largest profit years are removed, the average profit is $9.6 million, still virtually three times the average loss of $3.4 million. The consistency of the profit-making capacity of the large speculator is impressive.

The hedger, during the 18-year period, shows a $6.5 million profit in the 23 Small Markets, yet his loss in the Large Markets is so large ($183.1 million) that he suffers an All Market loss of $176.6 million. Recent research by Working[5] is consistent with these findings. Working indicated that the major proportion of hedging losses may spring from market execution costs, which can be considerably greater than the reduced member commissions paid by most large hedgers. Because hedgers' orders tend to be large, any buys and sells would tend to make price bulges and dips which scalpers would trade. Such action, if true, renders understandable why the amount of speculation in a given market is closely tied to the amount of hedging. Hedgers may be the major source of income of the large speculator. Because most hedging is short hedging, most large speculator profits should come from the long side of the Large Markets. This may be verified by referring to Table 13-2.

If the annual rates of return to the participants are defined as gross profits as a percentage of contract value, Table 13-4 can present the trader with an idea of the individual rates of return by trading groups. Even though commissions, taxes, and capital reserves are omitted, the fact that margin requirements are only 5 or 10 percent of the contract value means that the actual returns on margin money may be as much as 10 to 20 times the returns indicated here. Regardless of the level of absolute profits, the relative profits of the different trading groups may be compared.

For All Markets the rate of return on the long open interest is 4 percent annually. The hedger makes about this amount on his net long positions so that the large speculator picks up what the small trader loses on the long side in Small Markets as well as what the hedger loses in the Large Markets. On the short side the large speculator wins from the small trader and the hedger in both Small and Large Markets. Again the large speculator is the

[5] Holbrook Working, "Tests of a Theory Concerning Floor Trading on Commodity Exchanges," *Proceedings of a Symposium on Price Effects of Speculation in Organized Commodity Markets, Food Research Institute Studies,* Supplement, 7 (1967), 5–48.

TABLE 13-4   AGGREGATE RATES OF RETURN BY
TRADING GROUPS (PER CENT)

Groups and positions	Large markets	Small markets	All markets
Total positions			
All groups	6.1	0.0	4.0
Small traders, long	5.6	−2.0	3.0
Small traders, short	−5.8	−0.0	−4.1
Large speculators, long	10.1	4.3	7.6
Large speculators, short	0.5	5.0	2.7
Hedgers, long	5.3	1.7	3.8
Hedgers, short	−7.1	−0.6	−4.3
Net positions			
Small traders, net	0.6	−1.2	−0.0
Large speculators, net	7.2	4.6	6.1
Hedgers, net	−3.0	0.1	−1.7

SOURCE: Rockwell, *op. cit.*, 122.

standout in the Large and Small Markets. His overall return of 6.1 percent
is earned because he does well in both his long and short positions and because the ratio of his long to his short positions is large during the periods
that short hedgers are losing. The small trader loses so much on his short
positions that the resulting profits on his long positions do not overcome the
deficit. If the hedger is offsetting existing or expected positions in the cash
market, the overall loss (−1.7 percent) may provide an insight into the
gross cost of placing a year-long hedge.

Until recently the risk premium concept, as developed in Chapter 4, was
the consistent, if overworked, springboard into any discussion of the distribution of profits and losses in futures trading. The naïve strategy (being
net long when hedgers are net short and being net short when hedgers are
net long) does not result in an acceptable explanation of the profit flow.
The failure to isolate and measure persistent evidence that speculators are
paid for merely playing the game implies that speculative profits must be
explained by reference to the trader's forecasting ability. Forecasting ability
however, may be defined as two broadly differing skills. The first refers
to the basic ability to be long in markets when prices are going up on the
average and net short in markets when prices are going down on the average. This measure of forecasting skill indicates the long-run ability of a
given trading group to stay on the "right" side of a given market and is referred to as "basic skill." On the other hand, a second level of forecasting
ability refers to the "special skill" that a trading group exhibits when it
makes profits from price movements that are shorter in duration than the
total period under observation.

Table 13-5 presents a division of the rates of return according to basic
and special skills. Small traders make important money only in the Large
Markets, where rising prices result in a positive figure for basic skill (R^B).
Small traders exhibit a consistent negative value for special skill (R^F).
Large speculators, as is obvious by now, make money on the evidence of

both skills. There are no "minus" values for the large trader in the Large Markets, Small Markets, or All Markets summary. Almost 80 percent of the total profits of the large trader comes from his special skill and only 20 percent from his basic skill. The large trader, then, is not rewarded chiefly by executing the strategy of buy and hold in an extended up move or sell and hold in an extended down move but rather by trading price changes in the relative short run.

Working's recent study[6] of the detailed record of one professional trader in cotton futures for a brief period is important for several reasons. In attempting to test the theory that most floor trading is scalping and that the execution costs of hedging are perhaps the chief source of income to speculators in futures markets, the definition of "scalping" was considerably enlarged to cover not only the smallest dips and bulges that occur but those that last up to a few days. In the large, well-traveled markets professional scalping tends to specialize sometimes into three distinguishable classes — unit-change scalpers, day-trading scalpers, and day-to-day scalpers. Unit-change scalpers, who stand ready to buy one tick below the last sale or sell one tick above it, almost invariably end the trading session in a zero net

[6] *Ibid.*

**TABLE 13-5   DIVISION OF RATE OF RETURN
ACCORDING TO BASIC AND SPECIAL
FORECASTING SKILLS BY NET TRADING
GROUPS* (PERCENT)**

Trading and skill groups	Large markets	Small markets	All markets
Small traders net			
Rate of return from special forecasting skill (R^F)	−0.1	−1.2	−0.4
Rate of return from basic forecasting skill (R^B)	0.7	0.0	0.4
Total rate of return (R^A)	0.6	−1.2	−0.0
Large speculators net			
Rate of return from special forecasting skill (R^F)	5.0	3.9	4.8
Rate of return from basic forecasting skill (R^B)	2.2	0.7	1.3
Total rate of return (R^A)	7.2	4.6	6.1
Hedgers net			
Rate of return from special forecasting skill (R^F)	−0.9	0.8	−0.6
Rate of return from basic forecasting skill (R^B)	−2.1	−0.7	−1.0
Total rate of return (R^A)	−3.0	0.1	−1.7

* In a given market the decomposition of the total actual rate of return (R^A) into basic forecasting skill (R^B) and special forecasting skill (R^F) is discussed in Rockwell, *op. cit.*, 127.

SOURCE: Rockwell, *op. cit.*, 127.

speculative position. Day traders tend to concentrate on dips and bulges of greater than unit size and may decide to hold some small percentage of their positions overnight. Day-to-day scalpers more often than not are pre-pared to carry most or all of their positions into the next trading session or for two or three successive days.

As indicated by the Stewart study, nearly all speculators, on or off the floor of the exchange, make some attempts at scalping. Price level traders may wait for price dips before getting long or for price bulges before initiat-ing a short position. These traders, of course, run the risk of missing the market completely in those trades that, by definition, are the most success-ful. An alternative is to place orders "at the market," which ensures some execution costs at the hands of floor traders who are, themselves, scalping. The small trader is not on the exchange floor and cannot easily, for ex-ample, buy "on a dip" while the dip is forming.

Because the professional scalper derives profits from trading dips and bulges of varying time lengths, it seems difficult to understand why the ability to recognize price trends is asserted by floor traders to be the most important requirement for successful scalping.[7] The adage, "Cut your losses and let your profits run," heard by every trader alive, including those who came down with the last rain, has always been regarded as a basic rule of successful trading. Yet the effort to comply with the directive is success-ful only for the trader who can consistently anticipate the continuation of price trends. Such success is highly doubtful for reasons considered at length in Chapters 4 and 7. How, then, can the concepts of scalping and trend following coexist?

Working's thoughts, following a study of a two-month record of floor trading by a professional trader, explains why the adage, "Cut your losses and let your profits run," combines in one statement two entirely different approaches that are important for different reasons:

> (a) because a "trend" is the converse of a dip or bulge, trend recognition is a means of recognizing dips and bulges; (b) a scalper recognizes, in order to partially offset the losses that he incurs from trends whose beginnings he mis-takenly regards as initial moves in a dip or bulge; and (c) the adage, "cut your losses and let your profits run," which is highly respected by floor traders, de-serves such respect even if its application cannot be made a source of net gains. By letting profits run, to the best of his ability, a scalper derives such profits as he can from the emergence of unpredictable trends that happen to be in his favor, partially offsetting inevitable losses from the emergence of trends that run against him. By setting a limit on the amount of loss that he allows himself to incur, per unit of the commodity, a scalper accepts unneccessary loss to a greater extent than he avoids further loss (a consequence of the supposition that brief price trends are a source of net loss); but the practice, while slightly reducing his overall rate of profit per unit of the commodity, allows him to

[7] *Ibid.*, 44.

trade safely on a scale several times as large as would be prudent if he did not thus limit his losses per unit . . . effort to deal as successfully as possible with brief price trends is necessarily an integral part of professional scalping; and therefore, evidence that a floor trader makes such efforts does not, by itself, warrant classing him as a trend trader.[8]

SKILLS OF THE TRADER

FORECASTING SKILLS

The bald, unyielding fact is that small traders, as a group, seemingly possess no basic forecasting or special forecasting skill. They hold 46 percent of the value of all contracts and their gross profits are zero. Substantial losses occur when commissions are included. On the average, then, a small trader has the expectation of losing money—the losses over a reasonable period to equal commissions. It is evident that small traders do not require a history of profits to continue trading. The explanation of such a phenomenon may take several directions. First, the needs of some small traders may be met by merely playing the game. Having something that is dynamic and fast-paced to get up for in the morning is so exciting that the trader may be more than willing to lose money for the privilege of speculating. Second, traders may continue to trade because they believe they can forecast prices. The fact that they cannot consistently do so does not deter them because they tend to remember profits and forget losses. Third, the small trader may continue to trade because his group is amorphous and consists not of a crowd, but of a parade. The successful small trader becomes large as a result of his competence, whereas the unsuccessful small trader is eventually forced to withdraw from the market and is replaced by new blood. Fourth, the small trader may be convinced that his latest mistake is also his last mistake and, having learned, there is nothing ahead but smooth sea and blue sky.

On the other hand, small traders have years in which they post impressive profits. Referring to Table 13-3, it may be seen that in the years 1950/ 1951 and 1960/1961, for example, small traders show returns four and six times larger, respectively, than the average profit of the five other profitable years. This performance may well be explained by the tendency of the small trader to rely on the existence of positive serial correlation as the basis for his trading strategy; that is, small traders tend to rely on long-run trend-following methods for profits, in which they assume that the tendency of a rising market is to continue to rise and the tendency of a falling market is to continue to fall. Such trading theories result in trading strategies of buying strength and selling weakness, which may enable the small trader to reap extremely high profits in years when such trends are of

[8] *Ibid.*, 45.

long duration. Unfortunately, in the long run, more markets are trading markets than long trending markets; that is, there seems to be more of a tendency for price reversal than for price continuation.

Large traders generally tend to view markets as trading markets rather than trending markets. They may rely more heavily on the presence of negative serial correlation; therefore they may tend to sell certain rallies and buy certain declines. Such a result is consistent with an examination of the returns of large traders in their biggest profit years, again 1950/1951 and 1960/1961. In those years large traders show a return, respectively, of 3 and 3.7 times the average profit of the other 13 profitable years, considerably lower than those for the small trader.

It should be emphasized that there is a considerable difference between a winner in any given year and a consistent winner over a significant period of time. Although the studies to date have indicated that a trader in any given year has an approximate probability of one in four of achieving a net profit, the probability of extending his supremacy consecutively drops precipitously. Of the 25 percent who win in any given year, only 2 percent manage their skills in a consistent manner that ensures their reappearance in a ratio approaching 15 of 18. For the remaining 23 percent *sic transit gloria*.

It is important to note that the dismal profitability of the small trader results in no small part as a consequence of his inability to manage money intelligently. Of the four elements of money management, the two discussed in detail in Chapter 10 are probably the chief culprits—the expectation of the game being played and the probability of ruin. The small trader seldom approaches the expectation of the game in the spirit of fair, good, and bad bets as determined by the profitability of the event occurring, the ratio of gain to loss, and the cost of playing the game. In his desire to play a speculative game to the hilt, in which results, either good or bad, occur quickly, the probability of ruin does not receive the cool reflection it deserves, and the small speculator remains generally unconvinced that he cannot change the mathematical expectation of the game by the way he plays the game.

There are quantitative and qualitative reasons for the supremacy of one trader over another. Many of the quantitative skills, which certainly may be acquired by patience and intellectual diligence, have been the subject of much of this book. Many of the skills that must be developed, however, deal with behavior and the reaction of the trader to on-going events and conditions.

BEHAVIORAL SKILLS

It is difficult to discuss the development of skills that cannot be internalized adequately except by experience. The fact that such behavioral skills exist is clearly illustrated by a neophyte who, having been sensitized to a particular behavioral skill may say, "Why didn't you tell me that before?" —

to which the professional trader replies, "I did." Men make markets. The nature and behavior of man, although not reducible to formula, is at least agreeable to analysis. The behavior of the trader should move toward the kind of behavior necessary to survive.

Past studies. Only three studies since World War II have dealt specifically with the behavior of traders. One, by Blair Stewart, has been examined. Another, by Ira Glick, deals with the professional trader, and the most recent effort by Seymour Smidt attempts to analyze the characteristics of the amateur speculator.

Glick's study[9] analyzed three styles of trading that professional traders on the Chicago Mercantile Exchange believed could lead to success:

> One successful pattern is exemplified by the scalper, and, from the trader's point of view, is probably the most difficult to realize. The typical scalper is thought of as young, relatively new in the occupation; flexible, aggressive and exhibitionistic in his behavior, and *always* minimizing losses.
>
> A second career pattern for success is the older, more mature trader, actively and in a large way engaged in some phase of the egg business. He has excellent sources of information and is regarded as intelligent, able to view and grasp the total market situation in terms of a span of time and a diversity of factors. He is thought of as being wealthy and as having many wealthy friends, probably some of whom are also in the cash egg business.
>
> A third successful career line is quite similar to the above type, but this type of successful trader does not often appear on the exchange floor. Instead, he is thought of as purposely staying away from the (physical) marketplace, developing his trading strategy and tactics on the basis of good sources of objective information and executing his purchases and sales through representatives on the trading floor. . . .[10]

Smidt's analysis[11] reported findings on many characteristics of 349 futures traders who were interviewed personally or by mail. Because of the difficulty of obtaining access to a random sample of the trading population, Smidt relied on cross tabulation of his data to identify valid relationships.

When traders were classified into chartists and norm traders, that is, technicians and fundamentalists, results indicated that chartists are (a) less likely to take long positions and more likely to close out positions before receiving a margin call, (b) less likely to put up additional margin if they do receive a margin call, and (c) more likely to trade in a larger number of commodities and to pyramid their profits.

Initial sources of trading information were furnished by personal friends and brokers, and most traders interviewed preferred commodities about

[9] Ira O. Glick, "A Social Psychological Study of Futures Trading," an unpublished Ph.D. dissertation, Department of Sociology, University of Chicago, 1957.

[10] *Ibid.*, pp. 245–246.

[11] Seymour Smidt, *Amateurs, Information and Speculation: A Study of Amateur Commodity Speculators and Speculation,* Agricultural Industries Research Program, Graduate School of Business and Public Administration, Cornell University, Ithaca, N.Y., 1962.

which they had some information. The majority indicated that they anticipated no great change in their habits, and only 12 percent considered the possibility of discontinuing trading as the result of losing money.

An interesting comment in the study concerned the limitations in information used by the amateur speculator in commodities. For most traders in Smidt's sample

> . . . the broker is the only source of information, available more frequently than once a week, which contains more detail than would be available in *The Wall Street Journal* or some other daily newspaper. Considering the volatility of commodity markets, and the degree of leverage involved in commodity trading, this is somewhat surprising. It suggests that traders who do not rely heavily on their brokers can be expected to lag by as much as a week in their response to new information."[12]

Although interesting information is contained in these studies, they do not provide a systematic insight into the behavior of the commodity futures trader. A systematic approach would be useful not only to explain the trader's present behavior but to outline useful paths for change in the future.

Transactional analysis. One systematic approach that may serve as an explanatory model of the role of feelings and thought and their interaction is available in a recent popular study.[13] The model, originally developed by Erich Berne, has been named "transactional analysis" and is based on the premise that in every person there are at least three different people — the Parent, the Adult, and the Child. The Parent is the recording in the brain of the individual's first five years. The data in the Parent are not edited and permanently record all the verbal and nonverbal admonitions that the child heard and saw in his own parents. The replay of the Parent is a powerful influence throughout every individual's life, and the imperatives given in the early years can be a burden or a blessing, depending on whether they have been updated by the Adult. The Child is the body of data of internal events that was recorded when the little person was dependent and clumsy and had no vocabulary to speak of. Because of this condition, the Child is composed of feelings and emotions. Harris maintains that the Adult develops as soon as a person begins finding out for himself what is different about life from the "taught concept" of life in his Parent and "felt concept" of life in his Child.[14] The Adult relies on a "thought concept," which examines and updates the data from the Parent and Child to determine whether it is true and applicable.

It is important for the trader to understand the implications of the Whitman quote at the beginning of the chapter. Just as there are important

---

[12] *Ibid.*, pp. 54–56.
[13] Thomas A. Harris, *I'm OK–You're OK*, Harper & Row, 1967.
[14] *Ibid.*, p. 29.

relationships that are external to the trader, many of which may be quantified and learned, there are transactions that take place internally and may be involuntary as well. The boundaries between the Parent, Adult, and Child are fragile, and the total person may not always know which person is going to respond to a given transaction.

One of the basic reasons for understanding the identity of his Parent, Adult, and Child is illustrated in the trader's need for a plan. When a trader enters a position, but does not plan an objective and a stop, the plan is incomplete. When queried about the omissions, the trader may reply "I'll watch it." The problem with "watching it" is that it is not a statement made by the Adult in the trader. If the trade goes badly, the amount of loss taken will probably be greater than the amount that would have been taken had the Adult required the trader to take the time to make a basic decision about the value of a complete plan. Just as it is impossible to teach navigation in the middle of a storm, it is impossible to build an optimum plan in the middle of a bad loss. The Adult, functioning as a probability estimator, *knows* that losses must be planned in advance. The Child wants the feeling of assurance that everything will be all right without the plan. The Child wants no truck with unsavory consequences. The Parent might get in the act by quoting maxims appropriate to the occasion, such as "Never meet a margin call" or some other rule that will be marked by "should" or "ought."

Having a plan originated by the Adult before the trade is a vital step to success. The trader must, however, recognize that the temptation to tamper with the plan is founded in his Child and its fears and vulnerabilities. The Child is responsible for pulling out a stop-order just before it is elected or wishing to cancel an objective because the market is "acting well." Such directives from the Child may be seen in orders marked "cancel when close" or "good until executed."

The way in which the trader confronts reality gives a basic clue to his eventual success or failure. The successful trader with a well-developed Adult is good at adapting to various market and trading conditions. He learns that stop-loss orders must be placed irrevocably or the question becomes not *whether* he will be ruined but *when* he will be ruined. The successful trader has learned to cope with his feelings of fear (Child), primarily that what is wanted most — money — can be lost or denied. He has controlled his feelings (Child), for he realizes that a victim of fear cultivated by greed can be lost to the stultification of hoping for much but acting to ensure little.

The unsuccessful trader copes with unpleasant reality in a far different way. He does not depend on changing himself but rather on fantasizing or changing the way he views reality. He tends to be selectively perceptive and retentive; that is, he tends to see and remember what fits his needs and expectations. The trader in this situation is dominated by his Child; for example, most easily constructed trading systems, trend-following or otherwise, will have long-run dollar results approaching 50 percent profits and

50 percent losses. When commissions and execution costs are subtracted, the normal expected path of such a trader's capital is a gentle downward slope that terminates considerably short of his capacity for self-deception. If such a trader eliminates but one loss that a newly devised filter would not only never have permitted but would have reversed for a profit, while including a profit that was virtually certain before an unfavorable news item caused a loss, his record on the trades becomes seven profits and three losses. Only a trader stripped of all vision, he reasons, can quit on a system that is 70 percent accurate. The capacity of the dominant Child for misinterpreting reality is virtually limitless.

No matter how successful a trader becomes, he still finds it difficult to live in the real world. Where members of the animal kingdom must adjust to the external environment on its terms, man can manipulate reality over a broad range by the use of symbolism. A trader must realize that desirable qualities can be bestowed by words alone and that such words can be affixed more readily to the occasion than the occasion can be modified to fit the actual meaning of the words. A trader does not enjoy being wrong. Besides ruining his credit balance, being wrong does not build a good image of the self. Yet mistakes must be constantly perceived and remembered for no other reason than that under no other conditions can they be controlled.

Successful trading is reached, if at all, by following a series of successive approximations. Early in the process ignorance is the rule, and the trader knows that he knows nothing. Following a sometimes long apprenticeship in which the vocabulary symbols are acquired, a false sense of competence spreads like a thin veneer and serves to entertain friends with the glibness of skills not yet acquired, though seeming to be. Given enough time, patience, and perseverance, the successful trader enters into that third state in which he believes he knows something and no more. In this state he is "inner directed" and not "other directed."[15] The "other-directed" man reacts to what others believe about him. His roles and values tend to be derived from what his peers expect of him. The "inner-directed" man holds to the Adult course he has set for himself. Rather than being solely radar-equipped, as in "other-direction," the "inner-directed" man relies on a gyroscope that is not at the mercy of whim or caprice. The successful trader's gyroscope is finely tuned. He realizes that without a well-developed Adult he faces the same problem as the German High Command in World War II, in which the invasion of Britain was planned but never executed, whereas the Battle of Britain was executed but never planned. Many traders never move beyond the point of development where they tend to execute trades that are never planned or plan trades that are never executed.

The trader must understand that decisions with favorable consequences (made by the Adult) become built into a trading approach only if they are consciously reduced to principles and followed with *great effort*. Traders

[15] David Riesman. *The Lonely Crowd,* Yale University Press, New Haven, Conn., 1950.

who buy or sell on impulse find sooner or later that mere feelings about trading are 50-50; that is, there is no significant statistical correlation between good feelings and profitable trades. Therefore to avoid the results of emotional activity the successful trader must be prepared to give up trading what he finds most rewarding in interpersonal relationships — good feelings. The propensity for the trader to resist such depersonalization is high, and there is a constant temptation to spill out over the boundaries of the well-defined role of trading. Good feelings will come as a result of the successful plans that the Adult conceives and executes.

The broker is equally well advised to understand that he has three people for a client, not just one. Perhaps the "suitability" rule should include not only a financial but a behavioral match-up as well. The first rule of communication is that when stimulus and response, in the P-A-C sense, make parallel lines the transaction is complementary and can continue indefinitely.[16] In other words, a transaction between broker and client may go on indefinitely as Parent-Parent, Adult-Adult, Child-Child, Parent-Child, Child-Adult, and so on:

1. *Parent-Parent Transaction*

CLIENT: Those people you have on the floor always get the worst fills possible.

BROKER: Makes you wonder where it will all end, doesn't it?

2. *Adult-Adult Transaction*

CLIENT: I don't know whether to buy the bellies here or wait until after the report.

BROKER: I'll wire Chicago and see if they have any information on expectations.

3. *Parent-Child Transaction*

CLIENT (Parent):   I see where the 3-day moving average in May cocoa crossed the 10-day moving average on the upside yesterday and so I took a long position. It's off a little today but the weekly chart is bullish and when the weekly says up, you just don't worry about any adversity in the daily signal, especially during the time when the seasonal trend is up. In fact, I think I'll scalp about 30 points on the upside today and buy it back on Thursday morning after the Wednesday break.

BROKER (Child):   Right.

4. *Adult-Parent Transaction*

CLIENT (Adult):   I know I have trouble leaving the stop in when the market is acting poorly. I want you to promise me you won't listen when I try to pull out the stop.

BROKER (Parent):   I won't change any stop for you during market hours.

[16] Harris *op. cit.*, p. 70.

The second rule of communication in transactional analysis is that when stimulus and response cross, in the P-A-C sense, communication stops.

CLIENT (Adult):   I have a long position in July platinum and have been notified of delivery. How do I handle that?

BROKER (Parent):   Who put you in July platinum?

The broker and client can't talk about how the delivery is going to be handled. They first have to decide who is to blame for the trade.

CLIENT (Child):   I'm short soybeans just like you said and they have been up the limit for three days. They should sell off today, shouldn't they?

BROKER (Adult):   The validation on that trade called for a 5-cent stop which you did not enter.

The client in this case is asking the broker to take the responsibility for a bad trade. The broker, speaking from his Adult, points out that the recommended stop was not entered and leaves the client with a tarnished self-concept.

As might be suspected by now, brokers and clients can play roles for varying periods of time, but a solid relationship between two people cannot be built or extended without the Adult. Perhaps the most significant assistance a broker can render to a client is to take the time to help him make the big decisions about how and under what conditions the broker-client relationship is to continue. This process makes a multitude of small decisions unnecessary and encourages the good feelings made possible by a meeting of the minds before, not after, situations occur that might create stress.

EPILOGUE

The problems to which the trader has set his face have developed because his aspirations are infinitely expansible; the solutions lie in the hope that his knowledge and behavior are infinitely perfectible. In between the recognition of the problems and the acquisition of the quantitative and qualitative skills for their solutions lies a series of searches that must, many times, include the experience of failure. Indeed, no successful traders the authors have known can follow their paths backward very far without running into failure. It is not the act of failure, however, that differentiates the ultimately successful or unsuccessful trader. Rather, it is that the successful trader gets up, spends a few days healing, reaffirms what he knows, and goes about the business of adding to his store of wisdom. In such a growth process the quality of persistence looms large and is virtually irreplaceable.

The person involved responsibly, both intellectually and behaviorally, with the experience of trading may, to paraphrase Theodore Roosevelt, know at his best the triumph of high achievement or, if he fails, will have failed while daring greatly, so that his place will never be with those timid souls who know neither victory nor defeat. Perhaps, then, in the final analysis, it may be as rewarding to travel as to arrive.

The Broker in the Game

There are at least two reasons for the inclusion of Chapter 14, "Building, Maintaining, and Servicing a Commodity Clientele." The first is the obvious one of providing the commodity broker with a guide to on-going activities which show no clear beginning or ending. In that sense the chapter will have served its purpose if it proves useful as a yardstick of the broker's individual performance. The second reason, however, is as important as the first. The chapter should be studied by the trader so that as a client he may be aware of the principles on which the performance of a knowledgeable broker is based. The setting of standards does two things: first, both broker and client will more readily recognize substandard performance because good performance is defined; second, avenues to better performance are explored by which improvement in the quality of services rendered may be effected as much by client awareness as by the broker's presentation.

CHAPTER FOURTEEN

Building, Maintaining, and Servicing a Commodity Clientele

> To profit from good advice requires more wisdom than to give it.

INTRODUCTION

The registered representative who specializes in commodities is, like his counterpart in the securities area, basically a salesman. He must build a clientele by effective prospecting methods, maintain it by replacing clients lost, and serve those who deal with him efficiently. It is a truly rare person who is so skilled and knowledgeable that he can perform capably as salesman and researcher at the same time. Both research and sales are full-time jobs for most people if done competently. The primary function of a commodity salesman is to locate potential clients who, because he serves them honestly and well, will continue to do business with him over time.

BUILDING A COMMODITY CLIENTELE

Sales personality. The impression made by a registered representative on his clients is based on attitude, appearance, and ability to communicate. The attitude that any salesman should have is obviously beyond dispute. He should believe that his product is good for all concerned; his client, his firm, and himself. The client's interests must come first, but the firm and the salesman should also gain from satisfactory service. Long-term success is virtually impossible if all three do not benefit adequately and fairly. The brokerage company must make a profit from its business, the registered representative must be able to earn an adequate living handling his accounts, and the customer must be financially or psychically rewarded to justify his trading. Some salesmen believe that no client ever profits in the long run. Others are so disturbed by the high percentage of traders who lose money that they are unable to function effectively. These salesmen would help all concerned, including themselves, by selling some other product or by making a living in some other way. If the salesman can accept the fact that trading commodities is right for some people and wrong for others and tell all with whom he deals the truth about the business as he knows it, assuming that they are interested in his knowledge, then he can show enough sincerity to sell effectively. If he induces people to trade who clearly should not trade or persuades others not to trade who might enjoy it, profit from it, or both, or pretends to know what he does not know, he is helping no one. The proper sales attitude for most good salesmen is derived in large part from the enthusiasm that comes from a real understanding of what they are selling and what motivates the people who are buying.

The salesman's appearance is dictated by the same standards that apply to anyone in the investment field. He should look successful enough to avoid having his customers wonder why he is offering financial advice when he looks like a failure himself. He should not, however, dress so extravagantly that he gives the impression he has acquired all the money that his clients have lost. Extremes of dress are almost certain to prove offensive to some people who may respond by patronizing a different salesman.

The salesman communicates with his customers personally or by telephone or mail. He must know how to speak, write, and spell. If his speech, vocabulary, or writing ability is inadequate, he should recognize the deficiency and do something about it beyond hoping that the office stenographer will note and correct his errors. Effective formal courses in speech are available, and most communities have clubs dedicated to the improvement of public speaking. Group prospecting, such as addressing a luncheon meeting of a civic club, is too effective a sales device not to be utilized merely because a salesman is too inexperienced or shy to learn to speak well. Vocabulary and spelling may also be improved by taking positive steps that can be fun as well as economically rewarding. Formal courses in letter writing are part of the program of virtually all business schools.

Product knowledge. It has been said that commodity traders pass through three stages. First, they know not and know that they know not. Then they know not and know not that they know not. Then they know and know that they know. The first and third stages are relatively safe, but most traders seem to enter the dangerous second stage rather quickly and stay there. Worse, many registered representatives are there as well and are even more dangerous than individual traders because of their influence on others. Many inexperienced traders are led to believe that a registered representative knows more than he really does because of his fluency in the language of the business and his knowledge of its mechanics.

Some brokers study securities and commodities constantly in a truly professional manner and are really well informed. Others who become quite humble when they realize how little they do know approach trading with the caution it deserves. Too many, however, cover their lack with glib pretense and superficiality. It behooves the trader to ascertain the category into which his registered representative fits.

To establish himself as a professional in the area of product knowledge a registered representative need not build a reputation for enriching all his clients or selecting winning positions infallibly. A client who hopes to find such a man to service his account is hopelessly naïve, unreasonable, or both. There are, however, some constructive steps that may be taken by a salesman. He can become thoroughly informed of the services offered by his firm and by the commodity exchanges. He can master the rules, regulations, and mechanical procedures that apply to his job and learn enough about the legal, accounting, and tax aspects of commodity trading to provide his clients with general guidance, but he should never try to replace a qualified accountant or lawyer. Some of this basic knowledge is necessarily possessed by most salesmen because of the requirement of many exchanges that an examination be passed (see the appendix at the end of this chapter). Like any professional, a salesman in the commodity field should keep pace with all developments and changes and be aware of the implications they may have for his clients. Different commodity futures become popular or unpopular. Sometimes new ones appear on the futures exchanges and the old become dormant or disappear completely. Areas of activity such as trading currencies on the commodity exchanges or the periodic resurgence of trading in commodity options may offer new opportunities.

An important step toward professionalism constitutes a familiarity with the old and new literature in the industry. In addition to the obvious sources of current information available in financial magazines, newspapers, and services, there is the scholarly work done in commodities and the closely related areas of probability, money management, and utility theory with all of which the salesman should become acquainted in order to better understand his product and the customer who buys it. It is not a matter of unreasonable expense or effort for the salesman to build himself a personal library of appropriate books and government and private research publications. The rapid rate of growth of commodity trading makes it mandatory for the salesman to keep abreast of all changes for his own and his clients' benefit.

Probably the most important word to learn in the area of product knowledge is "validation." Half-truths and unsupported opinions such as "Gaps on a chart must be closed" or "When a 3-day moving average line crosses a 10-day moving average line, a trading opportunity is evident" should not be inflicted on unsuspecting clients who will almost certainly lose their trading capital. The salesman who induces his clients to make decisions based on such fragile foundations will sooner or later lose them and his reputation and will well deserve to lose both. The same applies to thought-less advice in the area of money management. One of the most popular of these high-sounding but questionable concepts is "Always keep a cash reserve." Obviously a cash reserve is useless if it is never to be put to work. Even more common is the frequently offered advice to set profit objectives at some dollar multiple of the risk; for example, if a trader is to risk 4 cents in a corn trade, his objective should be no less than 8 cents. Hence he is ostensibly taking a favorable two-to-one bet. Actually this is meaningless if no weight is given to the odds of achieving the profit or suffering the loss. Trading corn with a stop of ¼ cent and a goal of $1.25 profit a bushel hardly offers a trader odds of 500 to one, whereas a position with a risk of 4 cents and a goal of 4 cents is well worth taking if the probability of achieving the 4-cent profit is four times the probability of suffering the 4-cent loss.

Knowledge of the firm. The salesman should realize that there is no ideal firm in terms of size or specialization. Each has its advantages and limitations, but he should make an effort to understand the strengths and weaknesses of his own company and capitalize on its strengths and compensate for its weaknesses. If the weaknesses prevail on balance, he would do well to make a change.

Basically, there are two types of firms in the commodity futures field. One is the full-line wire house which, in addition to commodities, offers stocks, bonds, mutual funds, and various other types of financial merchandise. The other is the commodity specialty house. The full-line house is usually considerably larger than the specialty house in terms of capital, offices and number of personnel. The salesman for the first can offer the client the advantage of doing more of his trading in various types of financial merchandise with one firm, thus simplifying record keeping and transferring funds for his various financial ventures. The salesman with the specialty firm can sometimes offer more sophisticated service in terms of speed, interpretation of news, and technical knowledge because neither he nor his back office personnel have to diversify in so many complex areas.

The salesman must thoroughly understand the structure of the firm with which he is associated. A client has the right to know whether a firm holding a significant amount of his capital is financially stable. The salesman should either be fully aware of his firm's financial condition or have a good reason to explain why he is not. He should know which exchange memberships are held by his firm and which of them are clearing memberships. If the number of memberships is relatively limited, the salesman should be prepared to deal with the questions of a client rightfully concerned about the possibility of having recommendations concentrated among the commodities traded on the exchanges to which his firm belongs rather than among those presenting the best opportunities.

The salesman should be familiar with his own firm's market letter and its other published material as well as that of its competitors. He should be able to take advantage of other services such as charts, floor information, commodity calendars, and offers of specific trading recommendations and should know how to interpret his clients' confirmations and monthly statements.

The one area in which nearly every salesman expects more than his firm can deliver is that of providing consistently successful specific recommendations of market positions. The life of the commodity salesman would be easy indeed if all he had to do was pass on the recommendations of his firm's research department to clients who would then make a significant amount of money within a short time. Telling the client the glad news of his latest important profit is among the pleasantest experiences a salesman can have, whereas breaking the news of the latest market catastrophe is among the worst. Regardless of the size or degree of specialization of his firm, the salesman must realize that its good intentions are probably beyond question. It would like its clients to make money in the markets because it profits from commissions paid and knows that it is easier to retain a satisfied client than it is to replace him with a new one, particularly as its reputation for losing clients becomes known. Furthermore, a client who is successful in the market has an ever-growing account, and the commissions he pays grow accordingly if he does not withdraw all his profits. In addition, he is far more likely to refer new accounts to the firm than if he were a loser.

The magnitude of the problems faced by a commodity firm, regardless of the purity of its intentions, should not be underestimated by its employees or its customers. Making profits in the commodity markets is possible for the skilled, disciplined trader who is carefully managing an adequate but not unreasonably large pool of capital. If the firm recommends positions and its recommendations are followed by many of its clients, it acts much as if it were loosely managing many accounts, each influenced to some degree by its owner. If the firm is consistently successful, the amount of money it influences will grow almost geometrically as the accounts of its customers grow and new customers are attracted by tales of success. Ultimately, the firm's own clients will drive prices so high when they buy and so low when they sell that the firm's recommendations will become self-defeating. Although the commodity markets are generally sufficiently liquid to handle the business of individual traders, they cannot absorb concentrated orders of unusual size without distortion. Despite this problem, customers almost invariably demand and receive trade recommendations from the firms with which they deal in addition to the more reasonable basic data and current market information. The fact that long-term success is virtually impossible does not seem to deter many customers or their salesmen from demanding specific trading advice. It is interesting to note in passing that customers who ask for valid and specific records covering significant periods of time are far more likely to receive a reason why the records are not available than to receive the records themselves. The salesman should be aware that customers who follow a firm's recommendations precisely over a period of time are quite likely to lose money and virtually certain to blame him for their losses. If they make money, customers are likely to credit their own wisdom in selecting trades wisely. The situation for the salesman is analogous to the teacher whose successful students invariably say "I got an A", whereas the losers say "He gave me an F." Many of these students grow up and become commodity traders.

Prospect knowledge. Identification of potential commodity clients is difficult except in a most general way. The Chicago Mercantile Exchange surveyed 4,000 traders in 1971 and found that the closest approach to a profile would be a man about 45 years old who had a college background, an annual income of more than $10,000, was employed as an executive or professional, and who traded few contracts at any one time. Most of the sample had traded over a relatively short period and had security accounts. Although an effort to describe the potential clientele for a business is laudable, the wide band of characteristics attributed to the trader to date is too general to be really useful to salesmen. Pure conjecture would lead one to the conclusion that potential clients should have adequate resources which would eliminate most young people who have not yet had time to acquire speculative capital as well as the older segment of the population who are often more concerned, and properly so, with capital preservation than with growth. Even the excess number of male traders over female will probably diminish in time.

The job of any salesman is to identify the buying motives of his clients and to present selling points that will appeal to these buying motives as much as possible. In a broad sense commodity clients are motivated by some combination of the desire to make significant money and to play an exciting game for the sake of playing it. The two most common conflicting motives with which the salesman must deal are greed and fear. Most investors would be glad to realize substantial gains from commodity trading but are afraid to pay the price, namely, the risk of loss.

Registered representatives should be prepared to give honest answers, whether the questions are actually asked or only implied. Most potential clients can be expected to ask what gains can be expected from successful trading. The salesman's answer should be based on something more than pure conjecture, hope, or selective perception but must in no way offer any assurance of profit. He should realize that the fear expressed by a prospective client may not be his basic one. Many people are concerned with possible substantial deficits, endless limit moves, or physical delivery of the commodity in which they are trading, but their real doubt is most likely based on simple ignorance or the apprehension attendant on losing money. They must be made to realize that the risk of loss must be accepted in any venture in which the profit potential exceeds the interest paid on a bank savings account. The salesman should neither fan the greed nor quell the fear beyond reason but should try to contain both within reasonable bounds. Clients who expect to double their money monthly and others who are afraid that opening a small commodity account could easily result in a fore-closure on their homes are equally guilty of faulty thinking and should be corrected.

One frequent problem centers around the question, expressed or implied, of the salesman's own success in the commodity markets. In effect, if the opportunities are vast as often implied, why is he not rich himself? Handling this question is neither so difficult nor embarrassing as one might think. Basically, the good salesman deals with this question as with all others; that is, merely by telling the truth. One possibility, of course, is that he *is* rich and has accumulated his wealth by following his own advice. There are many others, however. The salesman may be too young to have accumulated enough capital to justify speculating. He may be conservative in nature and more concerned with not losing than with the chance of winning. The salesman, like any other customer of a financial firm, should adapt his financial merchandise to his own nature. It is also possible that he has a talent for guiding others, although he cannot play the game well himself. This is analogous to the athletic world in which many excellent coaches have never been good players and many good players could never succeed as coaches. Other salesmen feel that trading their own accounts would create a bias in their handling of clients' accounts and that they would have to make a choice between one direction or the other. They may conclude that in their own trading they would make important money four or five years out of six, which is true of most successful professional traders, but that by handling accounts of others they will make reasonably good money six years out of six.

The motivations and fears of his clients should be clear to the salesman. Both are described at considerable length in other chapters.

Salesmanship. In addition to natural talent, some training is necessary to develop an effective salesman. Procedures of the firm as well as the principles of salesmanship must be learned. Some of this training is the responsibility of the firm employing the salesman, although this responsibility is frequently abdicated by having inadequate classes conducted by people who have little more expertise in the subjects taught than the trainees themselves or by those with expertise but without the ability to teach. Regardless of the quality of his firm's training, a salesman should be willing to improve himself by learning what he can about the commodity area and how to present himself and his ideas effectively.

The principles of describing his product, meeting a client's objections, and closing sales in commodity positions are similar to those in selling any intangible product and are not presented here in detail. Most of them can be handled merely by knowing enough about the field to answer questions and making suggestions reasonably and honestly. Prospecting for new clients is so important and, for some, so difficult that it warrants some discussion.

When the thoroughly trained salesman has passed the necessary tests and obtained the required registrations, he is ready to begin prospecting. This is not a popular activity with most salesman, but in the investment business it is never ending. Not only would most salesmen like to have the largest clientele possible but they would also prefer to improve its quality.

Some sales managers reduce the subject of prospecting to its essentials: simply walk, talk, and meet the people. Finding customers thus becomes a simple numbers game. Approach enough people enough times and the result will be a number of interviews. Conduct enough interviews and the result will be the conversion of prospects to clients. Continue the process long enough and the result will be a large clientele of high quality. Basically, this philosophy of prospecting is quite correct, but the new salesman may well question the source of all the people to whom he is supposed to walk and talk. If 10 contacts ultimately result in one interview and three interviews produce one new account, a hard-working salesman can use up a great number of names within a short time. Replenishment of a real prospect list at reasonable cost is not so simple as it may appear.

Some firms rely heavily on newspaper advertising, particularly of the kind that requires some sort of reply. Favorites include the coupon that is returned for literature, an invitation to call a salesman who will provide desired information, or an invitation to a lecture. All of these usually provide names that result in new business and so are popular with salesmen. For their employers who pay for the advertisements, however, this method is somewhat less popular. Although most people interested in trading commodities read newspapers and magazines, most people, hence most readers, do not trade commodities, and a publication's advertising rates must be large enough to cover the cost of reaching its entire unspecialized audience. A small number of publications are devoted exclusively to commodities, but most of them appeal to those already engaged in trading rather than to those who are potential traders. When the cost of preparing, inserting, and following up an advertisement is considered, the expenditure for each new name placed on a firm's prospect list may approach or even exceed the revenues reasonably expected to be gained from new accounts. Some of this may be justified by the firm's desire to engage in institutional advertising simply to keep its name before the public. When this motive is combined with the effort to gain new business, the total cost may be judged reasonable.

Lectures, often dignified by the title "seminar" are sometimes effective but are also sometimes delivered by the wrong speaker to the wrong audience. Not infrequently they are given by people new to the business who have not yet developed a clientele to an audience that has not formulated an approach to trading. Alternatively, they may be presented by more experienced salesmen. Some may have changed locations or firms, and others may be trying to replace a clientele that has been lost. There may or may not be a correlation between knowledge of trading and skill of presentation, but sometimes glibness is confused with wisdom, and some members of "seminar" audiences have been damaged by what they thought was sound advice. Even well-promoted, effectively delivered, and efficently followed up lectures often result in the opening of only rather small, low-profit accounts, for sophisticated traders with large accounts seldom feel the need to attend. Workshops held regularly once or twice a week at the same location to examine current markets in a professional manner (not merely by indicating trend lines on a chart with a pointer) have proved quite successful for some brokers at a reasonable cost. The same prospective clients may return several times, thus allowing time for confidence to build, and they may bring friends. In addition, workshops tend to appeal more than general lectures to serious students of the market.

Conducting a seminar is a skill in itself and deserves some thought. Certainly the lecture should be carefully planned in every detail. A trader who will learn sooner or later that a well-prepared plan is the key to successful trading can hardly be impressed by a meeting at which the microphone does not work, the reading material is in short supply, the slides are shown upside down, or the number of chairs provided differs substantially from the size of the audience. Some problems can be avoided by asking for reservations by coupon or telephone. Although some who make reservations will not appear and others will come without reservations, a good approximation is at least possible. Some way of obtaining names and addresses inoffensively must be arranged if the productivity of the lecture is not to be defeated. Those who attend can sign in at the door or a door prize can be offered. Names and addresses can be written on the ticket stubs to be drawn.

If the audience contains people of varying degrees of sophistication, the level of the talk should be determined by the least knowledgeable but must move fast enough to hold the attention of those who are more familiar with the markets. If analogies are used, the speaker should be careful to go from the familiar to the unfamiliar and not from one unfamiliar activity to another. Slides and projections should be large enough to be seen clearly by those at the back and along the sides of the room. Questions should be answered at the end of the presentation to avoid breaking its continuity by permitting diversion into areas of interest to only small segments of the audience. When questions are allowed, answers should be concise. Longwindedness tends to stifle questions from other prospects who might open accounts if they could get just one more answer but are afraid that a question will result in another 20-minute speech and that they will never get home. Sixty seconds for each answer is usually long enough.

It is wise for a speaker to consider in advance the most frequent objections to his product. If an answer to the objection can be turned into a selling point by treating the objectionable aspect to better advantage, the salesman has nothing to fear if he knows his material and his answer is ready and well phrased. If questions that are difficult to treat favorably are expected, the speaker can do much to lessen their effect by raising them himself before the audience does and by phrasing them as favorably as possible, thus forestalling some of the adverse effect. Typical questions might involve the delivery of the cash commodity, the tremendous adversity caused by a series of limit moves against the trader's position, the Salad Oil Scandal of the early 1960s, and the instability of a small commodity firm, particularly if no financial statements are made available to its customers.

Mass mailing undoubtedly brings in leads but has most of the disadvantages of advertising in mass media; especially the high cost per lead. Because commodity traders have so few common characteristics other than speculative capital and a willingness to accept a risk, it is most difficult to define a mailing list that could prove especially useful, even presuming its availability. Lists of doctors, dentists, airline pilots, and those who have written commodity exchanges for information are especially overworked. Even salesmen who "work a list" often do so ineffectively. It is important to keep good records when contacts are made, eliminating names only when accounts are opened or when it becomes evident that they never will be. Too often a salesman is unwilling to approach prospects that would become accounts only after four, five, or even more contacts. It is usually unwise to attempt to sell commodity accounts or positions to people by mail or telephone. It is more productive to rely on interviews during which the sale of an account is easier. It is also easier to determine whether a prospect would make a suitable account at a face-to-face meeting.

Unannounced personal calls are unquestionably sometimes effectively made but are generally unpopular both with prospects and salesmen. Prospects, especially busy ones, often resent being disturbed at a time convenient only to the salesman, and many salesmen believe that the time consumed in seeking out a qualified prospect is beyond reason, especially in large cities. In addition, it places the salesman in a difficult psychological position. He is selling a trading activity that is supposed to present a handsome profit potential while he himself is walking door-to-door looking for customers. Any attempt to explain this away because one is new in the business is futile, for the customer will soon realize that he can pay his commissions to a salesman who is too well established to take the time to ring doorbells.

A more effective way to meet people is by personal radiation; that is, by joining and working in various organizations and gaining the friendship and respect of other members who might open accounts. It is important, of course, not to become an obvious "glad-hander" who is usually more avoided than patronized.

Many new salesmen believe that the difficult task of building a list of clients will take only a few months and that after a brief period a substantial clientele can be relied on to provide a good lifetime income with the commissions they will pay. This, however, is not the case. Attrition among traders, especially after a few recommendations have worked out badly, is the rule and not the exception. Referrals by satisfied clients provide less business than might be expected. Losers rarely make any. Even winners are sometimes reluctant to suggest highly speculative ventures to their friends for fear that they will be held accountable for any losses suffered and ultimately lose their friends with no hope of personal gain. (This fear is probably well founded.)

Salesmen employed by full-line wire houses are often able to convert some of their stock clients to commodity clients. Such conversions, typically constitute about 70 percent of the traders in commodities, but although speculators in the security markets provide an obvious source of clients, they are also a source of a number of problems. Sometimes the salesman becomes overenthusiastic about the opportunities in commodity trading and induces a stock client to trade commodities for whom commodity trading is unsuitable, and sometimes he overestimates the skill involved in his own or his firm's short-term success in selecting commodity positions and underestimates the risk, after which the client claims misrepresentation. Even in the case of a speculatively inclined client for whom commodity trading is suitable it frequently happens that an unsuccessful venture into commodity trading on a relatively small scale ultimately causes the loss of the larger stock account which might well have proved profitable over a period of years. It is for this reason that many executives of brokerage firms look unfavorably at such conversions. Some will separate security and commodity activities completely by having different salesmen handle the different products or even by maintaining entirely separate commodity and stock offices. Some will eliminate commodity trading from their firm's portfolio of products altogether, which might, however, have the effect of losing a stock account to another firm offering a more complete line of financial merchandise.

MAINTAINING A COMMODITY CLIENTELE

The ideal way to maintain a profitable commodity clientele would be to provide a continuous stream of highly profitable trade suggestions. If the salesman can do this, he will not need to be unduly concerned with servicing his clientele because he will have difficulty losing a customer, even intentionally. The registered representative with a trading method that has been validated in real time or who has a high degree of market judgment that permits him to select the positions of others will easily build and retain a substantial clientele. Just as surely the salesman who passes on shallow opinions based on superficial observation of a quote board, tape, or naïve chart cannot in a real sense succeed. Depending entirely on good trading results to maintain a commodity clientele will seldom lead to success. If the salesman suggests unprofitable trades, he will, of course, lose his clients because they will lose their money, faith or both. Even if his clients select their own positions, he will lose them sooner or later either because they will lose their capital or will find a way to justify blaming the salesman and his firm for the results, although neither had much to do with them. There are, however, some positive courses of action that the salesman can follow to help maintain his clientele.

A registered representative of most wire houses has a full line of merchandise. He should not induce his clients to trade in the parts of his line that he prefers either because they are most profitable to him or because they fit his personal biases, neither should he attempt to persuade them to avoid trading in areas in which he himself has not been successful. A salesman of investment and speculative vehicles would do well, in the long run, as would salesmen of anything else, to adapt his product line to the wishes and needs of his clients rather than to adapt the client to the items he prefers to sell. He should be careful neither to exaggerate nor to understate the profit potential of his security or commodity lines. A salesman who speaks convincingly of annual expectations of 100 percent or more will undoubtedly open many commodity accounts but will just as surely lose them when it becomes evident that he cannot possibly meet the standards he has set for his own performance. Understating objectives can be just as harmful to a client who has invested a small amount of money in a conservative venture yielding a small return when he might have made a greater gain in a more speculative venture. It is always best for a salesman to tell the truth about his merchandise, as far as he knows it, and not attempt to expound when he does not know the facts. He must stop short of the point at which the client makes his own decision concerning the amount of risk he chooses to take. The salesman should make every effort to provide honest guidance, but he should never try to be his brother's keeper.

As far as possible, the salesman should avoid becoming personally responsible for trades. Some may feel that the role of order taker is below their dignity and prefer to insert themselves into trades suggested by their Research Departments or by their customers, but this is seldom wise. Those who do will learn sooner or later the truth of the aphorism, "When I am right no one remembers—when I am wrong, no one forgets."

SERVICING A COMMODITY CLIENTELE

In the servicing of clientele one of the least popular but most important tasks is record keeping. If a client asks what his position is or when he established it and at what prices, he is entitled to a prompt and correct answer. The salesman who is days behind in his posting or does not do it at all does not deserve the continued patronage of his clients. Failure to maintain accurate records can result not only in the justified loss of clients because of poor service but also in costly errors. One of the most important ledgers is the holding record in which the name, account number, telephone number, and market positions, including prices and dates, as they are taken and liquidated for each client, are entered. This record book should be posted as confirmations are received or, at worst, at the end of each day. It should be available and open to the client's page while speaking to him. Relying on memory to fill an order can be a serious matter and using an erroneous account number can have surprisingly grave results. The client who places the order will not get a confirmation and will suspect that his order was neither promptly nor properly handled. Another of the firm's clients who did not place an order will get a confirmation and will wonder whether trading is being carried on in his account without authorization. The back office effort required to correct the error may cost the brokerage firm more money than it earned for its commission on the trade.

Much more serious, if a posting record is not maintained, is the possibility of allowing a client to think that he is liquidating a position previously liquidated, with the result that an unwanted position is created. A market order may be entered and an open order forgotten which, when filled later, can cause the same position to be established or liquidated twice. Misunderstandings in directions are easier if written records are not consulted. The salesman may find that he has tried to liquidate a short position by selling or a long position by buying. He will therefore have two positions instead of one. It may appear that the market will make the latter prove profitable half the time, but for some reason this seldom seems to work out. (Somehow, when someone drops a piece of toast onto the floor, it seems to have an uncanny way of landing buttered side down.) Losses incurred because of these or similar errors are almost invariably borne by the brokerage firm and, in turn, by the salesman himself, at least in part. In most cases the salesman deserves his loss.

It is also wise for the salesman to maintain a cross-file organized by commodities in order, if he wishes, to determine quickly which of his clients or prospects is interested in a given commodity. This record is especially important in the servicing of clients who rely on the advice of a brokerage firm. If a client enters a position that the firm later recommends should be liquidated and is not called promptly, he will not react happily to the news that he has suffered a loss or lost his profit because the salesman forgot that he had a position. When the salesman posts his customer's file, it takes only a few extra minutes to post the cross-file. If the newswires, financial journals, the government, or the firm itself release any information that could be of interest to clients holding positions in various commodities, it is easy for the salesman to identify them and convey the information to them by mail or telephone. For the salesman who is trying to increase the size of his clientele, it is also wise to post the positions of potential clients with whom he is in some communication in his cross-file and keep them informed of matters pertinent to them. His service may prove to be better than that offered by their present brokers who may be taking their business for granted. Eventually some or all of this business may be acquired. If a salesman ranks second on the lists of a large number of people who are determining where to place their business, he will ultimately receive a surprising number of accounts as the first choices fall out of favor. This happens frequently as customers become disenchanted with trade selections, when confirmations of trades are not received promptly or are considered to be unsatisfactory, when information is not passed on promptly or accurately, or when a check is not sent out quickly on request. Because a substantial number of commodity traders have more than one account or have traded with more than one broker, being next in line can prove to be most lucrative.

Because most accounts are opened after several contacts, it is important to maintain a lead file. This may be no more than an alphabetic filing of prospects, but it can prove to be invaluable. The best organized files also have a tickler section organized by date. If a prospect suggests calling back at a later time when he expects to have raised some capital or to have returned from a trip, the salesman can file his card under a future date to remind himself to call again at the proper time.

To service a client well, it is most important to determine what he will want when the account is opened. Some clients will prefer to follow the suggestions offered by the firm or the salesman. It is necessary to find out what kind of information they will need and when and where they wish to be called. Some of them will ask the salesman to trade for them when they cannot be reached, but if this is done the understanding between them and the salesman must be perfectly clear if problems are to be avoided when losses occur.

Other clients prefer to make their own decisions and do not care to be influenced even by comments about their own choices, much less have trades suggested to them. Presuming that such clients do not lose their money or decide to trade elsewhere for reasons beyond the control of the salesman, all that the latter need do is provide good service. This involves little more than maintaining accurate records, confirming a client's trades promptly, entering his orders properly, and making sure that the telephone is answered. A salesman who has many clients of this kind would do well to form a partnership of some sort with another registered representative to make sure that his phone is answered at once when he is away from his desk or office or on vacation.

It is in handling self-traders that brokers are really able to excel. This is especially true of young brokers who find no need to explain away their lack of experience as they would have to do with a customer who demanded more detailed direction. All that is necessary is to have a good working knowledge of the procedures of the business and to observe and pass on currently important information and facts rather than offhand opinions, glib guesses, and bluffs. The client who makes his own decisions has the right to expect really outstanding personal service in return for the often significant commissions he pays. The salesman who limits himself as much as possible to giving good service and passing on facts requested by his clients will not do so much business in the short run as his bolder counterpart who is willing to make specific suggestions, but he is quite likely to do more in the long run, build a better reputation, and sleep better at night.

Many salesmen may be dissatisfied with a role that is little more than order taker, but reflection may convince them that it can be more important than it appears. If a salesman has no reason to believe that neither his personal trade suggestions nor those of his firm will lead to long-term success, he is left with two functions that he can perform well, both of which are vital. One is the proper servicing of the customer's account. The other, and even more important, is acting as a customer's alter ego to help jog him along the right road; for example, a customer may tell his salesman that he believes every position taken should be protected immediately with a stop order, yet may omit placing such an order. The salesman who asks "Where do you want your stop?" and causes one to be entered may be performing a service far more important than that done by the salesman who calls his clients to tell them that wheat is acting well because it has been up for two days and that they should consider taking a long position.

The registered representative who guides his client toward logical money management can make a vital contribution to his success. He can avoid reinforcing his client's errors by acting as if all were well. If he does not know, he should say that he does not know. When a client shows loser's characteristics, the broker can take steps to induce him to change his ways before it is too late. "You never go broke taking a profit" warns of taking short profits. "I'm locked in" warns of a person who will not take a loss. "I'll watch it" is a clear indication of a lack of planning which is the most certain way to lose sooner or later. The salesman who learns the correct approach to trading, develops sufficient authority to warrant a hearing, and communicates well enough to deliver his message effectively can build a rewarding commodity clientele and serve and maintain it well.

Bibliography [1]

I. FUTURES TRADING AND COMMODITY EXCHANGES

Arthur, Henry B. "Economic Risk, Uncertainty and the Futures Market," in *Futures Trading Seminar*, vol. 3, Mimir, Madison, Wis., 1966.

Baer, J. B., and O. G. Saxon, *Commodity Exchanges and Futures Trading: Principles and Operating Methods*, Harper, New York, 1949.

Bailey, Fred, Jr. "What Every Banker Should Know About Commodity Futures Markets," reprint of the following articles from *Banking:* "What a Futures Market Is and How It Works (October 1967); "Hedging for Country Grain Elevators" (November 1967); "How Farmers Can Use the Futures Markets" (December 1967); "The Cattle Feeder and the Futures Market" (January 1968).

Bakken, H. H. *Theory of Markets and Marketing*, Mimir, Madison, Wis., 1953.

Blau, G. "Some Aspects of the Theory of Futures Trading," *Review of Economic Studies*, 7 (1), No. 31 (1944-1945) 1-3a.

Boyle, J. E. *Speculation and the Chicago Board of Trade*, Macmillan, New York, 1920.

Campbell, D. A. "Trading in Futures Under the Commodity Exchange Act," *George Washington Law Review*, 26, No. 2 (January 1958), 215-254.

Chicago Board of Trade. Futures Trading Seminar, Commodity Marketing Forum for College Teachers of Economics, Chicago, April 28-30, 1965, *Proceedings*, Erwin A. Gaumnitz, ed., Chicago Board of Trade, Mimir, Madison, Wis., 1966.

---

[1] Although individual works may encompass more than one subject classification, they are listed only under the *dominant* category.

Chicago Board of Trade. Futures Trading Seminar, Influence of Environmental Factors, Chicago, September 5–6, 1962, *Proceedings,* Chicago Board of Trade, Mimir, Madison, Wis., 1963.

Chicago Board of Trade, Symposium Proceedings, 1948 to date.

Commodity Trading Manual, Chicago Board of Trade, Chicago, Ill., 1973.

Cootner, Paul H. "Common Elements in Futures Markets for Commodities and Bonds," *Proceedings of the American Economic Association,* 51 (May 1961), 173–183.

Corbett, Caroline Louise (Phillips). *Economic Phases of Futures Trading: A Selected List of References,* Commodity Exchange Administration, Washington, D.C., 1937.

Dewey, T. H. *A Treatise on Contracts for Future Delivery and Commercial Wagers Including "Options," "Futures," and "Short Sales,"* Baker, Voorhis, New York, 1886.

Dow, J. C. R. "A Symposium on the Theory of the Forward Market. II. Addenda to Mr. Kaldor's Note," *Review of Economic Studies,* 7 (1939–1940), 201–202.

Dow, J. C. R. "A Theoretical Account of Futures Markets," *Review of Economic Studies,* 7 (1939–1940), 185–195.

The Economist (London). The London Metal Exchange, Whitefriars Press, Tonbridge, England, 1958.

Geiger, H. Dwight. "The Grain Futures and Cash Markets (and Some of Their Accounting Implications)," *The Arthur Young Journal* (Winter 1969).

Gold, G. *Modern Commodity Futures Trading,* Commodity Research Bureau, New York, 1966.

Gray, R. W. "Search for a Risk Premium," *Journal of Political Economy,* **69,** No. 3 (June 1961), 250–260.

Gray, R. W. "Some Current Development in Futures Trading," *Journal of Farm Economics,* **40,** No. 2 (May 1958), 344–351.

Gunnelson, J. A. *A Study of the Impact of Organizational Changes in Agricultural Commodity Markets,* Ph.D. Dissertation, Purdue University, 1970.

Harlow, C. V., and R. J. Teweles. "Commodities and Securities Compared," *Financial Analysts Journal* (September–October 1972).

Hawtrey, R. G. "Mr. Kaldor on the Forward Market," *Review of Economic Studies,* 7 (1939–1940), 202–205.

Heater, Nancy L. *Commodity Futures Trading, A Bibliography,* Department of Agricultural Economics, University of Illinois College of Agriculture, December 1966.

Hieronymus, T. A. "Should Margins in Futures Trading be Regulated?," *Commercial and Financial Chronicle,* **173** (5004) (April 19, 1951), 1648–1685.

Hoffman, G. W. *Future Trading upon Organized Commodity Markets in the United States,* University of Pennsylvania Press, Philadelphia, 1932.

Hoffman, G. W. "Past and Present Theory Regarding Futures Trading," *Journal of Farm Economics,* **19** (1937), 300–309.

Hoos, Sidney. "Future Trading in Perishable Agricultural Commodities, *Journal of Marketing,* **6** (1942), 358–365.

Houthakker, H. S. "The Scope and Limits of Futures Trading," in Moses Abramovitz et al., *The Allocation of Economic Resources,* Stanford University Press, Stanford, Calif., 1959.

How to Buy and Sell Commodities, a booklet published by Merrill Lynch, Pierce, Fenner and Smith, New York, January 1969.

Kaldor, Nickolas, "A Note on the Theory of the Forward Market," *Review of Economic Studies,* 7 (1939–1940), 196–201.

Larson, Arnold B. "Estimation of Hedging and Speculative Positions in Futures Markets," *Food Research Institute Studies,* **2,** No. 3 (1961), 203–212.

Lindley, A. F. "Essentials of an Effective Futures Market," *Journal of Farm Economics,* **19** (1937), 321–330.

Mehl, J. M. *The Development and Operation of the Commodity Exchange Act,* Commodity Exchange Authority, Washington, 1953.

Mehl, Paul. *A Rapid Method of Calculating Profits Made or Losses Sustained in Privilege Trad-*

ing on the Chicago Board of Trade, U.S. Grain Futures Administration, Washington, D.C., 1931.

Mehl, Paul. *Trading in Privileges on the Chicago Board of Trade,* USDA Circular 323, 1934.

Miller, Katherine D. *Futures Trading and Investor Returns; An Investigation of Commodity Market Risk Premiums,* Thesis, University of Chicago, 1971.

New York Coffee and Sugar Exchange. *History and Operation of the New York Coffee and Sugar Exchange, Inc., 1882–1947,* New York, 1947.

Phillips, J. "The Theory and Practice of Futures Trading," *Review of Marketing and Agricultural Economics* (June 1966).

Powers, M. J. "Effects of Contract Provisions on the Success of a Futures Contract," *Journal of Farm Economics,* 49, No. 4 (November 1967) 833–843.

Teweles, Richard J., and Charles V. Harlow: "The Commodity Futures Game: Who Wins? Who Loses? Why?" A two-part series in *The Journal of Commodity Trading,* 5, No. 1 (January–February 1970), 5, No. 2 (March–April 1970).

Teweles, Richard J., Charles V. Harlow, and Herbert L. Stone, *The Commodity Futures Trading Guide,* McGraw-Hill, New York, 1969.

U.S., 56th Congress, 2nd Session, House, *U.S. Industrial Commission Report* (1900–1901), House Doc. 94.

U.S., 85th Congress, 1st Session, House, *Hearings* before the Committee on Agriculture and Forestry, May 1–3, 1957.

U.S., 85th Congress, 1st Session, Senate, *Hearings* before a Subcommittee of the Committee on Agriculture and Forestry, August 12, 1957.

U.S., 85th Congress, 2nd Session, Senate, *Hearings* before the Committee on Agriculture and Forestry, March 22–26, 1958.

U.S., 88th Congress, 1st Session, House, *Hearings* on H.R. 904, April 8–10, 1963.

U.S., 89th Congress, 2nd Session, House, *Hearings* before the Subcommittee on Domestic Marketing and Consumer Relations of the Committee on Agriculture on H.R. 11788, April 4–6, 1966.

Venkataramanan, L. S. *The Theory of Futures Trading,* Asia Publishing, New York, 1965.

Working, Holbrook. "Tests of a Theory Concerning Floor Trading on Commodity Exchanges", *Food Research Institute Studies,* Supplement, 7 (1967), 5–48.

Working, Holbrook. "Western Needs for Futures Markets," *Proceedings of the Western Farm Economics Association* (1952), 95–98.

Working, Holbrook. "Whose Markets? Evidence on Some Aspects of Futures Trading," *Journal of Marketing,* 19, No. 1 (July 1954), 1–11.

II. HISTORY AND EVOLUTION OF FUTURES TRADING

Anderson, M. A. "Ninety Years Development: Fundamental and Technicalities of Futures Trading Explained," *Cotton Digest,* 21, No. 27 (March 26, 1949), 18–19, 42–43, 46–47.

Boyle, J. E. *Cotton and the New Orleans Cotton Exchange; a Century of Commercial Evolution,* Country Life, New York, 1934.

Cowing, Cedric B. *Populists, Plungers and Progressives: A Social History of Stock and Commodity Speculation, 1860–1936,* Princeton University Press, Princeton, N.J., 1965.

Dies, E. J. *The Plunger; A Tale of the Wheat Pit,* Covici, New York.

Dies, E. J. *The Wheat Pit,* Argyle, Chicago, 1925.

Irwin, H. S. *Evolution of Futures Trading,* Mimir, Madison, Wis., 1954.

Killough, H. B. "Effects of Governmental Regulation of Commodity Exchanges in the United States," *Harvard Business Review,* 11 (1933), 307–315.

Lermer, G. "The Futures Market and Farm Programs," *Canadian Journal of Agricultural Economics,* 16, No. 2 (June 1968), 27–30.

Miller, Norman C. *The Great Salad Oil Swindle,* Coward-McCann, New York, 1965.

Nimrod, Vance L. and Richard S. Bower. "Commodities and Computers," *Journal of Financial and Quantitative Analysis,* 2, No. 1 (March 1967).

Norris, Frank. *The Pit*, Doubleday, Page, New York, 1903.

Pine, L. G. "London: A Commercial History Since the Roman Occupation," Supplement to *The Public Ledger*, London, January 1960.

Robinson, H. G. *History and Evolution of Trading in Futures in Potatoes, 1930–1956*, Ph.D. Dissertation, Ohio State University, 1957.

Sowards, J. K. *Western Civilization to 1660*, St. Martin's, New York, 1965.

Taylor, C. H. *History of the Board of Trade of the City of Chicago*, Robert O. Law Co., Chicago, 1917.

Tomek, W. G. "A Note on Historical Wheat Prices and Futures Trading," *Food Research Institute Studies*, **10** (1971).

Working, Holbrook. "Review of H. S. Irwin, 'Evolution of Futures Trading,'" *Journal of Farm Economics*, **37** (1950), 377–380.

III. ECONOMIC THEORY AND EVIDENCE

Boulding, Kenneth. *The Skills of the Economist*, Clarke, Irwin, Toronto, Canada, 1958.

Brandow, G. E. *Interrelations Among Demand for Farm Products and Implications for Control of Market Supply*, Penn State Agricultural Experiment Station Bulletin 680, 1961.

Chamberlin, E. H. *The Theory of Monopolistic Competition*, Harvard, Cambridge, Mass., 1938.

Fama, Eugene F. "Efficient Capital Markets: A Review of Theory and Empirical Works," *Journal of Finance*, **25** (1970), 383–423.

Fama, Eugene F. "Mandelbrot and the Stable Paretian Hypothesis," *Journal of Business*, **36**, No. 4 (October 1963), 420–429.

Fishman, G. S. *Spectral Methods in Econometrics*, Harvard, Cambridge, Mass., 1969.

Foote, Richard J. *Analytical Tools for Studying Demand and Price Structure*, USDA Handbook 146, 1958.

Foote, Richard J., and Karl A. Fox. *Analytical Tools for Measuring Demand*, USDA Handbook 64, 1954.

Friedman, M. *Essays in Positive Economics*, University of Chicago Press, Chicago, 1953.

Gordon, D. F. "A Statistical Contribution to Price Theory: Discussion," *American Economic Review*, Papers and Proceedings, **48** (1958), 201–203.

Granger, C. W. J. and M. Hatanaka. *Spectral Analysis of Economic Time Series*, Princeton University Press, Princeton, N.J., 1964.

Gray, Roger W., and David J. S. Rutledge. "The Economics of Commodity Futures Markets: A Survey," *Review of Marketing and Agricultural Economics*, **39**, No. 4.

Houthakker, H. S. *Economic Policy for the Farm Sector*, American Enterprise Institute for Public Policy Research, Washington, D.C., 1967.

Johnson, D. G. *Forward Prices for Agriculture*, University of Chicago Press, Chicago, 1947.

Keynes, J. M. *The General Theory of Employment, Interest, and Money*, Harcourt, Brace, and World, New York, 1964.

Keynes, J. M. *A Treatise on Money*, Vol. 2, Harcourt, Brace, and World, New York, 1930.

Kogiker, K. C. "A Model of the Raw Materials Markets," *International Economic Review*, No. 8 (February 1967).

Nerlove, Marc. *Distributed Lags and Demand Analysis for Agricultural and Other Commodities*, USDA Handbook 141, 1958.

Nerlove, Marc. "On the Nerlove Estimate of Supply Elasticity," *Journal of Farm Economics*, **40** (August 1958), 723–728.

Nerlove, Marc, and William Addison. "Statistical Estimation of Long-Run Elasticities of Supply and Demand," *Journal of Farm Economics*, **40** (November 1958), 861–880.

Perrin, R. K. *Analysis and Prediction of Crop Yields for Agricultural Policy Purposes*, Ph.D. Dissertation, Iowa State University, 1968.

Schultz, H. *The Theory of Measurement of Demand.*, University of Chicago Press, Chicago, 1938 (reprinted 1957).

Selvestre, Helios. *Demand Analysis: An Attempt to Develop A Methodology for Detecting the*

Point in Time Where Structural Changes Took Place, Ph.D. Dissertation, Cornell University, 1969.

Taylor, F. M. Principles of Economics, 2nd ed., University of Michigan Press, Ann Arbor, 1913.

Watson, Donald. Price Theory and Its Uses, Houghton Mifflin, Boston, 1963.

Waugh, Fredrick V. Demand and Price Analysis: Some Examples from Agriculture, USDA Technical Bulletin 1316, 1964.

Weymar, F. Helmut: "The Supply of Storage Revisited," American Economic Review, 56 (December 1966), 1226–1234.

World, H., and L. Jureen. Demand Analysis: A Study in Econometrics, Wiley, New York, 1953.

Working, Holbrook. "The Investigation of Economic Expectations," American Economic Review, 39, No. 3 (May 1949), 150–166.

Working, Holbrook. "Theory of Price of Storage," American Economic Review, 39, No. 6 (December 1949), 1254–1262.

IV. TRADERS: BEHAVIOR AND RETURNS

Baruch, Barnard. My Own Story, Holt, New York, 1957.

Cantril, Hadley. The Invasion From Mars, Harper and Row, New York, 1966.

Cootner, P. H. "Returns to Speculators: Telser versus Keynes," Journal of Political Economy, 68, No. 4 (August 1960), 396–414, followed by L. G. Telser, "Reply," pp. 404–415 and P. H. Cootner, "Rejoinder," pp. 415–418.

Glick, Ira O. A Social Psychological Study of Futures Trading, Ph.D. Dissertation, Department of Sociology, University of Chicago, 1957.

Harris, Thomas A. I'm OK — You're OK, Harper and Row, 1967.

Houthakker, H. S., and L. G. Telser. Commodity Futures II: Gains and Losses of Hedgers and Future Speculators, Cowles Commission Discussion Paper, Economics No. 2090, December 1952.

Le Bon, Gustave. The Crowd, Viking, New York, 1960.

Lefevre, Edwin. Reminiscences of a Stock Operator, American Research Council, New York, 1923.

Longstreet, Roy W. Viewpoints of a Commodity Trader, Frederick Fell, New York, 1968.

MacKay, Charles. Extraordinary Popular Delusions and the Madness of Crowds, Page, London, 1932.

Market Vane Commodity Letter, Pasadena, Calif.

Matuszewski, T. I. "Trader's Behaviour — An Alternative Explanation," Review of Economic Studies, 25 (1958), 126–130.

Neill, Humphrey. The Art of Contrary Thinking, Caxton, Caldwell, Ohio, 1960.

Reisman, David. The Lonely Crowd, Yale, New Haven, Conn., 1950.

Rockwell, C. S. "Normal Backwardation Forecasting, and the Returns to Speculators," Food Research Institute Studies, Supplement, 7 (1967), 107–130.

Schwed, Fred, Jr. Where are the Customer's Yachts, John Magee, Springfield, Mass., 1955.

Smidt, Seymour. Amateur Speculators: A Survey of Trading Styles, Information Sources, and Patterns of Entry into and Exit from Commodity-Futures Markets by Non-professional Speculators, Cornell University Graduate School of Business and Public Administration, Ithaca, N.Y., 1965.

V. EFFECTS OF SPECULATION

Baumol, W. J. "Speculation, Profitability and Stability," Review of Economics and Statistics, 39 (August 1957), 263–271.

Emery, H. C. "Legislation Against Futures," Political Science Quarterly, 10, (1886), 62–68.

Emery, H. C. "Speculation on the Stock and Produce Exchanges of the United States," in the Faculty of Political Science of Columbia University, (Eds), Studies in History and Economics, Vol. 7, New York, 1896.

Emerson, P. M. and W. G. Tomek. "Did Futures Trading Influence Potato Prices?" *American Journal of Agricultural Economics,* 51, No. 3 (August 1969), 666–672.

Gray, Roger W. "The Attack Upon Potato Futures Trading in the United States," *Food Research Institute Studies,* 4, No. 2 (1964), 97–121.

Gray, Roger W. "Onions Revisited," *Journal of Farm Economics,* 45, No. 2 (May 1963), 273–276.

Gray, Roger W. "Price Effects of a Lack of Speculation," *Food Research Institute Studies,* Supplement, 7 (1967), 177–194.

Gray, Roger W. "Speculation Helps the Onion Grower," *Minnesota Farm Business Notes,* University of Minnesota, Institute of Agriculture, March–April, 1959.

Hieronymus, T. A. *Appropriate Speculative Limits for Soybean Oil and Lard,* Chicago Board of Trade, 1953.

Hieronymus, T. A. *Effects of Future Trading on Grain Prices,* Illinois Farm Economics No. 190–191, 1951, pp. 1150-1155.

Hooker, R. H. "The Suspension of the Berlin Produce Exchange and Its Effect Upon Corn Prices," *Royal Statistical Society Journal,* 64 (1901), 574–604.

Kaldor, N. "Speculation and Economic Stability," *Review of Economic Studies,* 7 (1939–40), 1–27.

Kemp, M. C., "Speculation, Profitability, and Price Stability," *Review of Economics and Statistics,* 45, No. 2 (May 1962), 185–189.

Marine, C. L. "Effects of Futures Trading on Price Variation," M.S. thesis, University of Illinois, Urbana, 1959.

Meade, J. E. "Degrees of Competitive Speculation," *Review of Economic Studies,* 17 (1950), 159–167.

Naik, A. S. *Effects of Futures Trading on Prices,* K. R. Samat for Somaiya Publications Pty., Ltd., Bombay, India, 1970.

Pavaskar, M. G. *Marketing of Cash Crops: Efficiency of Futures Trading,* Economics and Political Weekly, Bombay, India, 1971.

Powers, M. J. "Does Futures Trading Reduce Price Fluctuations in the Cash Markets?" *American Economic Review,* 60, No. 3 (June 1970), 460–464.

Stewart, Blair. *An Analysis of Speculative Trading in Grain Futures,* USDA Technical Bulletin 1001, October 1949.

Taylor, A. E. "Speculation, Short Selling, and the Price of Wheat," *Food Research Institute Wheat Studies,* (1931), 231–266.

Telser, L. G. "A Theory of Speculation Relating Profitability and Stability," *Review of Economics and Statistics,* 41 (1959), 295–301.

USDA, Commodity Exchange Authority. *Speculation in Onion Futures,* Washington, D.C., March 1957.

USDA, Economic Research Service. *Margins, Speculation and Prices in Grains Futures Markets,* Washington, D.C., December 1967.

Usher, A. P. "The Influence of Speculative Marketing Upon Prices," *American Economic Review,* 6 (1916), 49–60.

Vaile, R. S. "Speculation and the Price of Grain," *Journal of Marketing,* 12 (1947), 497–498.

Wesson, William T. *The Economic Importance of Futures Trading in Potatoes,* U.S.D.A., Marketing Research Report No. 241, Washington, D.C. June, 1958.

Williams, J. B. "Speculation and the Carryover," *Quarterly Journal of Economics,* 51 (May 1936), 436–455.

Working, Holbrook. "Futures Markets Under Renewed Attack," *Food Research Institute Studies,* 4, No. 1 (1963), 13–24.

Working, Holbrook. "Price Effect on Futures Trading," *Food Research Institute Studies,* 1, No. 1. (February 1960), 3–31.

Working Holbrook. "Price Effects of Scalping and Day Trading," *Proceedings of the Seventh Annual Symposium: Commodity Markets and the Public Interest,* Chicago Board of Trade, 1954.

Working, Holbrook. "Spoiling the Broth; Congress Acted Unwisely When It Banned Trading in Onion Futures," *Barron's*, 43, No. 5 (February 4, 1963), 11, 22.

Yamey, Basil S. "Speculation and Price Stability: A Note," and Robert Z. Aliber, "Speculation and Price Stability: A Reply," *Journal of Political Economy*, 74 (April 1966), 206–208.

VI. INDIVIDUAL COMMODITY STUDIES

Armore, S. J. *The Demand and Price Structure for Food Fats and Oils*, USDA Technical Bulletin 1068, June 1953.

Aronson, J. R. *The Soybean Crushing Margin, 1953–62: An Economic Analysis of the Futures Market, for Soybeans, Soybean Oil and Soybean Meal*, Clark University, Worcester, Mass., 1964.

Atwood, E. C., Jr. *Theory and Practice in the Coffee Futures Market*, Princeton University Press, Princeton, N.J., 1959.

Bakken, H., (Ed.) *Futures Trading in Livestock — Origins and Concepts*, Mimir, Madison, Wis., 1970.

Brand, Simon S. "The Decline in the Cotton Futures Market," *Food Research Institute Studies*, 4, No. 3, (1964).

Breimyer, Harold F. *Demand and Prices for Meat*, USDA Technical Bulletin 1253, 1961.

Brown, C. A. "Future Trading in Butter and Eggs," *Journal of Farm Economics*, 15 (1933), 670–75, followed by E. A. Duddy, "Discussion," 675–76.

Burrows, J. C., W. Hughes, and J. Valette. *An Economic Analysis of the Silver Industry*, Heath, Lexington, Mass., 1974.

Chapman, S. J., and Douglas Knoop. "Dealings in Futures on the Cotton Market," *Royal Statistical Journal*, 69 (1906), 321–364.

Danis, Tom. "An Economic Analysis of Egg Prices in 1969," The Chicago Mercantile Exchange, Research Report #1, April 1970.

Dominick, B. A., Jr., and F. W. Williams. *Future Trading and the Florida Orange Industry*, Florida Agricultural Experiment Stations, December 1965.

Drake, A. F., and V. I. West. *Econometric Analysis of the Edible Fats and Oils Economy*, Agricultural Experiment Station Bulletin 695, University of Illinois, Urbana, 1963.

"An Economic Study of the U.S. Potato Industry," *Agricultural Economic Report* No. 6, Economic Research Service, USDA, 1962.

Ehrich, Rollo. "The Impact of Government Programs on Wheat Futures Markets: 1953–63, *Food Research Institute Studies*, 6, No. 3 (1966).

Ertek, Tumay. *World Demand for Copper, 1948–1963: An Econometric Study*, Ph.D. Dissertation, University of Wisconsin, 1967.

Evans, W. S. "Canadian Wheat Stabilization Operations, 1929–35," *Wheat Studies*, 12, No. 7 (March 1926), 249–272.

Foote, R. J., John A. Craven, and Robert R. Williams, Jr. "Pork Bellies: Quarterly 3-Equation Models Designed to Predict Cash Prices," Texas Tech. University, 1971. Mimeographed.

Foote, R. J., J. W. Klein, and M. Clough. *The Demand and Price Structure for Corn and Total Feed Concentrates*, USDA Technical Bulletin 1061, October 1952.

Gallacher, William. "1973 Bellies–Priced to Clear," *Commodities* (March 1973).

Gerra, M. J. *The Demand, Supply and Price Structure for Eggs*, Technical Bulletin 1204, USDA, 1959.

Gray, Roger W. "The Futures Market of Maine Potatoes: An Appraisal," *Food Research Institute Studies*, 11, No. 3 (1972).

Gray, Roger W. "The Prospects for Wool Price Stability," *Proceedings: International Wool Textile Organization Conference*, Brussels, Belgium (June 1967).

Gray, Roger W. *Wool Futures Trading in Australia — Further Prospects*, University of Sydney, Department of Agricultural Economics, Research Bulletin No. 5, 1967.

Green, Leslie. "Understanding the Frozen Orange Juice Market," in Harry Jiler (Ed.), *Commodity Year Book*, Commodity Research Bureau, New York, 1968.

Gutman, G. O. and B. R. Duffin. "The London Wool Top Futures Market," *Quarterly Review of Agricultural Economics,* 8, No. 4, Bureau of Agricultural Economics, Canberra (October 1955), 185–192.

Harlow, Arthur. *Factors Affecting the Price and Supply of Hogs,* USDA Technical Bulletin 1247, 1964.

Hee, Olman. "The Effect of Price on Acreage and Yield of Potatoes," *Agricultural Economic Research,* 10 (1958), 131–141.

Hieronymus, T. A. *The Economics of Risk in the Marketing of Soybeans and Soybean Products,* Ph.D. Dissertation, University of Illinois, Urbana, 1949.

Hieronymus, T. A. *Farm Speculation in Soybeans,* University of Illinois Department of Agricultural Economics AERR 9, Urbana, 1965.

Hieronymus. T. A. *Futures Trading and Speculation in Soybeans,* University of Illinois Agricultural Extension Service AE-2777, 1951.

Hieronymus, T. A. "Futures Trading and Speculation in Soybeans by Country Elevators," *Grain and Feed Review,* 40, No. 7 (March 1951), 20, 22, 56, 57.

Honhon, Georges L. J. *An Econometric Analysis of the Corn Market in an Open Economy,* Ph.D. Dissertation, University of Illinois, 1970.

Houck, James P. *Demand and Price Analysis of the U.S. Soybean Market,* Agricultural Experiment Station Bulletin 244, Minnesota, 1963.

Houck, James P. "A Statistical Model of the Demand for Soybeans," *Journal of Farm Economics,* 46 (May 1964), 366–374.

Houck, James P. and J. S. Mann. *Domestic and Foreign Demand for U.S. Soybeans and Soybean Products,* Agricultural Experiment Station Technical Bulletin 256, University of Minnesota, Minneapolis, 1968.

Houck, J. P., M. E. Ryan, and A. Subotnik. *Soybeans and their Products: Markets, Models and Policy,* University of Minnesota Press, Minneapolis, 1972.

Johnson, A. C. Jr. "Whose Markets? The Case for Maine Potato Futures," *Food Research Institute Studies,* 11, No. 3 (1972).

Kofi, T. A. *Feasibility Analysis of International Commodity Agreements on Cocoa,* Ph.D. Dissertation, University of California, Berkeley, 1970.

Kohls, R. L. "A Technique for Anticipating Change in the Volume of Eggs Shortage," *Journal of Farm Economics,* 32, No. 4 (November 1950), 663–666.

Koudele, J. W. *An Economic Analysis of Trading in Egg Futures, 1934–1954,* Ph.D. Dissertation, Michigan State University, 1956.

Labys, Walter C. *Dynamic Commodity Models: Specification, Estimation, and Simulation,* Heath, Lexington, Mass., 1973.

Langemeier, L., and R. G. Thompson. "Study of Demand, Supply, and Price Relationships on the Beef Sector, Post World War II Period," *Journal of Farm Economics,* 49 (February 1967), 169–183.

Leuthold, R. M., A. J. A. MacCormick, A. Schmitz, and D. G. Watts. "Forecasting Daily Hog Prices and Quantities: A Study of Alternative Forecasting Techniques," *Journal of the American Statistical Association* 65 (March 1970).

Lowell, Fred R. *The Wheat Market,* Keltner Statistical Service, Kansas City, Mo., 1968.

Meinken, K. W. *The Demand and Price Structure for Wheat,* USDA Technical Bulletin 1136, November 1955.

Miracle, Diane S., "The Egg Futures Market: 1940 to 1966," *Food Research Institute Studies,* 11, No. 3 (1972).

Myers, L. H. *Economic Analysis of the Monthly Structure of the Hog Pork Sector of the U.S.,* Ph.D. Dissertation, Purdue University, 1968.

Peery, J. S. *Theory and Practice in the Forward Market for Shell Eggs,* Ph.D. Dissertation, Northwestern University, 1964.

Powers, Mark J. *An Economic Analysis of the Futures Market for Pork Bellies,* Thesis, University of Wisconsin, 1966.

Rourke, B. E. *Causes and Predictability of Annual Changes in Supplies and Prices of Coffee,* Ph.D. Dissertation, Stanford University, 1969.

Roy, Sujit. "Econometric Models for Predicting Short Run Egg Prices," Pennsylvania State University, University Park, Pa., 1971. Mimeographed.

Skadberg, J. M., and G. A. Futrell. "An Economic Appraisal of Futures Trading in Livestock," *Journal of Farm Economics,* 48, No. 5 (December 1966), 1485–1489.

Smith, J. G. *Organized Produce Markets,* Longmans, London, 1922.

Snape, R. H. *Protection and Stabilization in the World Sugar Industry,* Ph.D. Dissertation, University of London, 1962.

Sohn, H. K. *A Spatial Equilibrium Model of the Beef Industry in the United States,* Ph.D. Dissertation, University of Hawaii, 1970.

Telser, L. G. "Futures Trading and the Storage of Cotton and Wheat," *Journal of Political Economy,* 66, No. 3 (June 1958), 233–255.

Telser, L. G. "The Supply of Speculative Services in Wheat, Corn and Soybeans," *Food Research Institute Studies,* Supplement, 7 (1967), 131–176.

Telser, L. G. *The Supply of Stocks: Cotton and Wheat,* Ph.D. Dissertation, University of Chicago, 1956.

Tewes, T. "Sugar: A Short-Term Forecasting Model for the World Market, with a Forecast of the World Market Price for Sugar in 1972–1973," *The Business Economist,* 4 (Summer 1972), 89–97.

USDA, Agricultural Marketing Service. *Possibilities for Futures Trading in Florida Citrus Fruit and Products,* Marketing Research Report No. 156, Washington, D.C., February 1959.

USDA, Commodity Exchange Authority. *Trading in Frozen Pork Bellies,* Washington, D.C., October 1967.

USDA, Consumer and Marketing Service. *Fats and Oils Situations,* Washington, D.C.

USDA, Economic Research Service. *Demand and Price Analysis for Potatoes,* USDA Technical Bulletin 1380, July 1967.

USDA, Economic Research Service. "An Economic Study of the U.S. Potato Industry," *Agricultural Economic Report,* No. 6, 1962.

U.S. Federal Trade Commission, *Economic Report of the Investigation of Coffee Prices,* Washington, D.C.

U.S. Federal Trade Commission, *Report on the Grain Trade,* 7 vols., Washington, D.C., 1920–1926.

Uribe C., Andres. *Brown Gold,* Random House, New York, 1954.

Vandenborre, Roger J. "Demand Analysis of the Markets for Soybean Oil and Soybean Meal," *Journal of Farm Economics,* 28 (November 1946), 920–934.

Walsh, Joseph M. *Coffee, Its History Classification and Description,* Henry T. Coates and Co., Philadelphia, 1894.

Weiss, J. S. "A Spectral Analysis of World Cocoa Prices," *American Journal of Agricultural Economics,* 52 (February 1970), 122–126.

Weisser, M. *The Sydney Wool Futures Market,* Bureau of Agricultural Economics, Wool Economic Research Report No. 4, Canberra, June 1963.

Weymar, F. Helmut. *The Dynamics of the World Cocoa Market,* M.I.T., Cambridge, Mass., 1968.

Wickizer, L. V. D. *Coffee, Tea, and Cocoa,* Stanford University Press, Stanford, Calif., 1951.

Witherall, W. H. *Dynamics of the International Wool Market: An Econometric Analysis,* Econometric Research Program Memorandum 91, Princeton University Press, Princeton, N.J., September 1967.

Working, Holbrook. Economic Functions of Futures Markets, in H. Bakken, ed., *Futures Trading in Livestock—Origins and Concepts,* Mimir, Madison, Wis., 1970.

Working Holbrook. "Financial Results of Speculative Holding of Wheat," *Food Research Institute Wheat Studies,* 7, No. 81 (July 1931).

Working, Holbrook, "Futures Trading and Hedging as Applied to the Wine Industry," *Food Research Institute Studies,* (1953).

Yamey, B. S. "Cotton Futures Trading in Liverpool," *Three Banks Review,* No. 41, (March 1959), 21–38.

VII. PRICE BEHAVIOR

Alexander, Sidney. "Price Movements in Speculative Markets: Trends or Random Walks," No. 2, as reprinted in Paul Cootner, (Ed.), *The Random Character of Stock Market Prices,* M.I.T., Cambridge, Mass., 1964, pp. 338–372.

Armstrong, Charles E. "Testing Cycles for Statistical Significance," *Journal of Cycle Research* (October 1961).

Arnold, David B. *An Econometric Study on the Weekly Behavior of the Cash Basis for Corn at Chicago,* Thesis, University of Illinois, 1969.

Bachelier, Louis. "Theory of Speculation," reprinted in Paul Cootner, ed., *The Random Character of Stock Market Prices,* M.I.T., Cambridge, Mass., 1964.

Bear, R. M. *Martingale Movements in Commodity Futures,* Ph.D. Dissertation, University of Iowa, 1970.

Beckmann, M. J. "On the Determination of Prices in Futures Markets," reprinted in M. J. Brennan, (Ed.), *Patterns of Market Behavior,* Brown University Press, Providence, R.I., 1965.

Brinegar, C. S. *A Statistical Analysis of Speculative Price Behavior,* Ph.D. Dissertation, Stanford University, 1954.

Brinegar, C. S. "A Statistical Analysis of Speculative Price Behavior," *Food Research Institute Studies,* Supplement, 9 (1970).

Clough, Malcolm. "Relation between Corn and Wheat Futures," *Journal of Farm Economics,* 21 (1939), 500–502.

Cootner, Paul H., (Ed.) *The Random Character of Stock Market Prices,* M.I.T., Cambridge, Mass., 1964.

Cootner, P. H. "Stock Prices: Random vs Systematic Changes," *Industrial Management Review,* 3, No. 2 (Spring 1962).

Cowles, Alfred, and H. E. Jones. "Some A Posteriori Probabilities in Stock Market Action," *Econometrica,* 5 (1937), 280–294.

Dow, J. C. R. "The Inaccuracy of Expectations; a Statistical Study of the Liverpool Cotton Futures Market 1921/22–1937/38," *Economica,* n.s., 8 (1941), 162–175.

Ehrich, R. L. "Cash-Futures Price Relationships for Live Beef Cattle," *American Journal of Agricultural Economics,* 51, No. 1 (February 1969), 26–40.

Fama, Eugene. "The Behavior of Stock Market Price," *Journal of Business,* (January 1965).

Fama, E. F., L. Fisher, M. C. Jensen, and R. Roll. "The Adjustment of Stock Prices to New Information," *International Economic Review,* 10, (February 1969), 1–21.

Fielitz, B. D. "Stationarity of Random Data: Some Implications for the Distribution of Stock Price Changes," *Journal of Financial and Quantitative Analysis,* 6 (June 1971), 1025–1034.

Godfrey, M. D., C. W. J. Granger, and O. Morgenstern. "The Random Walk Hypothesis of Stock Market Behaviour," *Kyklos,* 17 (1964), 1–30.

Graham, R. W. *Cash-Future Price Relationships in Corn,* M. S. Thesis, University of Illinois, Urbana, 1954.

Granger, C. W. J. "What the Random Walk Model Does Not Say," *Financial Analysts Journal* (May–June 1970), 91–93.

Granger, C. W. J. "Some Aspects of the Random Walk Model of Stock Prices,"' *International Economic Review,* 9 (1968), 283–287.

Granger, C. W. J. and O. Morgenstern. "Spectral Analysis of New York Stock Market Prices," *Kyklos,* 16 (1963), 1–27.

Gray, Roger W. "The Characteristic Bias in Some Thin Futures Markets," *Food Research Institute Studies,* 1, No. 3 (November 1960).

Gray, Roger W. "Fundamental Price Behavior Characteristics in Commodity Futures," Futures Trading Seminar, Vol. 3, Madison, Wis., 1966.

Gray, Roger W. "The Relationship among Three Futures Markets," *Food Research Institute Studies,* 2, No. 1 (February 1961).

Gray, Roger W. "The Seasonal Pattern of Wheat Futures Under the Loan Program," *Food Research Institute Studies*, 3, No. 1 (February 1962).

Gray, Roger W. and S. T. Nielsen. "Rediscovery of Some Fundamental Price Behavior Characteristics," paper presented at meeting of Econometric Society, Cleveland, Ohio, September, 1963.

Gray, Roger W., and W. G. Tomek. "Temporal Relationships Among Futures Prices: Reply," *American Journal of Agricultural Economics* (May 1971).

Gusler, G. "Price Discovery II. How Egg Futures Affect Prices," *Egg Producer*, 91, No. 3 (March 1960), 8–9.

Heifner, R. G. "Temporal Relationships Among Futures Prices: Comment," *American Journal of Agricultural Economics* (May 1971).

Hendel, J., "Price Making in Organized Commodity Markets," Western Agricultural Economics Research Council, *Marketing Research Commission Report*, 5 (1963) 71–98.

Hoffman, G. W. *Future Trading and the Cash Grain Markets*, USDA Circular 201, 1932.

Hoffman, G. W. *Grain Prices and the Futures Markets*, USDA Technical Bulletin 747, January 1941.

Hoos, Sidney, and Holbrook Working. "Price Relations of Liverpool Wheat Futures with Special Reference to the December-March Spread," *Food Research Institute Wheat Studies*, 17 (1940), 101–143.

Houthakker, H. S. *Commodity Futures IV: An Empirical Test of the Theory of Normal Backwardation*, Cowles Commission Discussion Paper; Economics No. 2124, June 1955.

Houthakker, H. S. *Restatement of the Theory of Normal Backwardation*, Foundation Discussion Paper, Economics No. 44, December 1957.

Houthakker, Hendrik. "Systematic and Random Elements in Short-term Price Movements," *American Economic Review*, 51 (1961).

Irwin, H. S. "Seasonal Cycles in Aggregates of Wheat-Futures Contracts," *Journal of Political Economy*, 43 (1935), 34–49.

Irwin, H. S. *Seasonal Tendencies in Wheat Futures Prices*, Grain Futures Administration, Washington, D.C., 1938.

Jensen, Michael. "Comment," *Financial Analysts Journal* (November–December 1967), 77–85.

Jensen, Michael C., and George A. Benington. "Random Walks and Technical Theories: Some Additional Evidence," *Journal of Finance*, 25 (1970), 469–481.

Kassouf, S. T. "Stock Price Random Walks: Some Supporting Evidence," *Review of Economic Statistics* (May 1968).

Kendall, M. G. "The Analysis of Economic Times Series—Part I: Prices," *Journal of the Royal Statistical Society*, Series A (General), 116, No. 1 (1953), 11–25.

Keynes, J. M. "Some Aspects of Commodity Markets," *Manchester Guardian Commercial*, European Reconstruction Series, Section 13, March 29, 1923, pp. 784–786.

Labys, Walter C. *Commodity Price Fluctuations: A Short Term Explanation for Selected Commodities on the American Market*, Ph.D. Dissertation, University of Nottingham, 1968.

Larson, A. B. *Evidence on the Temporal Dispersion of Price Effects of New Market Information*, Ph.D. Dissertation, Stanford University, 1960.

Larson, A. B. "Measurement of a Random Process in Futures Prices," *Food Research Institute Studies*, 1, No. 3 (1960).

Larson, A. B. "The Quiddity of the Cobweb Theorem," *Food Research Institute Studies*, 7, No. 2 (1967).

Levy, R. A. "Random Walks: Reality or Myth?" *Fianancial Analysts Journal*, (November–December, 1967), 69–77.

Malkiel, B. G., and J. G. Cragg. "Expectation and the Structure of Share Prices," *American Economic Review*, 60 (1970), 601–617.

Mandelbrot, Benoit. "The Variation of Certain Speculative Prices," *Journal of Business*, 36, No. 4 (1963), 394–419.

Manderscheid, L. V. *Influence of Price Support Program on Seasonal Corn Prices*, Ph.D. Dissertation, Stanford University, 1961.

Margins, Speculation and Prices in Grains Futures Markets, Economic Research Service, USDA, December 1967.

McCain, Wesley G. *Price Effects of Margin Changes in Commodity Future Markets,* Ph.D. Dissertation, Stanford University, 1969.

Mehl, Paul. "Relationship Between Daily Price Range and Net Price Change, Opening to Close of the Dominant Corn Future and the Daily Volume of Trading in Corn Futures on the Chicago Board of Trade," U.S. Grain Futures Administration, Washington, D.C., 1938.

Mehl, Paul. "Trading in Futures and Price Fluctuations," *Journal of Farm Economics,* 16, (1934), 481–495.

Mehl, Paul. "Trading in Wheat and Corn Futures in Relation to Price Movements," *Journal of Farm Economics,* 22 (1940), 601–612.

Moore, Arnold. *A Statistical Analysis of Common Stock Prices,* Ph.D Dissertation, Graduate School of Business, University of Chicago, 1962.

Muth, John F. "Rational Expectations and the Theory of Price Movements," *Econometrica,* 29 (July 1961), 315–335.

Osborne, M. F. M. "Brownian Motion in the Stock Market," *Operations Research,* 7, No. 2 (March–April 1959), 145-173.

Osborne, M. F. M. "Some Quantitative Tests for Stock Price Generating Models and Trading Folklore," *Journal of the American Statistical Association* (June 1967), 321–340.

Parzen, E. *Time Series Analysis Papers,* Holden Day, San Francisco, 1968.

Peston, M. H., and B. S. Yamey. "Inter-temporal Price Relationships with Forward Markets: A Method of Analysis," *Economica,* n.s., 27 (1960), 355–367.

Pinches, George E., and William R. Kinney, Jr. "The Measurement of the Volatility of Common Stock Prices," *Journal of Finance,* 26 (1971), 119–125.

Praetz, P. D. "The Distribution of Share Price Changes," *Journal of Business,* 45 (January 1972), 49–55.

Roberts, Harry. "Stock Market 'Patterns' and Financial Analysis: Methodological Suggestions," *Journal of Finance* (March 1959), 4–5.

Rocca, L. H. *Time Series Analysis of Commodity Futures Prices,* Ph.D. Dissertation, University of California, Berkeley, 1969.

Samuelson, Paul A. "Intertemporal Price Equilibrium: A Prologue to the Theory of Speculation," *Welwirtschaftliches Archiv,* 79 (December 1957) 181–221.

Samuelson, Paul A. "Proof that Properly Anticipated Prices Fluctuate Randomly," *Industrial Management Review,* 6, No. 2 (Spring 1965), 41–49.

Samuelson, Paul A. "A Random Theory of Futures Prices," *Industrial Management Review,* 6 (June 1965).

Sargent, T. J. "Commodity Price Expectations and the Interest Rate," *Quarterly Journal of Economics,* 83 (February 1969), 126–140.

Shelton, J. P. "The Value Line Contest: A Test of the Predictability of Stock Market Changes," *Journal of Business* (July 1967).

Smidt, Seymour. "A New Look at the Random Walk Hypothesis," *Journal of Financial and Quantitative Analysis,* 3, No. 3 (1968), 235–261.

Smidt, Seymour. "A Test of the Serial Independence of Price Changes in Soybean Futures," *Food Research Institute Studies,* 5, No. 2 (1965).

Snape, R. H. "Price Relationships on the Sydney Wool Futures Market," *Economica,* n.s., 35, No. 138 (May 1968), 169–178.

Sobel, Eugene. "Approximate Best Linear Prediction of a Certain Class of Stationary and Non-Stationary Noise Distorted Signals," *Journal of the American Statistical Association,* 66, No. 334 (June 1971), 363–370.

Stein, J. L. "The Simultaneous Determination of Spot and Futures Prices," *American Economic Review,* 51, No. 5 (December 1961), 1012–1025.

Stevenson, Richard, and Robert M. Bear. "Commodity Futures: Trends or Random Walks?" *Journal of Finance,* 25, No. 1 (March 1970), 65–81.

Taussig, F. W. "Is Market Price Determinate?" *Quarterly Journal of Economics*, 35 (May 1921), 394–411.

Telser, Lester G. "Price Relations between May and New Crop Wheat Futures at Chicago Since 1885," *Wheat Studies*, 10 (February 1934), 183–228.

Teweles, Richard J., and Charles V. Harlow. "An Inquiry into Non-Random Elements of the Commodity Futures Markets," *Journal of Commodity Trading*, 4, (July–August 1969).

Tomek, W. G. and Roger W. Gray. "Temporal Relationships Among Prices on Commodity Futures Markets: Their Allocative and Stabilizing Roles," *American Journal of Agricultural Economics*, 52. No. 3 (August 1970), 372–380.

Turnowsky, Stephen J. "Stochastic Stability of Short-Run Market Equilibrium," *Quarterly Journal of Economics*, 82, (November 1968), 666–681.

12 Years of Achievement under Public Law 480, Economic Research Service, USDA, 1967.

Vaile, R. S. "Inverse Carrying Charges in Futures Markets," *Journal of Farm Economics*, 30, No. 3 (August 1948), 574–575.

Vaile, Roland. "Cash and Futures Price of Corn," *Journal of Marketing*, 9 (July 1944).

Vance, Lawrence. "Grain Market Forces in the Light of Inverse Carrying Charges," *Journal of Farm Economics*, 28 (November 1946), 1036–1040.

Weiss, Moshe. *Quantitative Analysis of Egg Price Quotations*, Ph.D. Dissertation, Cornell University, 1969.

White, G. R., "Some Statistical Aspects of Future Trading on a Commodity Exchange," *Royal Statistical Society Journal*, n.s., 99 (1936), 297–329.

Working, Holbrook. "The Post Harvest Depression of Wheat Prices," *Food Research Institute Wheat Studies*, 5 (November 1929).

Working, Holbrook. "Frontiers in Uncertainty Theory: The Evidence of Futures Markets; New Concepts Concerning Futures Markets and Prices," *American Economic Review Papers and Proceedings*, 51, No. 2 (May 1961), 160–163.

Working, Holbrook. "Memorandum on Measurement of Cycles in Speculative Prices," *Food Research Institute Studies*, (1949).

Working, Holbrook, "New Concepts Concerning Futures Markets and Prices," *American Economic Review*, 52, No. 3 (June 1962), 431–459.

Working, Holbrook. "New Ideas and Methods for Price Research," *Journal of Farm Economics*, 38, No. 5 (December 1956), 1427–1436.

Working, Holbrook. "A Note on Mr. Meade's Theory of Competitive Speculation," *Review of Economic Studies*, 18 (1951), 188–189.

Working, Holbrook. "Note on the Correlation of First Differences of Averages in a Random Chain," *Econometrica*, 28 (1960), 916–918.

Working, Holbrook. "Price Relations Between May and New-Crop Wheat Futures at Chicago since 1885" *Food Research Institute Wheat Studies*, 10 (1934), 183–228.

Working, Holbrook. "Price Relations Between July and September Wheat Futures at Chicago Since 1885," *Food Research Institute Wheat Studies*, 9 (1933), 187–238.

Working, Holbrook. "Professor Vaile and the Theory of Inverse Carrying Charges," *Journal of Farm Economics*, 31, No. 1 (February 1949), 168–172.

Working, Holbrook. "A Random-Difference Series for Use in the Analysis of Time Series," *Journal of the American Statistical Association*, 29, No. 185 (March 1934), 11–24.

Working, Holbrook. "Theory of the Inverse Carrying Charge in Futures Markets," *Journal of Farm Economics*, 30, No. 1 (February 1948), 1–28.

VIII. PRICE FORECASTING

Ainsworth, R. M. *Profitable Grain Trading*, Ainsworth Financial Service, Mason City, Ill., 1933.

Ashby, Andrew W. "On Forecasting Commodity Prices by the Balance Sheet Approach," *Journal of Farm Economics*, 46 (August, 1964), 633–643.

Ashby, R. B. "Cotton Futures as Forecasters of Cotton Spot Prices," *Journal of the American Statistical Association*, 24, No. 168 (December 1929), 412–419.

Bates, J., and C. W. J. Granger. "Combining Forecasts," *Operations Research Quarterly,* **20** (1969), 451–467.

Belveal, L. D. *Commodity Speculation,* Commodities Press, Wilmette, Ill., 1967.

Belveal, Lee Dee. *Commodity Speculation: With Profits in Mind,* Commodities Press, Wilmette, Ill., 1968.

Benner, Samuel. *Benner's Prophecies of Ups and Downs In Prices,* privately printed, Cincinnati, Ohio, 1875.

Bernstein, L. A. "How Commodity Price Charts Disclose Supply-Demand Shifts," *Commodity Year Book,* Commodity Research Bureau, New York, 1958, pp. 33–42.

Bolton, Hamilton. *The Elliot Wave Principle—A Critical Appraisal,* Bolton, Tremblay and Co., Montreal, 1960.

Bostian, David. *Intra-Day Intensity Index,* privately printed, Fort Benjamin Harrison, Indiana, 1967.

Brown, Robert. *Smoothing, Forecasting and Prediction of Discrete Time Series,* Prentice-Hall, Englewood Cliffs, N.J., 1963.

Busby, William T. *A Model for Speculation in Pork Belly Futures,* Ph.D. Dissertation, University of Southern California, May 1971.

Christian, Roy E. *New Methods for Long Term Stock Market Forecasting,* Physicians Market Letter, Aptos, Calif., 1966.

Cohen, A. *The Chartcraft Method of Point and Figure Trading,* Chartcraft, Larchmont, N.Y., 1960.

Collins, Charles. "The Elliott Wave Principle—1966 Supplement," *The Bank Credit Analyst,* Quebec, Canada.

Collins, Charles. "Market Ebb Tide," *Barron's* (March 1970).

Cowles, Alfred W. "Can Stock Market Forecasters Forecast?" *Econometrica,* 1 (1933).

Cox, H. *A Common Sense Approach to Commodity Futures Trading,* Reynolds, New York, 1968.

Dahl, Curtiss. *Consistent Profits in the Commodity Futures Market,* Tri-state Offset Co., Cincinnati, Ohio, 1960.

Devillers, Victor. *The Point and Figure Method of Anticipating Stock Price Movements,* Tender Press, New York, 1972.

Dewey, Edward R. *Cycles, The Science of Prediction,* Holt, New York, 1949.

Dewey, Edward R. "The 5½ Year Cycle in Corn Prices," *Cycles Magazine* (February 1955).

Dewey, Edward R. "Kick in the Pants Cycles," *Cycles Magazine* (August 1961).

Dewey, Edward R. "Samuel Turner Benner," *Cycles Magazine* (March, 1955).

Dewey, Edward R., and O. G. Mandino. *Cycles: Mysterious Forces that Trigger Events,* Hawthorne, New York, 1971.

Dines, James. *How the Average Investor Can Use Technical Analysis for Stock Profits,* Dines Chart Corp., New York, 1972.

Donchian, R. D. "High Finance in Copper," *Financial Analysts Journal,* 16, No. 6 (November-December 1960), 133–142.

Donchian, Richard. "Trend Following Methods in Commodity Price Analysis," *Guide to Commodity Price Forecasting,* Commodity Research Bureau, New York, 1965, pp. 48–60.

Drew, Garfield. "A Clarification of the Odd-Lot Theory," *Financial Analysts Journal,* (September–October 1967).

Dunnigan, William. *New Blueprints for Gains in Stocks and Grains,* privately published, San Francisco, Calif., 1956.

Edwards, Robert D., and John Magee. *Technical Analysis of Stock Trends,* John Magee, Springfield, Mass., 1961.

The Egg-spread Method, Market Research Associates, Pasadena, Calif., 1966.

Elliott, R. N. *Nature's Law—The Secret of the Universe,* privately published, New York, 1946.

Elliott, R. N. "The Wave Principle," *Financial World* (1939).

Farrell, M. J. "Profitable Speculation," *Economica,* n.s., **33**, No. 130 (May 1966), 183–193.

"The Fibonacci Numbers," *TIME* (April 1969).

Floss, Carl W. *Market Rhythm*, Investors Publishing, Detroit, 1955.

Gann, W. D., and J. L. Gann. *How to Make Profits Trading in Commodities; A Study of the Commodity Market, with Charts and Rules for Successful Trading and Investing*, W. D. Gann and Sons, New York, 1941; rev. ed., 1951.

Gardner, Robert L. *How to Make Money in the Commodity Market*, Prentice-Hall, Englewood Cliffs, N.J., 1961.

Gartley, H. M. *Profits in the Stock Market*, H. M. Gartley, New York, 1935.

Gotthelf, Edward B. *The Commodex System*, Commodity Futures Forecast, New York,

Granger, C. W. J., and O. Morgenstern. *Predictability of Stock Market Prices*, Heath, Lexington, Mass., 1970.

Granville, Joseph. *Granville's New Key to Stock Market Profits*, Prentice-Hall, Englewood Cliffs, N.J., 1963.

Hamilton, William Peter. *The Stock Market Barometer*, Harper, New York, 1922.

Harlow, Charles V. *An Analysis of the Predictive Value of Stock Market "Breadth' Measurements*, Investor's Intelligence, Larchmont, N.Y., 1968.

Hart, John K. *Commodity Trend Service*, Columbus, Ga.

Heiby, Walter. *Stock Market Profits Through Dynamic Synthesis*, Institute of Dynamic Synthesis, Chicago, Ill., 1965.

Hieronymus, T. A. *Economics of Futures Trading for Commercial and Personal Profit*, Commodity Research Bureau, New York, 1971.

Hieronymus, T. A. "Forecasting Soybean and Soybean Product Prices," in H. Jiler, (Ed.), *Guide to Commodity Price Forecasting*, Commodity Research Bureau, New York, 1965.

Hill, John R. *Technical and Mathematical Analysis of the Commodity and Stock Markets*, Commodity Research Institute, Chicago, Ill.

Hingorani, G. G. "Forecasting Economic Time Series Generated by Random Processes," *Proceedings of the Business and Economic Statistics Section of the Annual Meeting of the American Statistical Association*, 1966.

Houthakker, H. S. "Can Speculators Forecast Prices?" *Review of Economics and Statistics*, 39, No. 2 (May 1959), 143–151.

Irwin, H. S. "Technical Conditions are Important Factors in Short-Time Movements of Wheat Prices," *Journal of Farm Economics*, 18 (1936), 736–742.

Jarrett, F. G. "Short Term Forecasting of Australian Wool Prices," *Australian Economic Papers*, 4. (June–December 1965), 93–102.

Jevons, William Stanley. *The Periodicity of Commercial Crises and Physical Explanation*, University of Manchester, 1875.

Jevons, William Stanley. *The Solar Period and the Price of Corn*, University of Manchester, 1875.

Jiler, William (Ed.) *Guide to Commodity Price Forecasting*, Commodity Research Bureau, New York, 1965.

Jiler, William. *How Charts Can Help You in the Stock Market*, Commodity Research Publishing Corporation, New York, 1961.

Kaish, Stanley. "Odd Lot Profit and Loss Performance," *Financial Analysts Journal* (September–October 1969).

Keltner, Chester. *How to Make Money in Commodities*, Keltner Statistical Service, Kansas City, Mo., 1960.

Kewley, Thomas J., and R. A. Stevenson. "The Odd Lot Theory — A Reply," *Financial Analysts Journal*, (January–February 1969).

Labys, W. C., and C. W. J. Granger. *Speculation, Hedging and Commodity Price Forecasts*, Heath, Lexington, Mass., 1970.

Larson, Arnold B. "Price Prediction on the Egg Futures Market," *Proceedings of a Symposium on Price Effects of Speculation in Organized Commodity Markets*, Food Research Institute Studies, 7 (1967), 49–64.

Leslie, Conrad. *Guide for Successful Speculation*, Darnell Press, Chicago, 1970.

Levine, Irving. *Successful Commodity Speculation*, Levro Press, Newark, N.J., 1965.

Levy, Robert A. *The Relative Strength Concept of Common Stock Price Forecasting*, Investor's Intelligence, Larchmont, N.Y., 1967.

Lindsay, George. "A Timing Method for Traders," *The Encyclopedia of Stock Market Techniques*, Investor's Intelligence, 1965.

Lowell, Fred R. *Profits in Soybeans*, Keltner Statistical Service, Kansas City, Mo., 1966.

Mandelbrot, B. "Forecasts of Future Prices, Unbiased Markets and Martingale Models," *Journal of Business*, 39, Part 2 (January 1966), 242–255.

Markstein, David L. *How to Chart Your Way to Stock Market Profits*, Parker Publishing, West Nyack, N.Y., 1966.

Martel. R. F. *Charting Supply and Demand for Stock Analysis*, Martel., Reading, Pa., 1961.

Neill, Humphrey. *Tape Reading and Market Tactics*. Fraser, Burlington, Vt., 1960.

O'Connor, William. *Stocks, Wheat and Pharoahs*, Werner Books, New York, 1961.

Relative Volume Index, Trend Way Advisory Service, Louisville, Ky.

Rhea, Robert. *The Dow Theory*, Vail-Ballou, Binghamton, N.Y., 1932.

Rockwell, C. S. *Profits, Normal Backwardation, and Forecasting in Commodity Futures*, Ph.D. Dissertation, University of California, Berkeley, 1964.

Runner, Tim Jon. "Pit-falls of Computer Simulations," *Commodity Journal*, 6, No. 4 (July–August 1971).

Schabacker, Richard W. *Stock Market Profits*, Fraser, Burlington, Vt., 1967.

Schabacker, Richard W. *Technical Analysis and Stock Market Profits*, B. C. Forbes Publishing Company, New York, 1934.

Scheinman, William X. *Why Most Investors are Mostly Wrong Most of the Time*, Lancer, New York, 1970.

Schultz, John. *The Intelligent Chartist*, WRSM Financial Service, New York, 1962.

Seligman, Daniel. "The Mystique of Point and Figure," *Fortune*, March 1962.

Stoken, D. "Forecasting Pork Belly Futures," *Commodity Year Book*, Commodity Research Bureau, New York, 1966.

Shishko, Irwin, "Forecasting Sugar Prices," in H. Jiler, (Ed.), *Guide to Commodity Price Forecasting*, Commodity Research Bureau, New York, 1965.

Shishko, Irwin. "How to Forecast Cocoa Prices," in H. Jiler, (Ed.), *Guide to Commodity Price Forecasting*, Commodity Research Bureau, New York, 1965.

Shishko, Irwin. "Techniques of Forecasting Commodity Prices," *Commodity Year Book*, Commodity Research Bureau, New York, 1965, pp. 30–36.

Taylor, Robert Joel. "The Major Price Trend Directional Indicator," *Commodities Magazine* (April 1972).

Tomkins, Edwin H. *Systematic Stock Trading*, The Moore Guide, Riverside, Ill., 1969.

Unacek, Edward, Jr. *An Econometric Analysis and Forecasting Model for Pork Bellies*. Ph.D. Dissertation, Texas A. and M., 1967.

Van Horne, James, and G. Parker. "Technical Trading Rules: A Comment," *Financial Analysts Journal* (July–August 1968), 128–132.

Walters, James, and Larry Williams. "Measuring Market Momentum," *Commodities Magazine* (October 1972).

Weymar, F. H., "Cocoa, the Effects of Inventories on Price Forecasting," *Commodity Year Book*, Commodity Research Bureau, New York, 1969.

Wheelan, Alexander. "Point and Figure Procedure in Commodity Market Analysis," *Guide to Commodity Price Forecasting*, Commodity Research Bureau, New York, 1965.

Wheelan, Alexander. *Study Helps in Point and Figure Technique*, Morgan, Rogers and Roberts, New York, 1962.

Williams, Larry. *Accumulation–Distribution Studies*, Williams Reports, Carmel, Calif.

Williams, Larry. *The Secret of Selective Stocks for Immediate and Substantial Gains*, Conceptual Management, Carmel, Calif., 1973.

Working, Holbrook. "Quotations on Commodity Futures as Price Forecasts," *Econometrica*, 10 (1942), 39–52.

Working, Holbrook. "A Theory of Anticipatory Prices," *American Economic Review*, 48, No. 2 (May 1958), 188–199.

Wyckoff, Richard. *Studies in Tape Reading,* Traders Press, New York, 1972.

IX. MONEY MANAGEMENT AND RISK CONTROL

Barger, Harold. "Speculation and the Risk-Preference," *Journal of Political Economy,* 46 (1938), 396–408.

Barnes, Robert M. "A Statistical Method for Setting Stops in Stock Trading," *Operation Research,* 18 (July 1970), 665–688.

Blume, Marshall E. "On the Assessment of Risk," *Journal of Finance,* 26 (1971), 1–10.

Briloff, A. J. "Income Tax Aspects of Commodity Futures Transactions," in H. Jiler, ed., *Guide to Commodity Price Forecasting,* Commodity Research Bureau, New York, 1965.

Dalrymple, Brent B. *Risk Analysis Applied to Commodity Speculation,* Ph.D. Dissertation, Louisiana State University, 1970.

Epstein, R. A. *The Theory of Gambling and Statistical Logic,* Academic, New York, 1969.

Feller, W. *An Introduction to Probability Theory and Its Applications,* Vol. 2, Wiley, New York, 1966.

Goldberg, Samuel. *Probability: An Introduction,* Prentice-Hall, Englewood Cliffs, N.J., 1960.

Goldfein, Lawrence, and Lester Houchberg. "Use of Commodity Straddles Can Effect Impressive Tax Savings," *The Journal of Taxation,* 29, No. 6 (December 1968).

Hadley, G. *Introduction to Business Statistics,* Holden-Day, San Francisco, Calif., 1968.

Hardy, C. O. *Risk and Risk Bearing,* University of Chicago Press, Chicago, 1923.

Helmuth, J. W. *Futures Trading Under Conditions of Uncertainty,* Ph.D. Dissertation, University of Missouri, Columbia, 1970.

Hieronymus, T. A. *Principles of Inventory and Risk Management,* University of Illinois Agricultural Extension Service AE 2831, 1951.

Irwin, H. S. "The Nature of Risk Assumption in the Trading of Organized Exchanges" *American Economic Review,* 27 (1937), 267–278.

Knight, Frank H. *Risk, Uncertainty and Profit,* Houghton Mifflin, Boston, 1921 (reprinted 1957).

Markowitz, H. M. *Portfolio Selections: Efficient Diversification of Investments,* Wiley, New York, 1959.

Rinfret, P. A. "Investment Managers are Worth Their Keep," *Financial Analysts Journal* (March–April 1968).

Sandor, Richard L., and James E. Rhodes. "The Development of a Trading Strategy," *Commodities Magazine,* (July 1972), 22–28.

Schwartz, Marvin. "Scientific Money Management," *Commodity Journal,* 6, No. 3 (May–June, 1971).

Shackle, G. L. S. "An Analysis of Speculative Choice," *Economica,* n.s., 12 (1945), 10–21.

Sowders, A. G., Jr. "The Commodity Markets and Taxes," *Arthur Young Journal* (July 1960).

Standard Federal Tax Reporter, Code Volume, Commerce Clearing House, New York, 1969.

Thorpe, Edward O. *Beat the Dealer,* Random House, New York, 1962.

Von Neumann, John, and Oskar Morgenstern. *The Theory of Games and Economic Behavior,* Princeton University Press, Princeton, N.J., 1947.

Wilson, Allen N. *The Casino Gambler's Guide,* Harper and Row, New York, 1970.

Zweig, M. E. *An Analysis of Risk and Return on Put and Call Option Strategies,* Ph.D. Dissertation, Michigan State University, 1969.

X. HEDGING

Arthur, Henry B. "Inventory Profits in the Business Cycle," *American Economic Review,* 28, No. 1 (March 1938).

Arthur, Henry B. "The Nature of Commodity Futures as an Economic and Business Instrument," *Food Research Institute Studies,* 9, No. 3 (1972).

Brennan, M. J. "A Model of Seasonal Inventories," *Econometrica*, 27 (April 1959), 228–244.

Brennan, M. J. "The Supply of Storage," *American Economic Review*, 48, No. 1 (March 1958), 50–72.

Cootner, P. H. "Speculation and Hedging," *Food Research Institute Studies*, Supplement, 7 (1967), 65–106.

English, E. D. "The Use of Commodity Exchanges by Millers," *Proceedings of Fifth Annual Symposium, Chicago Board of Trade* (September 11–12, 1952).

Farmer Use of Futures Markets, Illinois Agricultural Experiment Station AE 3760, 1962.

Graf, T. F. "Hedging—How Effective Is It?" *Journal of Farm Economics*, 35, No. 3 (August 1953), 398–413.

Gray, R. W. "The Importance of Hedging in Futures Trading; and the Effectiveness of Futures Trading for Hedging," *Futures Trading Seminar*, Madison, Wis., Vol. 1, 1960.

Gruen, F. H. "The Pros and Cons of Futures Trading for Woolgrowers," *Review of Marketing and Agricultural Economics*, 28, No. 3 (September 1960), 1–12.

Hardy, C. O., and L. S. Lyon. "The Theory of Hedging," *Journal of Political Economy*, 31, No. 2 (April, 1923), 276–287.

The Hedger's Handbook: A Businessman's Guide to the Commodity Futures Market, a booklet published by Merrill Lynch, Pierce, Fenner and Smith, New York, 1970.

Heifner, R. G. "The Gains from Basing Grain Storage Decisions on Cash-Future Spreads," *Journal of Farm Economics*, 48, No. 5, (December 1966), 1490–1495.

Heironymus, T. A. "Four Ways to Make a Profit on Futures," *Better Farming Methods*, 35, No. 1 (January 1963), 22–25.

Hieronymus, T. A. *Hedging for Country Elevators*, Agricultural Economics Research Report 91, University of Illinois, March 1968.

Hieronymus, T. A. "How You Can Use the Futures Market," *Successful Farming*, 60, No. 4 (April 1972), 51, 70–71.

Hieronymus, T. A. *Making Use of Basis Changes to Earn Income*, University of Illinois Department of Agricultural Economics AE 3537, Urbana, 1959.

Hieronymus, T. A. *Uses of Grain Futures Markets in the Farm Business*, University of Illinois Agricultural Experiment Station Bulletin 696, 1963.

Hieronymus, T. A., F. S. Scott and W. J. Wills. "Hedging Cattle Feeding Operations," *Illinois Farm Economics*, No. 200 (January, 1952), 1272–1276.

Hobson, Karl. *Wheat Prices in 1964—How to Forecast Them, How to Insure Them*, Washington State University, Agricultural Extension Service E.M. 2332, 1963.

Hoffmann, G. W. *Hedging by Dealing in Grain Futures*, Ph.D. Dissertation, University of Pennsylvania, Philadelphia, 1925.

Howell, L. D. *Analysis of Hedging and Other Operations in Grain Futures*, USDA Technical Bulletin 971, August 1948.

Howell, L. D. *Analysis of Hedging and Other Operations in Wool and Wool Top Futures*, USDA Technical Bulletin 1260, January 1962.

Howell, L. D. *Influence of Certificated Stocks on Spot-Futures Price Relationships for Cotton*, USDA Technical Bulletin 1119, 1955.

Howell, L. D., and L. J. Watson. *Relation of Spot Cotton Prices to Futures Contracts and Protection Afforded by Trading in Futures*, USDA Technical Bulletin 602, January 1938.

Huebner, S. S. "The Insurance Service of Commodity Exchanges," in *Annals of the American Academy of Political and Social Science*, 155, Part 1 (May 1931), 1–6.

Irwin, H. S. *Speculation versus Hedging in Country Elevator Operation*, Commodity Exchange Administration, Washington, D.C., 1938.

Johnson, L. L. "Price Instability, Hedging, and Trade Volume in the Coffee Market," *Journal of Political Economy*, 45 (1957), 306–321.

Johnson, L. L. "The Theory of Hedging and Speculation in Commodity Futures," *Review of Economic Studies*, 27 (3), No. 74 (June, 1960), 139–151.

Johnson, Leland L. *Hedging, Speculation and Futures Trading in the Coffee Market Since World War II,* Ph.D. Dissertation, Yale University, 1957.

McKinnon, R. I. "Futures Markets, Buffer Stocks and Income Stability for Primary Producers," *Journal of Political Economy,* 75, No. 6 (December 1967). 844–861.

Paul, Allen B. "The Pricing of Binspace—A Contribution to the Theory of Storage," *American Journal of Agricultural Economics,* 52, No. 1 (February 1970), 1.

Rutledge, David J. S. "Hedgers' Demand for Futures Contracts: A Theoretical Framework with Applications to the United States Soybean Complex," *Food Research Institute Studies,* 10, No. 3 (1972).

Rutledge, D. J. S. *The Relationship between Prices and Hedging Patterns in the United States Soybean Complex,* Ph.D. Dissertation, Stanford University, 1970.

Schrock, Nicholas W. *A Portfolio Analysis of Straddle Operations in the Futures Markets,* Thesis, University of Oregon, 1967.

Schultz, Theodore W. "Spot and Futures Prices as Production Guides," *American Economic Review,* 39 (May 1949).

Snape, R. H., and B. S. Yamey. "Test of the Effectiveness of Hedging," *Journal of Political Economy,* 73, No. 5 (October 1965), 540–544.

Stevens, W. H. S. "The Relation of the Cash-Future Spread to Hedging Transactions," *Journal of Business,* 2, No. 1 (January 1929), 28–49.

Telser, L. G. "Safety First and Hedging," *Review of Economic Studies,* 23 (1), No. 60 (1955–1956), 1–16.

Working, Holbrook. "Futures Trading and Hedging," *American Economic Review,* 43, No. 3 (June 1953), 314–343.

Working, Holbrook. "Hedging Reconsidered," *Journal of Farm Economics,* 35, No. 4 (November 1953), 544–561.

Working, Holbrook. "Price Support and the Effectiveness of Hedging," *Journal of Farm Economics,* 35 (1953), 811–818.

Working, Holbrook. "Speculation on Hedging Markets," *Food Research Institute Studies,* 1, No. 2 (1960).

Yamey, B. S. "Addendum" to "An Investigation of Hedging on an Organized Produce Exchange," in P. T. Bauer and B. S. Yamey, *Markets, Market Control and Marketing Reform,* Weidenfeld and Nicolson, London, 1969.

Yamey, B. S. "An Investigation of Hedging on an Organized Produce Exchange," *The Manchester School of Economics and Social Studies,* 19 (September 1951), 305–319.

XI. PRICES AND RELATED STATISTICAL DATA

Boyle, J. E. *Chicago Wheat Prices for Eighty-One Years,* unpublished manuscript, 1922.

Chicago Board of Trade Annual Report, 1858 to date.

Chicago Board of Trade Year Book, Chicago Board of Trade, 141 West Jackson Boulevard, Chicago, Ill.

Chicago Mercantile Exchange Year Book, Chicago Mercantile Exchange, 444 West Jackson Boulevard, Chicago, Ill. 1923 to date.

Commodity Year Book, Commodity Research Bureau, New York (annual), 1929 to date.

Hoffman, G. W., and J. W. T. Duvel, *Grain Prices and the Futures Market: A 15 Year Survey,* USDA Technical Bulletin 747, January 1941.

New York Mercantile Exchange Year Book, New York Mercantile Exchange, New York.

Thomsen, F. L., and R. J. Foote. *Agricultural Prices,* McGraw-Hill, New York, 1952.

USDA, Commodity Exchange Authority. *Commodity Futures Statistics,* Washington, D.C., annual from 1947.

USDA, Commodity Exchange Authority. *Grain Futures Statistics 1921–1951,* Statistical Bulletin No. 131, Washington, D.C., 1952.

USDA, Consumer and Marketing Service. *Cotton Price Statistics,* Washington, D.C.

USDA, Consumer and Marketing Service. *Grain and Feed Statistics,* Washington, D.C.

USDA, Economic Research Service. *Statistics on Cotton and Related Data, 1925–62,* Statistical Bulletin No. 329, Washington, D.C., 1963.

Working, Holbrook. "Prices of Cash Wheat and Futures at Chicago since 1883," *Food Research Institute Wheat Studies,* 10 (November 1934), 103–117.

Working, Holbrook, and Sidney Hoos. "Wheat Futures Prices and Trading at Liverpool since 1886," *Food Research Institute Wheat Studies,* 15 (November 1938).

Index

Index

Catalog

If you are interested in a list of fine Paperback
books, covering a wide range of subjects
and interests, send your name and address,
requesting your free catalog, to:

McGraw-Hill Paperbacks
1221 Avenue of Americas
New York, N.Y. 10020